Rewriting Exodus

Decolonial Studies, Postcolonial Horizons
Series editors: Ramon Grosfoguel (University of California at
Berkeley), Barnor Hesse (Northwestern University) and S. Sayyid
(University of Leeds)

Since the end of the Cold War, unresolved conjunctures and crises
of race, ethnicity, religion, diversity, diaspora, globalisation, the
West and the non-West, have radically projected the meaning of the
political and the cultural beyond the traditional verities of left and
right. Throughout this period, Western developments in 'international
relations' have become increasingly defined as corollaries to national
'race relations' across both the European Union and the United States,
where the re-formation of Western imperial discourses and practices
has been given particular impetus by the 'war against terror'. At the
same time, hegemonic Western continuities of racial profiling and
colonial innovations have attested to the incomplete and interrupted
institutions of the postcolonial era. Today we are witnessing renewed
critiques of these postcolonial horizons at the threshold of attempts
to inaugurate the political and cultural forms that decolonisation
now needs to take within and between the West and the 'non-West'.
This series explores and discusses radical ideas that open up and
advance understandings of these politically multicultural issues and
theoretically interdisciplinary questions.

Also available

The Dutch Atlantic
Slavery, Abolition and Emancipation
Kwame Nimako and Glenn Willemsen

Islam and the Political
Theory, Governance and International Relations
Amr G. E. Sabet

REWRITING EXODUS

American Futures from Du Bois to Obama

Anna Hartnell

www.plutobooks.com

First published 2011 by Pluto Press
345 Archway Road, London N6 5AA

www.plutobooks.com

Distributed in the United States of America exclusively by
Palgrave Macmillan, a division of St Martin's Press LLC,
175 Fifth Avenue, New York, NY 10010

British Library Cataloguing in Publication Data
A catalogue record for this book is available from the British Library

ISBN   978 0 7453 2956 7   Hardback
ISBN   978 0 7453 2955 0   Paperback

Library of Congress Cataloging in Publication Data applied for

10   9   8   7   6   5   4   3   2   1

Designed and produced for Pluto Press by
Chase Publishing Services Ltd, 33 Livonia Road, Sidmouth, EX10 9JB, England
Typeset from disk by Stanford DTP Services, Northampton, England
Simultaneously printed digitally by CPI Antony Rowe, Chippenham, UK and
Edwards Bros in the United States of America

Contents

Series Preface

Writing about Barack Obama is no longer novel. Since 2008 the number of books published about the first African American US president have begun to resemble a veritable cottage industry among political commentators. Summarizing crudely the focus of this cottage industry seems inclined towards texts that involve either the re-narration of Obama's racial personal and political biography or the re-evaluation of the liberalism, pragmatism or populism of his administration. Nevertheless, whether romanticized from the Left or denounced from the Right, the seductive narrative effect of the Obama political phenomenon has been a conventional American story of exceptionalism. The post-colonial patriotic story of a once racially blighted democracy ultimately redeemed by Obama's election; a story of ever increasing and expansive American freedom, visualized, told, written or read from the perspectives of a hegemonically white America. Breaking with this parochial American approach *Rewriting Exodus* situates the political phenomenon of Obama within the pre-figurations and inheritances of African American political and religious discourses convergent around the trope of Exodus. This metaphorical analogy with the freedom aspirations of the ancient Hebrews under Egyptian slavery has long exerted a searing rhetorical influence on the critical imaginations of previously and formerly enslaved black populations. It is the narrative pivot on which the significance of this book turns.

In this sense *Rewriting Exodus* is a timely and compelling reminder that there have always been two antagonistic narratives of freedom in the United States, both intensely racialized, one hegemonic and the other disavowed. Ever since the United States was established initially as a settler colony and a slave society, its historical institutions of race and governance have been discursively repressed, only surfacing intermittently in public discourse as the exception proving the rule of a nation founded on life, liberty and the pursuit of happiness. Traditionally what is officially remembered and popularly recited in the US as emblematic of its institutions are the underwriting of the protection of personal freedom, the promotion of economic opportunities and the valorisation of political democracy. These memories and recitations have routinely foreclosed from any legitimate enunciation all but the merest traces of the longevity underlining the unrealized freedoms of both African Americans and Native Americans. Such foreclosures have enabled the most remarkable declarations to be made politically on behalf of the US as if it was unmistakably a global lighthouse of freedom. During the First and Second World Wars the US could still claim to be making the world safe for democracy, despite its earlier nineteenth century continental, imperial westward expansion and 'Indian wars'; its establishment of Jim Crow racial segregation; and its imperial annexation of the Philippines and Puerto Rico. If that was culled from a white hegemonic perspective of freedom, a black subaltern perspective was gestated in the long civil rights movement mobilized by African Americans from the late nineteenth century to the second half of the twentieth century. Although this critically expanded the meaning of American democracy, inexplicably it has never been represented as part of US iconography in these terms.

As the twentieth century drew to a close it became increasingly evident to scholars in African American studies, Ethnic Studies, Sociology and Political science, that the legislative successes of the civil rights movement co-existed with highly disproportionate racial disparities in poverty, HIV infections, unemployment, educational qualifications and incarceration rates affecting primarily African Americans and Latinos. However, these protracted 'facts of blackness' were not necessarily translatable either through activism or scholarship into the sound bites or headlines of a 24-hour news media. Indeed public indictments of racism were now becoming exclusively assigned to sensationally exposed locutions, featuring the tyranny of the verbal epithet or the textual insult. Once exposed mass media outrage and condemnation ensured they were treated as extreme interruptions of the accommodations achieved in media disseminations of cultural diversity. Although this projection of cultural diversity seemed very distant from racially segregated cities, racial profiling, racially punitive criminal justice and racially authoritarian immigration laws, it nevertheless could be found in the digital media-scapes that had not only witnessed but finessed the rise of commodified black popular culture from the early 1990s. The hyper-visibility of particularly African American males in sports, popular music and movies, spawned spectacles of corporate conviviality (especially in the commercial branding of blackness as the urban cachet of conspicuous consumption) that had never been greater or indeed more limited. Even though it seemed Black America in the twenty-first century had become symbolically more associated with the prominence of its celebrities, upper middle class and wealthy role models, it was also unspeakably more threatening in the greater urban accumulation of black people among the disenfranchised, the criminalized, the segregated and the poor. If the meaning of cultural diversity seemed obsessed with the allure of rapprochement between urbane blacks and whites, relegating 'ethnic others' to the position of unused extras, acute anxieties unleashed by the devastating impact of 9/11 and the 'war against terror'; as well as racial profiling mobilized in the virulent opposition to illegal immigration across the Mexican border, managed to consolidate and yet unsettle the exclusive racial grammar of the nation. Somehow an 'imagined community' of diverse American citizens could also find its unifying element against the *constitutive outsides* of the 'Muslim' and the 'Mexican'.

Nevertheless this denouement of race, more from national habit than critical analysis, still seemed to silently signify and stigmatize predominantly African Americans in public discourse, leaving untouched and uncriticised the hegemonic culture of whiteness. The first decade of the twenty-first century confirmed the resilience of a consensus in US public life regarding the unspeakability of race in politics and social stratification. But this was a consensus whose firmness became flimsy with the advent of Hurricane Katrina. The destruction of New Orleans in 2005 which decimated thousands of lives and homes throughout the coastal region brought to national TV screens images of destitute black people normally associated in the Western mind with the 'Third World'. These were black people who did not have the economic means to escape; black people whom the national media had difficulty acknowledging as socially neglected; black people who feeling disregarded and forgotten challenged insatiable broadcasters and newspaper reporters with the angry yet poignant lament, 'we are citizens, not refugees'. It was a stark if not sustained reminder of what was once described as 'The Two Americas'.

Rewriting Exodus is a powerful evocation of this contextual trajectory. It locates the phenomenon of Obama between the unspeakability of race in civil discourse and a new hyper-visibility of race inscribed on the corporeality and comportment of the US president that takes up permanent residence in political discourse like the proverbial elephant in the room. If anything, this is because the Obama phenomenon is also embodied in the imperfect union of a colonial and a liberal heritage shared ironically if unceremoniously with the nation itself. *Rewriting Exodus* challenges us to engage critically and reflexively with these racial thematics, analysing the intellectual, political and conflictual African American historical landscape to which current discussions of the Obama phenomenon owe their unacknowledged emergence. Perhaps its signal achievement is the calibration of a critical anamnesis of the nationally disavowed intellectual discourses of African American political and religious culture arising from the twentieth century, rewriting them as forms of histories of the racialized present, as well as contemporary commentaries on the contested and shifting meanings of freedom in the US. *Rewriting Exodus* exemplifies the best of inter-disciplinary scholarship in African American studies and Post-colonial studies, combining analyses of the 'fierce urgency of now' (Martin Luther King) with equally pressing problematizations of the contemporary 'quarrel with history' (Edouard Glissant). Throughout we are obliged to reflect on how Obama's bipartisan inheritance of presidential Americaness is also, like the nation itself, complicated by interruptions from the conflicting racialized traditions of Exodus in which all American intellectual, political and religious formations are deeply mired. Anna Hartnell has provided a memorable postcolonial prism through which to explore the post-Civil Rights era's complexities, highlighting Obama less as a proper name and more as a political phenomenon; inscribing the latter in intellectual discourses and debates emanating from the twentieth century archives of Black America that are all too often dismissed, euphemized or pathologized by recurrent obsessions with that momentous US presidential election of 4 November 2008.

Barnor Hesse
Chicago
February 2011

Acknowledgements

This book was shaped by the shadow of 9/11, the catastrophic aftermath of Hurricane Katrina and the meteoric rise of Barack Obama. The fear, devastation and hope to which these very different events gave rise seemed to bring to the fore long-running questions about the nature of American exceptionalism, its relationship to colonialism and its complicity in the post-slavery legacy of enduring and systemic racism. My aim here is to cast these key events of the early twenty-first century in the light of the prophetic traditions that have long shaped the black liberation struggle in the United States – to bring the moral force of anti-racist black political, religious and literary discourses to bear on these seemingly urgent questions. Written by a white person working from within British academic institutions, this book offers the perspective of an outsider.

There are many people who have helped me to write this book. It was working in the Department of English and Comparative Literature at Goldsmiths, University of London, that I was able to formulate some of the initial ideas for this project. In particular, I am indebted to Josh Cohen for his invaluable input into this project at this early stage, and thanks also to Kirsty Black and Padraig Kirwan for their friendship and advice.

The Department of American and Canadian Studies at the University of Birmingham provided a stimulating research culture that gave me the freedom to write the book I wanted to write. Thank you to all my colleagues and to all the students there. Special thanks to Steve Hewitt, who has not only been a great friend – who advised me on this project at the proposal stage – but whose vigilant eye to the internet ensured that throughout the presidential election campaign and beyond, I didn't miss any Obama-related news relevant to this book. Danielle Fuller could not have been a more generous and supportive mentor, Dick Ellis and Scott Lucas have been constant sources of encouragement, and incredibly wide-ranging conversations had with Sara Wood and Richard Langley always left me feeling more focused. Mags Conway has been a pleasure to work with. Many of the ideas for this book took shape while I was teaching a class on the African

American experience to undergraduate students during academic session 2008/9. Undoubtedly this book is indebted to the students in that class, and the lively and energetic debates that those classes led to. Contributing to the supervision of Lisa Palmer's PhD thesis on 'Loving Blackness' has also been a real privilege, and I have learnt a great deal from her that has in turn informed this book.

Particular thanks to Roger van Zwanenberg at Pluto Press, whose initial interest in this project was so encouraging, and to David Castle and Will Viney for their advice and patience. The work on the part of the production team has been invaluable, and the comments of the anonymous reviewers were also extremely helpful. Above all, I'd like to thank the series editor, Barnor Hesse, for a contribution to this project that went above and beyond the call of duty and which has without doubt made this a better book than it otherwise would have been. The dialogue I had with Barnor while writing this book often challenged my assumptions, and ultimately proved to be very productive. This book has benefited enormously from his intellectual insights.

While thinking about this book I made two trips to New Orleans in April 2008 and April 2009, and I am indebted to all of the people who generously gave up their time to help me understand events that no book could do justice to: in particular I'd like to thank Reverend Donald Boutte of St. John Baptist Church, New Orleans, Mai Deng of the Mary Queen of Vietnam Community Development Corporation, Darryl Malek-Wiley of the Sierra Club, Ashley Shelton of the Louisiana Disaster Recovery Foundation, Audrey Stewart of Loyola Law School's Katrina Clinic, and Mary Williams of the Deep South Center for Environmental Justice. Conversations with Linetta Gilbert of the Ford Foundation and Tonya Williams of the US Human Rights Network have also been invaluable. Thanks to Nick Duffy for accompanying me on the second trip and for always responding incisively to my work.

Finally, thank you to my family. Special thanks go to my father, John Strawson, for his unwavering support but also for his comments on drafts of this project, which have consistently opened up new angles that have helped shape the arguments of this book. Jonathan Lawrence, Ahmed Mehdi, Kate Hartnell, Gemma Lawrence, Catriona Ross and Melanie Newman have always been there for me. Huge thanks to Tara Keenan-Lindsay for being great in every way. I wouldn't have been able to finish this project without the love and support of Bart Moore-Gilbert. Words cannot express my debt to my mother, Caroline Hartnell, who has contributed to this project at every stage and on every level, and who has always been and remains my greatest source of inspiration. This book is dedicated to her.

Anna Hartnell
London
November 2010

Introduction: Rewriting Exodus

The election of the first African American president has breathed new life into a national narrative that has long sacralized the idea of freedom and cast the United States as an example to the rest of the world. Though often viewed with suspicion in the last few decades and outright hostility during the Bush administration, the story of American specialness has – for better or for worse – gained a new measure of credibility as articulated by Barack Obama. The irony is that Obama's black identity also makes him the unwitting reminder of the nation's failings – failings that were enshrined in founding documents which embraced slavery as part of America's unique experiment in democracy. Failings that were all too visible more than two centuries later when Hurricane Katrina laid bare a legacy of systemic racism that still traps disproportionate numbers of African Americans in what one black preacher characterizes as 'an abyss of hopelessness'.[1] Failings that have been vividly on display in the unseemly racist backlash that responded first to Obama's candidacy and then to his presidency. That an African American now occupies the highest office in the land occasions the opportunity to re-read America through the eyes of its black interpreters: and to re-examine the ways in which they have attempted to imagine a future that is not held hostage to the mistakes of the past.

This book revisits some of the major African American thinkers of the twentieth century – W.E.B. Du Bois, Martin Luther King, Malcolm X, Toni Morrison – and explores their re-telling of a myth central to America's national, religious and racial self-understanding: the Exodus narrative. Exodus, the second book of the Judeo-Christian bible, tells the story of the Hebrews' escape from Egyptian slavery. Led by Moses and guided by the benevolent hand of God, these slaves are crowned a 'chosen people', destined for a promised land where they will act as an example to the rest of the world, a 'light unto the nations'. Exodus is thus a narrative about freedom, one that speaks to the relationship between master and slave, between land, race and nation, while centralizing an account of divine election, the idea that a 'people' might be singled out to receive special favour in the eyes of God. This story of origins has shaped the mythology of one of the most significant nationalisms the world has ever seen. It stands behind George W. Bush's claim in the 2000 presidential election campaign that 'our nation is chosen by God and commissioned by history to be a model to the world';[2] it also suffuses Ronald Reagan's sense of America as a 'shining city upon a hill',[3] a sense that consciously echoes John Winthrop's vision of America as the latter led 700 pilgrims on their journey from England to their new promised land.

From the time of the first Puritan settlements that led to the founding of the United States, American patriots have mined the resources of this story to tell of their own nation's birth in flight first from religious persecution and then from the tyranny of British imperial rule. In turn, and simultaneously borrowing from larger black Atlantic traditions, African Americans have appropriated this same story to imagine their liberation from the suffering engendered by US slavery and its enduring legacy of racism. In many ways black America's rendition of the Exodus story is a deconstruction of the myth that stands at the centre of accounts of what many have characterized as an 'American civil religion'.[4] What Obama, following Martin Luther King, has termed America's 'original sin' of slavery entirely contradicts the nation's self-elected role as exemplar and guardian of liberty. It lays bare the paradox of the founding of the early Republic, which defined itself as an anti-imperialist endeavour while it embraced race-based slavery and a project of genocide that aimed to eliminate the nation's indigenous population. It is hardly surprising that in most African American renditions of the national story, America is not the promised land of the Exodus vision but rather the site of Egyptian oppression.

The embrace of the Exodus as a story which tells of the United States' postcolonial origins – its revolutionary overthrow of British rule – is thus fundamentally displaced by a black American counter-narrative that casts doubt on the presumptive 'innocence' that lies at the heart of the American project. As Roderick Bush suggests, the 'notion that the United States of America is a nation of immigrants, which, except for African Americans, has been a city on a hill, a shining light that has attracted people from every corner of the world to its welcoming shores', is not only 'facile and flattering' but obscures a reading of the United States as a settler-invader colony.[5] Thus while Hegel memorably described America as 'a land of desire for all those who are weary of the historical lumber-room of old Europe', his sense that America might really be the realization of freedom and the destination of history's 'end' is entirely contradicted by forms of subjugation that the early settlers exported to the new world.[6] In bearing witness to the fact that the New World did not constitute the New Jerusalem, black American renditions of Exodus not only re-signify the biblical story but also rewrite America as a nation defined not by an optimistic newness but as one that has yet to redeem its shameful past.

This book thus argues that the myriad versions of the Exodus narrative that have animated much black political rhetoric together encapsulate a negation of the nation's mythic 'flight from history' in the name of confronting past and present manifestations of white supremacy. In this sense we might usefully read black Exodus rhetoric as a form of what Michael Hanchard designates 'black memory', a form of memory that he argues works against the 'amnesia' and 'forgetting' that often characterizes 'state memory'. As well as preserving the memory of slavery and oppression against a system that routinely turns a blind eye to the origins of systemic racial inequalities, African American renditions of Exodus crucially 'remember' the experience of resistance, the defiance tradition that has shaped much African American culture. In imagining deliverance, the African American Exodus narrative thus represents a meeting point of a number of the 'symbols and rituals of national and transnational black imaginaries' that are deployed 'in the absence of state sanction and support'.[7] As African American historian Robin Kelley elaborates in relation to his own neighbourhood context in the 1970s:

> Whereas most Americans associated freedom with Western democracies at war against communism, free-market capitalism, or U.S. intervention in countries such as Vietnam or the Dominican Republic, in our neighbourhood 'freedom' had no particular tie to U.S. nationality.

'"Freedom"', writes Kelley, 'even became a kind of metonym for Africa.'[8] Black Exodus rhetoric – as a form of 'black memory' – is thus part of what Kelley identifies as African American 'freedom dreams', dreams that resist racial domination and instead construct imaginary homelands from the 'memories' of ancient Egypt, from the inspiration of decolonization movements in Africa, and even in the projection of utopias in outer space. At the very least, these dreams envisage the radical transformation of America. Such possibilities are very much at work in Du Bois' prophetic anticipation of a messianic 'day of reckoning',[9] in King's rhetorical transformation of the segregated South into a vision of the promised land; in Malcolm X's designation of Africa as 'the land of the future'[10] and in Toni Morrison's protagonists' vision of 'paradise' in her novel of the same name. These narratives of exodus can be read as forms of memorialization that keep 'visible the actual or imagined experiences of black peoples that would have been otherwise forgotten or neglected'.[11]

Yet the fact that the African American Exodus oscillates between visions of black self-determination – often imagined beyond the territorial borders of the United States – and the projection of a resolution via inclusion within the nation-state indicates, as Hanchard argues, that black memory, while distinct from state memory, nonetheless enables discursive crossovers between the two. As an African American who now occupies the office of US president, Obama can be seen as the literal embodiment of this crossover. Though Obama's electoral success relied on appealing to the rituals of black memory – in particular to the language and spirit of the Civil Rights movement – in order to garner vital support from the African American voting bloc, as US president he is now also the embodiment and mouthpiece of state memory. The extent to which his presidency necessarily subordinates black memory to the rituals of state memory is one of the primary questions that animates this book. While just under two years into Obama's first term is too soon to provide an answer to this question, this book maps the contours and distinctive characteristics of black Exodus rhetoric in the twentieth century, an exploration that not only illuminates Obama's own ideological and rhetorical positioning within black tradition, but which might also function as a measure against which Obama's rhetoric and action can be measured in the future.

Where Obama's presidency harbours the threat that 'non-statist' forms of memory might be subsumed by state memory, this possibility also lies at the heart of the biblical Exodus text. For while the assumption of the Exodus narrative as a central trope for America's transition from old world to new has so often been appropriated in the name of a linear and uncomplicated movement from bondage to freedom, from Egypt to the promised land, the Exodus narrative in fact encompasses two key moments that potentially render the story's development circuitous as opposed to linear, a process of dialectical exchange as opposed to a straightforward transition. The first moment enacts the Hebrew liberation into the desert, and the second is God's act of adoption of the Israelites as a chosen people. The one emphasizes the experience of oppression and the other is haunted by the possibility of assuming oppression's mantle; the movement is from liberation to nation-building. Certainly the story captures the possibility of the cycle of violence and oppression, the inevitable risk of the postcolonial moment. The seductive power of this story lies in its suggestion of the conjunction of innocence and power, which in the mainstream (statist) American rendition has all too often translated into a violent, racist chauvinism.

The Exodus event thus captures the problematic of group identity wherein a self-identified oppressed minority comes into its own as a majority. The crowning of the Hebrews as the Israelite nation – via God's act of adoption – grants religious sanction to a group identity grounded in the imperatives of race and nation. It is perhaps therefore unsurprising that the Puritans who settled America, the Zionists who laid claim to Palestine – the area that now comprises the State of Israel and the Occupied Territories – and the Afrikaners who made the trek to South Africa share a deep identification with this story. Though the Afrikaners' narrative has somewhat retreated since the end of apartheid in South Africa in 1994, the Exodus story continues to influence the national mythologies of Israel and the United States to the present day. Given that all three myths of settlement enabled various forms of often religiously sanctioned racism against non-white peoples, it perhaps seems an unlikely choice of motif through which African Americans might deconstruct US racism.

Clearly though, the Exodus myth is seductive because it endows the oppressed with power and agency. This point is elaborated in what follows via an exploration of the relationship between religious faith and political belief and action; while I argue that Exodus rhetoric, in its black nationalist and its liberal integrationist incarnations, is invariably put to work to resist oppressive state structures, I also explore the ways in which it can come to resemble a will to power that inadvertently reinscribes the logic it seeks to reject. Arguably this paradox – what might be characterized as an instance of 'forgetting' – is at work in the political vision of Marcus Garvey, which was drawn to the militarized aesthetics of state power and what Paul Gilroy describes as the rituals of 'racial becoming'.[12] Yet Garvey's populist 'back-to-Africa' movement was in no way morally or materially equivalent to the forms of racism and colonialism to which he was responding. Garveyism's mobilization of the symbols and rituals of popular – black – memory may have shared characteristics with state memory, but the movement did not wield state power but rather responded to the rough end of it. Rhetoric that appeals to Garveyite symbols is most commonly articulated not from the offices of the state but from the black church pulpit. Therefore this study of Exodus rhetoric is interested in measuring the distance and proximity not just between statist and non-statist forms of memory, but also, and often in a parallel move, between white supremacist mobilizations of the narrative of the chosen people and the black nationalist variant that, while on occasion problematic, for reasons of crucial power differentials cannot be named 'black supremacy' or described in terms of so-called 'reverse racism'.

These crucial power differentials have also mediated the sometimes intense identification with Jews and Judaism intrinsic to many black renditions of Exodus, and the commentary that twentieth-century black Exodus rhetoric has provided on the Middle East is part of the story that this book seeks to tell. Jews have frequently been viewed by US blacks as similarly inhabiting a location on the edges of western culture, yet since the founding of the State of Israel in 1948, this sense has gradually dissipated among African American activists, many of whom have increasingly seen the Jews in Israel as heir to the legacy of European colonialism. Shifting Middle East identifications in the mid to late 1960s led many black nationalists to jettison Judeo-Christian imagery altogether and to turn to alternate sources of identification in Islam and Afrocentrism. This alternative is characterized in this book by reference to the 'Egypt' trope. While this trope is apparently diametrically opposed to the Exodus identification, it has in fact long coexisted alongside the Exodus myth as a key component of black 'freedom dreams'. Again, Garveyism provides illustration: its centralization of the prophecy of Psalm 68:31 – 'Princes shall come out of Egypt; Ethiopia shall soon stretch out her hands unto God' – makes the redemption of Egypt and Africa more generally the horizon of the Exodus vision. Thus the 1960s is a key moment in which these collaborating stories are in a sense disentangled from one another and articulated as radically separate: the one supporting a separatist worldview emphasizing an African identity, the other leaning towards an integrationist worldview and an emphasis on America. That this separation is in many ways an illusion, that Exodus and Egypt function along a complex spectrum in black American thought, is demonstrated in the next chapter via an examination of the complicated religious and ideological frames that have informed the political identity of Barack Obama.

Chapter 1 acts as an extended introduction to this book by exploring the ways in which Obama enables us to re-situate some of the religious, political and transnational currents that permeate black Exodus rhetoric. The extent to which Obama's political vision is informed by black memory is viewed through the prism of his former church, as well as his identifications with the black, Jewish and Muslim diasporas. I suggest that while Obama undeniably endows the United States of America with the kind of redemptive agency imagined for Israel in the Exodus text, this is conditioned by an acute awareness of the consequences of state-sanctioned violence against national, religious and racial minorities that often transcend the imagined boundaries of the nation-state. Central to this awareness is the convergence Obama has staged between his postcolonial and African American identities – identities that enabled his presidential bid to lay claim to the legacy of the Civil Rights movement. This tension between black memory and state memory, the master narrative of American culture and the black American slave narrative, might be illuminated by what W.E.B. Du Bois designates in *The Souls of Black Folk* (1903) as African American 'double consciousness'. This dialectic speaks powerfully both to Obama's complex relationship to American identity and to the current scenario in which the presidency, faced with a right-wing backlash not incomparable to that which shaped the post-Reconstruction South that framed Du Bois' meditation in *Souls*, is being forced to view itself through the eyes of the white racist – in Du Bois' words, 'through the revelation of the other world'.[13]

Chapter 2 pursues this theme by examining the way in which Du Bois' re-enactment of the Exodus narrative highlights race as the organizing principle behind a master/slave dialectic that structures not only the rural American South but colonial relations across the globe. I argue that the radical irreconcilability of Du Boisian double consciousness – of being both African and American – finds its religious corollary in a prophetic rhetoric that refuses the redemptive trajectory of traditional American (Christian) renditions of the Exodus narrative. Instead, at many key moments, Du Bois' 'Exodus' is much more akin to the Jewish picture of an unredeemed world awaiting radical transformation. In this way Du Bois' thinking refuses to sanctify the status quo and instead can be allied with prophetic currents in black religious thought that have long fought for social justice.

Chapter 3 suggests that no other figure captures these religious effects of double consciousness more powerfully than Martin Luther King. As black America's most famous Christian, King's critique of the racism at the heart of American Christianity is often overlooked in favour of emphasizing the accommodationist tendencies of his 'dream'. At the heart of this dream was King's mobilization of the Exodus trope, which King saw as an allegory of the Civil Rights movement; while at certain points in his career King's vision seemed to be marked by Cold War liberalism and its attendant American exceptionalism, this was never uniformly the case. Many scholars now recognize in King's trajectory a radicalized later phase, but I suggest that the seeds for King's critique of America's imperial role on the world stage were sowed much earlier via a revised understanding of Christianity that staged an explicit encounter with Judaism. This encounter, I argue, guarded against the triumphalist rhetoric that was the hallmark of Cold War American exceptionalism. Instead King's critique not just of segregation in the American South but also apartheid in South Africa and the role of the US in the Vietnam war was advanced on the basis of a wider demystification of America's supposedly redemptive founding moment.

Chapter 4 suggests, therefore, that King's 'American dream' cannot be neatly counterpoised against Malcolm X's 'American nightmare'. Nonetheless, in contrast to Du Bois and King, Malcolm eschewed all forms of American exceptionalism in favour of transnational affiliations with African and Muslim diasporas. In so doing he outwardly rejected the Exodus trope of Judeo-Christian culture and instead identified with an equally mythological 'Egypt' – as the confluence of black and Islamic worlds. Malcolm in this sense is symbolic of the shift in African American culture, from what was perceived to be a domestically oriented Civil Rights movement to the internationalist bent of Black Power ideology, which emerged after Malcolm's death but which claimed his brand of black nationalism as its primary inspiration. Malcolm's religious and political transformations are thus read as precursors to the historic 'break' in the black–Jewish alliance that occurred in the late 1960s. This alliance had formed the backbone to the hugely successful Civil Rights coalition, and I argue that its demise, which was accompanied by a turn towards Islam in African American culture, was in part a response to the outcome of the 1967 war in the Middle East. However, as Malcolm's trajectory shows, the union between the politics of black empowerment and Islam is not necessarily any more straightforward than the union between anti-racism and Christianity. While the presidential election campaign of 2008 often simplistically implied that as an African American, Obama would struggle in his relationship with Jewish voters who would see him as somehow 'naturally' affiliated with the Muslim world and against the State of Israel, Malcolm's experiences show just how constructed and often strained these alliances actually are.

Chapter 5 explores some of these conflicts via a reading of Toni Morrison's 1998 novel, *Paradise*. Morrison's fictive all-black community not only parodies the ways in which the dual legacy of Civil Rights and Black Power have shaped contemporary African American culture. The community also stands in as a microcosm of the very nation that it supposedly fled via the staging of its own exodus event. *Paradise* traces the problematic fusion of religion and racial identity politics that haunts the Exodus text. It levels a profound critique at liberation movements that fail to decisively break away from the oppressive logic that they ostensibly flee, while demystifying the tendency of American exceptionalist discourse to sacralize and repeat the circumstances of the nation's founding. It is thus read here principally as a story of communal origins that includes a critique of patriarchal authority, analysis of which is notably elided in the national-religious visions of Du Bois, King and Malcolm X.

The class analysis at work in *Paradise* also raises the spectre of a post-Civil Rights landscape stalked by racial inequalities and in thrall to materialistic values that elevate property over and above human beings. This was the reality exposed by Hurricane Katrina in August and September of 2005. The highly racialized nature of the narrative that evolved from the storm is read in the concluding chapter as an event that has been partially assimilated into the archive of black memory. Following an overview of the way that the Katrina narrative has been conceptualized in relation to the specificities of New Orleans' racial, religious and colonial histories, I explore the post-Katrina experiences of exile and return that have disproportionately affected the city's poor black population. In particular the chapter explores the rhetorics of resistance that have emerged in response to what has often been perceived as a negligent and at times hostile state. It situates these rhetorics within the context of black Exodus tradition, thus illustrating that far from being a literary exercise, the mobilization of Exodus rhetoric in the black American imagination correlates to lived realities of dispersal and migration that have haunted the African American experience since the Middle Passage. Post-Katrina New Orleans thus returns us to the traumatic conditions of the nation's origins, and calls for the kind of reckoning with the past that so many hoped the Obama presidency might represent.

That much of the burden of New Orleans' rebuilding – in the face of severe government neglect – has been carried by African American churches speaks to the social justice mission that has animated significant sections of the historically black church. As argued throughout this book, the emphasis on social justice in the black religious tradition has manifested itself in a prioritization of the stories of the Old Testament – sometimes over and above those of the New – and particularly the Exodus narrative. The appropriation of a story that tells of the redemptive deliverance of a people from oppression is clearly a way of making available the rhetoric of the powerful for those traditionally blighted by the experience of powerlessness. Yet it is important to recognize that this is not the language of the everyday – it is a language spoken by designated leaders who have posed as custodians of a tradition. Where its most mainstream American articulations can now be heard from the mouths of US presidents, in the African American tradition it is voiced from church pulpits and by 'race leaders'. Consequently this book has self-consciously focused on those designated by Hazel Carby as 'race men'. As Carby pointed out in 1998, 'for a century, the figure of the race man has haunted black political and cultural thought'; this figure has bolstered the myth that representative black intellectuals and politicians are men – a myth that has occasioned the masculine monopolization of discourses of race, nation and religion. Carby argues that one of the ideological reasons for the perpetuation of the 'race man' myth is the promotion of the idea that African American society is afflicted by a crisis in black masculinity that needs remedying via affirmation of black male authority.[14]

It is precisely the symbolic power of Du Bois, King and Malcolm X – their perceived 'representativeness' – that makes them such compelling subjects for this book. Toni Morrison's own prophetic engagement in this discourse illustrates not only that the introduction of a gender analysis challenges the reification of race that can eclipse understandings of structures of oppression grounded in class and gender in the thought of 'race men'; it can also be read as a poignant comment on the problem of leadership, both inside and outside the black community, and the way that specific individuals can monopolize power and impose upon groups they ostensibly represent narrow or singular understandings of group identity. In this sense Morrison's novel can be read in sympathy with Carby's analysis and as a critique of black Exodus tradition. *Paradise* thus captures some of the ideological thrust of black feminist thought (though Morrison has pointedly evaded what she sees as the feminist label).[15] For like much black feminist work, Morrison's novel is, I argue, a form of 'redemptive critique' that challenges the black tradition from within by pointing up the ways in which an adherence to patriarchal values is indicative of not simply gender but also race and class investments that mimic the ideology of the wider nation.

Black Exodus rhetoric is thus read here as both religiously and ideologically complex, and illustrates that, as Melissa Harris-Lacewell writes, 'African American ideology cannot be easily constrained in a state-in vs. state-out dichotomy or an accommodation vs. militancy dichotomy that marks some traditional ways of approaching the study of black political thought'.[16] This idea also runs counter to the caricatured understandings of black political traditions circulated by the media during the 2008 presidential election. Michael Dawson challenges the commonplace assumption that the overwhelming preference for the Democratic Party among African Americans renders them politically homogeneous by identifying six specifically black ideologies: radical egalitarianism, disillusioned liberalism, black Marxism, black nationalism, black feminism and black conservatism. While black nationalism is the only ideology that places an absolute premium on race, Dawson argues that all black ideologies respond to the idea held by the great majority of African Americans that the fate of individual black lives are linked to that of the race.[17] While black Exodus rhetoric is most frequently articulated along the spectrum between black nationalism and black liberalism, a spectrum often identified with accommodationism vs. militancy or inclusion vs. separatism, other ideological outlooks have challenged and often nuanced these articulations. Harris-Lacewell's and Dawson's work is helpful not only for complicating the black ideological field but also for designating a 'black counterpublic' – a black public sphere that is to an extent defined by its oppositional relationship to the American mainstream. While black Exodus rhetoric, as already suggested, is largely an elite discourse, an understanding of its circulation in a black counterpublic is crucial for getting to grips with how and why the black articulation of the Exodus narrative – in its myriad forms – is often fundamentally different from its 'white' counterpart.

Writing in 1903 in *The Souls of Black Folk*, Du Bois argues for the centrality of black people in American life: 'there are to-day no truer exponents of the pure human spirit of the Declaration of Independence than the American Negroes';[18] veiled references to this idea abound in Obama's early speeches; in 2000 two of the most prominent contemporary African American intellectuals, Henry

Louis Gates and Cornel West, asked in their book, *The African-American Century*, 'Who could imagine the American Century without the African-American experience at its core?' In so doing they arguably supplement – rather than subvert – Henry Luce's prophetic announcement in 1941 that the twentieth century must be the 'American Century'; an idea that became central to Cold War triumphalism and later to the conception of a 'new American Century' envisaged by neo-conservatives associated with the Bush administration. In addition, Gates and West explicitly echo Du Bois' Hegelian tendencies by referring to the 'world-historical contributions of people of African descent in the United States of America that have repercussions around the world'.[19] Yet as my reading of Du Bois indicates, his oeuvre also categorically refuses the triumphalist logic that would name the United States 'the end of history'; though he shares with Gates and West an investment in American ideals which might be more fully realized if the nation honoured its promises to its black population, Du Bois' protest against US racism notably transgresses the traditional jeremiad.

As George Shulman explains, the 'jeremiad', which takes its name from the biblical prophet Jeremiah, is a form of protest by which 'prophets narrate conduct as a decline from origins'.[20] In the bible this originary moment is the covenantal relationship with God, forged as the Hebrew slaves make their exodus from Egypt. American Studies scholars such as Perry Miller and Sacvan Bercovitch have identified a 'uniquely American version of this rhetorical tradition' as playing a major role in shaping the myth of America. Bercovitch describes the Puritan-derived jeremiad as a *'political sermon'* that calls for social renewal and the revitalization of the American 'mission'.[21] Intimately connected to the idea that America is a chosen nation, the jeremiad has been invoked by a host of social movements in the US, along with successive American presidents, to ask the nation to live up to its founding ideals as enshrined in the Declaration of Independence and the US Constitution.

Bercovitch's influential work on the jeremiad underscores its essentially conservative role in maintaining America's sense of its own special destiny; he argues that there is no room for genuine dissent within this 'American ideology' because apparent protest is grounded in an ultimate consensus as to what 'America' stands for: a moral good. This rhetorical economy was a useful ideological counterweight to the fractious nineteenth-century context which explicitly excluded black people from the dominant narrative of 'Americanness'. Bercovitch's observations can be updated by observing the fact that this form of prophetic address was invoked after 9/11 by the right-wing Christian Jerry Falwell, who claimed that the tragedy was a divine punishment of a nation that had transgressed the covenantal relationship by throwing 'God out of the public square' and sanctioning abortion and homosexuality.[22] As Shulman notes, the 'legacy of Jeremiah' within American culture is often notably illiberal.

However, Eddie Glaude, whose *Exodus! Religion, Race, and Nation in Nineteenth-Century Black America* (2000) has been an important influence on this book, reminds us that the motif of 'chosenness' central to the Exodus narrative became the basis for a 'nation language' for black Americans in the nineteenth century. This was not a 'nation language' that could be reined into the economy of an 'American ideology' because the dominant narrative of nationhood was premised upon white supremacy. Glaude suggests that, according to Bercovitch, 'blacks and native Americans, although considered pariahs in antebellum America, may one day be considered true Americans if they adopt America's ideals':

> But this grossly underestimates the entrenched nature of America's racial beliefs, particularly the fact that the idea of chosenness was racialized such that members of the chosen people were all white men delineated or distinguished from those who were not chosen on the basis of race.[23]

Thus for Glaude, and contra Bercovitch, the Exodus rhetoric that undergirded the development of a distinctly black jeremiad in the nineteenth century transgressed the restricted racial economy of mainstream American jeremiads by naming blacks a chosen people. Glaude's conclusions seem to imply that this designation located blacks both inside and outside mainstream understandings of American identity – for while the designation of black chosenness was to an extent a claim to inclusion within the wider national discourse, it also laid the foundations for a separatist black nationalism.

This dual tendency, I suggest, can be seen in Du Bois' jeremiad. His sense that 'America is not another word for Opportunity to *all* her sons' points not only to the betrayal of America's founding ideals but also to an African heritage as partial solution.[24] Du Bois does not go as far as Malcolm X did in naming Africa, and not America, 'the land of the future', but his diasporic thrust does partially displace the geographical site of the American nation. Moreover, his steadfast refusal to accept that God wills the status quo guards against the triumphalism that defines exceptionalist discourse. As Shulman suggests, in seeking to break 'the vicious cycle of crime and punishment, Jeremiah imagines a new beginning ... he imagines a new Exodus, as if to inaugurate what Harold Rosenberg calls "the tradition of the new"'.[25] Yet this book argues that this call to 'newness' is consistently qualified in a black tradition that has routinely resisted the impulse to imaginatively wipe the historical slate clean. Even when Barack Obama as US president calls on America to renew itself, he gestures back to a moment of national founding that, as he himself has repeatedly pointed out, instituted racial slavery at the moment of its inception. Indeed, Wilson Jeremiah Moses, in his groundbreaking work on nineteenth-century black religious and nationalist traditions, defines the black jeremiad as 'the constant warnings issued by blacks to whites, concerning the judgement that was to come for the sin of slavery'.[26] While Obama's position in office precludes a more radical jeremiad, this book suggests the African American articulation often transcends the form itself; that is to say that where traditional expressions of the jeremiad maintain an absolute faith in the American ideal, if not the American reality, this assumption is very often itself subject to rigorous questioning in the black tradition.

This is in many ways because the black counterpublic has long occupied a unique place in the US racial formation. As Kelley writes, 'the marginal and excluded have done the most to make democracy work in America', and in both material and symbolic terms, African Americans have been and remain America's most marginal and excluded population.[27] In 1993, Toni Morrison wrote what has become an influential essay for *Time* magazine, which claimed that newly arrived immigrants to the United States achieve assimilation in part by learning discriminatory behaviour and practices towards African Americans. In this essay, poignantly entitled 'On the Backs of Blacks', Morrison writes that 'negative appraisals of the native-born black population' form the 'most enduring and efficient rite of passage into American culture'.[28] And as Thomas Sugrue argues in *Barack Obama and the Burden of Race* (2010), despite growing numbers of Americans who claim Hispanic and Asian descent, and 'immigration patterns' that have 'transformed urban and metropolitan geographies in ways that confound traditional racial categories', despite the fact that these populations do experience the rough end of racial discrimination in a variety of ways, 'by nearly every measure, African Americans stand alone'.[29] Possibly because they have stood to gain the least from American national ideology, studies have shown that more than any other minority, African Americans as a group have been least supportive of post-9/11 US foreign policy.[30] For these reasons, despite America's changing racial landscape, it still makes sense to talk about a black/white binary that has historically positioned blacks as whistleblowers in relation to US racism at home and imperialism abroad. As this book argues, some of the most powerful articulations of dissent have taken an explicitly religious form.

Manning Marable argues that 'the great gift of black folk to American politics and society has been that we have consistently fought for a more inclusive and humanistic definition of democracy, the relationship between people and the state.'[31] Here he not only echoes Kelley, Harris-Lacewell and Dawson in emphasizing the centrality of African Americans 'in shaping political debate and action in America'.[32] He also articulates the secular counterpart to Martin Luther King's sense that black America was chosen to 'save the soul of this nation'.[33] As Wilson Jeremiah Moses argues, the long tradition of black messianism – the idea that black suffering and ultimate deliverance might be the redemption of America – 'reconciles the sense of separateness that black people feel and their fundamental belief that they are truly American. It is the point at which their black nationalism and American nationalism overlap'. As Moses explains, black messianism, the idea of chosenness that sits at the heart of the Exodus narrative, does double duty as it not only provides a critique of America but it potentially fulfils its self-image as a redeemer nation.[34] Yet where the doubts that the Puritan jeremiad expressed about the American mission gradually gave way to a fundamentally self-certain vision of US world-historical destiny, black Exodus rhetoric has typically maintained a scepticism about the American project, and has thus fulfilled the moral function of enacting black memory in relation to the American state.

The relationship between blackness and Americanness is the theme of this book. One of the most memorable photographs to emerge from Hurricane Katrina features the now iconic image of a black woman waiting outside the New Orleans Convention Center wrapped in an American flag. It is hard not to read this image in the context of the wider African American experience on US soil; the face that the flag encircles captures a sense of misery that transcends its immediate temporal and spatial location. It is a picture that recalls the opening of Spike Lee's 1992 Malcolm X biopic, which shows the US flag being burnt into the shape of an 'X'. While some critics accused Lee of 'Americanizing' Malcolm, equally the image shows Malcolm's legacy to be seared into the national cloth in a way that is visually reminiscent of the crosses burnt by the Ku Klux Klan.[35] The union between America and the 'X' is born in flames, and while the flag apparently acts as a source of comfort for this woman sitting outside New Orleans' Convention Center, there is a deeper sense that it also represents her source of pain. Perhaps even more than the opening scene of *Malcolm X*, this photograph strains, questions, and possibly severs the relationship between blackness and the most potent sign of American nationalism.

That a black man now occupies the White House occasions this exploration of the genealogy of the Exodus trope in African American culture; one that seeks to trace the story's potential as both an entrance to and an exit from the privileged – and, so the story goes, redemptive – terrains of US national culture. Necessarily this book is an exploration of black intellectual traditions against the backdrop not only of the opening years of the Obama presidency but also of the post-9/11 US domestic and foreign policy to which Obama's presidential bid was so clearly responding. The fact that the resurgence of American exceptionalist discourse that occurred after 11 September 2001 coincided with a virulent Islamophobia is a poignant reminder that white supremacy has often been at the heart of US nationalism. Obama's rise tells a different story about America, but one that must be thought alongside a black Exodus tradition dedicated to revealing the extent to which racism has shaped the national mythology – pointing not to the celebration of a post-racial future but rather to the work yet to be done in the name of racial justice.

1
Re-reading America: Barack Obama

As Barack Obama took the oath of office and was sworn in as 44th United States President on 20 January 2009, he rekindled for many the romance of America. After eight long years of the Bush administration, and many more during which the nation's economic, political and military power seemed to more than hint in the direction of imperial ambition, distant memories of America's claim to be an inherently progressive project floated back into the momentarily magical space of the Washington mall, and the realms of the imaginable.

This space is also haunted by the ghosts of African and African American slaves; the National Mall marks one of a number of sites that during the eighteenth and nineteenth centuries oversaw the trade in human beings.[1] Fast forward to this cold and bright day in the first decade of the twenty-first century and one only needed to glance at the crowd that had gathered to witness the dazzling spectacle to realize that this historic event carried a very specific resonance for black Americans. They were there to get a glimpse of that 'better history' invoked throughout Obama's inaugural address, one that exemplifies, in the words of one commentator, a nation that 'still believes that even the darkest chapters in its past can be transcended'.[2]

The sense that the United States might be capable of redeeming its violent racial history was perhaps most powerfully captured on election night back in November 2008. Free of the ceremonial trappings that pervade inauguration day, Obama announced to Chicago's Grant Park that 'change has come to America' and proceeded to give one of the best oratorical performances of his career. Though his speech made clear that 'change' encapsulated much more than the election of the first African American US president, the significance of this feat echoed throughout the president-elect's narrative that was everywhere punctuated by the ideals and the rhetoric of the Civil Rights movement. What had become the mantra of the most successful grassroots presidential campaign in US electoral history became in this speech 'the timeless creed that sums up the spirit of a people', which was in turn rhetorically transposed onto the signature of the Civil Rights movement: '"We Shall Overcome." Yes we can.'[3]

In making the narrative of Civil Rights available to all Americans, Obama's election night speech demonstrated that his sense of standing on 'the shoulders of [Civil Rights] giants' was not simply an acknowledgement of his debt to the 1960s black struggle; it also evidenced the triumph of a movement that had advanced a dream of freedom central to the American project. Thus having evoked the challenges of 'two wars, a planet in peril, the worst financial crisis in a century', the president-elect borrowed imagery from the man who has come to symbolize the Civil Rights era. Obama declared: 'The road ahead will be long. Our climb will be steep. We may not get there in one year or even one term, but America – I have never been more hopeful than I am tonight that we will get there. I promise you – we as a people will get there.' The echoes of Martin Luther King's last speech in April 1968 are unmistakeable. The night before he died King told a crowd in Memphis: 'I've seen the promised land. I may not get there with you. But I want you to know tonight, that we, as a people will get to the promised land.'[4] Obama came of age in a post-Civil Rights milieu and his bid for the White House was of a different order to King's call for racial equality. What Obama shares with King is a propensity to place the African American experience at the centre of 'the American story' – in a way that fuses African American exceptionalism with the exceptionalist narrative that has long played a leading role in US national life. For King, the principal archetype for this redemptive national story – which claims the ideal of freedom, if not the reality, as a marker of American specialness – is the biblical Exodus. In echoing King's imagery, in which the American dream becomes synonymous with the promised land that represents the aspiration of the Exodus narrative, Obama pays lip-service to a long tradition whereby African Americans have retold the nation's origins from the perspective of the repressed.[5]

The inauguration of the first African American president occurred just over forty years after the assassination of the great Moses figure of the Civil Rights generation. Obama, the pre-eminent representative of what many have described as the succeeding 'Joshua generation', thus seemingly promised to lead the nation out of the wilderness period and into a post-racial future. The Civil Rights veteran Andrew Young explains his initial distrust of and eventual conversion to Obama in biblical terms: 'I had too many scars from Egypt and wandering in the wilderness to see clearly into the Promised Land.'[6] Young is among a number of commentators who have followed Obama's lead in appropriating the imagery of the Exodus story in order to link Obama's campaign with the Civil Rights movement and, in turn, the larger national story. Yet Young's initial doubts about the hope that an Obama presidency might inaugurate a Third Reconstruction are arguably confirmed by the frequent scholarly claim that Obama ran a race-neutral campaign and is now running a race-blind presidency.[7] Young's own cautionary words on election day indicate not only that Obama's promise has yet to be realized; they also point to the dangers of amnesia: 'When you get to the Promised Land – and we're with you when you go all the way – don't forget how you got there. Don't forget that it was God who parted the Red Sea, who fed you in the wilderness when you were hungry.'[8] Here we might read Young's injunction to remember as recognition of the tension between 'state memory' and 'black memory' – terms conceptualized by Michael Hanchard and discussed in the introduction to this book – and the fear that the imperatives of the former might eclipse those of the latter.[9] This threat is arguably intrinsic to a presidency that actively courted the idea that it might act as a vehicle of racial reconciliation.

This chapter is not an attempt to weigh Obama's presidency so far against this implicit claim of his campaign – to measure the extent to which the black struggle against racism has been, under the stewardship of the current administration, subsumed and possibly rendered invisible by the official story of America's inevitable progression towards freedom. Conclusions on this question seem premature. Rather, this chapter seeks to lay the groundwork for this future discussion by showing the way in which the current president, and the narratives that have emerged as consistent themes in his writings and speeches, help us situate – and think anew – the relationship between black liberation and American exceptionalism; the extent to which the nation's racial history haunts Obama's invocations of its purportedly biblically sanctioned journey towards freedom. For Obama has emerged as a quintessentially Janus-faced figure, viewed by different constituencies as simultaneously embodying the polar oppositions that have played a primary role in shaping both popular and scholarly conceptualizations of black political thought: between accommodation and militancy, the 'House Negro' and the 'Field Negro'. Or, as this book suggests,

identifications with the Judeo-Christian 'Exodus' or an African and/
or Islamic 'Egypt'.

Taking Obama's engagement with Exodus rhetoric as a starting
point, this chapter explores the ways in which Obama's writings and
speeches, as well as commentary on Obama, situate his narrative
in relation to the intersecting categories that animate the biblical
Exodus and its modern adaptations: nation, race, religion and
diaspora. The aim here is to assess the extent to which Obama's
rhetorical output – and thus his own self-understanding and self-
presentation – resonate with black Exodus, as opposed to statist
Exodus, traditions. Obama's relationship to US exceptionalist rhetoric, his affinities to his former church, and his attitudes
towards the African, Muslim and Jewish diasporas, are viewed
as brief case studies through which we might better understand
Obama's relationship to the often intersecting but sometimes
disparate discourses of US patriotism and the African American
critique of white supremacy. These case studies taken together
provide an extended introduction to the themes explored in more
depth throughout the rest of this book, and show the way in which
Obama's postcolonial legacy alongside his explicit self-identification
as an African American have enabled commentators to cast him as
both the embodiment and the antithesis of the American story. I
argue below that Obama's complex religious identity and ideological
affinities trouble the false dichotomies too often posed between
so-called 'black messiahs' and 'Uncle Toms'.

OBAMA AND AMERICA: THE MASTER NARRATIVE

As Obama stood at the centre of the inauguration ceremony – the
ritual that symbolizes the national civil religion like no other –
there was the suggestion that the apparently conflicting accounts
of liberation articulated by black and white America might have
transcended their differences. Certainly King's sometimes Hegelian
rendering of Exodus envisaged the eventual overcoming of the
master/slave dialectic via the integration of black and white. The
fact that Obama was able to so convincingly activate America's
revolutionary origins in the time-honoured tradition of presidential
inaugural addresses indicates that these traditions were equally
available to the new black president as they had been to his
predecessors. Indeed, many commentators complained that the
powerful oratory that we have come to expect from Obama was
drowned out by the well-worn lines and standard themes that

have come to dominate all but the most memorable inaugurals: sacrifice, courage, responsibility, renewal, etc. This sense gave rise to an idea that has since become something of a refrain in certain sectors of the media: that Obama often sounds remarkably similar to George W. Bush. Given the kind of rugged individualism the Bush administration practised at home and the violent interventions it undertook abroad, this association is designed to throw doubt on Obama's claim to advance a progressive politics that gives voice to the voiceless – one that, in terms of the Exodus dialectic, holds mastery in abeyance.

In many ways it is to be expected that Obama might sound closer to his presidential predecessor than the towering figure of the Civil Rights movement. Obama has studiously avoided the 'post-racial' label that insidiously stalked his election bid as a test of its viability for all – not just black – Americans. And he has consistently stressed that the work of the Civil Rights project has yet to be completed. Nonetheless, as the leading representative of the 'breakthrough' generation of black politicians – beneficiaries of the Civil Rights movement who rely on majority-white electorates for votes – Obama has rejected the idea that race should be the measure of his politics.[10] This has involved politically distancing himself from Civil Rights veteran Jesse Jackson, the man whose previous bids for the Democratic nomination for president undoubtedly helped pave the way for Obama's success. This potentially raises questions about Obama's appropriation of Civil Rights rhetoric to authenticate his claim to have brought 'change' to Washington. To what extent can the current US president lay claim to black political traditions?

That this authentication was crucial to Obama's electoral success is now widely agreed upon. Somewhat paradoxically given the enormous racial barriers Obama had to overcome in his bid for the presidency, his successful bid for an African American identity – amidst initial suspicions that his mixed heritage and his paternal links to a postcolonial as opposed to a post-slavery black identity rendered him at a distance from the African American experience – undoubtedly helped him secure the White House. For not only did Obama rely, as have all Democratic nominees since Franklin Delano Roosevelt, on the African American vote; arguably it was his hard-won status as a representative of black America that enabled him to convince the wider electorate that he might one day represent America as a whole. It seems highly likely that Obama's white heritage was hugely advantageous in terms of attracting some white voters; and his rich cultural heritage enabled Obama to pose as the symbol of a 'promised land' that had embraced immigrants from all over the world. Yet it also became increasingly apparent on the campaign trail that Obama's invocations of his black father from Kenya and his white mother from Kansas, his birth in Hawaii and part of his childhood spent in Indonesia, required balancing against the rooted sense of family and community that Obama had found on the South Side of Chicago. It seems that early on in his life, well before he glimpsed a political career, Obama realized that in a nation unable to sustain ambiguity when it comes to interpretations of the black/white binary, he must 'search' for 'a workable meaning for his life as a black American'.[11] This early desire to affirm his identity as an African American, an affirmation that enabled Obama to claim the legacy of King during his presidential campaign, was arguably crucial in his bid to succeed Bush as US president.

The following two sections of this chapter map the coordinates by which we might trace Obama's path between his Civil Rights legacy and presidential ambitions, and the way he has mobilized what Hanchard designates as 'non-statist' forms of black memory in order to become – and begin to carry out his duties as – the highest representative of the American state. One of the first things Obama did on gaining office was to replace the bust of Winston Churchill that sat in Bush's Oval Office with one of Abraham Lincoln, which was soon joined by a bust of Martin Luther King. The return of the Churchill bust to the UK was greeted as a snub by some sectors of the British press, though the White House claimed that the bust, loaned by former UK Prime Minister Tony Blair in the aftermath of 9/11 as a symbol of transatlantic unity, was due to be returned in any case. Nonetheless, I suggest that this switch is symbolic of Obama's wider project of rewriting 'America'; repudiation of the slave legacy, as opposed to friendship with the former colonial motherland and principal ally in the so-called war on terror, metonymically stands in for the national narrative. And yet the extent to which this move related to substance rather than style, the extent to which Obama is able, as US president, to stand up for the disadvantaged – as he has so often claimed to do – rather than represent the powerful, is highly constrained by the office he now occupies.

In his first inaugural address in January 2001, George W. Bush spoke of 'the story of a new world that became a friend and liberator of the old, a story of a slave-holding society that became a servant of freedom, the story of a power that went into the world to protect but not possess, to defend but not to conquer'. Obama's inaugural address tells a similar story. Bush told his fellow Americans: 'we are not this story's author, who fills time and eternity with His purpose. Yet His purpose is achieved in our duty, and our duty is fulfilled in service to one another.' By announcing that 'we renew that purpose today', Bush borrowed a trope from a long line of presidential addresses and reaffirmed Americans as a covenantal people – a 'chosen people' – who work hand in hand with God as beneficiaries of a special promise and harbingers of a special destiny. Following 11 September of that same year, Bush's concluding words gathered increasing significance: 'this work continues. This story goes on. And an angel still rides in the whirlwind and directs this storm.'[12]

By the time of Bush's second inaugural in January 2005, he felt compelled to explicitly reject the idea that the United States believes itself to be elected to a special task in the divine plan; he claimed that confidence in America's mission to 'carry the message of freedom' to 'the darkest corners of our world' must remain firm 'not because we consider ourselves a chosen nation; God moves and chooses as He wills.' Nonetheless, the speech's close – 'May God bless you, and may He watch over the United States of America' – leaves the listener in little doubt that this comprehensive reassertion of his administration's policy to wage war on terror could claim the sanction of God, or, to use a term that appeared earlier in Bush's address, 'the Author of liberty'.[13] As Jonathan Raban claims, inaugural addresses are a 'unique' literary form that grant their speakers licence to use words that 'would sound insane if spoken quietly, indoors'. Even so, the way a president chooses to blow this 'golden trumpet' is revealing, and there are times at which Obama's address seems to stick uncomfortably close to Bush's script.[14]

Obama claimed in his inaugural address that America's 'ideals still light the world', and his assertion that the United States is 'ready to lead once more' was unlikely to reassure those who in the previous eight years had found themselves on the wrong side of American leadership.[15] Indeed, Obama has struck this note with some consistency: writing in *Foreign Affairs* in the summer of 2007 – in an article entitled 'Renewing American Leadership' – Obama evoked a past when America had 'led and lifted the world' and declared that 'the American moment is not over, but it must be seized anew'. Renewing America's 'historic purpose in the world' involved resurrecting 'an America that battles immediate evils, promotes an ultimate good, and leads the world once more'.[16] Obama is clearly heir to an exceptionalist dream that unequivocally endows the United States with the task of moral leadership. As David Howard-Pitney claims, political rhetoric in the US is suffused by the belief in Americans as 'a chosen people with a historic mission to save and remake the world'.[17] As argued in the introduction to this book, successive American presidents have exhorted the nation to live up to its founding ideals, its covenantal calling. This classic form of exhortation, the jeremiad, was deployed by the Bush administration in order to marshal support for the 'war on terror'.

And yet part of Obama's appeal as a candidate was the extent to which he had challenged the Bush administration's variant of American exceptionalism; particularly beneficial to Obama's campaign had been his opposition to the US-led invasion of Iraq. In contrast to the certainty of Ronald Reagan's vision of a 'shining city upon a hill', in his election night address Obama nodded to the fallout from the so-called war on terror by evoking 'those who have wondered if America's beacon still burns as bright'.[18] Obama's rhetoric contrasts sharply with the now famous vision Bush articulated at West Point military academy in June 2002, which, as a prelude to the Iraq invasion, presents a picture of unbridled American power stamping its own reality onto the rest of the world. As Carl Pederson points out, what has become known as the 'Bush Doctrine' provides a precise illustration of the picture painted by theologian Reinhold Niebuhr, one of Obama's – as well as Martin Luther King's – favourite philosophers:[19]

A nation with an inordinate degree of political power is doubly tempted to exceed the bounds of historical possibilities, if it is informed by an idealism which does not understand the limits of man's wisdom and volition in history.[20]

In January 2008, Obama made it clear that his aim was not just to end the war: 'I want to end the mind-set that got us into the war in the first place.'[21] The way in which Obama conceived of this mindset was perhaps most clearly articulated in his Nobel acceptance speech in December 2009. As a number of commentators have noted, while Obama did not mention Niebuhr by name, he clearly invoked Niebuhr's sense of war as a 'tragic' choice that must mediate between the recognition that 'evil does exist in the world' and so 'war is sometimes necessary', with the knowledge that 'war at some level is an expression of human folly'. These 'irreconcilable truths', according to Obama, occasioned the Niebuhrian dilemma that any invocation of a 'just war' must be tempered by an awareness that 'we are fallible', that human assertion never fully transcends self-interest. For this reason, 'Holy War can never be a just war' because 'if you truly believe that you are carrying out divine will, then there is no need for restraint'. By stressing that this 'extremist' understanding of war has historically been at work in Christianity as well as Islam – Obama specifically mentions the Crusades – Obama made it clear that his object of attack included both Al Qaeda and western responses that framed their violent endeavours as the work of God.[22] Consequently a sense of the prudent limits of American power permeates Obama's rhetoric and leaves significantly less room for the kind of triumphalism that defined the Bush era. Unlike King, Obama does not map Niebuhrian philosophy onto a commitment to non-violence, but his appropriation of Niebuhr enables a rhetoric that rejects certitude as pride. In this way Obama's exceptionalist discourse can be distinguished from Bush's by the fact that his is a much more pronounced jeremiad, mobilized not to authorize but rather to challenge a status quo so often dictated by brute self-interest.

Obama's consistent counterbalancing of the ideal of the American promise versus the realities of American power is part of an analysis of American history that easily exceeds the political need to demonstrate the shortcomings of the eight short years of the Bush administration. During Obama's now famous keynote address to the 2004 Democratic Convention he claimed that Americans were called upon 'to reaffirm our values and commitments, to hold them against a hard reality and see how we are measuring up, to the legacy of our forbearers, and the promise of future generations'.[23] And as he addressed the 99th Annual Convention of the NAACP (National Association for the Advancement of Colored People) in July 2008, he stated that 'the true genius of America' is 'not that America is, but that America will be; not that we are perfect, but that we can make ourselves more perfect.'[24] While it might appear standard for a US president to lay claim to the future in this way, Obama's insistence that 'we have more work to do'[25] lays stress on the road ahead as opposed to sacralizing the moment of the Union's inception, the origins of the covenant – which Obama insists were not 'perfect'. Obama's sense that 'we do not have to live in an idealized world to still reach for those ideals that will make it a better place'[26] recalls King's invocation of Niebuhr's Christian realism as an idealism that cannot claim God's sanction – discussed in detail in Chapter 3 – and renders Obama's articulation of American exceptionalism far more complex than standard accounts.

As Raban's description of Obama's inaugural speech suggests, 'under the guise of noble platitude Obama was able to get away with murder, cloaking in familiar and emollient language an address that otherwise defied convention'. In this way Obama renewed the possibilities of exceptionalist discourse itself by resurrecting its role as a language of protest. Obama's call to remake America was hardly new, but the critical resources he mobilized to make this call amounted to a wholesale attack on the administration of the previous eight years, a move that is quite unprecedented in the history of presidential inaugurations. Like the storm evoked in Bush's first inauguration speech and comprehensively exploited in his second, Obama too claimed to be taking office 'amidst gathering clouds and raging storms', but this was cast as an opportunity to choose 'hope over fear'. Summoning the spirit of the revolutionary preamble of the American Constitution – 'we, the people' – Obama positioned himself against 'those in high office' who, he strongly suggested, had not remained 'true to our founding documents'. It was thus apparently on behalf of the American people that Obama issued a stream of implicit indictments of an administration that had offered a false choice 'between our safety and our ideals', ideals that had been plundered for 'expedience's sake'. Instead Obama promised to 'restore science to its rightful place', 'roll back the specter of a warming planet', keep a 'watchful eye' on a market that 'can spin out of control' and respect 'the rule of law and the rights of man'. For, Obama remarked, 'in the words of Scripture, the time has come to set aside childish things'.[27]

Raban elaborates:

> There was no triumphalism in this; there was, rather, a note of sombre regret. It was necessary for Obama to announce to both the United States and the rest of the world (and his inaugural was directed, unusually, at least as much to the foreign as to the domestic audience) that on Tuesday [20 January 2009] the Bush era had ended and that America, after a long, unhappy detour in the wilderness, was returning to its better history.

Even Raban's commentary cannot resist the biblical imagery of the wilderness – the place of exile to which the children of Israel are consigned in the book of Exodus prior to their realization of the promised land. The conclusion of Obama's speech also evokes a journey, though not explicitly that featured in the Exodus narrative – Obama's choice is more specifically located in the historical time of the nation. He pictures 'a small band of patriots huddled by the dying campfires on the shores of an icy river'; it is 'the year of

America's birth' and 'the enemy' is 'advancing'. Grafting the present moment onto the country's revolutionary origins, Obama exhorts Americans to 'brave once more the icy currents, and endure what storms may come':

> Let it be said by our children's children that when we were tested we refused to let this journey end, that we did not turn back nor did we falter; and with eyes fixed on the horizon and God's grace upon us, we carried forth that great gift of freedom and delivered it safely to future generations.[28]

As Raban suggests, this 'image of leaving the blood-stained snow behind to cross the freezing river' is more than 'a stirring call to arms to fight recession; he was placing between his incoming administration and that of the outgoing president a broad river packed with growling chunks of ice'. This portrait of endurance recalls the vision of the parting of the Red Sea in Exodus – which opens up an untraversable gulf between Pharaoh and his Egyptian army on the one hand and Moses and the departing Hebrews on the other. Obama's journey is similarly blessed by the grace of God and it crucially re-centres the experience of flight from imperialism in the American national narrative. Obama thus affirms America's origins in an anti-imperialist narrative, origins that the Bush administration, Obama strongly implies, betrayed. Obama thus re-ignites the Exodus narrative of American national mythology that casts the history of the United States as a postcolonial narrative. In so doing he apparently suppresses the reality that his rhetoric is elsewhere so aware of: the reality that meant, as Cedric Robinson writes, 'many thousands of Blacks', along with the majority of Native Americans, 'would fight against independence, not for love of imperial Britain but because they understood that Black freedom was otherwise unobtainable'.[29] Instead, and somewhat paradoxically, Obama's mythology of America appeals to the nation's 'better angels' in order to activate the narrative on behalf of all Americans, including those who have been oppressed in its name.

Obama's inaugural speech concludes at a moment just prior to the founding of the nation; the blessing received by God is that accorded to those Obama casts as the oppressed in flight as opposed to those on the verge of settling their new promised land. Obama thus closes his speech on a moment of possibility that anticipates future redemption for a promised land that has yet to be achieved. In so doing he signifies what I argue in this chapter is his rhetorical propensity to emphasize that which is yet to come – the always already unfinished process of history. Though he calls for a return to the nation's revolutionary origins in order to renew its historic project – Obama is by no means relinquishing claim to this – his call does not seem to indicate a desire to wipe the historical slate clean. While Obama's rendering of the revolutionary moment markedly suppresses its ambiguity for African and Native Americans, it is opened up as a new point of departure from which to think an American future that might be imagined otherwise. In this way Obama seems to share with King – and other African American thinkers who have made freedom their life's work – the intellectual, political and religious instinct to defer the redemptive moment in favour of emphasizing the work yet to be done in the name of social justice.

The gulf that Obama's speech opens up seems not to signal the gulf between America as the triumph of western progress and those 'darkest corners of our world' calling out to be liberated by the benevolent superpower. Earlier parts of Obama's speech make it clear that America extends the hand of friendship to other nations, and particularly the 'Muslim world' – in stark contrast to a Bush administration that projected an 'axis of evil' beyond the realms of American identification. Rather the gulf is between those who are able to exercise power responsibly and those who are not. In this he allies the incoming administration with earlier generations who

> understood that our power alone cannot protect us, nor does it entitle us to do as we please. Instead they knew that our power grows through its prudent use; our security emanates from the justness of our cause, the force of our example, the tempering qualities of humility and restraint.[30]

In response to the emerging Black Power movement four decades previously, King said something very similar: 'there is nothing wrong with power if power is used correctly'; 'power at its best is love implementing the demands of justice.'[31]

Thus Obama's rendition of the national story mobilizes a variant of state memory that claims for itself the logic but not necessarily the reality of freedom; in this way his exceptionalist rhetoric is comparable to that deployed by presidential predecessors but it is significantly mitigated by an awareness that America has not meant freedom for everybody. This alternative version of the Exodus story that shadows Obama's articulation of exceptionalist discourse is that which frequently populates African American letters. It is a version that subsequent chapters argue commonly lays stress not on the assumption of power but rather the moment of freedom. Emphasis on this perspective – drawn from the archive of black memory – was central to Obama's understanding of his bid for the White House.

OBAMA AND AMERICA: THE SLAVE NARRATIVE

Evidence of Obama's acute awareness of disadvantage, and his consequent reticence when it comes to identifying with an assertive US nationalism, is particularly apparent in a complex and somewhat convoluted passage in his 2004 preface to *Dreams From My Father* (1995). Obama begins this section of text by reflecting on a time when 'internationally, writers announced the end of history, the ascendance of free markets and liberal democracy, the replacement of old hatreds and wars between nations with virtual communities and battles for market share'. 'And then', he writes, 'on September 11, 2001, the world fractured.'[32] Obama's characterization of the violent fracture ushered in by 9/11 was similarly voiced by Bush in his 2005 inaugural address: 'after the shipwreck of communism came years of relative quiet, years of repose, years of sabbatical – and then there came a day of fire.'[33] The Obama of this 2004 preface is one headed for the Senate, seeking to place what is in many ways a radical book on US race politics under the acceptable sign of American patriotism. In this vein Obama then pierces his own somewhat unconvincing construction of history's end by setting the scene of a battle:

> Between the modern and the ancient; between those who embrace our teeming, colliding, irksome diversity, while still insisting on a set of values that binds us together, and those who would seek, under whatever flag or slogan or sacred text, a certainty and simplification that justifies cruelty toward those not like us.[34]

This, Obama's preface tells us, 'is the struggle set forth, on a miniature scale, in this book'. In so doing he places himself, and by implication the African American struggle for equality and recognition, on the 'right' side of a returned history, asserting an exceptionalist picture of the diversity of American democracy – in a vision that sits somewhat uneasily with the portrait of America's deep-seated racism that quietly unfolds in the proceeding memoir.

Yet even at this moment in the preface, Obama fails to tame the more radical currents of his own text. While his notion that 9/11 pitted forces modern and ancient against one another resonates with colonial accounts of bringing 'enlightenment' to 'backward' natives – a narrative that was clearly at work in the brutal passage of 'Manifest Destiny' that settled the United States – Obama here also pairs these forces with a perceived struggle between the 'worlds of plenty and worlds of want'; indicating that his analysis of 9/11 does dig a little deeper than his exceptionalist rhetoric would imply.[35]

Most revealing is Obama's sense that 'history returned that day with a vengeance ... in fact, as Faulkner reminds us, the past is never dead and buried – it isn't even past'. This reference to the uncanny history of Faulknerian narrative entirely deconstructs the prior allusions to a terminal postmodern condition, and could not be more different from Bush's invocation of 9/11 as the entirely context-less 'day of fire', a thunderbolt from nowhere. Instead this uncanny historical narrative carries the discomfortingly familiar traces of a repressed past that, moreover – claims Obama – 'directly touches my own'. These are the otherwise cautious words of an astute politician, positioning himself as a candidate that might unite America in its diversity against the violent simplicity of a pre-modern world. Yet it is hard to avoid the sense that this repressed past is a guilty one, and that it is those living in 'the worlds of plenty' that bear the burden of this guilt. It is also hard to avoid the conclusion that Obama's hedged account of 9/11 buries a repressed identifica-tion not with the 9/11 attackers themselves, but with the 'worlds of want' that lie somewhere behind them.[36]

This section argues that Obama's political identity is fundamentally shaped by an identification with the oppressed, an identification that often borders on casting the United States in a much less flattering light than its self-image as a moral leader. While the allusions in his preface to the 'worlds of want' that 'directly touch my own' are likely to be references to Obama's childhood experiences in Indonesia as well as to his Kenyan family, both of which have exposed him to the realities of third world poverty, Obama's writing and speeches are also forthright about the ways in which many African Americans exist at a substantial remove from the 'worlds of plenty'. Indeed, his memoir provides a lens through which black American poverty might be viewed in its global contexts – while visiting his Kenyan family in *Dreams From My Father*, Obama draws parallels between the poverty he finds in Africa and that he has witnessed in Altgeld Gardens on Chicago's South Side. While Obama resisted his mother's awkward attempts to educate him about black American history, it seems that her instinct to identify with the underdog, in productive tension with Obama's own understanding of his racial identity, played a significant role in her son's development. In 1983, while working for a publishing and consulting group that collected data on international business and finance, Obama wrote reports on economic conditions in third world countries, telling his mother that he was 'working for the enemy'; Obama's discomfort in this role led him directly to community organizing which, Obama writes, represented for him 'a promise of redemption'. Not only did community organizing put Obama on the 'right' side of history in his eyes; it also connected him to the Civil Rights movement, 'its heroes and martyrs' that he would stay 'up late at night thinking about' while at Columbia University.[37]

Throughout his presidential campaign Obama repeatedly referenced his role as a community organizer among the predominantly black communities of South Side Chicago – a location that acts as a stark reminder of persistent racial inequalities. It is significant that it was this experience that Obama consistently forwarded as formative in his political career, over and above his birth and upbringing in Hawaii, which got much less coverage. Hawaii emerges in popular accounts as a multicultural, Edenic paradise supposedly innocent of America's destructive racial 'knowledge'. An emphasis on Hawaii might have provided Obama with the opportunity to 'pass' as a quintessential product of the nation's mythic, egalitarian melting pot. That he did not choose this route seems to contradict Rickey Hill's claim that 'Obama did not want to be perceived by the white electorate as black'.[38] This assertion overlooks the fact that central to Obama's campaign was his repeated self-identification as a black man, a move that is at once personal and political, and which belies a denial of the enduring relevance of race. Indeed, as David Remnick recounts in his biography of Obama, many of Obama's former Hawaii acquaintances, insistent on the island's racial innocence, feel betrayed by the president's portrayal of Hawaii as a 'vexed and confusing paradise',[39] and his consequent insistence on his black identity. A similar sense of betrayal is reflected in an opinion piece written for the *Washington Post* entitled 'Why Obama should not have checked "black" on his census form'. In this piece Elizabeth Chang criticizes the president's decision to designate himself 'black' in the 2010 census, given that since the 2000 census Americans have been offered the option of self-identifying as more than one race. While Chang claims that this decision misses the opportunity to deconstruct the nation's racial binary by insisting on its multicultural heritage, equally it affirms Obama's political, as opposed to essentialist, understanding of racial identity – an opportunity that Chang misses when she implies that Obama's response to the census was 'inaccurate'.[40]

Obama's memoir offers a fascinating window onto his racial self-identifications. While the first edition was published in 1995, well before Obama ran for political office, it seems to chart a journey of racial self-discovery that has been perpetuated by Obama's political career. Remnick's account of *Dreams* places it in the long tradition of African American autobiography, beginning with the slave narratives, wherein an individual's life story is written not towards the end of their life but precisely as a beginning. Obama's own account indicates that his reading in the African American literary tradition – which emerges in *Dreams* as a notably male rendition – was extensive, and suggests that *The Autobiography of Malcolm X* (1965) was particularly influential in his own act of literary self-creation. Yet Obama's story lacks the lowly beginnings – the struggle against vicious racism, violence and poverty – that enabled Malcolm, via Alex Haley, to narrate what is now an archetypal neo-slave narrative, from the bondage of material deprivation and psychological slavery to self-knowledge and transformation. Borrowing Robert Stepto's characterization of the structure of African American autobiography as a 'narrative of ascent', Remnick argues that *Dreams*, which charts Obama's connections with a string of elite institutions – Punahou, Occidental, Columbia, Harvard Law School – sits uneasily within this tradition, despite Obama's attempts to 'darken his canvas'.[41] In many ways though *Dreams* is better understood as a 'narrative of descent', from these bastions of white privilege to a discovery of the extent of US racism in places like Harlem and the South Side.

Obama's biography spans an unsettled geography – the United States, Indonesia, Europe, Kenya – and is essentially a tale of home-coming. Where classic antebellum slave narratives like that of Frederick Douglass write the black slave into an American identity – albeit an identity often qualified with serious reservations about aspects of the national ideology – Obama's first concern seems to be to wrest a specifically African American identity from his larger American context. The search for Obama's father that animates *Dreams* is part of a larger search for Obama's 'story of race and inheritance', and the journey to Kenya acts as a crucial rite of passage. It is the story narrated by Obama's Kenyan 'Granny' in the book's concluding section that gives Obama's search a partial sense of closure. Granny begins by naming the origins of the family line encapsulated in a list of who begat who: 'Miwiru sired Sigoma, Sigoma sired Owiny, Owiny sired Kisodhi ...'[42] As Remnick elaborates:

> She tells the whole story: The family's migration from Uganda to Kogelo. Battles with the Bantu. The saga of Onyango. It is a story of Genesis, of Exodus, of generations – all recalled and told in the Luo language, with the sagacity of a village ancient.[43]

Granny's story thus assumes the shape of biblical epic, while telling a story reminiscent of Chinua Achebe's *Things Fall Apart* (1958): the appearance of white European traders, the introduction of a Christian God followed closely by guns, economic exploitation and a mechanized culture that challenges the old ways. Hers is a story of a loss of innocence that culminates with Barack and his sister Auma's examination of their grandfather's record of employment with the British colonial government; including a detailed list of Onyango's physical characteristics, this document will resonate with anyone familiar with the chilling documentation that accompanied bills of sale under chattel slavery. As with classic slave narratives, Onyango prizes the acquisition of literacy; 'to him knowledge was the source of all the white man's power, and he wanted to make sure that his son was as educated as any white man.'[44] Picking up the baton of this generational narrative of exodus, Obama's father thus finds his way to America, an experience that afforded him immense educational opportunities but which, his son imagines, left him partially alienated from his native Kenya – in a way that resonates with his own father's alienation from his family as a result of his comparative westernization. In a mirror image it is Barack junior's fate to experience partial alienation from his American identity as a result of his African heritage. Thus via a parallel between colonialism in Kenya and the slave system in America, Obama claims for himself a version of Du Boisian double consciousness – explored in the next chapter as a formulation which imagines African American identity as the site of a conflict between racial and national self-understandings – and in so doing writes himself into being as an African American.

Unlike Malcolm – whose 'hope of eventual reconciliation [with whites]', Obama suggests in *Dreams*, 'appeared in a distant future, in a far-off land' – Obama 'looked to see where the people would come from who were willing to work toward this future and populate this new world'.[45] That these dreams of a new world free from the oppressions of the old are yet to be fulfilled was clear, as Remnick points out, from the accusations towards the end of Obama's presidential campaign that he did not write his own autobiography.[46] These accusations recalled the fact that over 100 years earlier, the slave narrators had conventionally included white-authored prefaces that verified the fact that they were the authors of their own stories. These authentications were crucial in proving that the slaves were themselves capable of literacy, the acquisition of which, as Henry Louis Gates has written, proved to an Enlightenment culture that they were rational and thus fully human.[47] As Obama indicates in *Dreams*, his claim is to the other legacy of the Enlightenment: '*We hold these truths to be self-evident.*' His decision to leave community organizing for Harvard Law School was precisely to do battle with a classificatory system that sometimes seems to serve 'to regulate the affairs of those who have power'. For 'the law', Obama explains, 'is also memory; the law also records a long-running conversation, a nation arguing with its conscience':

> *We hold these truths to be self-evident.* In those words, I hear the spirit of Douglass and Delany, as well as Jefferson and Lincoln; the struggles of Martin and Malcolm and unheralded marchers to bring these words to life. I hear the voices of Japanese families interned behind barbed wire; young Russian Jews cutting patterns in Lower East Side sweatshops; dust-bowl farmers loading up their trucks with the remains of shattered lives. I hear the voices of the people in Altgeld Gardens, and the voices of those who stand outside the country's borders, the weary, hungry bands crossing the Rio Grande. I hear all of these voices clamoring for recognition, all of them asking the very same questions that have come to shape my life.[48]

Obama's narrative thus identifies the African American struggle against slavery and its legacy as an archetype by which oppressed people – inside and outside America – might understand race-based and class-based exploitation; exploitation sowed into the paradoxical foundations of an Enlightenment project that both established an exploitative capitalism fed in part by white supremacy *and* promised universal equality. As James Kloppenberg argues, Obama's attempts to mediate these contradictory legacies – his marked historicist sense of the imperfections of an inevitably incomplete American democracy – reveal continuities with the tradition of philosophical pragmatism that can be traced back to the writings of William James and John Dewey. Yet in the interests of his thesis, Kloppenberg peculiarly insulates Obama's (apparently universal, 'American') intellectual inheritance from his (particularist, 'African American') racial contexts. While Kloppenberg asserts that 'we should stop trying to differentiate the black from the white strands in American intellectual history', he casts the African American influences on Obama as largely 'literary' – Ralph Ellison's *Invisible Man* (1952) is singled out because of its emphasis on open-ended experimentation and the possibilities of American democracy.[49] In so doing Kloppenberg seems to downplay the central role African American literature has played in shaping black political thought, while he overlooks the fact that thinkers like Du Bois and King notably transformed some of the central tenets of pragmatism by way of prophecy. In order to fully understand Obama's intellectual coordinates – key to which has been his often prophetic understanding of oppression and particularly racial injustice – we must examine the way that his thinking intersects with black political and religious traditions.

Obama's is essentially a liberal vision of America – one that sustains a faith in the idea that the system encompasses the resources by which it might redeem itself. Yet the admission that white supremacy was central to the Enlightenment project and, by extension, the Declaration of Independence suggests that Obama's liberalism embraces a form of self-critique that Michael Dawson argues defines the 'disillusioned liberalism' so often found in black political thought. In addition Obama's consistent emphasis on equality, often over and above individual liberty, and his insistence on some form of government intervention into issues like health care and education, is indicative of a belief that the political grounds for equality, even if guaranteed, are not enough. This partially allies him with egalitarian tendencies that Dawson suggests often exceed American liberalism because, like the egalitarian tendencies of King, they pose, in Malcolm X's words, a '*version of freedom larger than America's prepared to accept*'.[50]

In this way Obama's early career and personal development, central to which was his initiation into Reverend Jeremiah Wright's Trinity United Church of Christ and his marriage to Michelle Obama, 'a daughter of the South Side',[51] seemingly encompassed a desire to revise the American exceptionalist master narrative via an acknowledgement of its underside. That said, Obama could not be described as a disillusioned liberal – his candidacy itself evidenced an inherent optimism in the American project. In response to a question posed by Michelle Obama as her husband was deciding whether to run for president – 'What do you think you could accomplish that other candidates couldn't?' – Barack Obama replied: 'When I take that oath of office, there will be kids all over this country who don't really think that all paths are open to them, who will believe they can be anything they want to be ... And I think the world will look at America a little differently.'[52] Not only was Obama well aware of the racial symbolism his election would carry and how his individual story could re-frame the national narrative; he presented it to his advisers as a primary reason for running.

Just one month into his presidential campaign, Obama was invited to speak at Brown Chapel in Selma, Alabama. This was to mark the anniversary of the voting rights march on Pettus Bridge, during which peaceful protesters were violently turned back by police who used tear gas, whips and clubs against them. A few months prior to this march, on 2 January 1965, in the midst of the voting rights campaign, King had come to Brown Chapel to tell the congregation that Selma had become 'a symbol of bitter-end resistance to the civil-rights movement in the Deep South'; on 4 March 2007, Barack Obama came to that same chapel to lay claim to the legacy of this struggle, and to present himself as a leader of a new Joshua generation who would 'finish the journey Moses had begun': 'today we're called to be the Joshuas of our time, to be the generation that finds our way across this river.' In this sentence Obama fuses the present moment with the Alabama River of the 1960s, both of which are in turn linked to the ancient mythology of the parting of the Red Sea. In so doing he unambiguously lays claim to King's Exodus vision.[53]

Obama's claim to be the next progressive chapter in America's history, one that will resonate with and complete the journey of the Civil Rights movement, is reliant on a certain rendering of American history and the national mythology. His candidness in the 2007 speech at Selma as to the consequences of systemic racism is matched by an evasiveness when it comes to the imperial legacy of the US. For example, though Obama's account of his emerging racial consciousness in Hawaii is not consistent with the idea that the island has escaped the racist consequences of the black/white binary that haunts the mainland, and his memoir evidences his understanding of the fact that America's youngest state – acquired in 1959 – is the object of US imperial conquest, the plight of the indigenous peoples of Hawaii has not become part of Obama's public rhetoric. Though evidence suggests that Obama wants his administration to repudiate the imperialist tendencies of Bush's 'war on terror', he has not thus far been able to close the prison at Guantanamo Bay, despite a promise to do so during his first day in office; as he committed the US to a massive surge in troops in Afghanistan, he summoned the spirit of national unity brought about by 9/11, the very unity and outraged virtue that sublimated the uncanny return of history that Obama was able to identify in his preface written just five years previously. 'Unlike the great powers of old', Obama told the US military in December 2009, 'we have not sought world domination. Our union was founded in resistance to oppression.'[54] And it seems that maintenance of this narrative is better served by the memories of Abraham Lincoln and Martin Luther King, memories that have been appropriated as emblematic of America's progressive trajectory, as opposed to Winston Churchill, a potent symbol of the British Empire – whose government led the brutal repression of the Mau Mau rebellion in Kenya – and who symbolically points to the US' ambiguous beginnings in that enterprise. Thus while Obama is able to draw comparisons between colonialism in Kenya and slavery and racism in the US, his story nonetheless draws a firm distinction between the different systems of oppression bred by Europe and America – the latter does after all represent the partial salvation of Barack senior and an even greater promise for his son – suggesting that redemption is more possible in a nation that imagined itself as the transcendence of Europe and the culmination of the Enlightenment project.

Consequently Obama's rhetorical output shows him to be suspended between two versions of the Exodus narrative, one statist and the other non-statist, one promoting an America defined by a peculiar mixture of triumphalism and innocence, the other painting a much more critical portrait of a nation that has yet to make good on its promises. I argue that the foundations of much of this latter critique, and its intersections with black Exodus rhetoric, derive from the prophetic traditions Obama encountered in his former church, to which this chapter will now turn.

OBAMA AND HIS CHURCH: THE WILDERNESS

One of the more recurrent features of the genre of the slave narrative is the motif of conversion. Most commonly slaves converted to Christianity. While often the slave narrators deployed their newfound religion to implicitly question the Christian character of their former owners and white America as a whole, these religious conversions nonetheless performed the function of qualifying the narrators for entry into the national-religious framework. Central to Obama's narrative is his religious conversion overseen by Reverend Jeremiah Wright, former pastor of Trinity United Church of Christ. Like the slave narrators before him, Obama's conversion ultimately performed a similarly ambivalent role wherein his Christianity both supported his critique of US racism and affirmed his place within a Christian nation.

In his 2006 book, *The Audacity of Hope*, Obama writes that 'it is a truism that we Americans are a religious people'.[55] For those hoping that the election of a Democratic president might mean the relegation of religion from the public to the private sphere, Obama's attitudes towards faith are likely to be a disappointment. Sceptical about religion until well into his adult life, Obama's account of his conversion to Christianity indicates that it was precisely religion's role in the social world that drew him to Trinity. As is now widely recognized, part of Obama's enormous electoral success lies in the fact that he was able to recapture a leading role in the debate about values and public morality for the Democratic Party. His principal route into these debates was via religious discourse. The black church traditions mobilized by Obama's campaign created what many have seen as a collaboration between US churches and the cause of progressive politics comparable to that which fuelled the Civil Rights movement and, before that, the abolition of slavery. The success of this coalition though was by no means guaranteed, and during the campaign for the Democratic primaries it looked likely that Obama's church affiliations would irreparably fracture his bid for the nomination. Paradoxically, the religious identity acquired through his church was one of the primary vehicles by which Obama was able to claim the legacy of King, yet unlike King's Christianity, and despite the fact that Trinity's gospel is not inconsistent with King's, Obama's chosen church was not deemed an acceptable association for a viable presidential candidate. In contrast to the liberal integrationist traditions King is often called upon to represent, Trinity was portrayed in the US media as adhering to a threatening brand of black nationalism more akin to the politics that animate popular caricatures of Malcolm X. This section argues that this portrayal of the church reduces the complexities of the black religious traditions that Trinity embodies. It was at Trinity that Obama was comprehensively exposed to black

Exodus traditions, traditions that have painted the post-Civil Rights landscape as a wilderness period. The following situates Trinity within these traditions and shows the way in which they were crudely misinterpreted by the media as counter to the mainstream American national mythology.

In *Dreams From My Father*, Obama's religious conversion is the second of three moments of partial 'enlightenment' around which the text is structured. During Obama's first sermon at Trinity he hears the 'stories of ordinary black people merging with the stories of David and Goliath, Moses and Pharaoh, the Christians in the lion's den, Ezekiel's field of dry bones':

> Those stories – of survival, and freedom, and hope – became our story, my story; the blood that had spilled was our blood, the tears our tears; until this black church, on this bright day, seemed once more a vessel carrying the story of a people into future generations and into a larger world.[56]

The merging of the stories of black people with biblical narrative that occurs in Wright's sermon anticipates Obama's Kenyan Granny's biblical rendering of the family epic, one in which Obama also hears multiple voices returning to 'that single course, a single story....'[57] Where Granny's story offers him a narrative by which he might claim his Kenyan family and African heritage, Wright's story becomes a primary route through which Obama can claim a black church community and his African American heritage. Obama's unease about his absent father and consequent hazy sense of familial heritage are matched by anxieties related to the absence of God and a wider religious community in his life. During his time as a community organizer Obama is aware that his acceptance among the communities in which he is working is hampered by his lack of church membership, but Obama's conversion seems to have been motivated by something more fundamental than political convenience.

Located in the heart of Chicago's South Side, Trinity in many ways represents the revered black church tradition that has placed social justice at the centre of its ministry. As Melissa Harris-Lacewell claims, 'the study of African American religiosity and political behavior has largely centered on the question, does Christianity encourage or discourage political activism among African Americans?'[58] This question is rooted in the contradictions passed down from slave religion, which was influenced by the slave owner's message that the slaves should await their rewards in heaven, but equally inspired by the revolutionary message espoused by some slave preachers that slavery was a sin, Jesus was committed to ministering to the needy, and Old Testament narratives, particularly Exodus, bore witness to an earthly deliverance. While the majority of scholarly and popular accounts have tended to see the historically black church as heir to the latter legacy, and thus black churches as places that mobilize African Americans for (largely progressive) political action, it is important to recognize that black churches do not represent a monolith. Indeed, recent tendencies among some black churches tell a different story. As Harris-Lacewell writes, from the mid to late 1990s, the media began reporting on the fact that thousands of largely middle-class black Christians located in predominantly suburban areas were being attracted to megachurches which preach a version of the prosperity gospel, the idea that wealth is evidence of God's blessing. The conservative emphasis of these churches is on individual as opposed to collective salvation, and consequently, as Harris-Lacewell points out, many observers argue that 'these churches have lost sight of a black religious tradition' and exhibit a historical amnesia as to the role black churches have played in the black freedom struggle. This theme will be explored in more detail in Chapter 5; here it is sufficient to note that Trinity United Church of Christ, Obama's chosen church, was decidedly not of this mould. Rather, it represents the kind of politicized black church that sees itself, in Eddie Glaude's words, 'as a repository for the social and moral conscience of the nation'.[59]

On his first visit to Trinity Obama was greeted by a sign just outside reading 'Free South Africa', one that would in all likelihood have appealed to him given that some of his earliest forays into progressive politics involved anti-apartheid activities. On meeting the church's pastor, Obama finds himself impressed with the range of social projects that Wright had initiated at the same time as overseeing a rapidly expanding congregation – that included sections from both the most and the least affluent of the communities living on the South Side. Trinity's new pastor, Reverend Otis Moss, continues Wright's work on poverty, homelessness, HIV/AIDS. It is not hard to see how a church that draws energies for its progressive agenda from its critique of capitalism and white supremacy at home and abroad would have appealed to Obama, the community organizer, who was determined to work on behalf of the disadvantaged. Crucially Obama is impressed by the church's 'Black Values System', one that indicates the church's black nationalist and

2222222

Afrocentric orientations. Trinity's current website explains: 'We are an African people, and remain "true to our native land," the mother continent, the cradle of civilization.' In its account of the church's history, the website highlights the specific plight of African Americans: 'God has superintended our pilgrimage through the days of slavery, the days of segregation, and the long night of racism'; the idea that God has cultivated a special relationship with black America also pervades the church's mission statement, which claims that 'as a congregation of baptized believers, we are called to be agents of liberation not only for the oppressed, but for all of God's family'. 'We are called out to be "a chosen people."'[60]

These statements suggest that, as Wright tells Obama in *Dreams*, the church is influenced by academic scholarship that many churches disdain. In particular the church draws on black liberation theology, a set of ideas that has received its most authoritative and systematic articulation in the work of James Cone.[61] Cone's core thesis is that God is on the side of the oppressed – a precise reversal of the prosperity gospel that implies that God favours those already in possession of material wealth. Cone argues that the Old and New Testaments demonstrate that the motivating force in providential history is liberation. The Exodus narrative and the realization of the divine promise in the ministry of Jesus Christ are underscored as evidence of this proposition. Cone contends that in order for a Christian theology to be relevant to black people, it must not only address the experience of racism, but Christ must also be understood as black. This is essential in order to illustrate God's identification with the oppressed – which, in the US context, means primarily black people. This thesis reflects Cone's belief that 'white American "Christian" values are based on racism'.[62]

Though black liberation theology specifically sets itself against American racism, its larger critique is of a racist Christianity as manifested in the European 'civilizing mission'. Albert Cleage's *The Black Messiah* (1968) opens with the contention that 'for nearly 500 years the illusion that Jesus was white dominated the world only because white Europeans dominated the world'. Cleage cites with approval Marcus Garvey's moves to counteract this tendency in the African Orthodox Church by 'including a Black God, a Black Jesus, a Black Madonna, and black angels'.[63] The Exodus motif and the notion of the 'chosen people' was also central to Garvey's 'back-to-Africa' movement which gained a mass following in urban areas in the US in the 1920s. Yet as will be discussed in more detail in Chapter 4, Garvey also emphasized the apparently opposing trope of Egypt, an emphasis that was adopted by the Nation of Islam which sought to draw Garveyism outside of the imaginative geography of the Judeo-Christian West. And while black liberation theology was, at least from Cleage's point of view, an attempt to show black nationalists that there was a viable religious alternative to Islam, it shares with Garveyism and the Nation of Islam a markedly non-western orientation – one that includes the elevation of ancient Egypt as the cradle of civilization, an idea that would become a hallmark of 1980s and 1990s Afrocentrism. Indeed, Jeremiah Wright contests Cone's contention that the black church 'symbolizes a people who were completely stripped of their African heritage as they were enslaved by the "Christian" white man'; rather than needing to cultivate a greater understanding of the continent, according to Wright's variant of black liberation theology, slave religion has passed to the contemporary black church an 'underground theology' that is a marker of an African heritage.[64]

Black liberation theology, Harris-Lacewell argues, has been linked to progressive agendas including the call to end the Iraq war, tax cuts that favour the rich and the prison-industrial complex, as well as a commitment to health care and development activities in Africa and the Caribbean. Harris-Lacewell's analysis of data collected in the 1994 National Black Politics Study suggests that 'those who perceive Christ as the Black Messiah are significantly more likely to participate politically'.[65] Yet it was precisely Trinity's theological emphasis on blackness that was seized on by Obama's critics as evidence of the church's supposedly reactionary politics and so-called 'reverse racism'. The controversy that erupted in March 2008 cast Trinity as an unlikely site from which the Democratic Party's claim to the national civil religion might be renewed. The phrase 'God damn America' was among the controversial soundbites that were extracted from Wright's sermons and treated to wide circulation on all major news networks, in the US and around the world. Played in an endless loop, clips of Wright not only damning America but also claiming that the US was responsible for 9/11 and unleashing HIV/AIDS on Africa, seemed to cast doubt on the judgement of a presidential candidate who had chosen to listen to the author of this inflammatory rhetoric for over twenty years. Trinity's self-definition as 'Unashamedly Black and Unapologetically Christian' was cited as evidence that Obama's church was racially divisive and un-American. This critique of Trinity also incorporated a crude version of the academic tendency – exemplified by E. Franklin Frazier's seminal yet somewhat misleading work, *The Negro Church in America* (1963)

– to view black religious behaviour as a function of black politics.[66] In so doing, right-wing sections of the US media, in contrast to the spirit of Frazier's scholarship, undermined Obama's religious identity in thinly veiled attacks not only on his racial identity, but also on the religious legitimacy of the black church.

Cone's ground-breaking *Black Theology and Black Power* (1969) was written in the shadow of King's assassination and was an attempt to make King's Christian insights relevant to the Black Power generation, which either gravitated towards Islam or the view that religion was irrelevant. Cone's attempt to bring together the legacies of Civil Rights and Black Power, the legacies, as he sees it, of Martin and Malcolm, is clearly at work in Jeremiah Wright's sermons. In 'Audacity to Hope', the sermon which inspired the title of Obama's second book, Wright claims 'I was influenced by Martin King, yes, but there was this other guy named Malcolm, and I tried one brief time being a Muslim: "As salaam alaikum." Anything but a Christian.'[67] As Darryl Pinckney points out in the *New York Review of Books*,

> Wright, at least in some of his statements, seems to see his ministry as a continuation of the radicalization King underwent after the profound disappointment of the white reaction to the Poor People's campaign in Chicago and to the striking garbage workers in Memphis.[68]

Yet this link to the legacy of Civil Rights was almost wholly ignored by the media in favour of viewing Trinity's black nationalist tendencies as evidence of the church's alien, anti-American underpinnings. In this way Trinity's centralization of the Exodus narrative – so pivotal both to a dominant American culture and to a Civil Rights movement retrospectively domesticated and absorbed into the larger national narrative – was rendered unrecognizable and unfamiliar by its associations with Africa and Islam, associations that I suggest in this book might usefully be thought in relation to the 'Egypt' trope. Consequently some commentators not only suggested that Trinity was un-American; it was also suggested that it was not properly Christian either.

One of the most influential expressions of such views appears in Jerome Corsi's 2008 book, *The Obama Nation: Leftist Politics and the Cult of Personality*. Coming from a far-right position that viewed many of George W. Bush's policies as too 'liberal', Corsi's book was promoted by a Republican consultant and reached the number one spot on the *New York Times* bestsellers list.[69] Though widely dismissed as 'poisonous crap', the Obama campaign deemed it important enough to release a 41-page document on Corsi's journalistic practices called *Unfit for Publication* – which concludes that Corsi's 'record of attacks is disgusting and false, and so is this book'.[70] Consequently *The Obama Nation* can be seen as an important example of the three-pronged and interlinked attack on Obama's religious, racial and national identity. Corsi's critique of Obama works via suggestion and insinuation, but much of the book rests on the deeply problematic assumption that any politics forwarded in the name of black identity is evidence of 'reverse racism' and anti-Americanism. Moreover, while Corsi makes clear that the play on words in the title of his book is fully intended, he then proceeds to offer an unconvincing contextualization of the world 'abomination' which completely dilutes its meaning, claiming that the election of Obama would result in an '*abomination*' in terms of US domestic and foreign policy. He thus evades the inordinately more personal and indeed theological possibilities of this word. The *Oxford English Dictionary* suggests as its first definition 'a feeling or state of mind of disgust and hatred; detestation, loathing, abhorrence'; and secondarily: 'abhorrent behaviour; a loathsome or wicked act or practice; a detestable vice.' These rather more extreme meanings of the word recall its usage as denoting spiritual corruption, a usage that has historically been deployed by southern white churches as an attack on black humanity. Ironically given Corsi's dismissal of black liberation theology, it nods in the direction of the racist biblical tradition that Cone and Cleage's theology was designed to resist.[71]

Corsi in particular fixates on what he sees as Obama's 'Islamic' connections in an attempt to unravel the veracity of his claim to be a Christian. Corsi points out that Trinity honoured Louis Farrakhan, the leader of the Nation of Islam, with one of the church's annual awards in 1982. This, along with the Muslim identity of Obama's Kenyan grandfather and Obama's own middle name, 'Hussein', is part of the picture Corsi builds to strongly imply that Obama is in fact a Muslim. While the question posed by Colin Powell amidst such 'accusations' – 'Is there something wrong with being a Muslim in this country'?[72] – is the appropriate response to Corsi's insinuations, the means by which Corsi attempts to undermine Obama's Christianity points to a significant aspect both of Obama's faith and its relationship to black religion. Corsi's suggestion that Obama's conversion is not genuine is largely based on the implication that the black church's emphasis on the particulars of the black experience eludes the universality of the Christian message. Moreover, citing the epigraph to *Dreams* – '*For we are strangers before them, and sojourners, as were all our fathers*' (I Chronicles 29:15) – Corsi writes:

> The Christian Bible, even in the chapter of Chronicles that Obama quotes, urges us to resolve this feeling of alienation with the realization that we are all children of God. With the New Testament, we are further advised that only in Christ and through Christ can we find our true identity. If Obama is on a search for identity, then our question must be this: How does Obama resolve the crisis of abandonment and identity that his life experience so poignantly causes him to feel? Is it in Christianity, as Obama solidly proclaims?[73]

The implication here is that to be a true Christian one must be fully reconciled to worldly realities. Any sense of alienation from society's mainstream indicates that an individual has not accepted Christ. Arguably on these grounds Corsi's book disqualifies not just the entire black church but all oppressed people from the Christian faith. It is hard to reconcile this view with the rich and varied traditions that have called on Christian theology in the name of social justice and equality. Yet here Corsi inadvertently highlights an important aspect of Obama's Christianity, one that consistently questions the redemptive certainties that lie at the heart of much – particularly Pauline – Christian thinking.

Obama openly writes of the fact that his entry into the Christian church 'came about as a choice and not an epiphany; the questions I had did not magically disappear.' For Obama, it was the realization that 'religious commitment did not require' him to 'suspend critical thinking' or 'disengage from the battle for economic and social justice' that enabled him to kneel 'beneath that cross on the South Side of Chicago'.[74] His conversion was thus made possible precisely because of the realization that faith alone is never enough. The chapters that follow suggest that Obama's cautious words echo intellectual currents in the African American religious tradition, the history of which tells against the idea that the promised land has been achieved, a tradition that, in Obama's words, has had 'too many quarrels with God to accept a salvation too easily won'.[75] The rejection of the idea that God might have sanctified the status quo is the origin of the black jeremiad, a form of rhetoric that has consistently refused to collapse the difference between the American ideal and the American reality.

Arguably this was the form of address Obama delivered on 18 March 2008, when, in what is now considered to be a major speech on race, Obama called for 'a more perfect union' in an attempt to defuse the media storm that had centred on Wright's church by providing some much needed context. This speech was an elaboration of the position that Obama had maintained since the media storm had begun – that the controversy issued from a fundamental misunderstanding of the black church on the part of white America. Obama's address returned to the drafting of the Declaration of Independence and reminded Americans that the document on which the Union was founded had incorporated the 'original sin of slavery' – the consequences of which, Obama told his Philadelphia audience, survive into the present day. Obama accounted for the surprise felt by some Americans at the seemingly incendiary nature of Wright's speeches by the fact that 'the most segregated hour in American life occurs on Sunday morning'. 'Trinity', Obama asserted,

> embodies the black community in its entirety … the church contains in full the kindness and cruelty, the fierce intelligence and the shocking ignorance, the struggles and successes, the love and yes, the bitterness and bias that make up the black experience in America.

He told the crowd that he could no more 'disown' his pastor 'than I can disown the black community'. That Obama did ultimately feel compelled to resign from the church's membership in May of that same year led some commentators to view his actions as a betrayal and repudiation of black church traditions.[76]

These traditions are still very much in evidence in Obama's language and rhetoric. In July 2009, Obama addressed the centennial convention of the NAACP in what was widely billed as his first address to black America as president. In a tone that led the *New York Times* to dub the speech a 'fiery sermon',[77] Obama preached to black parents about their role in preventing their children from internalizing a narrative of racial failure. This talk recalled his 2008 Father's Day speech, where from the pulpit of a black church Obama lectured African American men on their parental responsibilities – drawing criticism from Jesse Jackson that he was 'talking down to black people' and from others that his focus on individual responsibility elided the much more real issue of systemic racism.[78] While systemic racism did make it into Obama's NAACP address, his sense that black America had yet to be delivered into the 'promised land' was largely met by a message of self-help and self-reliance; the very conservative emphasis on individual responsibility espoused by some black churches, those same churches that have been accused by some of stepping away from their prophetic calling.[79] Indeed, in June 2010, African American religious studies professor Eddie Glaude wrote a provocative piece entitled 'The Black Church is Dead' for *The Huffington Post*, which responded not only to the rising social conservatism among some black church groups but also to the fact that, as Samuel Freedman puts it, 'the election of Barack Obama, a black Christian, as president has complicated if not blunted the black church's traditional role of confronting the establishment, "speaking truth to power"'.[80]

Glaude's obituary of the black church is a jeremiad which challenges the black church to live up to its covenantal calling. In a not dissimilar vein, Obama's presidency is increasingly being accused of drifting from the more radical agenda of his campaign. Yet if Trinity represents one of the progressive links Obama was forced to abandon in order to get elected, its vilification also exemplifies the pressure Obama as both candidate and as president has come under from all sides. And while Obama's eventual resignation from his church and the conservative notes that he has struck since can be interpreted as a betrayal of what Trinity stands for, including the black struggle against racism, conservatism should not be seen as alien to the diverse field of black ideologies. Indeed, as Harris-Lacewell argues, there is an established tradition of specifically black conservatism; while it enjoys considerably less support among African Americans, in part, as Harris-Lacewell suggests, because its account of racism centres as much on what it perceives as black pathology as it does on white racism, it in fact exhibits a number of crossovers with black nationalism, an ideological field that most obviously centralizes black interests against white supremacy.[81] The consequent lineage that links Booker T. Washington, Marcus Garvey and the Nation of Islam might thus caution against the idea that Obama's emphasis on self-help is inevitably alienating to his black constituency; rather, it might be read as a version of what Kevin Gaines has described as 'uplift ideology', an often paternalistic and condescending critique but one that is offered from the perspective of the insider.[82]

The debate about Obama's church affiliation and religious rhetoric can sometimes give the false impression that black religious traditions are irreconcilable with the American civil religion. At the extreme ends of the debate, the idea that these are mutually exclusive traditions either casts Obama as a traitor to his race or a traitor to his nation. This apparent disjunction between race and nation, one that is often exacerbated by religious affiliation, will be explored further in the following section. This briefly examines Obama's identifications with the African, Muslim and Jewish diasporas, and the extent to which he is able to reconcile these identifications with his understanding of state memory and black memory, the Exodus of mainstream American exceptionalism and that which animates the African American counter-narrative.

DIASPORIC IDENTIFICATIONS: OBAMA AND THE POST-AMERICAN WORLD

On 19 November 2008, just two weeks after Obama's election victory, Al Qaeda released a video in which the terrorist organization's second in command, Ayman al-Zawahiri, accused the president-elect of being a 'House Negro'. In recalling Malcolm X's famous description for black Americans who are happy to do the bidding of whites to get ahead, Al Qaeda raised a question mark over the next president's ability to authentically represent the interests of Americans of any hue in the Middle East. Not only was al-Zawahiri suggesting that Obama was betraying his racial identity – by contrasting him with a black American for whom solidarity with the non-white and Muslim worlds, constituencies Al Qaeda claims to represent, was a natural position for US blacks. The suggestion was also that Obama's motives for carrying forward the US foreign policy agenda in the Middle East were driven more by personal ambition than genuine loyalty to America. There was something incongruous, Al Qaeda was suggesting, about a black man's entry into the White House.

Al Qaeda's video was a precise mirror image of the cover of a July 2008 edition of *The New Yorker* which, as Rickey Hill recounts,

featured Barack and Michelle Obama celebrating with a fist bump in the Oval Office in front of a portrait of Osama bin Laden and an American flag burning in the fireplace. Michelle Obama is portrayed as a militant radical with a bushy Afro hairstyle and an AK47 hanging from her back. Barack Obama is portrayed in full Muslim garb.[83]

While *The New Yorker* claimed that the image was a satire of the view of Obama from the perspective of his right-wing critics, it nonetheless perpetuated a set of racial caricatures that linked Barack and Michelle Obama to black nationalism and Islam, affiliations that the image paints as both violent and anti-American. This set of associations can be linked to the one-dimensional lens through which their former church was viewed, and in particular its connection to what this book characterizes as the Egypt trope, one that I have suggested is often simplistically rendered in opposition to that which is represented by the Exodus narrative. Trinity United Church of Christ's complex theological orientations tell against this opposition, but the church's critique of US domestic and foreign policy, particularly the support of the US for the State of Israel, was deployed as part of a narrative that reinforces it. By thus painting a picture of Trinity that alienated it from its Judeo-Christian underpinnings as well as its roots in the Civil Rights movement, Obama's critics associated his church with a threatening, caricatured black nationalism that has long been vilified not only for its perceived anti-Americanism but for its perceived anti-Semitism as well. As Chapter 4 elaborates, the misleading association of black nationalism with anti-Semitism emerged in the late 1960s and coincided with the widespread critique of Israel as a colonial oppressor that developed among Black Power activists after 1967. It has also been resurrected more recently in the aftermath of 9/11 – which gave rise to a reductive 'clash of civilizations' thesis that seemed to inject new meaning into the black nationalist critique of the West. Obama's connections to his former church, alongside his professed admiration for figures like Malcolm X and Frantz Fanon, led critics to associate him with a crude caricature of black nationalism during his presidential campaign. Though Obama explains his eventual rejection of an unqualified black nationalism in *Dreams* and is forced to reject Trinity, Obama has been judged 'guilty by association' by his right-wing critics while being branded as a traitor – as a result of his repudiation of these links – by many on the left. This section explores the contexts that have created the false binaries by which Obama's politics are often judged, and argues that his imaginative identifications with the African, Muslim and Jewish diasporas tentatively point to a vision appropriate not to a post-racial but rather to a post-American world.

Cedric Robinson's influential work on black social movements posits that from the second half of the nineteenth century, two distinct black political cultures had emerged: one largely assimiliationist, the other largely separatist. Robinson is critical of both formations – the adoption of capitalistic individualist values on the one hand and, when times were tough, tendencies towards xenophobia on the other. Yet it is clear that Robinson privileges the politics of the latter:

> Communities of free Blacks gravitated toward the privileged political and social identities jealously reserved for non-Blacks. At the same time, on the plantations and in the slave quarters, slaves tended to form a historical identity that presumed a higher moral standard than that which seemed to bind their masters.

'For the former, America was an unfulfilled promise; for the latter, America held little special significance.'[84] While Robinson's is a nuanced account of different black political traditions, the binary by which he understands them – separatism versus assimilation, militancy versus accommodation – are often employed reductively in popular and journalistic accounts as markers of racial authenticity, markers that tend to pit blackness and Americanness against one another. Aspects of Malcolm X's analysis of US race relations played into this binary: his distinction between compliant 'House Negroes' and rebellious 'Field Negroes' is consistent with his sense that 'I'm not an American. I'm one of the 22 million black people who are the victims of Americanism.'[85] While Malcolm's distinction was in some ways about class differences among black Americans, as Dawson suggests, it 'had more to do with the racial loyalties of each class than the class interests of either'.[86] And for Malcolm the loyalties of black people should not lie with the United States.

As Wilson Jeremiah Moses writes in *Afrotopia* (1998), the idea that the key to the black American future might lie in Africa as opposed to America – politically, metaphorically and spiritually, if not literally – runs from slavery into the present day.[87] Martin Delaney and Edward Wilmot Blyden wrote of Africa's importance to black America in the nineteenth century. W.E.B. Du Bois' understanding of African American links with the black diaspora was apparent in his work at least since 1921 when he organized the second Pan-African congress. Marcus Garvey, preaching both a spiritual and literal return to Africa, attracted a mass following of urban black Americans in the 1920s. Penny von Eschen argues in *Race Against Empire* (1997) that the 1930s and 1940s saw unprecedented links between black American anti-racist activists and anti-colonial movements in the diaspora and beyond.[88] After a brief interlude which saw the repression of leftist movements in

the US as a result of the domestic front of the Cold War, the Civil
Rights movement and particularly the black nationalist movements
of the late 1950s, 1960s and 1970s forged explicit black diasporic
alliances. The Afrocentrism that emerged in the 1980s, and which
has been identified with the work of Molefi Kete Asante more
than any other, differs from these earlier developments in that its
orientations are primarily cultural as opposed to directly political.
As Moses suggests, most varieties of US black cultural politics that
have centralized 'Africa' have drawn either implicitly or explicitly on
Jewish intellectual traditions, a fact that has often been repressed on
all sides as a result of worsening relations between blacks and Jews.

The rise of the Nation of Islam and the emergence of Black Power
hastened the break-up of the black–Jewish Civil Rights alliance of
the late 1950s and 1960s; black nationalists increasingly identified
the divergent socio-economic fortunes of African Americans and
Jewish Americans – and the fact that the assimilationist model had
proved inordinately more successful for the latter – as evidence
that Jews were part of a white American power structure rather
than allies in the struggle against racism. The commentary on the
emergence of Afrocentrism in the 1980s and the popularity of Louis
Farrakhan in the 1990s, amidst fractious debates about affirmative
action, exacerbated the notion that blacks and Jews, rather than
identifying as a consequence of common histories of oppression –
and, for some, a shared dream of realizing a national homeland – are
somehow natural rivals.

The desire shown by some Afrocentrists to purge the black cultural
link with Jews has on occasion amounted to patent anti-Semitism
– and should be viewed as part of a larger project whereby 'Africa'
is reclaimed as a pure origin for black identity untainted by the
experiences of slavery or colonization brought into being by a Judeo-
Christian West. Yet it is important to note contrary tendencies. For
example, Martin Bernal's *Black Athena: The Afroasiatic Roots
of Classical Civilization* (1987), which became a key text for
Afrocentrists, argues that the rise of the 'Aryan model' in nineteenth-
century interpretations of the ancient world – as a result of anti-black
racism *and* anti-Semitism – suppressed the centrality of ancient Egypt
in favour of emphasizing Athens as the origin of civilization. Moses,
who is himself critical of what he sees as Egyptocentrism (though
not Afrocentrism as a whole) – on the grounds that it romanticizes
'pharaonic dominion' – argues that because Afrocentrism's critics
have wanted to 'associate Afrocentrism with anti-Semitism', they
have ignored 'the influence of Jewish scholars on the evolution

of Afrocentrism'.[89] British scholar Stephen Howe's *Afrocentrism: Mythical Pasts and Imagined Homes* (1998) is a prime example of this; according to Howe, 'the ideologies of political Zionism and of Pan-African or Afrocentric assertion, despite (or perhaps because of) their substantial shared ancestry, have long been bitterly opposed'.[90] He thus not only collapses the long and varied histories of Pan-Africanism and Afrocentrism into a singular entity – alongside the various forms of black Islam that his book also discusses – but also overlooks the long history whereby Pan-Africanists have identified with Zionists and vice versa. Howe is thus complicit with the more problematic strands of the Afrocentrism that he critiques, by presenting the cultural politics of blacks and Jews in the United States as radically separate.

Writing in 1993 in his seminal *The Black Atlantic*, Paul Gilroy suggests that a greater awareness of the intellectual links between black and Jewish diasporic thinking might help heal the fractured relationship between blacks and Jews; he observes that 'it is often forgotten that the term "diaspora" comes into the vocabulary of black studies and the practices of pan-Africanist politics from Jewish thought'. Gilroy supports his point by noting that the black identification with the Exodus narrative is waning, and that 'blacks today appear to identify far more readily with the glamorous pharaohs than with the abject plight of those they held in bondage'.[91] Where Egypt, according to Gilroy, represents for Afrocentrists a return to a pre-slavery Africa and thus circumvents the defining experience for blacks in modernity, the Exodus narrative is a vehicle through which slavery might be confronted. By this account, the fact that the civilizations of slave-holding pharaohs might appeal to some black people represents historical amnesia if not the imagination of a power reversal. While Chapter 4 argues that the imagination of Egypt in black American thought has led to diverse ideological outcomes and cannot simply be equated with amnesia about slavery or a crude will to power, Gilroy's critique of the Egypt identification is important in that it recognizes that some forms of Afrocentrism seek to enact a retreat from ambiguity.

The complex nature of Obama's understanding of African American identity rejects simplistic accounts of black identifications – with America, Africa and Jews – forwarded by some Afrocentrists and their critics. His very direct link with Kenya seems to have prevented him from investing in a homogenized or romanticized vision of the continent; yet his decision that Ghana and not Kenya should be the destination of his first state visit to Africa was arguably not just a comment on contemporary Kenyan politics but also indicative of the president's awareness of the symbolic import of West Africa for African Americans. During a visit to Cape Coast Castle on the Ghanaian coast in July 2009, President Obama thanked the people of Ghana for 'preserving this history' – the history of the slave trade. As Obama pointed out, 'it is here where the journey of much of the African American experience began'.[92] Having noted the African heritage of black America alongside its traumatic passage to the United States, Obama then remarked that the tour of the castle, where captured slaves had been imprisoned prior to auction, was 'reminiscent of the trip I took to Buchenwald because it reminds us of the capacity of human beings to commit great evil'. Obama thus points to a historical analogy between the enslavement of Africans and the Holocaust of European Jews. Analogies between the Holocaust and slavery have in recent years engendered competition – centred on a hierarchy of pain – as opposed to identification, largely because the memorialization of the Holocaust has become a public ritual all over the world, whereas the West has yet to fully confront its role as architect of the transatlantic slave trade. Obama's act of identification in Ghana is suggestive of a desire to restore neglected links between blacks and Jews – a desire that arguably goes deeper than the obvious political gains to be made from negating the atmosphere of accusation and recrimination that defined relations between blacks and Jews in the 1980s and 1990s, and which lingers on into the present day. Rather, the black diasporic link with Jews is manifest not only in Obama's identification of a shared history of suffering, but also in his understanding of his own religious identity and its relationship to the experience of exile and the allure of homeland.

That a diasporic consciousness has shaped Obama's own self-understanding is clear from the epigraph of his memoir. As argued above, the sense of rootlessness that the epigraph points to – 'For we are strangers before them, and sojourners, as were all our fathers' – seems to have played a role in shaping Obama's understanding of religious faith. These lines are written about the experience of exile, an experience acutely captured by traditions of diasporic Judaism, many of which cultivated an understanding that an alienating world remained radically unredeemed. This sense of the provisionality of worldly experience yields a paradox: it both demands action (to make the world better) and undermines the very grounds of that action (redemption is yet to come). This bears similarities to the Niebuhrian paradox of the religious requirement to act without knowledge of God's intentions, a paradoxical understanding which arguably in part formed the context for Niebuhr's close personal and intellectual friendship with Rabbi Abraham Joshua Heschel – who as Chapter 3 explores, was also friends with King. In turn, this paradox seems to similarly structure Obama's understanding of the relationship between faith and action, as illustrated by a passage in *The Audacity of Hope*.

In this passage Obama evokes a world devoid of redemptive guarantees by summoning the ghosts of Abraham Lincoln and those buried at Gettysburg, to 'remind us that we should pursue our own absolute truths only if we acknowledge that there may be a terrible price to pay'.[93] In other words, we might always be wrong. Yet as Obama also recognizes, sometimes it is those who eschew such balancing acts that carry history forward: 'it has not always been the pragmatist, the voice of reason, or the force of compromise, that has created the conditions for liberty.' Obama recalls the 'unbending idealism' of William Lloyd Garrison and the actions of Denmark Vesey, Frederick Douglass and Harriet Tubman 'who recognized power would concede nothing without a fight'. In acknowledging 'that deliberation and the constitutional order may sometimes be the luxury of the powerful', Obama concedes that 'the cranks, the zealots, the prophets, the agitators, and the unreasonable – in other words, the absolutists' have often been the shapers of a better world. 'I am robbed', he writes, 'even of the certainty of uncertainty – for sometimes absolute truths may well be absolute.'[94]

Here Obama posits the leap of faith by which religious impulses are translated into worldly actions. In so doing he traces the potentially violent path by which the unknowable is pronounced knowable, the infinite rendered finite. Obama does not here explicitly identify with Jewish history, but he charts in African American history the aporetic path between exile and homeland, one that is clearly part of Obama's personal story and at work in the tension between Jewish diasporic traditions (that emphasize an unredeemed world) and a yearning for Zion (that imagines the biblical redemption of historical time). Kloppenberg reads Obama's emphasis on history and the provisionality of human experience – the tempering of faith with doubt – as evidence of his anti-foundationalist leanings, and yet I suggest that, like Niebuhr and King, Obama is no relativist. Everywhere his writings suggest that good and evil do exist, and that human beings, though imperfect, are united by 'that spark of the divine that stirs within each of our souls'.[95] In this vein, in May 2009, he told students at Notre Dame University that they ought to embrace their teacher's sense that the institution is 'both a lighthouse and a crossroads'. The 'lighthouse' evolves in Obama's speech as the beacon of faith, of example, but it is to be tempered – humbled – by the thought of the 'crossroads':

> Remember, too, that you can be a crossroads. Remember, too, that the ultimate irony of faith is that it necessarily admits doubt. It's the belief in things not seen. It's beyond our capacity as human beings to know with certainty what God has planned for us or what He asks of us. And those of us who believe must trust that His wisdom is greater than our own.[96]

This dialectic between the 'crossroads' and the 'lighthouse' might be mapped onto the disparate figures of exile and homeland, difference and identity. And as Obama's emphasis on the role of the absolutist in shaping a better world reminds us, African American history is also conditioned by the paradox of the lighthouse and the crossroads, the knowledge that a profoundly imperfect world calls out for worldly deliverance – it is full of people seeking to force their way into the promised land. I suggest that Obama's claim during his campaign to 'understand the Zionist idea' might be seen in the light of his understanding of the tension that insinuates a dream of homeland at the heart of the experience of exile – an understanding that has been central to African American religious identifications with Judaism explored in subsequent chapters – and not simply as a result of his evident desire to garner Jewish American votes.[97]

Obama's conciliatory gestures towards American Jews during his campaign – often by way of expressions of support for the State of Israel – were read as pure political opportunism from both left and right, largely as a result of the anachronistic perception that a black candidate can have no organic affiliation to the Jewish community.[98] Obama's most prominent gesture of support for Israel during the campaign came in a speech he made to AIPAC (American Israel Public Affairs Committee) in June 2008. In this speech Obama offered his 'unwavering' support for Israel and committed himself to an 'undivided Jerusalem' (though later Obama did clarify and partially retract this latter pledge). Many viewed the speech as a cynical and opportunistic move to pander to the so-called Israel lobby. Undeniably the speech was politically motivated; Obama's analysis of the Middle East in this speech was attentive only to Israel's perception of the security threat. But his claim to understand Zionism along with his embrace of the Jewish redemptive project of *tikkun olam*, repairing the world, as the impetus behind social justice work which might renew the Civil Rights alliance between blacks and Jews, seems to be consistent with his understanding of the analogy between the ethnic and religious orientations of the two groups.

Many left-wing commentators on the AIPAC speech strongly implied that it affirmed John Pilger's January 2008 characterization of Obama as a 'glossy Uncle Tom'[99] who was destined to betray 'brown-skinned people', particularly the Palestinians. In a different register, Grant Farred compares Obama to the biblical figure, Pontius Pilate, for failing to speak out, while president-elect, against the Israeli attacks on Gaza in December 2008.[100] Here Obama's perceived betrayal relates not to his racial identity – as does Pilger's analysis – but rather to his professed progressive politics. A comparable sense of betrayal was also apparent in the reaction to Obama's major address in Cairo in June 2009. Pilger further revealed his understanding of Obama's politics as somehow inauthentic by characterizing the speech as a 'smile on the face of the tiger';[101] at the same time Obama's right-wing critics raged against a president they perceived to have sold America down the river.

Obama's speech in Cairo also failed to specifically condemn Israel's most recent attack on Gaza, in spite of the fact that by this time he had been inaugurated as president and was now in a position to do so. And while Obama's administration has raised the possibility of the US government negotiating with Hamas – the group that was democratically elected to the Palestinian assembly but which is also perceived by many western powers as a terrorist organization – it has rhetorically remained faithful to the Bush administration's line that 'Palestinians must abandon violence'. Interestingly though, in his speech in Cairo Obama makes this point by referring to the Civil Rights movement: 'for centuries, black people in America suffered the lash of the whip as slaves and the humiliation of segregation. But it was not violence that won full and equal rights. It was a peaceful and determined insistence upon the ideas at the center of America's founding.' Obama may strike a note of condescension here but he also implicitly compares Palestinian self-determination to the black American struggle for equality within the US, while drawing the Israeli oppression of the Palestinian people alongside America's failure to guarantee the rights of its black population. Neither nation, he seems to suggest, has heeded its covenantal calling. While Obama has consistently drawn on the narrative of the Civil Rights movement to gesture towards improved black–Jewish relations, in Cairo this highly prized narrative is loaned to the people of Palestine in order to forge an equivalence between them and black America.[102]

Obama matched his insistence on America's support for Israel and the 'cultural and historical ties' to the Jewish state with the recognition that 'the situation for the Palestinian people is intolerable' and stated America's commitment to 'not turn our backs on the legitimate Palestinian aspiration for dignity, opportunity, and a state of their own'. This was accompanied by the assertion that 'the United States does not accept the legitimacy of continued Israeli settlements', a US position that has since been reasserted in the face of the continued expansion of Israeli settlements in the West Bank and East Jerusalem. But perhaps more important than his allusions to a changing tide in US Middle East policy was the fact that the speech represented an unprecedented address to the Muslim world on the part of a US president, and its call for 'a new beginning' was anything but a call to wipe the historical slate clean; rather, in significant ways it marked a desire to reintroduce history into the paralysed and polarized terms of the 'clash of civilizations' debate.

In Cairo Obama took the unprecedented step of apologizing for America's role in overthrowing a democratically elected government in Iran during the Cold War. This anticipated Obama's address to the Ghanaian parliament in July 2009, in which his condemnation of European colonial practices resists the temptation to extract the US from the litany of blame by making it clear that as part of 'the West', America has inherited the colonial attitude of viewing 'Africa as a patron or a source of resources rather than a partner'. Twice in Ghana Obama articulated the phrase 'Africa's future is up to Africans'; a phrase which echoes Marcus Garvey's signature phrase, 'Africa for the Africans'.[103] Some commentators accused Obama of reducing both Africa and the Muslim world to homogeneous entities in his respective addresses in Ghana and Egypt. Writing in *Pambazuka News*, an influential online newsletter that claims to showcase 'Pan-African Voices for Freedom and Justice', Marieme Helie Lucas accuses Obama's Cairo speech of 'essentialising Islam' in precisely the vein of Muslim fundamentalists who claim to speak in its name. Lucas claims that in counterpoising 'America' and 'Islam', Obama sets up an opposition between a country and a religion, thus implying that '"the West" is composed of countries, while "Islam" is not'.[104] Yet Lucas overlooks the fact of Obama's own diasporic identity that transcends national boundaries. Just as he was able to declare in Accra 'I have the blood of Africa within me', Islam is also part of his experience – not only from his

'Kenyan family that includes generations of Muslims' and the years he spent in Indonesia as a child, but also from the time he spent as a community organizer in Chicago; he tells his Cairo audience that 'Islam has always been part of America's story'. Lucas is right to insist that western modernity has overwhelmingly privileged those who can uncomplicatedly slide into the identities afforded by the geographical boundaries of the nation-state, but she forgets that she is listening to a man who himself belongs to a group that has never been afforded this privilege. While the term 'Muslim world' undoubtedly homogenizes diverse communities under one label, it is equally clear that Islamophobia – particularly virulent since 9/11 – does not discriminate between different Muslim groups, in the same way that anti-Semitism does not differentiate between different forms of Jewish self-identification. Moreover, the question of Palestine has inflamed Muslim sensibilities the world over in a way that is comparable to the extent to which the question of Israel has the ability to unite diverse communities of Jews. This is not to pose a false equivalence between the two very different scenarios. But it is to suggest that Obama's imaginative identifi- cations seem to work analogically in a way that not only shows him to be loaning concepts and themes central to the narrative of American exceptionalism; his flexible rendering of these analogies is also comparable to the function of the Exodus and Egypt tropes in African American thought.

In fact, it is clear from the opening of Obama's speech that his decision to speak from Egypt was itself based on a complicated understanding of the nation-space. Many criticized Obama for choosing to speak from Egypt at all – which is hardly a model for democracy. But Obama makes a point of thanking not the Egyptian government but rather Cairo University and the 'people of Egypt' for their hospitality. By invoking 'the timeless city of Cairo', Obama distances his address from the contemporary regime that resides in Cairo, and the city emerges in his text as a transhistorical symbol – comparable to that which has long functioned in African American thought as a symbolic meeting point between Muslim and African worlds. What Obama's rhetoric seems to do consistently is to cast other nations and 'civilizations' in the same glow that he casts America, and in so doing mitigates his own exceptionalist discourse. So where in Cairo he talks of 'civilization's debt to Islam', in Accra he tells Ghana 'freedom is your inheritance'; 'the world will be what you make of it ... yes you can.' America undoubtedly takes centre-stage in Obama's rhetoric, but his investment in the mythologization of other geographical spaces appears to go further than a superficial respect for or romanticization of other cultures; his speeches in Egypt and Ghana show that the supposedly American theme of 'renewal' is not reserved for Americans only. In other words, America might be both a 'lighthouse' and a 'crossroads'.

While American exceptionalist discourse has in the past been deployed to advance a Euro-American project of white supremacy in the name of God, Obama's rhetoric disables the neat equivalences between faith, race and nation that this discourse has historically assumed. As Obama notes in Ghana, the borders of modern African nations are the result of 'a colonial map that made little sense' and 'helped to breed conflict'; on his visit to Cape Coast Castle, he noticed that 'there was a church above one of the dungeons – which tells you something about saying one thing and doing another'.[105] By acknowledging that the collaboration between Christianity, race-based slavery and colonialism, and the rise of the nation-state have in conjunction oppressed people of the black, Jewish and Muslim diasporas, all of which in part transcend the ethnic and religious boundaries marked by the nation-state, Obama's own brand of national-religious exceptionalism must delve into what it recognizes as deeply compromised legacies in order to re-write America. Because Obama's nuanced historical understanding exhibits an awareness that his own categories are always already sullied, this act of rewriting, of renewal, is conditioned by a sense of provisionality unknown during the Bush years.

The complexity of Obama's 'America' thus eludes the shallow caricatures projected by Al Qaeda and *The New Yorker*. What emerges instead is altogether more appropriate for what looks likely to be a post-American century, one in which the United States will probably have to share power with rising eastern nations, particularly China. One that, as Carl Pederson suggest, will highlight the 'war on terror' of the Bush years as a throwback to the nation's post-1945 dominance as opposed to a sign of things to come. Pederson argues that while Obama has rhetorically remained faithful to the idea that the twenty-first will be 'another American Century', he is also showing 'signs' that he 'is willing to adapt to the geopolitics of the twenty-first century' which may well call for a 'post-exceptionalist' US foreign policy. Obama's role in ushering in this new era would be particularly fitting given that, as Pederson suggests, the start of the first American century might be dated from the overthrow of Hawaii in 1893, a moment that shone a light on the US' imperial ambitions in the Pacific, having 'closed the frontier' and thus consolidated its continental empire.[106] At present we can only speculate about what might be the result of the turn to foreign policy that is likely to characterize the second phase of Obama's first term in office; the battering from the right in the domain of domestic policy, which culminated in significant Democratic defeats in the 2010 mid-term elections, suggests that Obama's room for manoeuvre is increasingly constrained. We might also note that Obama's propensity to loan highly prized American themes to other cultural spaces threatens to flatten his rhetoric of diversity by reining it back into an economy of the same. But certainly the vision Obama offered in Cairo was one that generously conceded ground to worlds beyond America.

CONCLUSION: A PROMISED LAND DEFERRED

Writing in *The Independent* of London, Robert Fisk opens his article on Obama's Cairo speech with the following words: 'Preacher, historian, economist, moralist, schoolteacher, critic, warrior, imam, emperor. Sometimes you even forgot Barack Obama was the President of the United States of America.'[107] Obama's public persona seems to have absorbed both the presidency and a stature comparable to some of the great black American leaders of the twentieth century. As Harris-Lacewell writes, 'African American cultural and political life is shaped by a reliance on and respect for oral communication' and consequently, she claims, citing Charles Henry, the '"search for black ideology must begin with the oral tradition"'.[108] In tracing Obama's relationship with the Exodus rhetoric that pervades the sometimes overlapping terrains of American exceptionalist discourse and the black Exodus tradition, this chapter has focused on Obama's account of himself and his role in his public utterances, an account which I argue provides insights into the beliefs, values and ideological orientations that inform his presidency. One of the contentions of this chapter has been that Obama has consistently privileged the narrative of the black Civil Rights movement, not only writing his own story into its lineage and loaning its legacy to other modern liberation movements in acts of imaginative identification, but also encouraging the suggestion that his election might be its fulfilment. By way of conclusion, these tendencies will be thought in relation to the debate about reparations for slavery, demand for which has been central to the contemporary black Civil Rights movement. Not only has this debate brought Obama into a triangular conflict involving black, Jewish and Muslim worlds; most significantly for this discussion, the issue of reparations brings to the fore a direct clash between the imperatives of 'black memory' and 'state memory'.

In April 2009, the Obama administration decided to boycott the UN conference on racism. This decision was taken ostensibly because the conference was too closely associated with the first conference on racism held in Durban in 2001, a conference that after the event became overwhelmingly associated with the issue of Israel–Palestine. As Naomi Klein argues, the memory of the Durban conference was in effect hijacked by this issue and branded as anti-Semitic for largely strategic reasons. Anti-Semitic cartoons and slogans did make it into the Durban conference's NGO (non-governmental organization) forums, and problematic formulations equating Zionism with racism were proposed as part of the Durban Declaration. But as Klein points out, these sentences 'had no chance of making it into the final draft'. She argues that both the 2001 conference and what became known as 'Durban II' were conveniently dismissed by the United States and a number of European countries because they raised the very real issue of reparations for slavery. According to Amina Mohamed, the chief negotiator for the Africa bloc, Durban was Africa's 'rendezvous with history', a sense that Klein argues was embraced by the US Civil Rights movement 'which had regarded the first Durban conference as an historic turning point'. According to Klein the boycott of the Durban Review conference in 2009 was 'Obama's most explicit betrayal since taking office'.[109]

Klein imagines Durban II as the setting for a 'minority death match' between blacks and Jews which the latter, as the more powerful group, won. Certainly since the late 1950s black activists for reparations have been pointing to the creation of the State of Israel and the German government's decision to compensate Holocaust victims as historical precedents that the US government should follow. The evasion of the reparations issue thus reinforces the sense that memories of slavery are routinely suppressed in contrast to the strict observance of the injunction to remember the Holocaust on the part of the international community. What Klein does not fully account for is the fact that the issue of slavery reparations at the UN conferences was not simply crushed by overwhelming concern for Israel and for Jews. It got caught in the cross-fire between two actors in the Middle East. Arab and Islamic states – particularly Iran – have provided fuel for the narrative that has simplistically cast the conference as an anti-Israel talking shop. This is not to suggest that the UN should not provide a forum for the discussion of the Israeli occupation and the brutal denial of Palestinian self-determination. Rather it is to suggest that ever since its 1975 resolution that branded Zionism as racism, the UN has been shadowed with questions about its legitimacy on this issue, questions that have done irreparable harm to the institution's ability to act as an effective organ of anti-racism.

Du Bois in particular saw the UN as an opportunity to challenge the idea that individuals only have rights as citizens of nation-states. From Du Bois to King to Malcolm X, the UN has occasioned moments of black internationalism that have seen the collaboration of anti-colonial and anti-racist movements. Obama's refusal to attend the UN's historic conference on racism as the first African American president is a sobering repudiation of this vision. In a climate in which Obama's health care reforms were being cast as 'slavery reparations by stealth', it is hard to see how it would have been possible for Obama to take a stand on this issue, even if he were committed to the practical implementation of reparations. Obama has in the past stated that while he agrees with the principle of reparations, the complexities of actually trying to implement them make the idea 'unworkable'.[110] Even so, the evasion of a discussion about the principle of reparations can be seen as an instance of sacrificing black memory to the imperatives of state memory. Rather than being understood primarily as a betrayal of the Civil Rights movement – interpretations of which are of course highly contested – Obama's decision not to attend the conference on racism might better be seen as a necessary reminder that a representative of the state is never going to be the state's most effective opposition, even if that representative is an American president uniquely predisposed to name the sins of the nation's past.

'Reparation', as Dawson writes, 'has been the quintessential black demand for arousing broad and deep support among blacks and hostility among whites.'[111] Manning Marable elaborates by explaining that reparations would 'force whites to acknowledge the brutal reality of our common history, something white society generally has refused to do'.[112] The demand for reparations among black Americans has existed in the US ever since the government reneged on the promise of 'forty acres and a mule'. For most of the twentieth century it has largely been associated with black nationalist movements, and the mainstreaming of the reparations movement within the African American Civil Rights movement is a relatively recent phenomenon. The demand for financial compensation for slavery within the US involves illustrating 'the central role of the

US government and various state and local governments in creating the legal frameworks for the systemic exploitation of African-Americans, perpetrated by white corporations and throughout American society'.[113] While expressing reservations about certain understandings of reparations – including the danger that they might seem to offer a sense of closure on the issue of racism, or reinforce an individualist as opposed to collective vision of black life, one that is rooted in ideas of capitalist accumulation – Robin Kelley nonetheless views reparations as a potentially key aspect of black 'freedom dreams':

> If we think of reparations as part of a broad strategy to radically transform society – redistributing wealth, creating a democratic and caring public culture, exposing the ways capitalism and slavery produced massive inequality – then the ongoing struggle for reparations holds enormous promise for revitalizing movements for social justice.[114]

Kelley claims that reparations would herald a 'genuine day of reckoning' for the nation, a vision that resonates with black messianic traditions in which Obama himself has been cast. Indeed, while evading the specific form of reckoning that Kelley calls for, Obama has tentatively painted himself as a redeemer figure before the nation's pre-eminent (though comparatively conservative) Civil Rights institution. On the occasion of the 99th Annual Convention of the NAACP in July 2008, Obama, having told the organization that their work represents the highest form of patriotism, claimed:

> I will come back here next year on the 100th anniversary of the NAACP, and I will stand before you as the President of the United States of America. And at that moment, you and I will truly know that a new day has come in this country we love.[115]

Obama does not quite say, as King did, that the redemption of black America would be the salvation of the nation as a whole, but there are shades of that here. As Wilson Jeremiah Moses writes, the idea that a specific people might hold out redemptive powers for the rest of the world, adapted from Judaism as well as more directly from American messianic traditions, has played a key role in African American revolutionary rhetoric. Moses' argument in *Black Messiahs and Uncle Toms* (1982) revolves around the observation that while the 'Uncle Tom' figure has been appropriated as the epitome of the anti-revolutionary, he started his life in Harriet Beecher Stowe's novel as precisely a 'black messiah'. Moses claims that 'the humble heroism of old Uncle Tom has been transmuted into racial treason by the subtle alchemy of social amnesia'.[116] What is fascinating about Moses' thesis is its implication that the line that separates the perception of accommodation from radicalism is sometimes a fine one, one that is consistently transgressed by the cooptation of particular images of black humanity for specific political agendas. The black messianic imagination, in contrast to the 'Uncle Tom' caricature, has been largely, though not wholly, associated with black nationalism, and has often been perceived as racial chauvinism – as the recent media reaction to black liberation theology, which includes distinct messianic strains, exemplifies. Yet paradoxically, historically black messianism has also been the subject of romanticization among white Americans of all political stripes – as Stowe's novel demonstrates. In the eighteenth and nineteenth centuries the white elevation of black messianism often went hand in hand with the racist championing of the 'return' of US blacks to Africa; more recently the appropriation of Martin Luther King as an agent of American redemption has threatened to diminish the sense of white responsibility for slavery and its legacy.

This is the fine line that Obama is being forced to tread. While he may insist that his election is only a beginning, others are committed to appropriating his notes of triumph to promote the idea that he is the resolution – the redemption – of the nation's 'race problem'. And while, as Kevin Gaines suggests, 'Obama's victory was a triumph of the black freedom movement', his presidency is being assailed by patently racist anti-government forces bent on obstructing his agenda.[117] The consequent perception of a timid presidency on the part of Obama's own constituencies has led to a corresponding narrative of betrayed expectations. That Obama's presidency has to answer to these opposing voices recalls the memory of Abraham Lincoln, the president who held together two contradictory Americas, and to whom Obama has most consistently turned in his writings and speeches. Lincoln seems to appeal to Obama precisely because he was not perfect. A reluctant abolitionist, Lincoln refused to punish the defeated South in a graceful act of national reconciliation that also anticipated the seriously compromised freedom of the newly emancipated slaves. In *The Audacity of Hope*, Obama recalls Lincoln's 'unyielding opposition to slavery and his determination that a house divided could not stand' but reminds us that 'his presidency was guided by a practicality that would distress us today'. 'I like to believe', writes Obama, 'that for Lincoln, it was never a matter of abandoning conviction for the sake of expediency':

> Rather, it was a matter of maintaining within himself the balance between two contradictory ideas – that we must talk and reach for common understandings, precisely because all of us are imperfect and can never act with the certainty that God is on our side; and yet at times we must act nonetheless, as if we are certain, protected from error only by providence.[118]

The rest of this book explores the articulation of this balancing act in black Exodus traditions – a balancing act that highlights tensions between religious faith, political action and the imperatives of group identity politics – traditions that have shaped Obama's personal, political and religious identity. It argues that where, in spite of Obama's largely candid reading of American history, his insistence on its 'better angels' can have the apparently unintended effect of seeming to redeem its worst chapters – in a scenario that threatens to put black memory into the service of state memory, and wherein the ideal paves over the real – the other figures discussed in this book largely avoid this by remaining in an adversarial position in relation to the American state, one that enables them to exceed the form of the jeremiad. The next chapter turns to the thought of W.E.B. Du Bois, whose formulation of double consciousness captures the paradoxes of Obama's position at the crossroads of American and African American exceptionalism.

2

Double Consciousness and the Master/Slave Dialectic: W.E.B. Du Bois

W.E.B. Du Bois' unfolding of the master/slave dialectic via his famous articulation of double consciousness offers a window through which we might better understand the parallel racial universes that shape contemporary America and thus perspectives on Obama's presidency. Throughout the nineteenth and twentieth centuries, African American thinkers have imagined the transformation of what one of Orlando Patterson's novelistic characters identifies as a 'white world of grief' into the 'Zion' of black religious hopes and America's elusive promise;[1] this dream has been revived in the early decades of the twenty-first century by those who dared to hope that the election of the first black president might herald this redemption. That this transformation remains consigned to an as yet to be realized future is everywhere apparent. Currently a White House official need only hint in the direction of the enduring salience of 'race' and the administration is accused of 'reverse racism'.[2] While most academic definitions of racism are founded on a link between prejudice and power, and while it is clear that the elevation of one black individual into the White House does not even begin to redress the imbalance of economic, social and political power that exists between black and white Americans, the so-called 'Tea Party' activists and their sympathizers are bent on identifying black racism emanating from the White House. These accusations fail to provide a smokescreen for the fact that, as Kevin Gaines writes, the agenda of these anti-government conservatives itself has a clear racial subtext.[3] Thus in sharp contrast to the world that Du Bois witnessed a century ago, in which the black/white divide was dramatized via barely disguised racial violence, 'postmodern racism', as David Theo Goldberg asserts, is in denial about its own existence:

> Born again racism reappears whenever called upon to do the dirty work of racist politics but purged of its categorical stiffness.

66

Indeed, shed of its stiff categoricality, raceless racism operates in denial, anywhere and anytime.[4]

'Born again racism' means that, as Lisa Palmer claims, 'Obama has to navigate his presidency through a minefield of racial time bombs that are easily escalated and combustible and threaten to derail him at any given moment.'[5] Nonetheless, as Gaines suggests, the current right-wing revolt against the administration, which he characterizes as 'the convergence of older narratives of white supremacy, updated by post-9/11 xenophobia', shows a marked nostalgia for the 'whites only' model of citizenship that Du Bois was confronting in the post-Reconstruction South. Indeed, as Gaines points out, much of the energy for the recent legislative attack on birthright citizenship – an attack that began with the 'birther' movement's claim that Obama himself is not a US citizen and therefore not a legitimate president – has come from the former Jim Crow states. For these reasons Du Bois' understanding of African American double consciousness, which responded to the backlash of white racism which followed on the heels of Emancipation, speaks powerfully to the present moment, which was also prematurely hailed by some as a moment of racial redemption.

In *The Souls of Black Folk* (1903), Du Bois translates the master/slave dialectic from the slave system into the new 'Egypt' of Jim Crow segregation. In so doing he conceptualizes the parallel racial universes wherein blacks must reside behind a 'vast veil', at a distance from the opportunities afforded to whites but consistently vulnerable to the pain of white racism. Yet this 'vast veil' also creates the opportunities for an independent black life, one that both responds to and exceeds the reach of white supremacy. Du Bois' notion of double consciousness thus affirms a valorized understanding of race, one that this chapter argues is not parasitic on the biological essentialism that permeates white racism. Du Bois' Exodus rhetoric arrives at a configuration of black agency that is not only instructive for the current moment, in which any allusion to 'race' on the part of a black presidency might be equated with 'racism'; it also provides a crucial coordinate for understanding Obama's own investments in black Exodus traditions – investments that were, as argued in the previous chapter, largely formed during his time at Trinity United Church of Christ. The debate about the race politics of Obama's former church was an early example of Obama being forced to view his commitments, in Du Bois' words, 'through the revelation of the other world', to accommodate the perspectives of many white Americans in an asymmetrical relationship that would never require them to do the same.[6] In this vein, double consciousness is a psychological and spiritual condition that mirrors the Hegelian 'unhappy consciousness' which names a subjectivity at war with itself – one that has been forced to internalize the positions of both slave and master. What Du Bois characterizes as African American 'second-sight' points to a situation in which the black subject identifies as both 'African' and 'American', her inclusion in the 'American' system resting on the paradoxical premise of her constitutive and violent exclusion on the grounds of her 'African' heritage. So while, Du Bois suggests, her primary identification is with the oppressed and the exploited – the 'slave' position' – she is also forced to recognize the perspective of the 'master', and thus is constantly faced with a view of the self imagined from the standpoint of the other. And yet, implicit in Du Bois' text is the Hegelian insight that the slave's knowledge of freedom, via its negation, is fuller than that of the master. This insight, the following chapter argues, emerges in *Souls* not just through a re-working of the Hegelian master/slave text but through a narrative that also appears to be central to Hegel's dialectic: the biblical Exodus.

In *Souls* Du Bois envisages the American South as a biblical landscape and sacralizes the idea of freedom, an idea that, this chapter argues, *Souls* strongly implies is most fully cognized by black America. In endowing freedom with religious meaning that is in turn first and foremost the inheritance of US blacks, Du Bois insinuates a proximity between black people and the divine that directly counters the white supremacist distortions of the bible, which render blackness as the antithesis of a white Jesus.[7] In so doing Du Bois anticipates the varieties of black liberation theology that are united by a shared understanding that God is on the side of the oppressed, for whom freedom is destiny. Thus this chapter argues that for Du Bois as for Obama, it is the religious dimension of his thinking that most fully captures his deeply ambivalent sense of an eclipsed national dream.

In his landmark 1903 text, Du Bois surveys 'the crimson soil of Georgia' and meditates on a land 'which is to-day the centre of the Negro problem, – the centre of those nine million men who are America's dark heritage from slavery and the slave-trade'. The 'gloomy soil' of this 'unknown world' was once called, we are told, 'the Egypt of the Confederacy'. As a 'foreigner' from the North, Du Bois thus attempts to ventriloquize what remains inarticulate in this 'silent scene', and to glimpse for this 'scarred land' its long-awaited promise of freedom. As he travels deeper into Georgia Du Bois encounters what resembles 'a Land of Canaan', which gives him the 'comfortable feeling that the Negro is rising'; and yet 'the fields, as we proceed, begin to redden and the trees disappear'. Rather what emerges is an over-worked soil that still claims the blood of Georgia's so-called 'freedmen'; for 'a pall of debt hangs over the beautiful land'.[8]

A century before Obama made his mark on the US political landscape, Du Bois gazes on the failure of the Reconstruction period in the South that took place in the wake of black Emancipation. In this period newly freed slaves were able to make inroads into the economic, social and political fabric of southern society in the immediate aftermath of the Civil War. Yet southern white opposition to black participation was violent and so this period of progress was brief; by the mid 1870s it was clear that African Americans were to be sacrificed on the altar of national reconciliation, and the white South was ultimately given licence to crush the recently discovered freedoms of its former slaves. So while the black belt Du Bois meditates on at the turn of the century is almost entirely deserted of the bodies of its former white masters, their influence persists as a ghostly presence; 'the shadow-hand of the master's grand-nephew or cousin or creditor stretches out of the gray distance to collect the rack-rent remorselessly.' And so Du Bois powerfully captures the South reneging on its promise to blacks by continuing to bind them to an indentured existence. Asking of the former 'Cotton Kingdom' 'and where is the King?' Du Bois finds his answer in a curious return to the terrains of Pharaoh.[9]

The Exodus that is imagined for African Americans in *Souls* has not been occasioned by Emancipation. In material terms the promised freedom is still to come, and the register of Du Bois' text is one of profound alienation. Yet *Souls* also strains towards healing the rupture between people and place to which it bears witness. Du Bois poses as a prophet seeking to transform the wilderness into a lost Zion. The nebulous location of this 'Zion' will form the subject of this chapter. Du Bois has been dubbed an 'American prophet' by Edward Blum, and certainly a contemplation of America was central to his vision in *Souls*. By insisting that 'America is not another word for Opportunity to *all* her sons', Du Bois seemingly voices the classic black jeremiad.[10] In imagining the transformation of 'Egyptland' into 'Canaan', *Souls* apparently does not seek to jettison but rather widen an 'American dream' to include its black citizens. Yet much more than Obama's, Du Bois' text is a negation of the 'state memory' – via the centralization of 'black memory' – discussed in the previous chapter.[11] Indeed, this early text arguably contains the seeds for his later commitments to Pan-Africanism that led him to ultimately abandon America for Ghana sixty years later. The very duration of Du Bois' career means that his ideological leanings were diverse. The prophet who projected a sometimes liberal vision of the American promise was also the advocate of separate black institutions and has consequently been lauded by black nationalists who instead emphasize his identifications with the African diaspora. Alongside his elevation of ancient Egypt and his sense of black chosenness, Du Bois sustained a life-long identification with Jews and Judaism – believing Jews to be the 'natural political and moral allies' of black people.[12] Du Bois thus apparently straddles the space between liberalism and black nationalism, Exodus and Egypt, flirting in his earlier career with elitist ideas derived from his admiration for Bismarckian authoritarianism, while much later in his career he became an advocate for various forms of black Marxism. It is fitting that the concept for which this expansive thinker is best known is one that elaborates an identity shaped by existential conflict.

This chapter argues that the key to unlocking the vexed issue of racial identity that is the preoccupation of most Du Bois scholarship is the much less frequently discussed question of Du Bois' religious sensibilities. This issue has only recently begun to gain the attention it deserves, with the publication of Phil Zuckerman's edited collection of Du Bois' writings on religion in 2000,[13] and Edward Blum's *W.E.B. Du Bois: An American Prophet* in 2007, the first religious biography of a man who is only now emerging as one of the twentieth century's major thinkers of religion. My focus on Du Bois' appropriation of the Exodus trope and rhetorical figures of religious election contributes to this effort, and throws fresh light on his elaboration of the master/slave dialectic that he saw structuring racial inequalities across the globe. The chapter begins by summarizing the debates about Du Bois' long career as a thinker on the subject of race, his sense of racism's collaboration with organized religion, and how what he saw as this 'unholy alliance' between religion and racism came to undergird his thinking on colonialism. It will then trace the way in which Du Bois reconstructs a validated sense of group identity which, contrary to much thinking on Du Bois that dismisses him as an atheist, also involves the reha-bilitation of certain problematized religious concepts. I explore this movement through Du Bois' oft-noted engagement with Hegel, but then suggest that quite in contrast to Hegel's projected merging of Christianity with the state – in the name of a unified national spirit – Du Bois hangs on to radical discontinuities and so rejects Hegel's colonizing logic. For it seems that ultimately for Du Bois, the world, and not just America or even the African diaspora, remained his preferred horizon. The thrust of Du Bois' thought is markedly transnational – with a view to achieving freedom for the minority within a transfigured conception of the nation-space. *The Souls of Black Folk* is my focus throughout, but my reading will be supplemented by other writings within Du Bois' diverse body of works.

RELIGION, THE 'RACE CONCEPT', AND THE COLONIAL CRITIQUE

That Du Bois gave his semi-autobiographical 1940 text, *Dusk of Dawn*, the subtitle *An Essay Toward an Autobiography of a Race Concept* signals the absolute centrality of race to his life and thought. This reads:

> My life had its significance and its only deep significance because it was part of a Problem; but that problem was, as I continue to think, the central problem of the greatest of the world's democracies and so the Problem of the future world.[14]

Here Du Bois not only indicates his sense of America's dominance – and, interestingly, its 'greatness' – in relation to the wider world, he also re-states the essence of what is possibly his most famous line recorded almost forty years earlier in *The Souls of Black Folk*: 'the problem of the Twentieth Century is the problem of the color line.'[15] As Richard H. King points out, Du Bois' statements on race span a period which saw dramatic alterations in scientific and academic understandings of race, and so his thought is notoriously difficult to pin down.[16] What is perhaps most surprising about Du Bois, however, are the consistencies in his thinking on race: his prophetic 1903 statement on the centrality of the 'color line' remained the cornerstone of his thinking until his death in Ghana in 1963. Du Bois was convinced that slavery and colonialism – crucial stages, as he saw it, in the history of western capitalism – were linked by the overarching discourse of white racial superiority. Inextricably linked to this discourse, argued Du Bois, are religious myths of divine favour.

In a 1944 address to Talladega College, a black liberal arts college in Alabama, Du Bois offers the story of Jacob and Esau as a biblical parable for the power struggles and inequalities that structure the modern world. In this address Du Bois questions the conventional wisdom that casts Jacob as a hero for in effect stealing his brother's birthright. In Genesis of the Hebrew bible, Esau comes to Jacob faint with hunger, and Jacob offers him food in return for his older brother's birthright. The fact that Esau 'sold out' to Jacob is traditionally seen as indicative of Esau's disdain for his father, Abraham, and the Jewish lineage that Abraham would come to symbolize. In contrast, for Du Bois, Jacob represents raw power, Esau the weak and the hungry. The legacy of Esau, according to Du Bois' revisionist reading, is one of exploitation, resentment and the desire for revenge; Jacob on the other hand stands over the tradition that saw the Jews marching 'north after escaping from slavery in Egypt' and taking up a patch of land in the name of a 'Great Plan' masterminded by 'its own God'. This new conquering Israelite nation, in the spirit of Jacob, 'looked upon all its neighbours, not simply with suspicion, but with the exclusiveness of a chosen people, who were going to be leaders of earth'. Du Bois writes that 'Jacob's war of cold acquisition and power' should be seen 'not simply as a Jewish idea, but more especially as typical of modern Europe'.[17]

For as Du Bois points out, where 'the poor little Jewish nation was dispersed to the ends of the earth by the overwhelming power of the great nations that arose East, North, and South and eventually became united in the vast empire of Rome', it was left for others to capitalize on the legacy of this colonial idea. 'A British Empire … came near to dominating the world', and 'colonial imperialism swept over the earth and initiated the First World War, in envious scramble for division of power and profit.' Du Bois thus echoes Lenin's sense of the imperialist origins of the First World War. In so doing Du Bois argues for the all-pervasive nature of colonial relations which he persistently linked to 'the race concept' and the specificities of American racism. Du Bois' 1944 address reads:

> Whatever was begun there of ethical wrong among the Jews was surpassed in every particular by the white world of Europe and America and carried to such length of universal cheating, lying and killing that no comparisons remain.[18]

The color line is thus drawn between the diverging destines of Jacob and Esau. Religious myths that teach 'the despising of men who are not the darlings of our particular God'[19] are inseparable in this particular address from myths of racial superiority, and race emerges as the principal category through which Du Bois understands both European colonialism and American slavery. In 'The Souls of White Folk' published in *Darkwater* (1920), Du Bois writes 'the discovery of personal whiteness among the world's peoples is a very modern thing'. While slavery was part of the ancient world, its race-based nature is a decidedly modern phenomenon which shares with colonialism the desire to exploit 'the darker world'; for colonialism itself is 'slavery in all but name' and similarly espouses 'the doctrine of the divine right of white people to steal'.[20] Thus Du Bois designates the scramble for Africa part of a 'Christian colonial system' that found its historical antecedent in the New World, where the enslavement of black people was also carried out in the name of its 'civilizing', Christian, mission. The incredulity with which Du Bois treats this collaboration between religion and racism was a note he was to sound throughout his life.

For the purported link between 'godliness and whiteness' that the civilizing mission implied was foundational to white religion in the South – experienced first-hand by Du Bois as a young man. It is the book of Genesis that stands at the centre of a racist discourse which justified gross human inequalities via the word of God. Claiming variously that black people were the descendants of Ham, or the bearers of the mark of Cain, many white southern churches construed them as a people cursed by God, endowing the 'race concept' with spiritual meaning and in turn justifying slavery and then segregation. The white church's flagrant support of the racist foundation of the American South is, according to Du Bois' unfolding analysis, part of a global picture that signifies for him 'the utter failure of white religion'.[21] As he puts it in *The World and Africa* (1946):

> There was no Nazi atrocity – concentration camps, wholesale maiming and murder, defilement of women or ghastly blasphemy of childhood – which the Christian civilization of Europe had not long been practicing against colored folks in all parts of the world in the name of and for the defense of a Superior Race born to rule the world.[22]

As Richard King suggests, here Du Bois anticipates the arguments of Hannah Arendt and Aimé Césaire, which also construe National Socialism as the effects of European colonialism coming home to roost. [23] The Aryan idea emerges in Du Bois' oeuvre as testimony to Nazism's ironic embrace of a conception of the 'chosen people' that evolved from Jewish origins. Du Bois thus shows that the bible's elevation of one 'people' over another in the name of God can sanction the most vicious racist violence. The logic of divine chosenness – initiated explicitly in the book of Exodus – is therefore thoroughly complicit in slavery and colonialism as well as horrors committed closer to the heart of white Euro-America. As Du Bois writes in the wake of the Great War: 'This is not Europe gone mad; this is not aberration nor insanity; this *is* Europe; this seeming Terrible is the real soul of white culture.'[24]

Despite his sophisticated understanding of the destructive power of the 'race concept', Du Bois did not eschew 'race' as a descriptive category. Indeed the title of his most famous book implies that this 'soul of white culture' finds its corollary – and possibly its corrective – in 'the souls of black folk'. The most obvious evidence for the fact that Du Bois himself was a committed 'race man' appears in his 1897 text, 'Conservation of the Races', which argued for the coherence and importance of the concept of race. Much debate has centred on the extent to which Du Bois' early understanding of race drew on social Darwinism and was grounded in the same biological rationalizations that were being used to justify white racism from the latter stages of the nineteenth century. And yet as Richard King concludes, though Du Bois did at this stage invest race with a biological dimension – in 'Conservation' he defined 'race' as 'a vast family of human beings, generally of common blood and language' – for him the foundation of race was never primarily biological.[25] Even in 1897, Du Bois named history and tradition as the more important indicators of shared racial heritage. By 1940 Du Bois was to write in *Dusk of Dawn* that 'it is easy to see that scientific definition of race is impossible'.[26]

Nonetheless, in this same text Du Bois endows his African heritage with a quasi-mythological status that seems to transcend what he also characterizes as the primarily historical origins of race:

As I face Africa I ask myself: what is it between us that constitutes a tie which I can feel better than I can explain? Africa is, of course, my fatherland. Yet neither my father nor my father's father ever saw Africa or knew its meaning or cared overmuch for it. My mother's folk were closer and yet their direct connection, in culture and race, became tenuous; still, my tie to Africa is strong.[27]

As Paul Gilroy suggests, Africa emerged for Du Bois – as early as *The Souls of Black Folk* – 'as a mythic counterpart to modernity in the Americas'. In *The Black Atlantic* (1993) Gilroy notes that the title of Du Bois' 1903 literary masterpiece indicates that it was the souls of all black folk – and not just African Americans – that preoccupied him even at this early stage.[28] Thus the romantic racialism that characterizes Du Bois' writings on black America in *Souls* and *Darkwater* was arguably already part of a wider vision that became increasingly apparent as Du Bois forged links with the diaspora. Segun Gbadesgesin explains that Pan-Africanism, a movement to which Du Bois contributed substantially, started life as an American idea, issuing from 'the perception of race as the basis of the African degradation and thus the most important basis for Pan-Africanism'.[29] But what Ghadesgesin characterizes as a potential 'Pan-Negroism' was for Du Bois not just based on the mutual experience of race-based oppression but also had an important spiritual dimension. Rather than endorsing a biological understanding of race, Du Bois believed, as Richard King writes, that 'each race has a purpose, a telos, a meaning, which it seeks to realize in history'.[30] King's insight can be supplemented with the idea that for Du Bois, this journey of special destiny – which African Americans share with the diaspora – has a markedly religious dimension. In *Dusk of Dawn* Du Bois playfully writes:

> This race talk is, of course, a joke, and frequently it has driven me insane and probably will permanently in the future; and yet, seriously and soberly, we black folk are the salvation of mankind.[31]

So where Du Bois vehemently objected to the evils of a white racism nurtured at the heart of white Christianity, he never gave up on the concept upon which racism is based, believing that a valorized understanding of 'race' was also integral to the work of anti-racism. Neither did he sever his own discourse on race from religious rhetoric, for precisely the same reason – *Darkwater* is suffused with images of a black Christ that acts as a bulwark against demeaning images of black humanity emanating from a white racist biblical theology. Rather than rejecting notions of religious election, then, Du Bois rehabilitates and revises the idea of chosenness. Ahead of a Pan-African conference held in 1919, Du Bois insisted that the conference was not a call for racial separatism or the mass emigration of American blacks to Africa, but he nonetheless claimed that 'the African movement means to us what the Zionist movement must mean to the Jews, the centralization of race effort and the recognition of a racial fount'.[32] Thus resurfaces the Zionist idea of the Exodus narrative that elsewhere Du Bois so definitively rejects.

Most of Du Bois' biographers have been keen to claim that his critique of religion forecloses the possibility that he himself was anything but an atheist. This view is typified by Arnold Rampersad, who asserts that Du Bois' 'belief in science came ... at the expense of religious faith'.[33] Yet just as Du Bois allowed a validated concept of race to emerge from his powerful anti-racist agenda, so too, I suggest, did he embrace a transfigured sense of religious destiny. Indeed, he appropriated the white racist tendency to endow racial categories with spiritual meaning to the opposite effect; as Blum suggests, even the title of *The Souls of Black Folk* was a direct challenge to racial extremists in the South who asserted that black people did not have souls at all.[34] *Souls* counters this notion not only by vividly portraying black people as the purveyors of a 'divine spark', but by suggesting that this spark is even more divine than that which attends a white humanity so compromised by its role in slavery and colonialism. So is this claim – that black people are somehow *more* 'divine' than their white brethren – simply a reversal of the master/slave dialectic, the move by which a black God supplants its white counterpart? Does Du Bois reject biblically sanctioned white racism while claiming religious superiority for black America? While so much scholarship has focused on Du Bois' possible investments in the biological premises of race, I suggest that it is his investments in the religious meanings of race that more fully situate his discourse in relationship to white supremacy – and illuminate the myriad critical resources he mobilized to resist it.

The rest of this chapter argues, via a close reading of *The Souls of Black Folk*, that Du Bois' apparent reversal of white racist religious rhetoric is in fact something much more complex than a straightforward contradiction. The next section turns to the encounter that Du Bois stages with the master of contradictory logic, G.W.F. Hegel. As the architect of some of the most important conceptual dragons of postcolonialism, Hegel's influence on Du Bois is of real significance here. As Robert Young argues in *White Mythologies* (1990), Hegel does not invent the dialectic but rather describes a logic already manifest in history; the simultaneous projection and disavowal of difference central to Hegel's system is clearly a basic thrust of colonizing movements – which in effect both usurp and negate indigenous cultures.[35] Yet where for Hegel the dialectic constitutes the stuff of 'progress', for postcolonial studies it is the pressing problem of modernity. The next section will explore whether Du Bois' rendition of double consciousness seeks to champion or defeat the master/slave dialectic.

AN ENCOUNTER WITH HEGEL

Hegel's sense of America as the destination of History's end is categorically refuted by Du Bois' theory of race history. In *Darkwater* Du Bois pours scorn on the exceptionalist crusade that imagines an exemplary America making the 'World Safe for Democracy'.[36] Far from having 'mastered' the domain of history, America, a pivotal player in the racial drama, is the scene of its greatest strife. This emerges most clearly in *The Souls of Black Folk*, an eclectic mix of autobiography, fiction, essay and sermon which, as early as 1903, glimpsed the Pan-African idea by casting black America as part of a wider diaspora borne of the triangular trade. Du Bois thus not only rejects narratives of New World exceptionalism espoused by this philosopher of Old Europe, he also challenges Hegel's designation of Africa as a historical void – anticipating his later role as 'one of the earliest Africanist historians'.[37] In spite of this, Du Bois' vision of black American destiny figures a 'world-historical people' that undoubtedly draws on the spirit of Hegel. Moreover, in *Darkwater* Du Bois indicates that his thinking has not transcended idealized notions of a national-religious community; he writes 'a nation's religion is its life, and as such white Christianity is a miserable failure.'[38] Here Du Bois rejects Hegel's triumphalist celebration of America, but he nonetheless sounds the note of a distinctly Hegelian rhetoric by idealizing the possibilities of group life.

The section that follows will explore the nature of Du Bois' well-known appropriation of Hegel's master/slave dialectic, and will consider the extent to which Hegel's logic infuses Du Bois' elaboration of African American double consciousness. This will have important consequences in terms of assessing Du Bois' attempt to escape the logic of racial and national exceptionalism – discourses which he identifies as intimately bound up with the logic of colonization. For his life-long efforts to forge links between anti-racist and anti-colonial movements find their starting point in a vision of a black exodus from the racial violence of the American South. Yet if Hegel was Du Bois' starting point, what hope did Du Bois really have of imagining a region that might circumvent colonial violence? As Hegel himself points out, 'the one who merely flees is not yet free; in fleeing he is still conditioned by that from which he flees.'[39]

Souls does not project a bodily exodus from the oppressions of the South; instead, deliverance is imagined in both psychological and spiritual terms. Du Bois stages his re-enactment of the Exodus story, his own version of the dramatic confrontation between master and slave, in the consciousness of a 'freedman [who] has not yet found in freedom his promised land'. While the exodus imagined in *Souls* clearly has a material dimension, it also recalls the Christian belief that the promised land resides in our souls, as well as Hegel's spiritual quest for absolute knowledge. Du Bois describes 'book-learning' and the mounting tide among African Americans of the 'longing to know' as the 'dawning' of 'self-consciousness, self-realization, self-respect'. And yet discovery, 'at last' of 'the mountain path to Canaan' remains 'the dreams of a credulous race-childhood', dreams that can only be realized when the ideals of 'physical freedom, political power, the training of brains and the training of hands' are 'melted and welded into one'. Metaphors of integration – reminiscent of Hegelian synthesis – thus seem to foreshadow the solidification of a unified group identity.[40]

While Canaan may appear 'always dim and far away', it is nonetheless designated by Du Bois as destination for a black America which must establish its 'place in the world' by remaining true to itself 'and not another'.[41] *Souls* thus charts the African American journey towards a higher providential destiny via a painfully heightened self-awareness. Through his use of biblical tropes, the promise of freedom acquires sacred status, and yet this is the projection of an exodus which is decidedly yet to come. In 1907 Hallie Queen, an African American studying at Cornell University, wrote to Du Bois that *Souls* 'reminded her of the One hundred and thirty seventh Psalm – "By the Rivers of Babylon."' As Blum explains:

> This reader disclosed a great deal about how she and many others understood *Souls* when she invoked Psalm 137. It is one of the most powerful and disheartening selections in the Hebrew Bible. Driven from their Promised Land and serving in a foreign kingdom, the Jews moaned in despair. They had lost their nation, their sense of community, and perhaps their connection to God.[42]

Souls resonates deeply with this biblical vision of exile and the longing for return, just as it incorporates the cadences of the Hebrew text. Yet it also offers diagnosis of a spiritual condition that not only traces the master/slave dualism, but which gestures towards its overcoming. Du Bois names this condition, which implies both exile and redemption, 'double consciousness'. Du Bois' complex depiction of double consciousness, I argue, locates African American identity as the site of divine chosenness – this entails not only pride but burden too, as it is a condition of responsibility that points to the possibility of redemption for both self and other, master and slave; for, as cited above, 'we black folk are the salvation of mankind'. Cast as Hebrew slaves, Du Bois' black folk still reside in the confines of an 'Egyptland', and yet through a re-figuring of Hegel's allegory Du Bois reverses the trajectory of the Exodus narrative by portraying African Americans as always already God's chosen people. So unlike the Israelites of the biblical narrative, Du Bois' modern-day Hebrews bask in divine favour and as a consequence emerge as a defined collectivity *prior* to reaching the promised land. In making this gesture Du Bois introduces a notion of alterity based on a kind of 'slave ethic', whereby the contradictions that attend the Hegelian quest for absolute knowledge stubbornly refuse to melt away.

Du Bois opens the first essay in the collection, 'Of Our Spiritual Strivings', by figuring a complete impasse between the worlds of black and white. In a concretization of Hegel's extended metaphor, these radically opposing identities are wedded, by history, to their positions as master and slave engaged in a 'life-and-death struggle'. In *Phenomenology of Spirit* (1807) Hegel suggests that it is the bondsman, he who can only 'possess his independence in thinghood', who most fully realizes his self-consciousness. This emerges somewhat counter-intuitively from the fact that the bondsman finds no comfort in illusions of self-sufficiency, he is only too aware that his inner identity as a slave is thrust upon him from the outside. This painful exposure to otherness means that the bondsman fully registers the whole of which he is only a part.[43] The lord by contrast fails to recognize that his position as master is largely upheld by the acknowledgement of his servant; his freedom thus lacks self-consciousness and remains determined, insufficient, whereas for the slave the ideal of a fully satisfied freedom survives as a possible future. Experienced only as a negation, the slave nonetheless possesses knowledge of freedom. So paradoxically, it is the slave who holds the potential to achieve *true* freedom for self-consciousness, because this requires the knowledge acquired, in Du Bois' words, by viewing the self 'through the revelation of the other world'.[44] Faithful to Hegel's formula, this is precisely the condition that befalls black Americans in the dramatization of the master/slave dialectic recounted in *Souls*.

This then is not a relationship that engenders power for the slave but it does bequeath the possibility of agency. In the concluding section of *Slavery and Social Death* (1982), Orlando Patterson suggests that the master/slave dialectic, rather than being characterized as 'a relation of domination', might be better conceived as a case of 'human parasitism' – precisely because slavery renders the master dependent on the slave:

> Parasitisim emphasizes the asymmetry of all such unequal relations: the degree to which the parasite depends on the host is not necessarily a direct measure of the extent to which the host is exploited in supporting the parasite. A parasite may only be partially dependent on its host, but this partial dependence may entail the destruction of the host.[45]

This I suggest is comparable to Du Bois' revisionist reading of Hegel, which also turns the racist lexicon of the 'white man's burden' on its head. As is much remarked, Du Bois' rendering of double consciousness draws heavily on Hegel's description of the 'Unhappy Consciousness', an 'agonizing' state whereby consciousness is '*broken in two*' by in effect internalizing the master/slave dialectic.[46] Du Bois' well-known elaboration of this 'peculiar sensation, this double-consciousness', reads:

> One ever feels his twoness, – an American, a Negro; two souls, two thoughts, two unreconciled strivings; two warring ideals in one dark body, whose dogged strength alone keeps it from being torn asunder.[47]

The inescapably physical nature of this spiritual zone is captured by Frantz Fanon when, in *Black Skin, White Masks* (1952), he hears the words 'Look – a Negro!' and experiences what he memorably describes as the 'epidermalization of being' on realizing that the finger is pointed at him.[48] And yet just as Patterson's understanding of slavery as parasitism captures the pain associated with the terms 'domination' and 'exploitation' while refusing the sense of passivity that those terms imply, for Du Bois, life lived in the US 'within the Veil', mediated by 'the contradiction of double aims', is emphatically not 'weakness'. Almost as soon as this doubled consciousness descends on Du Bois, he 'had thereafter no desire to tear down that veil, to creep through'.[49]

At first glance Du Bois' description of African American self-division emerges as remarkably in keeping with Hegel's critique of a certain kind of Christianity that conditions the unhappy consciousness. For Hegel this – decidedly 'weak' – theology constitutes 'the movement of an infinite yearning' that longs for an 'unattainable *beyond*', one that might heal the sense of an intangible rupture.[50] For Du Bois too the white 'beyond' of 'the other world' remains master by establishing unattainable ideals that made the black worker 'ashamed of his lowly tasks'. Moreover, Du Bois' critique of the religion offered to slaves by their masters is identical to Hegel's portrayal of Christianity as thwarted dream: Du Bois writes, 'the Negro, losing the joy of this world, eagerly seized upon the offered conceptions of the next.' This 'comforting dream', according to Du Bois, implanted a 'deep religious fatalism' about life in bondage, one that severs the link between religion and worldly action.[51] And yet where for Hegel the unhappy consciousness is one of the 'ideologies', as Alexandre Kojève explains, by which the slave 'seeks to justify himself, to justify his slavery, to reconcile the *ideal* of Freedom with the *fact* of Slavery',[52] double consciousness as a form of self-division finds a very different inflection in *Souls*. In fact it works in precisely the opposite direction by ensuring that the ideal of freedom, far from being reconciled to the fact of slavery, remains in constant tension with it.

Unlike Hegel, who is dealing with historical abstractions, 'Du Bois is caught here between a transcendence of and a simultaneous entrapment in concrete existence'.[53] For while Hegel portrays lordship and bondage as dynamic positions that we occupy dialectically within the movement of self-consciousness, Du Bois' account relies on concretizing the metaphor. African Americans may encompass the contradictions of both mastery and slavery – as well as the cultures of both black and white – yet their physical lives are lived as metaphorical, and indeed at one point in history very literal, slaves. Du Bois thus ontologizes – fixes – what in Hegel is a crucially dynamic condition. The universal drama described by Hegel – the movement of self-consciousness through the different positions as both master and slave – becomes in *Souls* a particular attribute of black America. Du Bois thus locks his protagonists into a drama of consciousness that is rendered static by the social conditions of America, and particularly the South; so while the unhappy consciousness entails an internalization of the positions of both master and slave, it is nonetheless a 'slave ideology' by which black and *not* white America carries the burdens of the nation. This divided knowledge that glimpses both black and white life means that African Americans more fully cognize 'America'.

To an extent, then, Du Bois' elaboration of an ontologized version of the master/slave dialectic *freezes* its progress; there is a sense in Du Bois of the absolute irreconcilability between black and white life. Joel Williamson, paraphrasing what he sees as the tendency of Du Bois' thought, writes: 'if black life was to have meaning, to have value, it would have to be a separated life.'[54] This vision of ultimate separation could not be further from the logic of the Hegelian *telos*, which is driven by the synthesizing impulse to integration.

Where for Hegel thought goes through various stages of alienation before it can achieve identity with itself, African Americans, rather than *thinking* their own dispossession, experience it at the most basic level. The 'knowledge' portrayed by Du Bois as African American 'second sight' is achieved on an intuitive level, thus issuing from the very trappings of physical life from which Hegel's reason seeks to escape. While double consciousness is an unhappy consciousness – clearly characterized by pain in *Souls* – this early stage of Hegel's dialectic is nonetheless valorized in *Souls* in a gesture that can only be described as un-Hegelian. For Hegel the unhappy consciousness finds resolution in its own transcendence towards a higher stage of understanding; for Du Bois, ambivalent as he is on the dilemma of double consciousness, 'resolution' is not a possibility. Thus Du Bois does not, ultimately, champion the abstractions of a Hegelian 'insight' uncontaminated by the physical world, but rather celebrates a condition that has yet to transcend its own contradictions.

Du Bois' account of African American subjectivity in the Jim Crow South thus suggests that black consciousness is not returned satisfactorily to itself: the promised land remains suspended towards an uncertain future, the substance of a dream that remains incomplete. Yet Du Bois is determined to celebrate this difference, to turn its potential negative into a positive – not through Hegelian synthesis, but rather by highlighting this difference as divine.

As a child Du Bois perceived that white life beyond the veil offered 'dazzling opportunities', indicating, perhaps, that God's favour was 'theirs, not mine'. And yet I suggest that these associations linking this 'beyond' to both the worlds of white mastery *and* religious fulfilment only superficially undermine Du Bois' implicit assumption of African American chosenness. For in spite of 'the fond imaginings of the other world which does not know and does not want to know our power', black America 'knows that Negro blood has a message for the world'.[55] White America for Du Bois embodies Kojève's remark that 'Mastery is an existential impasse',[56] while African Americans have seemingly been favoured with the gift of self-awareness that equals a gift to the world. If, as Williamson claims, for both Du Bois and Hegel, 'ignorance is the measure of the distance of our separation from God',[57] then God has seemingly chosen black America for divine proximity. And yet unlike Hegel's *telos* of a God incarnate, Du Bois' text – devoid of a materialized promise – must hold the future radically open. So contra the *Phenomenology*, the mismatch between human mind and divine spirit – the real and the ideal – is productive in *Souls*, proximity to God accompanied by a seemingly untraversable divide.

The anxious question – 'why did God make me an outcast and a stranger in mine own house?' – thus echoes as a refrain throughout the text and hints at the possibility of a failed theodicy, that is, the sense that God's goodness has *not* been vindicated.[58] For in marked distinction to Hegel, Du Bois suggests that for African Americans, self-knowledge cannot be equated with freedom. And the experience of freedom, seemingly the preserve of whites, cannot reflect – and certainly must not vindicate – the will of God.

In 'Credo', a piece that prefaces *Darkwater*, Du Bois states: 'I believe in God, who made of one blood all nations that on earth do dwell'; he thus unequivocally refutes claims made by many of his subsequent commentators that he was an atheist, and places faith in a universal religious vision that transcends human categorization. Yet he also writes 'especially do I believe in the Negro Race: in the beauty of its genius, the sweetness of its soul, and its strength in that meekness which shall yet inherit this turbulent earth.' Belief in human beings and indeed human groupings is given here equal – if not more – weight than belief in God. Given that the work of 'the Devil and his angels' is so evident in 'the wicked conquest of weaker and darker nations by nations whiter and stronger', religious concepts are borrowed from a seemingly silent – if not absent – 'Prince of Peace' and loaned to the face of an all too evident human suffering. Thus while Du Bois asserts that 'all distinction not based on deed is devilish and not divine', he tempers this with an apparently contradictory investment in transcendent terms: 'I believe in Pride of race and lineage and self.' This compromise between human equality and belief in divine chosenness thus emerges here as profoundly provisional. In a world notably bereft of redemptive guarantees, human beings must nonetheless struggle for divine ideals and quite literally wrestle with a 'God' who threatens to remain silent on the subject of that pivotal question: 'Why did God make me an outcast and a stranger in mine own house?' Equality may be the goal, but in the absence of its realization, human work – inevitably conditioned by bias – must be its substitute: echoing *Souls*, Du Bois' 'Credo' reads:

> I believe in the Training of Children, black even as white; the leading out of little souls into the green pastures and beside the still waters, not for pelf or peace, but for life lit by some large vision of beauty and goodness and truth; lest we forget, and the sons of the fathers, like Esau, for mere meat barter their birthright in a mighty nation.[59]

Thus unlike Hegel's ideal, which eventually masters and transcends contradictory knowledge, Du Bois' religious vision remains conditioned by paradox. Where later Du Bois will equate the colonized and the hungry with the legacy of an Esau he champions, here he shuns 'mere meat' for the seductions of a 'mighty nation'. These contradictions, however, evidence their own brand of 'logic' in that they issue from Du Bois' refusal to equate racial realities with the dream of racial equality. Consequently in the next section I argue that Du Bois departs decisively not only from the Hegelian text but from the Christian one too. Blum writes that '*Souls* entered the U.S. cultural landscape as a sacred text',[60] and what follows will discuss the extent to which its vision resonates with Christianity.

A CHRISTIAN 'CREDO'?

If Hegel's vision of the ideal state is synonymous with the overcoming of the master/slave dialectic, then the human God of Christianity – towards which Hegel's 'system' clearly moves – is the foundation of this mythic egalitarian polity. These idealized visions of equality are clearly shared by Du Bois. Yet both Hegelianism and Christianity project this vision not as an aspiration but as an already realized dream awaiting recognition; in this Du Bois cannot share. Where for Christianity redemption is always already achieved, Du Bois' vision of an African American exodus holds out the hope for future redemption. I have tried to show that Du Bois' dream of freedom from racial inequities and colonial conquest is couched in a peculiarly religious register, yet does this make him a Christian thinker?

The extended metaphor of the veil – drawn on by Shamoon Zamir
to note that Du Bois' drama of consciousness issues from its descent,
Hegel's from its ascent[61] – has strong religious connotations and
becomes the symbol through which Du Bois discusses the segregation
of American life. African Americans live 'behind', 'within', 'below',
a 'vast veil' that lies between them and the white world. In their
constant struggle to 'escape both death and isolation', the veil
threatens to shroud black American existence.[62] On the subject of
this powerful Du Boisian trope, Werner Sollors writes:

> Du Bois imaginatively adapted two biblical images of the veil as
> a division within the temple [Exodus 26:33] and as the cover that
> the divinely inspired Moses wore when he came back from Mount
> Sinai and spoke to the people [Exodus 34:33–35]. Both images
> are typologically focused in Paul's second letter to the Corinthians
> [3:13–18], a passage which promises a universal revelation once
> the Old Testament veil has been sundered in Christ.[63]

Sollors maps the trajectory of Du Bois' veil typologically – i.e. he
suggests that the Old Testament anticipates and is fulfilled by the
New – and so affirms a Christian reading of *Souls*. And yet this
reading projects the veil's sundering as the Du Boisian *telos*, its
endpoint and its aim. But the idea that the removal of this differential
consciousness – the eradication of what Blum characterizes as a
racial 'cosmic sight' – is the desired end is given only ambivalent
expression in *Souls*. Such an unveiling is of course the end in Hegel,
for whom transcendence of difference through knowledge, and thus
the end of contradiction, is the ultimate goal. As Rowan Williams
writes, for Hegel 'scripture and doctrine must be unveiled for what
they truly are, and this is the destiny of philosophy'.[64] However,
while Du Bois clearly prizes knowledge, it does not follow that
increased wisdom would be the consequence of the act of unveiling
described here. In fact, in Du Bois it is the veil itself which confers
this heightened awareness, suggesting not only that knowledge is
always textured and never absolute, but also that we cannot fully
cognize the absolute through knowledge.

Du Bois' difference from Hegel is perhaps captured by Phillip
Blond's sense that 'for Hegel what is not known does not matter'.
For Du Bois, who is describing a world of segregated systems of
knowledge that is yet to redeem itself, 'what is not known' – or
not yet realized – clearly does matter. In his counter to Rowan
Williams' construal of the Hegelian dialectic as a true affirmation

of a 'Trinitarian grammar', Blond outlines the risk involved in what he sees as the reduction of 'God to the level and shape of our own mental life'. Blond writes:

> To avoid a simple immanentism such a position would have to claim that mental life can indeed come to a full knowledge of the absolute without constructing that absolute, as the absolute has already fully actualised itself in history. Since God does not stand apart from us, He stands for Hegel as already fully present and historically completed. Human cognition, rather than constructing this objectivity, has merely to come to an awareness of it being already existent.

Blond claims that the Hegelian account denies a futural trajectory to mental life, and he contends that 'to base a religious life on this is to have a theology without a future'.[65] Given that Du Boisian hope lies in the dream of future change, Hegel's invocation of a completed universe waiting to offer itself as freedom to self-consciousness is an unappealing one in this context, contradicted as it is by material realities. As J.N. Findlay notes, Hegel's claim is that 'time is the destiny and the necessity of the as yet not perfected Spirit'; 'Time simply is the form of this self-realizing process. Until Spirit reaches the end of the requisite temporal process it cannot achieve complete self-consciousness.' There is a relentless and inexorable quality to Hegel's system which is quite out of keeping with the interruptive temporality invoked by Du Bois. Where Hegelian consciousness transcends and thus redeems the alienated world by realizing inwardly the existence of the 'Divine Man or Human God', Du Boisian double consciousness is much more inclined to follow Sojourner Truth – who, during an abolitionist convention, asked Frederick Douglass 'Is God dead?' – in echoing the unhappy consciousness in its cry that 'God is dead'.[66] For the generative principle in Du Bois as compared to Hegel is not reconciliation with reality but rather the reverse.

What Hegel derides as 'the hard-edged, abstract, out-thereness of religion, its presentative character',[67] clearly emerges in Du Bois' repeated lament: 'Why did God make me an outcast and a stranger in mine own house?' Yet in *Souls*, African American double consciousness remains fundamentally *unreconciled* to its everyday realities, and Hegel's sense that 'evil' is nothing other than 'the first step in the direction of good' imagines God *as* history rather than one that flies in its face. As Kojève explains, Hegel argues that 'the Christian synthesis must be effected not in the

Beyond, after death, but on earth, during man's life'; with this, Du Bois is clearly in agreement. But Kojève goes on to explain that the '*transcendent* Universal (God) ... must be replaced by a Universal that is immanent in the World. And for Hegel this immanent Universal can only be the State.' It is here that Du Bois parts company with Hegel, because in his view the bodies of African Americans have already been subsumed by a sacralized notion of statehood. Where Hegel, according to Kojève, seeks to 'eliminate the Christian idea of transcendence' in the interests of the state, Du Bois figures a transcendence of the state itself.[68] In this sense he seeks to break out of Hegel's colonizing logic; whether he does so by mobilizing the Christian idea of transcendence against the state is though questionable.

In 'Of the Faith of the Fathers' Du Bois breaks the boundaries of the traditional jeremiad by identifying black America's radical roots not with the founding fathers of the nation but rather with African and African American slaves. It is these roots, Du Bois suggests, that set the standard against which black spirituality must measure up, and not those of the American civil religion. Du Bois' essay charts the insinuation of a Christian ideology of passive acceptance into the original African religions. Yet he also notes a change in the evolution of this submissive Christianity as Emancipation looms on the horizon and 'freedom' appears to the slave as 'a real thing and not a dream. His religion became darker and more intense, and into his ethics crept a note of revenge, into his songs a day of reckoning close at hand.' Here Du Bois describes the beginnings of a radical current in black religious expression. Quite in contrast to the 'religion of resignation and submission' encouraged by slave owners, 'the dream of Abolition' became 'a religion to the black world'. 'Thus', writes Du Bois, 'when Emancipation finally came, it seemed to the freedman a literal Coming of the Lord.' Emancipation is experienced not as the fulfilment of the state but rather as an interruption from the future. Quite unlike Hegel's map of freedom, liberation for Du Bois will be an event occasioned by the unknown.[69]

Du Bois underscores the church's centrality to the development of black consciousness on American soil, because 'as a social institution it antedated by many decades the monogamic Negro home'.[70] So upon realization of the disappointments of Emancipation, Du Bois blames the black churches for nurturing a combination of bitterness and apathy that blunts black radicalism. Nonetheless, Du Bois concludes this essay on a note of defiance:

But back of this still broods silently the deep religious feeling of the real Negro heart, the stirring, unguided might of powerful human souls who have lost the guiding star of the past and are seeking in the great night a new religious ideal. Some day the Awakening will come, when the pent-up vigor of ten million souls shall seep irresistibly toward the goal, out of the Valley of the Shadow of Death, where all that makes life worth living – Liberty, Justice, and Right – is marked 'For White People Only'.[71]

So in contrast to the Hegelian sense of divinity which has already arrived on 'the guiding star of the past', I suggest that Du Bois invokes the dream of a God to come, of 'a new religious ideal' emerging from 'the great night'. Many Christian theologians have of course rejected the notion that the Hegelian acceptance of history as the construct of a 'Human God' is in fact an elaboration of 'true' Christianity. Kojève supports this view when he claims that 'according to Hegel, one can realize the Christian *anthropological* ideal (which he accepts in full) only by "overcoming" the Christian *theology*'.[72] And Blond voices this rejection when he writes, contra Hegel, that 'for Christianity, all that has occurred in history, all the satanic negations of human life, all the death and crushed possibility, is not a negative that can be turned into a positive'.[73] Likewise Du Bois entirely rejects the crushing experience of American racism which he describes in the passage above as the experience 'of the Valley of the Shadow of Death'; this is not a negative that can be turned into a positive but rather a life-defying existence that demands an 'Awakening'.

Blond explains: 'there are some events, some death events, that one should never be reconciled with. And what is Christianity if it is not this, this refusal to accept death?'[74] Blond thus claims for Christianity what often appears to be lacking in Hegel: the critical ability to counterpoise what *is* with what *ought* to be. And yet interestingly, while Du Bois rejects death on this metaphorical level and instead demands exodus, part of the radical thrust of *Souls* lies in an acceptance of literal death as a form of worldly exit, an exit that holds no redemption of this world by the next but one that nonetheless achieves liberation.

'On the Faith of the Fathers' is followed in Du Bois' collection by a moving account of the death of his son, 'Of the Passing of the First-Born'. The image of black America rising from the 'Valley of the Shadow of Death' is thus followed by the event of birth and the hopes embodied 'in his baby voice' heard by his parents as 'the voice of the Prophet that was to rise within the Veil'.[75] That the hopes inspired by 'the joy of creation' are not destined to be fulfilled within the material world recalls the fate of first-born sons in Genesis who, from Cain to Reuben, are seemingly 'passed over' by a God who continually favours younger siblings; that Du Bois discusses the 'passing of the first-born' in relation to slavery and freedom points to several moments of comparison with the Exodus text as well.

Du Bois' early hopes that his first-born might 'rise within the Veil' recalls God's assurances to Moses that 'Israel *is* my son, *even* my firstborn' (Exodus, 4:22). And indeed, following his son's death, Du Bois comforts himself with the thought that his son *has* been chosen for freedom: 'my soul whispers ever to me saying, "Not dead, not dead, but escaped; not bond, but free."' For as Du Bois' hopes for his son were accompanied by a vision of 'the shadow of the Veil as it passed over my baby', so his death might well be this blessing: 'well sped, my boy, before the world had dubbed your ambition insolence, had held your ideals unattainable, and taught you to cringe and bow.' Du Bois' essay is clearly riddled with grief and such suggestions are coupled with questions addressed to 'God' to the opposite effect: 'are there so many workers in the vineyard that the fair promise of this little body could lightly be tossed away?' What seems clear in these protestations is that regardless of Du Bois' sorrow, his child has nonetheless escaped the all-encompassing net of power that would have put his body to work.[76]

In the first chapter of Exodus, Pharaoh, anticipating the moves of Hegel's master/slave dialectic, abates the perceived threat posed by the Israelites – who seemingly confront Egypt with the possibility of death – by enslaving them. Yet he simultaneously orders the execution of every Hebrew boy (Exodus, 1:22), in essence murdering his own potential slaves. As David Gunkel notes, 'in so doing, he interrupts the institution of slavery. He annihilates a negativity that shall never serve Egypt in bondage.'[77] Pharaoh's actions thus in part disrupt the structure of mastery which in Hegel relies on the survival of the 'other' in the form of the slave. Du Bois detects a similar interruption in the event of his son's death. As David Levering Lewis explains, Du Bois' work had brought he and his wife 'to a city practically devoid of doctors of their own race – a city where white physicians refused to treat even desperately sick black children'.[78] Burghardt's consequent death means that his body will forever reside beyond the economy of 'the blood-red land'.[79] The effects of racism are thus fatal here, but the event of death nonetheless counteracts the project of racial slavery.

On the subject of the birth of Du Bois' first-born son, Lewis writes, 'like another birth nearly two thousand years earlier, Burghardt's coming foretells eventual deliverance of a people, symbolizing faith in some ultimate transcendence of the Veil by the African American millions'.[80] In this sense Du Bois' account of the birth of his son anticipates the next essay, which characterizes Alexander Crummell as an exemplary, Christ-like figure, and together these essays cast black people in the shape of the divine in a way that arguably anticipates the black liberation theology of the 1960s.[81] Yet I suggest that Du Bois does not cast the death of his son in the redemptive light that defines the Christian story. Du Bois writes: 'better far this nameless void that stops my life than a sea of sorrow for you.'[82] This does not seem to be equivalent to the moment in Exodus when Pharaoh, in horror at the loss of Egypt's first-born, essentially 'converts' to belief in the Israelite God and asks that Moses 'bless me also' (Exodus, 12:32). Neither is Burghardt's death a Christ-like sacrifice that can be put to work. Rather than being a negative that can be turned into a positive, his death seems to evade the economy of redemption. In this sense it is a fitting response to 'the faith of the fathers' which here is not affirmed but rather shattered by the notion that slavery might just be a fate worse than death.

It is important here to note that Du Bois was writing during a time in which the South was structured not around the brutalities of legalized slavery but rather 'lynch law'; where the 'peculiar institution' conferred a significant cash-value on the heads of African Americans, their release from bondage meant the cheapening of black blood to the point that literally thousands of African Americans, mainly men, were lynched by white mobs at the turn of the century. Where chattel slavery did obviously rely on living blacks – who desired to go on living – the system of indentured service that followed could afford to lose countless black bodies to satisfy the appetites of bloodthirsty racists. Nonetheless, lynching was clearly another way of performing white control over the black body, whereas an active turning towards death on the part of African Americans denied whites agency in the arena of black desire, just as it deprived them of this power during institutionalized slavery. Gilroy links the trend in black American writing that offers 'representations of death as agency' to archival material on the practice of slave suicide; he writes:

> This turn towards death as a release from terror and bondage and a chance to find substantive freedom accords perfectly with

Orlando Patterson's celebrated notion of slavery as a state of 'social death.' It points to the value of seeing the consciousness of the slave as involving an extended act of mourning.[83]

In this way, and in the aftermath of official slavery in the South, Du Bois continues to give voice to a strain of resistance in African American letters which is marked by a turning towards death. Thus Du Bois' vision of an ultimate exodus refuses the comfort of the certainty of a Christian heaven – on the basis that the afterlife would redeem earthly suffering; for the redemption of suffering makes way for its acceptance, something Du Bois' oeuvre consistently refuses to do. The description of a world 'ever haunted by the shadow of a death that is more than death' depicts a scenario which will not sustain the Hegelian master/slave dialectic – which after all relies on the *desire* to evade death at all costs.[84] And while Phillip Blond argues that this dialectic does not reflect a truly Christian vision of the future, Du Bois' refusal of an economy of redemption departs significantly from Blond's portrait of Christianity as a 'refusal to accept death'.

Williamson claims that in *Souls*, Du Bois predicts that 'when black people know their souls, they will know Truth, Beauty, and, the ultimate reality, God. When they know themselves, they will know whiteness too, and they will be at peace with the whiteness that is within them.'[85] And yet it is difficult to read such a vision as a 'prediction' in the context of Du Bois' racially divided world in which it sometimes appears 'just as though God really were dead'.[86] The communication with God that I suggest Du Bois does infer through the gift and burden of African American 'second-sight' seems much closer to the veiled addresses of Moses to his people than to an unmediated relationship with Jesus Christ. Just as the Israelites cannot bear to look on at the divine radiance that illuminates Moses' face, neither can Du Bois fully comprehend a God that might claim the lives of the first-born – as she does mercilessly in the tenth plague against Egypt – as a stage on the way to freedom. I argue that Du Boisian double consciousness implies that black America *is* God's 'first-born', but its redemption is yet to be achieved; the relation with God is thus one experienced at the level of loss, of mourning.

Gilroy's notion of slave consciousness as mourning can thus be extended to Du Boisian double consciousness, in which black Americans mourn an elusive freedom, just as they mourn an elusive God. The sacralization of freedom in *Souls* not only implies a close relationship between God and freedom, it also figures an intimate relationship between these concepts and black America. Patterson's account elaborates this apparent paradox found in Du Bois' text:

> The first men and women to struggle for freedom, the first to think of themselves as free in the only meaningful sense of the term, were freedmen. And without slavery there would have been no freedmen.[87]

This 'extended act of mourning' signals the death of the national dream and indeed the collapse of the discourse of the jeremiad within Du Bois' thought – for his suggestion is that the coming exodus would figure not a fulfilment but rather an interruption of 'America'. Unlike Obama then, discussed in the previous chapter, Du Bois' text evades the risk that state memory might eclipse black memory. Rather the memory – or afterlife – of slavery interrupts any uncomplicated investment in America's promise.

So while the experience of oppression has led Du Bois to appropriate the motif of the 'chosen people' for African Americans, the terms of this chosenness remain shrouded in mystery, clothed in the veil of divine mediation, the inaccessibility of which seems to refuse the triumph of Hegel's knowledge or Christian revelation. 'The Nation', Du Bois writes, 'has not yet found peace from its sins'; it remains fatally divided against itself, as indeed does the very nature of the divine.[88] African American double consciousness, then, reflects not only the deepest knowledge of a troubled America – a knowledge seemingly undetected by whites – but also mirrors a disrupted 'God'.

CONCLUSION: BETWEEN EXODUS AND EGYPT

Souls imagines the utopian possibility of transforming freedom experienced only as a negation into something quite different. The Christian promise of death *as* life encompasses just this kind of radical hope. Yet the fact that Hegel himself drew heavily on Christianity as the model for his own 'system' cautions against the notion that the Christian vision always speaks candidly to liberation movements. Indeed the Christian church's complicity in slavery, colonialism and race-based oppression – eloquently elaborated by Du Bois – perhaps makes it no surprise that Hegel would effortlessly draw on Christian tropes as the archetype for a logic that would similarly legitimize the consequences of colonial violence. For Hegel's colonizing logic – by which weaker historical trends are incorporated into the logic of stronger ones, their contradictions thus transcended – derives from the Christian notion that a negative can be radically turned on its head and made over into a positive, that death could really mean life. While undeniably attractive, the Hegelian consequence is that Esau is put to work for Jacob, colonized for colonizer. The slave master must learn from his servant – who possesses knowledge he lacks – but ultimately it is the master that triumphs in a philosophy that notoriously sanctifies the status quo.

Unlike Hegel, Du Bois did not identify with the powers of white Europe but rather with a black world – both within and exterior to 'America' – bearing the legacy of Esau. Du Bois' convoluted and doubled discourse is testimony to the fact that while 'freedom' currently bears the face of Jacob, the transcendence of the spirit of Esau would also mean the death of group solidarity so crucial for African American and Pan-African unity. The result is a provisional repudiation in *Souls* of any destination that would terminate the contradictions of racial difference. Paradoxically then, Du Boisian spirituality in part suspends the redemptive moment of equality in favour of a group distinction that elsewhere – in other guises – he himself abhors. But this suspension seems not to be a choice but rather necessity: in the face of a reality that brazenly refuses to step in line with an ideal freedom, Du Bois rejects what in Hegel seems to be a premature sighting of redemption, a sighting that in effect serves the interest of current power relations. Thus Du Bois, the virulent critic of race-based oppression, particularly that which is underscored by distorted religious doctrine, names blacks in general and African Americans in particular members of a race favoured by God. In this sense race trumps nation as a category of analysis. Du Bois' invocations of Exodus in *Souls* and elsewhere thus demonstrate that the text is stalked by the possibility of dialectical reversal. I have argued though that this is not the effect; Du Bois' thought is so adept at hanging onto two contradictory ideas simultaneously that the one is not allowed to eclipse or subsume the other.

In *Darkwater* Du Bois cites Psalm 68:31, 'Princes shall come out of Egypt; Ethiopia shall soon stretch out her hands unto God', showing that black identification with Hebrew slaves need not preclude invocations of a proud Africa, and might even involve the redemption of the very Egypt that enslaved them. For while Du Bois conjures a contemporary Africa brought to her knees – 'prostrated, raped, and shamed' – he evokes the spirit of an Egyptian queen to imagine a future Africa returned to the ancient glories of the land of the Pharaohs.[89] Unlike black nationalists like Marcus Garvey, whose invocation of Psalm 68 and a black Zion often wrote over the parallel Hebraic story as much, if not more, as it identified with it, Du Bois remained a steadfast supporter of a Jewish homeland until his death in 1963. Writing in *Crisis* in 1919 he wrote that 'the African movement means to us what the Zionist movement must mean to the Jews'.[90]

While a number of critics have claimed that Du Bois was guilty of stereotyping Jews and even expressing hostility towards them, writing in 2002 Benjamin Sevitch marshals a diverse array of evidence spanning Du Bois' long career to argue convincingly that he was in fact a lifetime opponent of anti-Semitism. Sevitch writes that 'Du Bois was among the most prescient American observers of the Holocaust; and he never retreated from sounding the alarm.'[91] Du Bois' role in reporting the path to genocide in Europe was foreshadowed by many years during which he consistently viewed Jews as fellow victims – alongside diasporic blacks – of a racist West. And his identification with Jews clearly travelled the distance from a spiritual affinity via the Exodus text and the experience of suffering through to political support for Jewish statehood, a fully materialized 'promised land'. Writing in the *Chicago Defender* in 1948, one day after the State of Israel was declared, he states:

> Here is a comparatively small group of people noted in ancient history for their high religious concepts, for their clear thinking, and the splendid results of their family life. They have met with opposition for thousands of years, not on account of laziness and inefficiency, but on account of their determined will to survive and to be spiritually free.[92]

Du Bois' support for Jewish national self-determination is entirely consistent with the black/Jewish analogy he repeatedly drew via the Exodus narrative, which is after all not only a story about suffering and slavery but also one about the laying down of roots, of the ingathering of the exiles into one unified national community. For Du Bois' references to black chosenness, as well as his embrace of the African diaspora, are poignantly laced with a longing for home, the sustenance of roots, longings which also propel the most successful projects of nation-building. Yet as the Israeli story unfolded it became harder for Du Bois to reconcile the competing strands of his thought that simultaneously identified with the experiences of suffering *and* with power, Jacob *and* Esau, the spiritual *and* the material implications of Jewish biblical tradition, Exodus *and* Egypt. This is captured by Du Bois' literary response to the Suez crisis of 1956, a crisis that brought the new Israeli state and Nasser's Egypt into direct conflict:

> Young Israel raised a mighty cry
> 'Shall Pharoah ride anew?'
> But Nasser grimly pointed West,
> 'They mixed this witches' brew!'
> ... Israel as the West betrays
> Its murdered, mocked, and damned,
> Becomes the shock troops of two knaves
> Who steal the dark man's land.[93]

Du Bois' admiration both for Nasser's Egypt and for Israel leads him to cast Israel as the dupe of the racist imperial powers. This is because in spite of the paradoxes and apparent contradictions that attend Du Bois' meditations on race, religion and nation, his firm belief in the need to acquire power and agency was rooted in a life-long sense of solidarity with the oppressed, a solidarity that issued from his affiliation first and foremost to black America.

Ultimately Du Bois' articulation of the African American narrative must tell of displacement: it is almost as if in the absence of roots – which his prose incessantly dreams of – Du Bois makes do with routes. His writings make it patently clear that in the absence of a promised land made flesh, the colonized subject must articulate the reality of a world that offers not home but rather exile. In this his religious vision is more akin to the Jewish picture of an unredeemed world than a Christian vision of eternal salvation. Indeed it is precisely the triumphalist possibilities of discourses of salvation that form the ethnocentric threads of mainstream American (and some Israeli) renditions of the Exodus narrative – against which Du Bois implicitly counters his own. Du Bois thus provides a systematic rationale for Obama's tendency to lay emphasis on the inherently incomplete nature of history – an emphasis that is at odds with renditions of Christianity that claim to cure human alienation from reality via the equivalence between man and God.

The exodus glimpsed in *Souls* thus defies a self-serving American Christianity in favour of spiritual links forged with the wider world. In 1952, four years after Israel's founding, but still within ten years of the horrors of Auschwitz, Du Bois claimed that his encounter with 'the Jewish problem' in post-war Poland led to 'a real and more complete understanding of the Negro problem'.[94] For Du Bois Jews remained representative of a quintessentially *unhoused* identity. This identification with Jewish history that Du Bois expressed in 1952 was anticipated half a century earlier in a text which bears a distinctively Hebraic character. What this Hebraic text indicates, perhaps, is that while some renditions of Christianity may embrace the workings of the state, Judaism's relationship to the state – Jewish or otherwise – is inherently problematic. For, as the next chapter will explore, Hebraic religion often shows a marked resistance to the declaration of this-worldly redemption upon which nationalist discourses rely. Du Bois' appropriation of a decidedly Hebraic biblical narrative of the going out of Egypt by necessity casts the acquisition of 'roots' into a radically uncertain future, unsettling the stability of place, nation and the foundations of a 'people'.

In this sense Du Bois is a figure at the crossroads: his thinking on race was crystallized largely prior to the period that saw the establishment and then the break-up of the black–Jewish Civil Rights alliance, and he died before Israel had taken its place in the black American imagination as a symbol of racist colonialism.[95] The religious and philosophical contradictions that thus attend his combination of Hebraic religion, Zionism and Pan-Africanism remain largely uncomplicated by the political divisions that were to come later. And so Du Bois' Hebraic rendition of the Exodus narrative, which both deconstructs and affirms the Zionist dream, is overlain with a longing for an Africa symbolized by 'Egyptian' greatness. The 'Egypt' metaphor thus uneasily collaborates with aspirations to Zion, as both are animated by the allure of national and racial exceptionalism. As argued in the previous chapter, all of these elements infuse the theological-political currents that shape Obama's former church. It is, however, the political climate of the intervening years, and particularly that which unfolded following the establishment of the State of Israel, that has rendered these nuances invisible via one-dimensional understandings of black political affiliation and religious identity. This formative period in the black American narrative will be explored in the next two chapters via two pivotal figures: Martin Luther King and Malcolm X. That Du Bois' thought clearly anticipates that of the symbol of 'liberal integrationism' *as well as* that of the most potent symbol of 'black nationalism' demonstrates just how hollow these shallow characterizations have become.

The Egypt thread will be picked up in Chapter 4, where I argue that it pushes the religious tenor of black nationalism towards conversion to Islam. The chapter that follows this one will develop suggestions forwarded here about the black religious encounter with Hebraic religion. Taken together, these chapters explore some of the diverse religious influences that shape politicized black Christianity today. The next chapter argues that Martin Luther King, a figure much more readily embraced by white America than Obama's pastor, shares with Jeremiah Wright a flexible and highly unconventional approach to Christian doctrine, one which bears the strain of a deep ambivalence towards a religion so heavily implicated in America's race history.

Where the Du Boisian text resonates with anti-theodic strains that bear witness to a failure to deliver on the promises of freedom, Martin Luther King's dream was increasingly cast in the shadows as his rhetoric grew more apocalyptic, more prophetic and, arguably, less recognizably 'Christian' in the eyes of a white American mainstream. Where Du Bois invests in rehabilitated versions of categories he simultaneously rejects, King too proves not to be immune to ideas of racial exceptionalism as he faces the glaring failures of a national dream. Thus 'the fiction of the Elect and the Superior'[96] – that Du Bois so effectively critiques *and* rehabilitates – proves curiously persistent even in the rhetoric of America's most famous voice of inclusion. In this sense then King's powerful rendition of the Exodus narrative is heir to the paradoxes of double consciousness that haunted Du Bois' career as a biographer of race and key combatant in the fight against racism.

3
Excavating the Promised Land: Martin Luther King

No other African American figure has captured the image of racial reconciliation as powerfully or memorably as has Martin Luther King Jr. The speech that now constitutes a defining landmark in twentieth-century oratory projected a promised land wherein the overcoming of the master/slave dialectic is synonymous with the overcoming of the black/white binary. King's 1963 masterpiece famously imagined a nation in which his children might be judged not 'by the color of their skin but by the content of their character'. Where Du Bois' theory of double consciousness refused to surrender the concept of racial difference, King's vision in 'I Have a Dream' is one in which the differences between human beings are melted away. And where Du Bois' religious instincts only ambivalently embraced Christianity, King's was undoubtedly a Christian vision. The biblical landscape that thus emerges as a resurrected America in King's speech testifies to his belief that integration is a principle divinely ordained by God. It is for this vision that King is remembered – as a Moses figure who sought to lead an exodus that would redeem both black and white America.[1]

This frozen image of King is now celebrated in an annual national holiday and embraced right across the US political spectrum. The irony is that the continuing potency of King's message lies precisely in the knowledge that his vision of racial transcendence has yet to be realized. This irony was written all over the media coverage of Barack Obama's speech to the Democratic Party Convention on 28 August 2008, in which he accepted the party's nomination for president on the 45th anniversary of King's most famous sermon. Alive to the myriad ways in which this address would be a defining moment in US history, Obama's campaign team staged his acceptance speech against a backdrop of Greco-Roman architecture. Any suggestion that the moment at which Obama delivered his address – entitled 'The American Promise' – might signify the realization of King's dream was dispelled by the fact that the spectacle was widely ridiculed by the national and international media.

This reaction was perhaps best exemplified by the *New York Post*, which featured a satirized image of Obama in a toga, thus visually capturing the prevailing idea that the Greek columns that framed the nominee's speech betrayed political hubris and delusions of grandeur.[2] The fact that the columns alluded not only to ancient Greece, but also much closer to home, to the neo-classical architecture of the White House and to the Lincoln Memorial – from which King made his own epoch-defining speech – seemed to carry no weight for those commentators who insisted that Obama's stage was 'alien' and 'foreign'. Symbols that appear to chart a perfectly logical path for Obama to claim – from what is widely perceived to be the birthplace of democracy, to the US presidency and the Civil Rights movement – were cast as somehow unavailable to this particular presidential candidate. While John F. Kennedy was also ridiculed for deploying such imagery, more recently, in 2004, the Greek columns that framed George W. Bush's convention speech – in which he accepted the Republican nomination for president – were not widely remarked upon. It is hard not to conclude that Obama's racial identity contributed to the sense that the Greco-Roman tradition was just not compatible with anything he might represent.

The inability to reconcile Obama's figure with imagery that goes to the heart of US democracy recalls a narrative that has all too often framed King's engagement with the western intellectual tradition. This narrative has surfaced in the work of a number of King scholars who claim that the supposedly 'stilted' and 'derivative' prose in which King framed his mobilization of western philosophy is evidence of the fact that he was in some sense out of his depth. These same scholars stress the linguistic skills King displayed from the pulpit, showing him to be, in contrast, entirely 'at home' in the black church tradition. The fact that King seems to have plagiarized sections of his PhD thesis and frequently failed to acknowledge his sources in much of his writing has been forwarded to support the view that King's scholarly aspirations betray a dis-ease with the rigours of the western academy. This deeply patronizing tendency is noted by Richard Lischer, yet even Lischer's otherwise excellent study of King, which acknowledges that King's intellectual legacy was substantive as opposed to aspirational, seems strangely resistant to the idea that the western tradition is an integral part of a black American's intellectual inheritance. Lischer claims that King 'appears to have embraced' the western intellectual tradition 'as

an alternative to the strong medicine of his own religious tradition';
having 'thoroughly absorbed its vocabulary and values', King was
then able to 'come "home" to his own tradition with his horizons
considerably widened'.[3]

It is certainly true that King's narrative of African American
liberation was couched in the language of the black church and
western philosophy, but his engagement with the latter should be
seen as part of his American heritage, hardly a transgression into
'alien' territory. Nonetheless, as King's Civil Rights achievements
in the South were followed by a string of disappointments in the
North, his words did increasingly bear witness to a persistent
friction between blackness and Americanness. While King believed
that US blacks were entitled to lay claim to the full range of the
American experience, including the intellectual traditions of the
West, he was forced to confront the fact that many white racists
continued to deny this fact. Thus by 1967 King was to claim that
'most Americans are unconscious racists'[4] – a stunning reversal
from his earlier positions that revealed what seemed to be a genuine
optimism about the transformative possibilities of white liberal
guilt. And while King continued to resist what he saw as potential
racial chauvinism on the part of the Black Power movement, by
1968 he claimed 'when I speak of integration, I don't mean a
romantic mixing of colors, I mean a real sharing of power and
responsibility'[5] – a statement that contrasts sharply with his 1963
meditation on a colour-blind society. Indeed, in 1968 he pointed out
that colour blindness itself could be racist – in rhetoric that spelled
out a clear case for affirmative action.[6] So while King is steadfastly
remembered for his investment in the American dream, its failure
to materialize for US blacks within his own lifetime, the endurance
of deep-seated racism masquerading behind the invocation of false
universals, led him to speak the language of racial particularity, so
much so that his understanding of African American identity just
prior to his death sounded remarkably close to Du Bois' theory of
double consciousness. In a posthumously published essay written
in 1968, King wrote:

> I have come to hope that American Negroes can be a bridge
> between white civilization and the nonwhite nations of the
> world, because we have roots in both. Spiritually, Negroes
> identify understandably with Africa, an identification that is
> rooted largely in our color; but all of us are a part of the white
> American world, too.

'So,' King continued, 'although in one sense we are neither, in another sense, we are both Americans and Africans.'[7] King's consequent sense that black America held the key for the redemption of white America – and *not* the other way round – recalls the theological thrust of Du Boisian thought. It suggests that King's understanding of 'the American promise' had undergone a distinct shift, from an inclusive framework whereby US blacks were granted insider status, to a sense that African Americans had a very particular role to play in the story of national redemption. As discussed in more detail below, this is a theology of liberation that partially resonates with that of James Cone, an association that does little to service the prevalent memory of King as a peace-loving symbol of racial harmony, who posed no real threat to the existing order.

Scholars have long contested the sanitized image of King that still permeates contemporary culture, one that dilutes his radical legacy by casting him as the quintessential American liberal, the acceptable face of 'racial progress'. The story that is most often told in academic literature is that King's later disappointment with the pace of change and the persistence of racism fuelled an increasingly prophetic outlook that betrayed a deep alienation with America. While I agree with this portrait of King's political evolution, this chapter argues that King's increasing emphasis on the disenchanted world of the prophets is entirely consistent with the theological orientation of King's earliest writings as a student at Crozer Theological Seminary. These writings consistently resist the Christian assumption of an already realized redemption in favour of an exodus that is yet to come. Such an emphasis is comparable not only to Du Bois, but also to Obama's insistence on the unfinished nature of history – an insistence which similarly springs from a deep-rooted commitment to social change.

King's Christianity undoubtedly formed the centrepiece of his thinking on freedom, but, as I argue below, he often privileged the Exodus motif over and above the figure of Jesus – indicating that the materialized promise embodied by the latter was a premature symbol for a dream that remained out of reach. King's desire that America make good on the promises of democracy – the ideals captured in the timeless imagery of Hellenic culture – was articulated via a decidedly Hebraic rendering of the Exodus text. King's famous jeremiad thus remains firmly rooted in the traditions of the so-called 'West' – quite in contrast to Du Bois' Pan-African impulses – yet I argue that his understanding of western culture is profoundly shaped by a sense of the otherness that resides at its heart. This understanding occasioned for King a deep identification with Jews and Judaism – for his theological-politics of non-violence is, I suggest, first and foremost targeted at a racist culture fuelled by the Christian church, a culture that has historically persecuted both blacks and Jews alike.

So while King's legacy is routinely dissociated from black nationalism, his central role in forging the fragile black–Jewish Civil Rights alliance led to his staunch support for Jewish nationalism. And where the emerging forces of black nationalism were condemning Israel's role in the 1967 war, King not only countenanced the violence intrinsic to that war but saw the outcome as the fulfilment of biblical promise. In many ways King's problematic position on Israel deconstructs the neat opposition that casts the militant face of the black struggle as that which broke away from a moderate, non-violent, domestically oriented Christian Civil Rights movement that had forged an alliance with white liberals.

In fact, many of King's later statements bear more similarities to the apparently inflammatory rhetoric of Reverend Jeremiah Wright than they do to the gentler message for which King's dream has come to be known. King's increasingly vocal opposition to the Vietnam war is comparable to Wright's view of the US-led invasion of Iraq. And King's statement in 1968 that a nation that could condemn the Japanese to internment camps in the 1940s is capable of putting black people in concentration camps could just as easily have issued from the lips of Wright, Louis Farrakhan or Malcolm X – all of whom have been vilified for what have been deemed as controversial racial messages. Moreover, as King's career-long criticism of apartheid South Africa and admiration for post-Independence India shows, his conception of the Civil Rights movement was never hermetically sealed off from the global contexts of decolonization as many historians have implied. His was never a wholesale accommodation with the culture of the West, a culture that for King constituted an entirely legitimate but nonetheless difficult heritage.

And yet quick readings of King's support for Israel from today's perspective seem to ally him with conservative and even reactionary US foreign policy positions, and the complacency of the western powers on the question of Palestinian self-determination. This chapter argues that such a reading is anachronistic in terms of the constellations of power in the Middle East, and fails to grasp King's complex understanding of Jewish victimization and the consequent need for self-determination – an understanding that complicates what are often easy readings of the way in which left/right positions translate into identifications with actors in the Middle East. Moreover, King's identifications with both Jews and Israel offer a window through which to re-examine his understandings of race, nation and religion, as well as the master/slave dialectic that sits at the heart of the Exodus narrative – a narrative that has played a very particular role in scripting the cycles of violence that plague the Middle East.

This chapter begins by outlining King's engagement with the Exodus narrative, which demonstrates the ways in which King's theological-politics bring him much closer to the liberation theology of Obama's former church than his popular image allows for. The section that follows shows that King's understanding of Christianity's racist possibilities led him to emphasize Jesus' Jewish contexts, an emphasis that somewhat departs from the radical black church that James Cone saw resulting from a union between the religious impulses of Civil Rights and the political orientation of Black Power. The third section charts the ways in which this difference manifested itself in King's identification with the religious, political and national aspirations of the Jewish diaspora – identifications that offer up a lens through which to examine King's critique of colonialism.

King emerges here as a much more complicated touchstone for Barack Obama than many commentators will admit – one that resists the amnesia intrinsic to the state memory that has held the figure of King hostage. It may well be that the Greek columns that framed Obama's address to the Democratic Convention were a rather superficial gesture towards the 'history' his campaign wanted to evoke – even though they pointed to a tradition that Obama was entirely justified in calling his 'own'. There is a sense that the visual imagery of ancient Greece is frozen in time, recalling the stasis of the ideal forms so revered in Platonic philosophy. But I suggest that 'the young preacher from Georgia' that Obama evoked in his acceptance speech stages an intimacy between the two figures that is far from superficial.[8] This is not the sanitized version of King trapped in popular memory, but rather one for whom the dynamism of history, and the hope of an unknown future, was the substance of a radical dream that he consistently cast in the shapes of the Exodus narrative.

THE THEOLOGICAL-POLITICS OF EXODUS

King consistently equated the Civil Rights movement with the Exodus story, imagining the progression towards black freedom as

part of a larger picture of providential history. As one commentator
puts it, in his sermons King 'explained the Exodus as nothing less
than God's repeating liberatory act, an archetypal event spiralling
through history'.[9] Famously, King claimed that God was working
through the movement in Montgomery, and in asserting that 'God
struggles with us' King anticipated James Cone's contention that
God is on the side of the oppressed.[10]

   For Cone the Exodus is proof of this: 'beginning with the exodus,
God's righteousness is for those who are weak and helpless.'[11] Thus
both King and Cone articulate a black American identification with
the Exodus that dates back to slave religion when memories of the
Middle Passage were not so distant. The appropriation of Exodus
for black liberation therefore speaks of the titanic effort by which
African and African American slaves overcame the deadly waters
of slavery in order to articulate a counter-narrative by which the
sea providentially opens up the path of freedom. And yet as Du
Bois' deeply ambivalent writing on slave religion testifies, the slave's
relationship to Christianity was not straightforward. Not only
was it envisaged by slave owners as a potentially pacifying force,
but various moments in the Old and New Testaments explicitly
foreground the racist potentialities of the notion of election central
to the Exodus narrative. The very discourse of the chosen people,
which anticipates a corresponding and deeply divisive narrative
of the damned and the saved, was forwarded in the South as
justification for slavery and then segregation. The ways in which
King's theology attempted to counter the threat of chauvinism –
the potentially exclusive notion of God's elect – at the heart of the
very story he took to be an allegory of the Civil Rights movement
is the subject of this section, which argues that King's initial point
of departure is remarkably similar to that which animates the more
radical currents of black religion today.

   The racist theology that permeated white southern churches,
and which King and Cone both sought to challenge, appropriated
biblical imagery to mark black people as losers in a cosmic battle
between 'good' and 'evil'. Commenting on what he sees as the
development from slavery onwards of the 'South's gospel', Timothy
Caron explains:

   The white Southern church relied upon several biblical texts (or
   biblical silences) to justify slavery. The ancient Israelites possessed
   slaves; Jesus makes no pronouncements against slavery in the
   New Testament; Paul and other New Testament writers admonish

slaves to obey their masters – all of this was taken as solid 'proof' by the white South that chattel slavery was divinely ordained by God. Much of this same rhetoric survived well into twentieth-century pulpits.[12]

While the Exodus narrative dramatizes the divinely willed liberation of Hebrew slaves, God's act of adoption of the children of Israel as a chosen people, the second stage of Exodus, arguably anticipates this ethnocentrism. In King's view, such ethnocentrism, and the failure to speak out against it, was blasphemous. Thus at a conference on Religion and Race in Chicago in 1963, King claimed that 'America's segregated churches come dangerously close' to losing 'the capacity to distinguish between good and evil'.[13] Not only did racism reside at the heart of southern white Christianity, but the southern white church's overwhelming emphasis on individual piety and salvation starkly contrasted with the dominant tendency of black churches to insist on the primacy of social justice – the environment from which King's theology clearly evolved.

And though the tone of Cone's rhetoric differs markedly from King's, this is a black church legacy that the two men clearly share. Cone's notion of a specifically *black* theology would likely have been rejected by King – particularly in his earlier phase – but it too 'refuses to embrace any concept of God which makes black suffering the will of God',[14] just as King rejected the South's racist biblical determinism. For King as for Cone, it was imperative that the church be judged on the basis of its actions in the world, and in this both men echo the assertions of the Social Gospel movement that eschewed the idea that faith alone can bear genuine witness to the Christian message. Consequently King was repeatedly chastised by southern white evangelical preachers for neglecting souls in favour of the needs of the flesh. As Jerry Falwell put it in 1964 – in a statement that warned against his own political interventions in right-wing politics in later years – 'preachers are not called to be politicians but soul-winners'.[15]

So when, in his widely celebrated 'Letter from Birmingham Jail' of April 1963, King looks to the white churches of the South and demands to know 'who is their God?'[16] his charge of idolatry is aimed at multiple targets. King's famous letter is focused on an explicit critique of the church's 'other-worldly' disengagement from the consequences of vicious racism. But the letter also implies that the fact that such racism was enshrined in law was not unconnected to the decidedly 'worldly' pronouncements of southern churches, pronouncements that justified black subjugation on the basis of 'God's word'. King's point was that the blind eye southern churches turned to racial injustice in effect sanctified a status quo that white Christian theology had played a large role in shaping. King's letter does extend the hand of friendship to white churches in the spirit of non-violence, yet it also clearly registers his fury at their hypocrisy, a fury that signifies not the caricature of facile Christian forgiveness, but rather the 'stern love'[17] King deemed necessary for non-violent resistance.

So although the black liberation theology of James Cone largely rejects King's message of non-violence and the spirit of forgiveness that King did undoubtedly champion, the anger that fuelled King's Civil Rights agenda should not be discounted, nor should the similarities between King's and Cone's unreserved condemnations of white racist theology. What is often overlooked in the characterization of King as the black preacher who told his flock to love white America is the fact that in his view, non-violent resistance endowed Civil Rights activists with a moral superiority, just as his message of forgiveness asked black America to forgive the unforgivable. For the racist ideology of the South was in King's view pathological and required what he consistently described as excessive love. Writing in the shadow of King's own violent death, Cone announced this commitment bankrupt, but remained true to King's sense that:

> Any religion which professes to be concerned about the souls of men and is not concerned about the social and economic conditions that scar the soul is a spiritually moribund religion only waiting for the day to be buried. It well has been said: 'A religion that ends with the individual ends.'[18]

The strong this-worldly thrust of much African American religiosity is evidenced by King, Cone and Jeremiah Wright alike in the consistent tendency to cast black Americans as actors in the stories of the Old Testament. As Eugene Genovese explains, this tendency has its roots in slave religion, which, rather than elevating the New Testament above the Old – as do narratives of Christian supersession[19] – instead established a complex relationship between them. Slave religion's treatment of the figures of Moses and Jesus illustrates this: 'the slaves did not draw a sharp line between them but merged them into the image of a single deliverer, at once this-worldly and otherworldly.'[20]

As a symbol of suffering, Jesus was a crucial point of identification and comfort for slave religion, and this is the image of Christ that King seemed to inherit; King wrote that 'the most precious thought in Christianity is that Jesus is our daily friend, that he never did leave us comfortless or alone, and that we may know his transforming communion every day of our lives.'[21] He insists that 'Jesus remains the most persistent, inescapable, and influential figure that ever entered history' for 'God used him to reveal his divine plan to man'.[22] Nevertheless, for King, like the slaves, while Jesus spoke to the spiritual life of those in bondage, it is Moses who most adequately addressed their material conditions. Writing of the figure who is widely perceived to be the founder of the Christian church, and whose epistles are the earliest record of Christianity, pre-dating the composition of the Gospels by several decades, King asserts:

The Apostle Paul – along with all of the early Christians – believed that the world was coming to an end in a few days. Feeling that the time was not long, the Apostle Paul urged men to concentrate on preparing themselves for the new age rather than changing external conditions. It was this belief in the coming new age and the second coming of Christ which conditioned a great deal of Paul's thinking. Early Christianity was far from accepting the existing social order as satisfactory, but it was conscious of no mission to change it for the better.[23]

Thus it seems that King shared the slaves' reluctance to entirely embrace the social message of the New Testament, a tendency that he arguably inherited from Howard Thurman. In his 1949 book *Jesus and the Disinherited* – often hailed as an early work of black liberation theology – Thurman describes the antipathy with which his grandmother, who was born into slavery, viewed Paul's letters. Thurman recounts the fact that after years of reading the bible aloud to his grandmother – who could neither read nor write – he decided to ask her why she would not allow him to read this crucial section of the New Testament. Her response was that during the days of slavery, Paul's letters were consistently invoked by white preachers to impress upon slaves obedience to their masters. As Thurman surmises:

It cannot be denied that too often the weight of the Christian movement has been on the side of the strong and the powerful and against the weak and oppressed – this, despite the gospel.

A part of the responsibility seems to me to rest upon a peculiar twist in the psychology of Paul.[24]

Thurman points to the fact that whereas Jesus was a member of an oppressed minority, Paul was a citizen of Rome. While Thurman expresses admiration for Paul's declaration of a universal church, which 'certainly included all men, bond and free', he is suspicious of Paul's identification with the powerful. King is rumoured to have carried a copy of Thurman's *Jesus and the Disinherited* on his journeys in the South, and I suggest that his non-violent Christianity contains strong echoes of Thurman's account of what he liked to describe as 'the religion of Jesus' – a religion that in both Thurman's and King's accounts was in many ways distinct from that of Paul.

Central to Pauline politics is a conversion narrative – the 'thunderbolt' that summons Paul on the road to Damascus – which leads to Paul's central revelation: 'Christ is risen.' The consequence of this experience is Paul's claim that 'faith, not works' must be the ultimate human justification before God (Galatians, 2:15–3:14). Yet as the southern church showed, this was not simply the road to political quietism. The heir to this conversion experience, the book of Revelation which closes the New Testament, is one of the principal sources for the violent discourse of salvation that shaped the religiously justified racism that King was challenging in the South. In this book the idea of election initiated in the book of Exodus reaches what is possibly its logical conclusion – Christ is crowned king and descends to earth as a warrior with the task of separating the sinners from the saved. While there are of course many ways of reading this enigmatic text, it is the generative text of Christian apocalyptic thought and as such has been identified by a number of scholars as central not just to the religion of white Baptists in the South but also to the triumphalism that characterizes some brands of the American civil religion. Arguably the end of the Civil War occasioned in the white South a deeply pessimistic politics that manifested itself in the religious imagining of an apocalyptic end – this is the backwards-facing South that emerges in the writings of William Faulkner.[25] But on a national scale the trope of resurrection has been mobilized to cast America as the destination of a global future, and this imperial claim has bred anything but political inaction on the world stage. Indeed, in his study of American apocalyptic religion, Michael Northcott claims that the text of Revelation was mobilized by the Bush administration in support of the so-called war on terror.[26]

King's own understanding of Christianity thus emerges in stark contrast to the kind of biblical literalism that he saw plaguing American Christianity in general and southern theology in particular. For this highly literal religious worldview is grounded in the kind of absolute faith that Paul called for, and it seems that King's novel brand of Christianity in fact questioned the very basis of Pauline certitude: the incarnation and the resurrection.

Jesus emerges in King's writings as by far the most significant of the Jewish prophets, but like the prophets that preceded him, he remains distinct from God. The doctrine of Jesus as deity, one that gradually evolved in the visions of the early Christians, is explained by King as largely the result of the power of Jesus' personality over his followers. In his early years at Crozer Theological Seminary, King claimed that 'it was the magnetic personality of this historic Jesus that caused men to explain his life in a category beyond the human'. For, he writes, 'most of us are not willing to see the union of the human and divine in a metaphysical incarnation'; it is Jesus' 'filial consciousness', and not a 'substantial unity' with God, that constituted his human realization of a 'divine calling'. King therefore does not deny the divinity of Christ, but his Christology relies on the contention that 'this divine quality or this unity with God was not something thrust upon Jesus from above, but it was a definite achievement through the process of moral struggle and self-abnegation'. For King, Christ's example is indeed 'the way' to the divine, but Jesus himself is not of the divine, he is not God but rather fully human.[27] In claiming this King rejects what James Cone, along with contemporary commentators like Slavoj Žižek, view as the materialist core of Christianity. This is an interesting move for a preacher seeking religious grounds for radical politics.

King wrote that 'to say that the Christ, whose example of living we are bid to follow, is divine in an ontological sense is actually harmful and detrimental.'[28] An editorial note that accompanies the essay from which this quotation is taken reads: 'by establishing Jesus as human, King allows for the possibility of progressive improvement in earthly society through individual action.'[29] And yet another crucial consequence of this statement is the fact that the progression King envisages cannot claim the sanction of God. This is a sanction claimed by racist white churches as well as Cone's powerful response to that racism. For Cone's investment in the human God is key to his understanding of the resurrection, an understanding that differs from King's in fundamental ways. Cone claims:

Christian freedom is the recognition that Christ has conquered death. Man no longer has to be afraid of dying. To live as if death has the last word is to be enslaved and thus controlled by the forces of destruction. The free are the oppressed who say no to an oppressor, in spite of the threat of death, because God has said yes to them, thereby placing them in a state of freedom.[30]

In contrast the resurrection appears in King's theology only in very muted terms. Parallel to his rationalization of the belief in Jesus as deity, the doctrine of the literal resurrection of Christ becomes in King's vision a metaphor for the continuing survival of Jesus' spirit. For what King describes as 'the ultimate Christian conviction: that Christ conquered death' to his mind 'raises many questions'. He writes, 'in fact the external evidence for the authenticity of this doctrine is found wanting.' King explains the evolution of the doctrine among Jesus' early followers thus: 'in the pre-scientific thought pattern of the first century, this inner faith took outward form.' The resurrection therefore emerges as internal rather than external and points to the survival of Christ's spirit: King writes 'through his spirit Jesus brought the immortal hope to light.'[31] So in some ways ironically, while King's theological-political project is utterly this-worldly, it in part rejects the aspect of Christianity identified by a whole range of thinkers as intrinsic to its revolutionary power.

Cone's emphasis on the human God is echoed in the contemporary work of Žižek, just as his investment in the Christian resurrection recalls the work of Žižek's intellectual ally, Alain Badiou. Badiou's influential work on Saint Paul casts the resurrection so central to Pauline politics as the quintessential 'event' which clears the ground for radical action.[32] This is an 'event' that at first glance might be not only analogous with, but also the culmination of, the Exodus event so central to King's understanding of the black liberation struggle in the US. Yet King refuses the very 'event' designated by Badiou as Paul's site of political agency – on the grounds that it was just this kind of agency that had enabled white racism.

King was undoubtedly a Christian seeking a Christian platform from which to engage in social action, but I suggest that King's theology was deeply informed by Howard Thurman's sense that there is a 'lurking danger' within the faith. According to Thurman 'it is the sin of pride and arrogance that has tended to vitiate the missionary impulse and to make of it an instrument of self-righteousness on the one hand and racial superiority on the other'.

No Christian figure better exemplifies this impulse than Paul, whose conversion narrative – which undoubtedly transcends barriers of race and class – is nonetheless 'available to those who wish to use the weight of the Christian message to oppress and humiliate their fellows'.[33] Interestingly, Albert Cleage makes a similar point in *The Black Messiah* (1968) when he claims that 'Paul preached individual salvation and life after death. We, as black Christians suffering oppression in a white man's land, do not need the individualistic and otherworldly doctrines of Paul and the white man.'[34] Unlike Cone's variant of black liberation theology, for Cleage Jesus was primarily a historical figure defined by his ministry as opposed to the 'otherworldly' doctrines of the resurrection and incarnation.

While the politics of Cone poses an undeniable challenge to white racism, his portrayal of Jesus' resurrection as the grounds for political agency nonetheless embraces the politics of rupture – of radical newness – that enables theological-political violence. Cone's black liberation theology makes no secret of the fact that it has departed decisively from the philosophy of non-violence, and the assertive tone in which it is couched speaks to the radical certainty that the Pauline conversion enables. For as Badiou's work indicates, Paul's thinking was based on the utter conviction that the (first) resurrection of Christ was non-negotiable truth. I suggest that King's rejection of the literal resurrection is in part a rejection of the certainty to which it gives rise, a certainty that is premised on the announcement of a historical break and a new kind of theological-politics. For while it seems likely that King would have agreed with Žižek's sense that 'freedom is not a blissfully neutral state of harmony and balance' – it is, rather, the constant struggle for social justice – King's non-violent Christianity is anathema to Žižek's description of 'Christian love' as 'a violent passion to introduce a Difference'.[35] And this difference, according to many readings of Pauline Christianity and central to Badiou's, is precisely a difference from Judaism.

As the next section will argue, rather than capitalizing on the radical potential of Jesus as human God, King instead emphasized the empirical life of Jesus and his kinship with the Jewish prophets. It was on these grounds, I suggest, and not the Christian politics of rupture, that King fashioned a non-violent Christianity. Exodus politics in the black tradition is about the translation of faith into action in this world. In many ways the black Exodus, in different ways and at different moments in history, attempts to counter the version at the centre of American civil religion that not only justifies but also in part created the racism intrinsic to the status quo. I have argued that King's engagement with the black counter-narrative was not original, and neither did its legacy die with King – it lives on in the politicized black churches of today that are products both of Civil Rights and Black Power. Yet King's religious justifications for action in the world do differ markedly from those claimed by Cone's variant of black liberation theology. In contrast to Cone, King's understanding of Exodus politics was not dependent on Jesus Christ as the ultimate ground for redemption. This insight – that would lead many to discount King's Christianity as heretical – had significant implications for King's view of the role of non-violence in the Civil Rights movement, and speaks to the different understanding of human agency that marks King's thought out from the Black Power context that shaped Cone's theological-politics, as well as some of the politicized black churches that followed in King's wake. Testimony to this difference is the fact that where Cone's – and Cleage's – liberation theology insists that Christ must be black in an attempt to provide a counterweight to white supremacist claims, for King, whose reading of the New Testament is led more by logic than metaphysics, Jesus is better understood not as white or black but rather Jewish.

EXCAVATING CHRISTIAN HISTORY

Jesus was a Jew.
It is impossible to understand Jesus outside of the race in which he was born. The Christian Church has tended to overlook its Judaic origins, but the fact is that Jesus of Nazareth was a Jew of Palestine. He shared the experiences of his fellow-countryman. So as we study Jesus we are wholly in a Jewish atmosphere.[36]

King wrote these words in 1949 as a student at Crozer Theological Seminary, and in so doing he echoes – sometimes word for word – Thurman's *Jesus and the Disinherited*, which was published that same year. Unlike many Christian theologians who see Christianity as a radical break with the traditions of Judaism, and Jesus himself as the point of rupture, King follows Thurman in viewing the ethics of Christianity as in large part continuous with Jewish ethics[37] – King claims that 'there is no justification of the view that Jesus was attempting to find a church distinct from the Synagogue'.[38]

Vincent Harding suggests in his foreword to *Jesus and the Disinherited* that only a superficial encounter with the title of

Thurman's text would 'lead us to anticipate a 1940s version of liberation theology'.[39] Thurman's complex meditation on Jesus and non-violence imagines the resistance of Israel to Roman oppression as an apparently binary choice: 'become like the Romans or be destroyed by the Romans. They chose the former.'[40] There are ways in which this is the route taken by Cone and some black liberation theologians who argue for a racially specific theology – which is precisely their initial object of critique. Yet it is also important to realize not only the nuances of the approaches of theologians like Cone and Cleage, but also that black liberation theology is not monolithic. Where, as Melissa Harris-Lacewell asserts, the blackness of Cone's Christ is 'ontological rather than biological'[41] – blackness is a marker of an oppressed status with which Jesus identifies – for Cleage it is an ethnic distinction. Consequently Cleage's is a historical Jesus whose ministry is emphasized over and above the resurrection and incarnation, while for Cone the metaphysical status of Jesus – as human God who has conquered death – is crucial. King's liberation theology combines aspects of both. Contra Cleage's sense that Jesus was ethnically black, and Cone's emphasis on the metaphysical nature of Christ, King follows Thurman's very different sense that as a member of an oppressed minority in the Roman world, Jesus is a fully human figure who stands in for all the disinherited – for all those, in Thurman's memorable phrase, 'with their backs against the wall'.[42]

Noting the propensity of historical Christianity to side not with the disinherited but with the powerful, Thurman wonders if the religion harbours within itself a 'basic weakness', and I suggest that both Thurman and King respond to this possibility via a profound engagement with the religion that Christianity has itself so violently disinherited. This section argues that in his repudiation of Christian violence, which, as I have suggested, involved the rejection of some of Christianity's central tenets, King also challenges the religion's initial repudiation of Judaism itself. As will be discussed below, King's Exodus politics are better thought in relation to the figure not of resurrection – which for many thinkers, beginning with Saint Paul, is the crux of Christian theology and the grounds for Christian social action – but of excavation.

In his study of Saint Paul, Badiou explains that following Paul's dispute with Peter and the 'Judeo-Christians', it is clear that for Paul, 'Law has *become* a figure of death'.[43] Law for Paul is life according to the flesh, whereas faith in the Christ-event is life according to the spirit. The ultimate destiny of the flesh is death, whereas Christ's resurrection signals eternal life. In his Epistle to the Romans, Paul claims that 'if we have been planted together in the likeness of his death, we shall be also *in the likeness* of *his* resurrection' (Romans, 6:5). Paul thus insists that the resurrection signals the establishment of principles which are completely new, and yet when he asks 'do we then make void the law through faith?' he responds: 'God forbid: yea, we establish the law' (Romans, 3:31).

For Paul the law is fulfilled in the death and resurrection of Jesus Christ; he writes 'while we were yet sinners, Christ died for us' (Romans, 5:8) – and thus cleared the grounds of human (original) sin which necessitated the commandments of Jewish law. So in fact, while Paul poses as the preserver of the law, he actually abolishes it, an act he justifies by claiming that in a redeemed world, sin is itself conjured by the law: 'for by the law *is* the knowledge of sin' (Romans, 3:20); 'For until the law sin was in the world: but sin is not imputed when there is no law' (Romans, 5:13). Jewish law becomes almost interchangeable with the 'sin' it ostensibly legislates against, and thus encapsulates the figure of death, the very figure over which Paul sees Christianity triumphing. Badiou cites Paul's analysis of the role of the law approvingly, and comments: 'Paul does not much like Moses, man of the letter and the law.'[44]

King's divergence from this is evident. In a world that King believed to be radically *un*redeemed, Moses remained a crucial touchstone for King's understanding of theological-political leadership. For though the Exodus narrative is in many ways a story of redemption, it is also a story that defers the redemptive moment – as symbolized by Moses' dying glimpse of the promised land. Israel may be God's chosen nation, but as the prophets that would come later illustrate, it is far from living up to its divine calling. Thus in King's view, Christ did not sacrifice his life in order to atone for human sin. King explains, 'if Christ by his life and death paid the full penalty of sin, there is no valid ground for repentance or moral obedience as a condition of forgiveness. The debt is paid; the penalty is exacted, and there is, consequently, nothing to forgive.'[45] If Christ redeemed humanity, humanity plays no role in the task of redemption. In his 'Letter from Birmingham Jail', King suggests that 'we will have to repent in this generation not merely for the hateful words and actions of the bad people but for the appalling silence of the good people'.[46] It is not enough therefore to rely on the idea that love is now inscribed on the human heart, as the Pauline text often suggests; 'good' people does not equal 'good' politics.

Unsurprisingly, King's sermons show that he, like his mentor Howard Thurman, was drawn to Paul's universalism that emphasizes the equality of all peoples before God. Yet King's theological-politics was in many ways driven by the opposite impulses to those which led to Paul's founding of a new church and the heralding of a new Christian era. His politics relied not on the kind of violent rupture that might wipe the historical slate clean – an idea foregrounded by Badiou who poses Christ's resurrection as *the* metaphor for change – but was instead premised upon the need to excavate racism's troubled history in order to activate white guilt. King's sense of this guilty history is illustrated in the following words, which offer an uncompromising indictment of US racism that is quite different from the images of comfort that so often crowd out King's more radical legacy:

> Our nation was born in genocide when it embraced the doctrine that the original American, the Indian, was an inferior race. Even before there were large numbers of Negroes on our shores, the scar of racial hatred had already disfigured colonial society. From the sixteenth century forward, blood flowed in battles over racial supremacy. We are perhaps the only nation which tried as a matter of national policy to wipe out its indigenous population. Moreover, we elevated that tragic experience into a noble crusade. Indeed, even today we have not permitted ourselves to reject or to feel remorse for this shameful episode.[47]

And it seems that King's commitment to bearing witness to the nation's race history and the complicity of the Christian church also involved excavating Christianity's founding repression. For at the heart both of US racial history and the Christian 'overcoming' of Jewish difference is a missionary impulse that encompasses different but nonetheless related forms of colonization. Though never explicitly acknowledged by King, that Paul's epistles in effect claim to have rendered Judaism redundant is a fact that has long been noted. While Badiou himself insists on the universal possibilities of Paul's declaration, it is qualified by no acknowledgement that it definitively excludes Jews practising Judaism. So with Paul, Badiou reads the Old Testament as entirely contingent upon the New – he claims that Paul's preference for Abraham over Moses 'anticipates what could be called a universalism of the Jewish site'.[48] Jewish subjectivity universalized is not only no longer Jewish but seemingly makes no space for a Jewishness untouched by Christianity.

In contrast, King's Christianity betrays an acute awareness of its Judaic conditioning, as evidenced by the fact that the Jesus that populates King's writings and sermons is overwhelmingly the Jewish Jesus of the Gospels.[49] This differs markedly from the religious vision of Paul, who discounts the value not only of its Jewish legacy but of the empirical life of Jesus as well, which goes practically unmentioned in Paul's epistles, as do Jesus' famous parables. For King on the other hand, the Jesus of the Gospels is central as a transitional figure not between life and death but rather as one that links Christianity to the world of the prophets. King's Exodus politics does not look ahead to the essentially Greek narrative of a God made flesh – which is most definitively described in John's Gospel. Perhaps ironically for a prophet who has come to symbolize reconciliation of all kinds, King rejected the ultimate reconciliation between human and the divine, thus maintaining the otherness of God. In this respect King, the inveterate synthesizer, rejects Hegel, whose conception of Christianity without question supersedes its Judaic beginnings.

King's project of religious excavation can be helpfully illuminated by a brief look at Sigmund Freud's highly eccentric account of Jewish biblical history. Freud's account of the post-Exodus biblical history in *Moses and Monotheism* (1939) tells a story in which the children of Israel murder Moses for trying to enforce the second commandment – the ban on images of God. But after a period of back-sliding during which the Israelites worship Yahweh, the tribal God, the repressed traumatic event – the murder of Moses – surfaces belatedly in the reassertion of the second commandment. For Freud this commandment is the pivot of the Jewish ethical tradition. But as his version of biblical history suggests, the violent transgression of this commandment, and the guilt that this transgression occasions, is precisely the origins of morality.

Freud admits that Judaism's descendant and adversary, Christianity, is, as it claims, a 'resolution' of Judaism in the sense that it replaces the law of the father with that of the son, and resolves the guilt occasioned by what is in effect the idolatrous murder of God, via the atonement. As Freud writes, 'the murder was not remembered: instead of it there was a phantasy of its atonement, and for that reason this phantasy could be hailed as a message of redemption.' The atonement that Paul was so eager to declare is, in Freud's view, 'delusional'. It establishes a false sense of innocence that is, moreover, dangerous. For in the absolution that Christians claim to derive from the 'confession' of their original 'crime', they let go of the guilt that Freud identifies as the source of ethical religion.[50]

King's strong sense of the need to strive towards social justice resisted the idea of the atonement for very similar reasons. As his respect for Christian theologian Reinhold Niebuhr indicates, King's theology was deeply imbued with a sense of the human capacity to participate in 'the glaring reality of collective evil'. While King thought that Niebuhr 'had over-emphasized the corruption of human nature', he nonetheless maintained that Niebuhr's theology 'is a persistent reminder of the reality of sin on every level of man's existence'.[51] Niebuhr's insights pointed in a very similar direction to the ban on images central to the Jewish tradition, and King also learnt from him – as Obama did later – that the reason human action can never claim the sanction of God is that it is always in part enmeshed in the workings of pride and self-interest. Thus while segregation and racism consistently emerge in King's lexicon as 'sinful', as many have pointed out, his own non-violent philosophy was itself paradoxically premised on the human capacity to do violence. For non-violence responded to the violence of a racist order by provoking yet more violence. This in turn underscored the moral superiority of the non-violent resister. Such a dynamic underscores the fact that human action is inevitably conditioned and compromised by historical foundations that are themselves never innocent of selfish motive. So quite in contrast to the Christian politics of rupture as outlined above, King's non-violent philosophy relied, like Freud's story of a murdered Moses, on the generation of productive guilt, guilt rooted in a repressed history. The ultimate aim was of course the interruption of that violence. But for King, the redemption most Christians read from the incarnation, resurrection and the atonement was irreconcilable with the unredeemed history of US racism. Its message was fundamentally premature.

Freud wrote his novel account of Jewish biblical history on the eve of the Holocaust, and his narrative was in many ways an attempt to come to terms with the violent repetitions that have historically plagued the Jewish people. I suggest that Freud's *Moses and Monotheism* offers a helpful way in to understanding not only King's identification with the Jewish religious tradition, but also the way in which this tradition squared with his non-violent philosophy as well as his commitment to the black–Jewish Civil Rights alliance. For King, like Freud, held a deeply pessimistic view of violence *as* history. The optimism people often find so appealing in King issues from his dream that the cycle of US racial violence might one day be broken, but as many critics have suggested, King's later years indicate increasing disillusionment with the ultimate goal of his Civil Rights vision: the transcendence of racial difference. Unlike black nationalists who reached the same conclusion, King did not abandon non-violence and neither did he advocate separate organizations and institutions for black people. King continued to view Jews as a central component of the coalition of the disinherited that he believed must be mobilized against racism not just in the US but around the globe. As the next section argues, his support for Jewish nationalism – which in turn both throws light on and emerges in tandem with his gestures of support for 'Third World' decolonization movements – suggests that his continued identification with Jews was part of his increasing radicalism, rather than, as in the view of many commentators, indicative of a stubborn attachment to a now defunct alliance with white liberals.

BLACK–JEWISH RELATIONS AND THE ANTI-COLONIAL STRUGGLE

King shared his understanding of historical violence, and the constant ethical need to reawaken its memory, with his friend and Civil Rights ally the Jewish Rabbi Abraham Joshua Heschel (who was himself a close friend of Niebuhr's). Heschel's thinking was profoundly shaped by the Nazi Holocaust. The bond between Heschel and King thus involved an understanding of oppression that linked the histories of slavery and the Holocaust, as well as a shared reverence for biblical history. As Heschel's daughter Susannah Heschel writes, 'the preference King gave to the Exodus motif over the figure of Jesus certainly played a major role in linking the two men intellectually and religiously; for Heschel, the primacy of the Exodus in the civil rights movement was a major step in the history of Christian-Jewish relations.'[52]

This section outlines King's role in the so-called 'black–Jewish alliance', an alliance that is as much fable as reality. By the end of King's life what had always been a troubled alliance had largely fractured along the lines of colour and descended into mutual distrust. For King the influence of Jewish culture extended far beyond the religious sphere. King liked to draw on Jewish intellectual sources – he often described segregation as a violation of Martin Buber's 'I–Thou' relation which proposed equality as the founding condition of human interaction.[53] And King's support for the State of Israel, including its role in the 1967 war, was unqualified. I argue below that King's embrace of Jewish nationalism throws light on his understanding of the Exodus narrative as an allegory for decolonization. Not only does this analysis highlight the limits of an approach that threatens to collapse the difference between historical and biblical reality. It also shows the potential generosity of King's Exodus vision, which he consistently extended to the world beyond Israel and America.

In 1948, incidentally the year of the State of Israel's founding, James Baldwin wrote that 'the Negro identifies himself almost wholly with the Jew. The more devout Negro considers that he is a Jew, in bondage to a hard taskmaster and waiting for a Moses to lead him out of Egypt.'[54] Heschel reciprocated this long history of theological-political identifications between blacks and Jews when he told the 1963 Chicago conference on Race and Religion – that King also attended – that King was a modern-day Moses. Yet as early as 1948, prior to the main achievements of the Civil Rights era, the seeds of the factors that would play a significant part in the dissolution of the fragile alliance between blacks and Jews were being sown in the Middle East.

As Jonathan Kaufman explains, in the 1950s and 1960s, memories of the Holocaust were still very fresh in people's minds, and there was a sense among American Jews that 'what had happened in Germany could happen anywhere. As the twentieth-century's ultimate victim, Jews would more easily identify with other victims of oppression and injustice.'[55] King was well aware of the enormous benefit Jewish allies yielded for the Civil Rights movement, and consistently stressed their commonalities with blacks, commonalities rooted in events rather less remote than the Hebrew exodus from Egypt:

> There are Hitlers loose in America today, both in high and low places. As the tensions and bewilderment of economic problems become more severe, history's scapegoats – the Jews – will be joined by new scapegoats, the Negroes. The Hitlers will seek to divert people's minds and turn their frustrations and anger to the helpless and the outnumbered. Then whether the Negro and Jew shall live in peace will depend upon how firmly they resist, how effectively they reach the minds of decent Americans to halt this deadly diversion.[56]

King's deployment of Jewish fears about US anti-Semitism – still widespread in the 1960s – which he here brings into comparison with anti-black racism, betrays the fact that the alliance between blacks and Jews during the Civil Rights campaigns was always considerably strained. While the history of Jewish persecution predisposed some Jews in America to identify with oppressed African Americans, this coexisted with a feeling among some groups that the footholds Jews had gained in American society were threatened by their association with the black struggle. This was particularly the case in the South. 'You people are like Hitler,' one southern Jew told a representative of a national Jewish organization which had supposedly 'coupled Jew and Negro in the public mind', 'you're stirring up anti-Semitism down here'.[57] Writing of Jews in Montgomery following the integration of the bus system, Marc Schneier notes that 'the overall Jewish response was not to rock the boat ... The lack of Jewish response did not go unnoticed. For many blacks, it spoke of the Jewish community's failure to step up to its divine calling.'[58] These complexities were overlain by the fact that the socio-economic position of American Jews was on average much higher than that of African Americans, a trend that was accelerated following the Second World War as the status of Jews in America rose sharply.[59]

These domestic issues were exacerbated in the late 1960s by very different assessments of the outcome of the 1967 war in the Middle East, a conflict that sparked a direct confrontation between the 'Israel' and 'Egypt' that had long played a metaphorical role in the imagination of black liberation. The Holocaust had overcome much Jewish resistance to Zionism, and many American Jews saw the defence of the State of Israel as continuous with the need to resist the threat of annihilation intrinsic to the chilling aims of Hitler's 'Final Solution'. Yet, as the next chapter explores in more detail, as black nationalists gained ascendancy within the black struggle in the mid to late 1960s, Israel was increasingly cast by Black Power advocates as a symbol of colonial oppression. What they saw as Israel's aggressive role in the 1967 war led them to re-think the origins of the state not as the culmination of a national liberation movement but rather as equivalent to racist colonial narratives that had consolidated illegitimate acts of statehood: just as the Puritans had perpetuated the myth of North America as an 'empty land' – a myth also deployed by the Afrikaaners in South Africa – now Jewish settlers were talking of making the desert bloom in Palestine.[60]

King in contrast imagined the events in the Middle East as a biblical drama playing out in the Holy Lands. In an article that appeared in the *Saturday Review* in August 1967, King claimed that 'all men of good will will exult in the fulfillment of God's promise, that his People should return in joy to rebuild their plundered land'. For King this promise involved securing for a historically oppressed people the safety of a much yearned for national home. Unlike many Black Power activists who saw the 1967 war as the outcome of Israel's opportunistic and aggressive bid to acquire more territory, King believed that Israel fought the war in self-defence, and thus it did not appear to pose a problem for his pacifism. For King believed Zionism to be 'nothing less than the dream and ideal of the Jewish people returning to live in their own land'.[61] Interestingly this comes close to the view of earlier waves of black nationalism in the US that had explicitly identified with the Jewish dream of repatriation to a national homeland.

The greatest irony of King's position on Israel is that at the very moment that he declares the Jewish state the redemption of biblical history – as a literal enactment of the Exodus narrative – he eschews the Judaic insight that I have argued is so central to his theological outlook. For by claiming that the State of Israel is the work of God, he articulates a markedly Christian understanding of worldly redemption.[62] Thus the theologian who, along with Thurman, seemed to reject the Roman equation of religion with the state – and thus the sword – here does precisely this. Though he rejects this move on American soil, it seems that King's identifications with Jewish culture rendered him unwilling to distinguish between 'Israel' – perceived by King as a religious and moral entity – and 'state'. This was at a moment when many religious Jews were describing the essentially secular Zionist movement as blasphemous – because it envisioned the 'ingathering of the exiles' in what was in their view an unredeemed world.[63]

This apparent contradiction can perhaps be explained in part by the fact that though King's religious thinking – like Du Bois' and the Jewish religious traditions that influenced King – is marked by a continual sense that the world remains unredeemed, unlike the anti-theodic strains in Du Bois' thinking, King remained a believer in salvation history. This was a belief that King shared with Heschel, who differed from other post-Holocaust Jewish thinkers who felt that theodicy – i.e. the vindication of God's goodness – was no longer a tenable position after the Nazi death camps. Both he and King were therefore caught in the contradiction engendered in the notion of a 'divine plan', one that logically necessitates both joy and suffering – good *and* evil – be founded on an ultimate 'good'. As Zachary Braiterman writes of Heschel's *Israel: An Echo of Eternity* (1967), Heschel expressed deep despair before the memory of Auschwitz. It would be blasphemy, he knew, to accept the establishment of the State in 1948 and its military victory in 1967 as a 'compensation.' And yet Heschel experienced the rebirth of a Jewish State after the Holocaust as nothing less than a resurrection. Its existence, he argued, 'makes life less unendurable.' Its rebirth calls for a renewal of trust in the God of History and holds out hope in the messianic promises that alone could make life meaningful.[64]

Heschel's inadvertent claim that suffering be the basis of reward and thus made 'meaningful' is after all the self-conscious foundation of King's non-violent philosophy, which echoed Gandhi's belief that 'unearned suffering is redemptive'. Yet, while King's pacifistic philosophy should be seen as an all-encompassing commitment, as he consistently presented it – not simply as a 'tactic' – his embrace of non-violence did not have the rigour of the Gandhian system to which King so often attributed his own philosophy. As Leela Gandhi explains, Mohandas Gandhi's notion of *ahimsa* – non-violence – 'frequently fails to address the human cost of totalizing morality'. As an example of such blindness she cites his claim 'that he is able joyfully to "countenance ... thousands losing their life for *satyagraha* [non-violent resistance]," on the grounds that "it ennobles those who lose their lives and morally enriches the world for their sacrifice"'.[65] In 'Pilgrimage to Nonviolence' (1958), which sets out in writing King's most systematic analysis of his own philosophy of non-violence, he claims that 'Gandhi was probably the first person in history to lift the love ethic of Jesus above mere interaction between individuals to a powerful and effective social force on a large scale'.[66] Yet for King this was the most important thing, that non-violence makes its way into the social sphere. For Gandhi – and arguably Jesus – the most important forum for this 'renunciative project'[67] is *not* its externalization, but rather its internal presence within the human being; as a check on the self's (destructive) desires for Gandhi, inscribed on the human heart for Jesus. King's vision of non-violence seems to be less purist than this; in 'Pilgrimage' he writes:

> After reading Niebuhr, I tried to arrive at a realistic pacifism. In other words, I came to see the pacifist position not as sinless but as the lesser evil in the circumstances. I felt then, and I feel now, that the pacifist would have a greater appeal if he did not

claim to be free from the moral dilemmas that the Christian nonpacifist confronts.[68]

Within this context, it is perhaps easier to understand how King could support the Israelis in the 1967 war, while black nationalists from SNCC (Student Non-Violent Coordinating Committee) to the Nation of Islam talked of 'Nazi-like tactics exercised by the Zionists against the defenceless civilian population in the occupied Arab lands'.[69] The next chapter argues that the stark conclusions reached by some black nationalists simplified an extremely complex historical moment. But it is also clear that King's attachment to the logic of the Exodus narrative led to comparable simplifications. His theological-political identifications with the Jewish people rendered him blind to the obvious plight of the Palestinians. Writing in his memoir, *Out of Place* (1999), Edward Said mentions Martin Luther King 'whom,' Said writes, 'I had genuinely admired but was also unable to fathom (or forgive) for the warmth of his passion for Israel's victory during the 1967 war'.[70] Where for Said, analysis of the Palestinian situation was coextensive with his understanding of colonialism, it seems that Israel played a parallel role in King's critique of colonial relations.

The Civil Rights movement identified with King is characterized by most historians as a domestically oriented, anti-Communist affair. In *Race Against Empire* (1997), Penny Von Eschen identifies the emergence of the Civil Rights movement in the mid 1950s as the moment at which anti-colonial activity is eclipsed as a major force animating African American politics; Du Bois is one of the intellectuals that Eschen identifies at the heart of the internationalist black political project that she argues extended from the late 1930s to the early Cold War. Eschen is convincing in her claim that black Civil Rights liberals engaged in a brand of Cold War era American exceptionalism in basing their arguments on the notion that the US could not claim to be the leader of the free world while supporting Jim Crow. Yet her attendant claim that the Cold War 'effectively severed the black American struggle for civil rights from the issues of anticolonialism and racism abroad' ignores the fact that King himself consistently compared the Civil Rights struggle to anti-colonial struggles abroad.[71] Nowhere is this clearer than in his partial embrace of Gandhian non-violence, and the identification with the Indian struggle for independence from the British Empire that this clearly entailed.

In *Jesus and the Disinherited*, Thurman describes a 1935 'pilgrimage of friendship' he undertook 'from the students of America to the students of India, Burma, and Ceylon'. In Ceylon he was challenged by the principal of a college he visited with the question 'what are *you* doing over here?' The principal began by rehearsing the Christian involvement in the slave trade and concluded with the words:

> I am a Hindu. I do not understand. Here you are in my country, standing deep within the Christian faith and tradition. I do not wish to seem rude to you. But, sir, I think you are a traitor to all the darker peoples of the earth. I am wondering what you, an intelligent man, can say in defense of your position.[72]

The evidence suggests that the discomfort this moment occasioned for Thurman would have been shared by King. As argued above, King had absorbed his mentor's suspicion of Christianity's colonization of another religion, and had translated these insights into his critique of the violent missionary drives that settled the United States, drives that King, like Thurman, also saw at work in overseas colonial projects. King himself was not immune to the missionary impulse – he talked of the ways in which Christianity along with modern technology had heightened expectations across the developing world[73] – but he did chastise not only the timidity of Christianity in the decolonizing world, he also spelled out the complicity of the white South African church in a racist colonial system. As early as 1957, King had become a member of the American Committee on Africa (ACOA), thus recognizing the bonds between continental Africans and African Americans. Ten years later, King was to write in *Where Do We Go from Here* (1967) that US blacks had been 'caught up by the spirit of the times, and with his black brothers of Africa and his brown and yellow brothers in Asia, South America and the Caribbean, the United States Negro is moving with a great sense of urgency toward the promised land of racial justice'. In this same publication King rejects 'the convenient temptation to attribute the current turmoil and bitterness throughout the world to the presence of a Communist conspiracy' and, sounding very much like Du Bois, King declares racism a global phenomenon that 'knows no geographical boundaries': 'racism and its perennial ally – economic exploitation – provide the key to understanding most of the international complications of this generation.'[74]

Admittedly, King was unique among Civil Rights leaders in his propensity to compare the struggle, even in the early days, to those of overseas national liberation movements. South Africa took centre-stage in King's analysis of racism's international coordinates because he saw direct parallels between the apartheid system and segregation in the South. In fact, as Lewis Baldwin points out, 'King equated both with "the struggle of Moses" and "his devoted followers as they sought to get out of Egypt." As he put it, "This is something of the story of every people struggling for freedom."'[75] For King nowhere could this be more clearly underscored than in the struggle taking place on what is assumed to be the actual geographical site of the Exodus narrative. Had King survived past 1968 his support for the State of Israel would soon have come into conflict with his championing of the anti-apartheid movement in South Africa – the emergence of strategic alliances between the Jewish state and the white minority-ruled regime in South Africa was under way before King's death and was very apparent by the early 1970s. But throughout the 1960s the situation was much less clear. While there had long been support for Zionism within the South African government, in the early 1960s anti-Semitic attacks in South Africa were on the increase due to disproportionate Jewish involvement in the anti-apartheid struggle. The State of Israel was at this stage still trying to form friendships with black African states and it would not be until the early 1970s that its anti-South African voting patterns in the United Nations went into reverse gear.[76] For in spite of the fact that the apparently more 'militant' wing of the black struggle sided with the Palestinians against the Israelis in the 1967 war, in 1948, the year of Israel's establishment, this was not a foregone conclusion. Indeed, King's steadfast support for Israel, at least up until 1967, was entirely in sync with those on the left in both America and Europe who, as George Orwell said in 1945, were 'strongly committed to support the Jews against the Arabs'. This was in light not only of the widespread sense that the Holocaust more than justified Jewish desires for the security of a national home; it was also connected to the strong socialist bent of the early Zionist vision.[77]

Yet as Orwell also suggested in 1945, 'the Palestinian issue is partly a colour issue' which means that 'an Indian nationalist, for instance, would probably side with the Arabs'.[78] This was not the case for King and neither was it immediately the case for black nationalists. Du Bois' ambivalent response to the Suez crisis – cited in the previous chapter – is illustrative of the fact that many black

Americans who identified with anti-colonialism abroad were pulled in two directions by the issue of Israel–Palestine. King's championing of the black–Jewish alliance along with his support for Israel as, in his eyes, a decolonizing movement of national liberation, was part of his wider commitment to transcending this colour line. King's aspiration to transcend racism was intimately linked to his desire to transcend religious division. While his ecumenical racial and religious vision was in crucial ways tied to the American dream, it did, as I have argued, have a markedly transnational aspect apparent from the movement's early days in Montgomery. Exodus emerges in King's thought as a vehicle through which both transnational and national identifications were forged. As many critics have noted, King's transnationalism became increasingly pronounced alongside his alienation with the American system, an alienation that, as the concluding section will outline, arguably signified the eventual collapse of the jeremiad – and thus faith in the American project – in King's thought. Ultimately, and like Du Bois, King was not prepared to prematurely announce the arrival of a post-racial promised land.

CONCLUSION: THE AMERICAN NIGHTMARE

In a sermon given on Christmas Eve 1967, King referred to his famous 1963 speech and claimed that 'not long after talking about that dream I started seeing it turn into a nightmare'.[79] King's evident disillusionment towards the latter stages of his life did nothing to diminish, and in many ways invigorated, his vision of justice for black America. Where in his assessment of Israel King had succumbed to the temptation to collapse the difference between the real and the ideal and in effect declare the nation redeemed – a tragically premature declaration for a man so committed to ending cycles of violence – this was not the case with America. In the ghettoes of Chicago, which became the base of King's campaign in the mid to late 1960s, King encountered not his dream of racial transcendence but rather an urban dystopia haunted by intransigent racism and systemic racialized poverty. That much of Chicago's South Side is now even more of an abandoned wasteland than it was in the late 1960s – just blocks from the home of the current US president the streets are stalked by a deadly combination of poverty, drugs and guns[80] – is a grim epilogue to the despair of King's late years.

In the speech delivered the day before he died King was at his most prophetic and most apocalyptic: he declared 'the world is all messed up. The nation is sick. Trouble is in the land. Confusion all around.' And yet he also claimed that he had 'been to the mountaintop' and had 'seen the promised land'. Nowhere is King's merging with the voice of Moses more pronounced than in this sermon; this is perhaps King's most rousing and militant speech, but in spite of its apocalyptic tone, King eschews the purgatory violence that this might imply. He tells his audience:

> We aren't engaged in any negative protest and in any negative arguments with anybody. We are saying that we are determined to be men. We are determined to be people. We are saying that we are God's children. And that we don't have to live like we are forced to live.[81]

Richard Lischer goes as far as to claim that 'the terrible secret that the prophet began to tell in his last desperate years was this: it doesn't matter if America has or has not lived up to its principles, because the principles themselves are a lie'. It is certainly true that where King's 1963 speech talked about coming to Washington to cash the 'promissory note' of equality as enshrined in the nation's founding documents, in a 1968 sermon to Ebenezer church in Atlanta he wonders, as Lischer notes, whether black Americans will be able to celebrate the Bicentennial and muses that the Declaration of Independence has 'never had any real meaning in terms of implementation in our lives'.[82]

Noting a 'terrible ambivalence in the soul of white America',[83] in his last few years King in effect stopped appealing to the super-ficialities of 'white liberal guilt' – often synonymous with mere 'nerves' – and his tactics of non-violent resistance could no longer be interpreted as a 'therapeutic' experience for the conscience of the white South. As Michael Eric Dyson suggests, the rhetoric of recognizing the 'true' humanity at the core of southern whites was only flattery on one level, and 'in time this led to a greater backlash because it suggested King's and black people's moral superiority'.[84] King thus moved from the belief that whites might be able to redeem themselves to the sense that America's salvation lay in redemption by black America. King's thinking did not emphasize blackness as a marker of oppression in the vein of black liberation theology. At the end of his life his imagination was fired by the idea of a 'Poor People's Campaign' that would create an interracial human rights coalition. Nonetheless, by 1968 if not before, the influence King was to have on black liberation theology is apparent in his belief that because black Americans had been so exploited by the system, they 'bring a special spiritual and moral contribution to American life – a contribution without which America could not survive'.[85]

In this vein, and responding specifically to what he saw as the racist war in Vietnam, King claimed that a properly 'integrated' foreign policy might best be led by someone who is not of the 'white West':

> I honestly feel that a man without racial blinders – or, even better, a man with personal experience of racial discrimination – would be in a much better position to make policy decisions and to conduct negotiations with the underprivileged and emerging nations of the world.[86]

Whether or not the election of Barack Obama – which necessarily involved mobilizing large sectors of the white vote precisely in the vein of King's multiracial alliance politics – will fulfil King's expectations in the realm of foreign policy remains to be seen. The fact that Obama now shares with King the distinction of being a Nobel peace laureate is a premature indicator of Obama's performance in the global arena. And the Niebuhrian notes that Obama consistently sounded throughout his December 2009 Nobel acceptance address may have done little to placate the ghost of the non-violent Civil Rights giant who seemed to be watching over Obama's shoulder as the latter eloquently made the case for 'just war' – in relation to a conflict in Afghanistan that has increasingly been dubbed by the media 'Obama's Vietnam'. The Nobel judges attempted to dilute this paradox and justify their choice by explaining that in his first nine months in office, Obama had created an international climate conducive to 'hope' for a more peaceful future. Yet Obama's prize was awarded in part for his restoration of America's image in the eyes of the rest of the world, whereas by the end of his life King's Exodus politics in many ways took on the task, as Lischer claims, of demythologizing the American civil religion. Nonetheless, King's increasingly global vision did not give up on the hope of future change. Indeed, at the end of his 1968 essay, 'A Testament of Hope', King invoked the Jesus who represented 'the poor and the despised' and imagines a revolution that ushers in justice, brotherhood, peace and 'abundance for all':

When we have won these – in a spirit of unshakable nonviolence – then, in luminous splendor, the Christian era will truly begin.[87]

Clearly in King's view, the world was not there yet. King's words here might be an appropriate response to Jerome Corsi who, as outlined in Chapter 1, questions Obama's Christianity on the grounds that his personal narrative is stalked by a sense of alienation unknown to the 'true' Christian who has found identity in Christ. For King's rhetoric of redemptive deferral – informed by the sense of struggle still ahead – maintains the ultimate Christian vision of reconciliation as the stuff of future hope. Though in very different tones to late King, Obama's vision of the 'American promise' – which was framed by the neo-classical columns – is also one 'that makes us fix our eye not on what is seen, but what is unseen, that better place around the bend'.[88] As US president Obama is far from abandoning the rhetoric of the American civil religion – arguably he is currently its highest custodian – but I suggest that his rhetoric too refuses to collapse what is into what ought to be. This refusal was very clearly on display when Obama accepted his Nobel peace prize not as recognition of achievement but as a call to action.

Looking back on King's 'Poor People's Campaign' it is hard not to imagine him applauding the current president's efforts to pass a bill on health care that would provide access to millions of uninsured Americans, a group overwhelmingly made up of ethnic minorities. The much diluted bill that has now been passed is far from the radical re-structuring of society that King imagined in his later years – which would lead some commentators to suggest he was a Marxist – but it does anticipate reforms that have led many to brand Obama 'un-American'. In a not dissimilar vein, during the last years of his life King was not the popular figure embraced by the American establishment today. He was persecuted by FBI surveillance on the one hand and death threats from white supremacists on the other. Obama himself is of course highly unlikely to find himself on the receiving end of the kind of treatment dealt out to King by the FBI, but, as mentioned in the previous chapter, his legitimacy as president has been questioned by a growing chorus of voices dubbed the 'birther movement', who claim that the president is not a US citizen. Their assertion that Obama is in fact a citizen of Kenya would be laughable if it were not for the fact that it is part of an insidious and racialized discourse that has also led to lynched effigies of the president – along with his Democratic allies – that are reminiscent of the racism that responded to the Civil Rights movement. Indeed the vicious threats against Obama's life that have stalked him since the earliest days of his candidacy led some, highly ironically, to suggest that – in the shadow of the assassinations of Martin and Malcolm – a black man should not stand for president.

Anti-government opposition to Obama's proposed health care reforms was so strong during the summer of 2009 that campaigners wielded images of the president made over into the face of Adolf Hitler. This is the result of the idea that Obama's proposals would amount to a socialized system that would in effect ration health care in a 'survival of the fittest' contest dubbed 'death panels' by the former Vice Presidential Republican candidate Sarah Palin. Apart from the gross mischaracterization of Obama's original plan, the merging of Obama's image with that of the author of the Nazi death camps is overlain with a nexus of painful ironies. The game of calling antagonists Nazis is of course a common one – as the Middle East conflict, in which the tactics of both Jewish settlers and Palestinians have been compared by opponents to those of the Nazis – illustrates. Yet the fact that the campaign against Obama's policies is a personal attack with clear racial overtones gives this round of name-calling a particularly vicious edge.

The relationship between anti-black racism and anti-Semitism has been particularly prominent in the US, and it is a link that has survived beyond the upsurges of anti-black racism among some American Jewish groups and anti-Semitism amongst some black American groups. As Algernon Austin points out, the following quote from Hitler's *Mein Kampf* (1925) appeared on the website of a US-based white supremacist organization, Aryan Nations, in 2004: 'I believe that I am acting in accordance with the will of the Almighty Creator by defending myself against the Jew, I am fighting for the work of the Lord.' As Austin claims, 'much white supremacist thought is based on religious, not biological, ideas'.[89] The prime example in the US context is the Ku Klux Klan, which is a white Christian organization. The National Socialists in Germany did of course base much of their racism in a warped pseudo-scientific language which harboured an extreme biological agenda – as those who campaigned against Obama's health care plan seemed to realize. But as this quote from Hitler illustrates, there was a distinct religious element to Nazism – indeed the nationalist fervour it demanded of Germans meant that Christianity was itself largely squeezed out in favour of religious symbols that deified the Third Reich itself.

The Aryan idea is of course a highly racialized version of the chosen people. As Freud attempted to grapple with accelerating Nazi violence against the Jews on the eve of the Holocaust, he suggested that it is the Jewish religious idea of the chosen people that has historically antagonized other religious and national groupings. Freud's atheistic rendering of the Exodus story leads him to offer the human image of an Egyptian Moses, one that signals the possibility of overcoming the binary between master and slave, gentile and Jew, and which might lead to a genuinely universal counter-revolution against the evils of tribalism. In a religious register, this symbol also captures the vision of King's dream. King's desire to witness the worldly fulfilment of biblical promise led to his premature embrace of the State of Israel as that realization. This move ironically over-stepped the careful safeguards constructed by his encounter with Judaism. But in America King was in no danger of collapsing the real into the ideal. Integration may have been his ultimate aim but his thought refuses the Hegelian synthesis whereby the historically weaker trend is put to the service of the stronger one – Judaism subsumed by Christianity, 'black memory' usurped by 'state memory'.[90] Consequently, King's politics bore witness to the fact that black and white life remained distinct. For King, like Du Bois, black America's relationship to America was comparable to the messianic role that Judaism imagines Jews to play in relation to the rest of the world. In contrast to the messianic bent of the national civil religion, and similar to Du Bois' brand, this redemptive role involved fighting for social justice against the status quo of unequal power relations. King thus veritably exceeded the liberal tradition in which he is regularly remembered by naming the system 'sinful' and increasingly questioning its ability to redeem itself. In the same vein as Freud, at no stage did King's non-violent philosophy absolve whites of their guilt in support of the myth of American innocence; the idea that America is an inherently anti-imperialist nation is unequivocally displaced by King's Exodus vision.

For this reason it may be that the Obama campaign's choice of a Greco-Roman backdrop for his Democratic Convention speech did not do justice to the legacy of King's dream spoken exactly 45 years earlier. While Greek architecture clearly recalls the origins of democracy, some have argued that neo-classical imagery so often drawn on by US politicians brings into focus a parallel between the US and the Roman Republic's decline into imperialism.[91] It is possible that Thurman had the same comparison in mind when he rejected Rome's equation of Christianity with the sword. Without doubt, such imagery recalls the spectre of violent state power, a spectre out of sync not only with Obama's stated desire to restore American leadership in the world – not by force but by exercising restraint – but also with King's repudiation of violence of any kind, particularly that identified with the state. And yet, as I have argued, while Obama's invocations of an unfinished history do echo King's prophetic – and decidedly Hebraic – invocation of a redemption that is yet to come, the fact that his name has become synonymous with American state power, and in particular is closely associated with the war in Afghanistan, is suggestive of a far more compromised career. King's famous citation of Amos – 'we will not be satisfied until justice rolls down like waters and righteousness like a mighty stream'[92] – is appropriate for a Moses figure who resides outside the walls of power.

Neither Obama nor King are comprehensible outside of western traditions that have been shaped not only by Hebraic and Hellenic tendencies, but by non-western cultures too. This latter claim has been pivotal to a stream in African American thought that has strongly contested both the location of ancient Greece and Judeo-Christian tradition as the origin of 'civilization' – and this stream takes centre-stage in the next chapter. This chapter has argued that King himself embraced the implications of his western inheritance, but that his theology to an extent unravelled the problematic 'Judeo-Christian' construct that has long privileged the latter over and above the former. This meant that King's Christianity was largely resistant to the most Hellenic of transformations of 'the religion of Jesus': the incarnation. In turn this made King's theological-politics peculiarly suited to a 'decolonial thinking' that in fact showed him to be much more influenced by and bound up with black diasporic thought and politics than he is usually given credit for. Branded an 'Uncle Tom' by Malcolm X, King was by far the most influential African American advocate of black messianism. The idea that blacks have a special role to play in the divine plan was also central to the organization that launched Malcolm X's political career. While Malcolm ostensibly rejected his western legacy, the next chapter suggests that his privileging of Egypt – as both African and Islamic, and over and above the Judeo-Christian trope of Exodus – was far from the straight reversal of King's politics that Malcolm is so often called upon to represent. Popular memory has held that it was Malcolm X who articulated 'the American nightmare', but as this chapter has argued this vision also appeared in King's rhetoric – and in much sharper focus than the distant hope of his dream.

4
Reclaiming 'Egypt': Malcolm X

Malcolm X's life and legacy stand as the most powerful indictment of white American Christian nationalism in the black tradition. For Malcolm black people were lost in what he frequently referred to as 'this wilderness of North America', but the freedom that lay ahead was not for him the promised land of Judeo-Christian culture. Malcolm's rhetoric transforms the terms of the Exodus text by underscoring that the emptiness of the wilderness period – which in the bible is a period of interregnum between Egyptian bondage and the promised land – is precisely the site of oppression. It symbolizes a loss that might be restored via the plenitude of the highly complex 'Egypt' trope, one that, this chapter argues, signifies a politics of restitution that resurrects a wall against the destructive drives of white supremacy.

This is a liberation politics that only superficially reverses the master/slave dialectic of the Exodus text by holding up Egyptian masters, and not Hebrew slaves, as source for black identification. While the coordinates of the Judeo-Christian story never completely disappeared from Malcolm's narrative, his principal reference points were Islamic and African. For him, Egypt stood at the crossroads of non-western traditions that held out the hope of redemption for US blacks within a wider framework of Pan-African and postcolonial politics and religion. Where for King Exodus was reclaimed from the hands of white racists as a narrative of decolonization, the Egypt metaphor fulfilled a similar function for Malcolm. Thus while King sought to purge his Christianity of its violent origins, Malcolm found the religion of western colonialism and race-based slavery to be beyond redemption: 'Christianity has failed us 100 percent.'[1] In this way, in contrast to King, who remained a steadfast albeit highly revisionist Christian, Malcolm followed the logic of Du Bois' doubts about Christianity – and went considerably further in his repudiation of it. His complex affiliation to black nationalism – a philosophy which in its myriad forms has been generally pessimistic about the possibilities of mitigating white American racism – meant

133

that unlike King's gradual alienation from the terms of the national dream, Malcolm's was a wholesale rejection of US exceptionalism.

Arguably in the period 1960–63, when Malcolm X was the most prominent spokesperson for the Nation of Islam (NOI) and King's Civil Rights campaign was in full swing and in the ascendancy, these two figures that tower over the black tradition stood for its most extreme poles. The one a Muslim, the other a Christian, one preaching the necessity of separate black institutions while the other claimed for integration the sanctity of God; the one advocating resistance by any means necessary and the duplicity of white 'devils', the other philosophically committed to non-violence and love for one's enemies. Yet these shallow caricatures cannot do justice to two incredibly complicated political figures, both of whom espoused views at the ends of their lives that were inconceivable at earlier points in their careers.

As Richard Lischer argues, by 1967 'King was self-consciously crossing the boundary from reform to revolution, liberalism to liberationism', and where earlier in his career he might have condemned rioting, 'his later sermons condemn the system that makes riots inevitable'. At this stage he is, writes Lischer, 'no longer the double-voiced one. He is past signifying.'[2] If late King in many ways eschewed the contradictions of his earlier appeals to white racists, Malcolm's later renunciation of the controversial 'white devils' thesis and consequent willingness to cooperate with white allies in the struggle against racial injustice arguably brought him more squarely within the dilemmas of double consciousness that Du Bois so eloquently described. Like King, Malcolm increasingly critiqued the underlying causes of inequality and translated his critique into global, as opposed to national, terms. But Michael Eric Dyson's assessment of their respective relationships to America seems to be apt when he suggests that 'Malcolm was the prodigal son who strayed far from home before his partial return', whereas 'King was the son who never left but grew to question his inheritance'.[3]

And yet the fantasy of rapprochement between the two – had they not met with their violent deaths – that is entertained by so many scholars, and which is visually captured in a March 1964 photograph which pictures the handshake of their only meeting, belies enormous differences, not only in their political agendas and styles, but also in the type of legacy they left behind. It should be remembered that Malcolm was assassinated in February 1965 prior to the major shift that would mark King's career. Those who want to see Malcolm's politics as an extension and radicalization of King, or as the embodiment of the Black Power period, call on the memory of his extraordinarily fertile afterlife. While the lives of both men were tragically cut short, Malcolm's remarkable intervention into black politics was in the public eye for little more than five years. His legacy thus works in fundamentally different ways. Where King is judged on the basis of at least ten years of Civil Rights successes – from the Montgomery bus boycott of 1955 to the Voting Rights Act of 1965 – as well as his evolutionary phase from 1965 to 1968, Malcolm is more often seen in the light of what might have been. Though he was personally responsible for bringing the little-known organization of the Nation of Islam to national prominence, as well as vastly expanding its membership, the dramatic transformations that he underwent in 1964 following his break with the NOI led to the articulation of a political vision that was never fully worked out or realized in practice. Writing in a special issue of *Black Digest* in 1969, Carolyn Gerald described Malcolm as 'the epic hero of our struggle ... His significance, far more than historical, is mythological.'[4]

Consequently Malcolm X's legacy has proved inordinately flexible and, possibly to an even greater extent than King's, has been appropriated by a huge range of often competing and contradictory political and religious agendas. A primary inspiration not only for the Black Power movement of the late 1960s and early 1970s, Malcolm was also central to the Afrocentrist cultural vision that then developed, most notably in the work of Molefi Kete Asante, whose writings came to prominence in the 1980s and 1990s. Malcolm has been elevated as a cultural, political and religious hero by groups of Sunni Muslims, both in the US and beyond, but he has also been rehabilitated, somewhat ambiguously, by the very Nation of Islam that was in all likelihood partially responsible for his death. And, as we have seen, he is claimed by James Cone as the central inspiration for black Christian liberation theology. Malcolm's critique of capitalism has been claimed by Marxists, black and white, the world over; and as Chapter 1 explained, his distinction between 'House Negroes' and 'Field Negroes' was adopted by Al Qaeda in the context of post-9/11 global politics and the election of Barack Obama.

Possibly Malcolm has received the most uniform posthumous treatment in the mainstream US media and the public school system, which with few exceptions has cast him as a one-dimensional prophet of black rage, violence and so-called 'reverse racism'. This negative portrayal speaks to the huge gulfs that exist between black and white Americans. As Michael Dawson argues, the assessment of 'the importance of Malcolm X as a black leader' – alongside 'the prevalence of white racism' and the 'desirability of independent black organizations' – is one of the indicators of consensus among ideologically diverse African Americans, indicators that highlight the distance between 'black ideologies' and those likely to circulate among white Americans.[5] Among black Americans Malcolm's memory, like King's, generally commands huge respect. And in some ways this respect is less complicated than that accorded to King, whose near universal appeal across the racial divide – as well as the cooptation of his memory by the state and the feeling among some that he had 'sold out' to white liberals – has made him much less of an exclusively black cultural hero.

That Malcolm might be more easily claimed by black Americans than King is further reinforced by the canonization of his life in *The Autobiography of Malcolm X* (1965). King left behind a vast collection of writings but it was left to Clayborne Carson to piece together the story of his life into a cohesive narrative.[6] Malcolm's life story was narrated to Alex Haley – who had the final editorial control of the manuscript following Malcolm's death – and arguably evidences Haley's own political biases, yet it does seem to capture something of the 'authentic' Malcolm; when compared to transcripts of his speeches, the *Autobiography*'s style and tone rings true. Though clearly the creation of Haley's imagination, this sense of authenticity makes for an extraordinarily powerful narrative that has been read widely around the world and considered a landmark in American literature. As discussed in Chapter 1, Obama's memoir indicates that Malcolm's *Autobiography* was an important touchstone for clarifying Obama's own expanding race consciousness. The *Autobiography* is singled out for discussion as one of the few African American texts Obama read that does *not* corroborate the 'nightmare vision' of a black man's destiny in a 'white man's world':

> His repeated acts of self-creation spoke to me; the blunt poetry of his words, his unadorned insistence on respect, promised a new and uncompromising order, martial in its discipline, forged through sheer force of will.[7]

Obama distinguishes his own story from Malcolm's by the fact that he cannot share Malcolm's 'wish that the white blood that ran through him, there by an act of violence, might somehow be expunged', and neither does he share Malcolm's sense that true equality lies in 'a distant future, in a far-off land'. Yet Obama rehabilitates the much vilified popular image of Malcolm by claiming that his 'talk of blue-eyed devils and apocalypse' can be dismissed as 'religious baggage that Malcolm himself seemed to have safely abandoned toward the end of his life'.[8]

That Obama not only admires Malcolm X himself but is also aware of the cultural purchase Malcolm's name carries among African Americans in general was clear on the campaign trail. On a number of occasions during 2008, Obama told voters they had been 'hoodwinked' and 'bamboozled' by his opponents – referring variously to Senators Hillary Clinton and John McCain. The use of these two unusual words in succession seems to be a clear reference to Malcolm X via Spike Lee's film of the same name. Malcolm is not reported to have actually used these words himself, but they are spoken by Denzel Washington who plays Malcolm X during a memorable speech to an all-black Harlem crowd in Lee's biopic.[9] These references were first noted during a January 2008 address to a mostly African American crowd in North Carolina, prompting some commentators to draw parallels between Obama's speech and the wider contexts of Lee's fictive Malcolm – who was warning black folks not to trust white folks with the running of their communities.[10]

It may be that this was Obama's own version of signifying – sending out a message with double-edged meaning that would in all likelihood play rather differently to black and white audiences. Certainly the fact that Obama used two terms associated with black America's most famous Muslim to bat away the erroneous claim that he was himself a Muslim suggests that his speech was laced with intriguing double-entendres. This is particularly so given the fact that the speech in Lee's film features Malcolm claiming not to be standing before the crowd as a Democrat or a Republican, Christian or Jew, or even an American: 'I have to stand here today as what I was when I was born: a black man.' Here Lee's fictive Malcolm echoes many statements made by the historical Malcolm – that highlight natural, 'god-given', (human) rights over and above those accrued by citizenship – and captures one of the historical functions of black nationalism: the articulation, as Wahneema Lubiano writes, of 'black Americans' awareness of their place in the state's intentions'.[11] Obama's candidacy was in part an attempt to subvert these intentions by placing an African American at the centre of the state apparatus and in so doing counteract the continued denigration of black Americans within the US racial formation. And yet the fact that the racist attacks on Obama both prior to and after his election have primarily been forwarded in an attempt to undermine his claim to American citizenship, and the fact that his administration has shied away from speaking openly about systemic racism supported by institutions of the state, demonstrates the persistent relevance of Malcolm's self-understanding and the attendant black nationalist critique.

While this chapter argues that Malcolm's rejection of America was not as clear-cut as his own statements often imply, it is also evident that his vision of freedom was animated by geographical locales beyond the United States. This is reflected in the Afrocentric orientations of Obama's former church as well as the 'third worldism' of the black liberation theology that undergirds much of that church's religious vision. Both Jeremiah Wright and James Cone lay explicit claim to Malcolm's internationalist outlook, an outlook that began to develop when Malcolm came under the influence of the Nation of Islam – which taught that Egypt, and not America, or ancient Greece or Rome, was the origin of civilization. What I describe here as the Egypt trope has no source text comparable to the Exodus narrative and will thus receive a different treatment here. This chapter approaches the set of identifications captured by the Egypt metaphor – that I argue, following Melani McAlister, functioned in the 1960s as an alternative identification for black Americans to the Judeo-Christian narrative of Exodus – by assessing its intersections with the life and legacy of Malcolm X. Through Malcolm's *Autobiography*, letters and speeches, I explore the way in which Malcolm participated in the black nationalist project of detailing 'for black Americans an origin and a destiny outside the myth of "America"'.[12]

As Chapters 2 and 3 argued, both W.E.B. Du Bois and Martin Luther King express a marked ambivalence towards this myth and the liberal vision that shapes it. They engage in varieties of black Exodus rhetoric not only by historicizing the categories of race, nation and religion that animate the often racist variants of the national civil religion; their rhetoric also invests in transcendent terms – in spiritualized, messianic understandings of blackness – in order to ground an understanding of black agency that might be mobilized against a racist state. While both thus imagine a redemptive role for black America based on a moral superiority to white supremacy, both also, and in different ways, maintain a scepticism about redemptive politics, a politics that might sanction an unjust status quo by endowing it with a sense of closure. This chapter attempts to explore the extent to which Malcolm X's reclamation of a black Egypt invests in and resists a politics of redemption. It deploys Malcolm's life as a prism through which to view the black nationalist analysis of, and attempt to intervene in, the workings of the master/slave dialectic that figuratively reflects America's race relations. Malcolm is of interest here not only because he is known as America's most famous advocate of black nationalism, but also because, rather than exemplifying black nationalist ideology, Malcolm increasingly articulated positions that challenged it from the inside.

The first section traces Malcolm's investment in a variant of black chosenness under the auspices of the NOI, and his evolving sense that Islam, and not Christianity, is the 'natural' religion for oppressed black Americans. The section that follows complicates this sense by showing the way in which Malcolm's shift from the Nation of Islam to Sunni Islam led to a marked tension between his religious and political commitments, tensions that question some of his former theological certainties and threaten to unravel the 'Egypt' trope that holds together what Malcolm initially supposed were the complementary commitments to Islam and Pan-Africanism. Thus in contrast to Du Bois and King, Malcolm becomes increasingly ambivalent about the role religion might play in the fight for racial justice. The implications this has for Malcolm's assessment of the Middle East conflict is explored in the third section. This suggests that by looking back to the roots of black nationalism in black Exodus politics, it is clear that the philosophy inherited by Malcolm X has partially invested in the colonial cultural logic of the West that it outwardly rejects. The repudiation of parts of this legacy in Malcolm's final phase, which, according to a number of scholars, was the progenitor of a 'revolutionary nationalism',[13] will be tracked in the concluding section, which considers Malcolm's progressive legacy as instructive for problematizing the unhelpful East/West binary of a post 9/11 world.

FROM EXODUS TO EGYPT

The Autobiography of Malcolm X is, as discussed in Chapter 1, an archetypal neo-slave narrative, encapsulating as it does many of the key features of the genre that functioned in antebellum America as literary contributions to the cause of abolition: the movement from slavery to freedom, ignorance to enlightenment, is the major structuring device that Malcolm's autobiography shares with the classic slave narratives, which usually encompass some kind of religious conversion and dramatic scenes of reading that signify the acquisition of literacy. And yet while the text penned by Alex Haley on behalf of Malcolm X includes these generic features, it also entails crucial differences: where classic antebellum slave narratives consciously wrote themselves into the narrative of American identity, Malcolm's writes himself out of it. And where antebellum slave narratives usually involve compulsory expressions of allegiance to the Christian faith, Malcolm's text is in many ways dedicated to negating the validity of Christianity for black Americans. Malcolm's story of liberation thus fundamentally revises the redemptive trajectory not only of the slave narrative but also of the American civil religion, which in turn takes its cue from what is *the* archetypal slave narrative of Judeo-Christian culture, the Hebrew exodus out of Egypt.

In his ground-breaking study of nineteenth-century black American expressions of the Exodus narrative, Eddie Glaude argues that the story functioned as a form of black 'nation language' that emerged within the context of the 'nation within a nation' that is the black church. Though often conducive to political quietism, the nineteenth-century black church was also a force for political radicalism which acted as a buffer between blacks and the state as well as providing an alternative space of 'national' allegiance.[14] This was the religious model on which Marcus Garvey's so-called 'Back-to-Africa' movement capitalized, which struck a populist chord among particularly urban black Americans in the 1920s – including Malcolm's parents. Drawing on the revolutionary potential of both the black church and the Exodus narrative, Garveyism formed the major religious context for Malcolm's childhood.

Michael Dawson describes Garvey as 'the founder of modern black nationalist movements',[15] while Wilson Jeremiah Moses situates Garveyism as the height of what he describes as the 'golden age of black nationalism'. According to Moses, central to this 'golden age' was the 'mystical' prophecy of Psalm 68:31: 'Princes shall come out of Egypt; Ethiopia shall soon stretch out her hands unto God.'[16] This psalm casts the redemption of Africa as the horizon of the Exodus vision. While the transformation of Hebrew slaves does not necessarily make them *Egyptian* princes, somewhat paradoxically the place of slavery sows the seeds of royalty. In this way Garveyism converted a story about suffering and slavery into one about power and prestige, one in which black people are not only God's chosen people but God is also black. Contrary to popular perception, Garvey himself did not advocate the mass emigration of black Americans 'back' to Africa, but he believed that all blacks must work to build a future 'African nation'. As David Howard-Pitney writes, Garveyism was 'a potent, black, civil religion promulgating the idea that there was no promising future for blacks in America'.[17] Unlike the interracial vision that motivated King's black Exodus rhetoric, for Garvey, the centrality of race – 'as *the* fundamental category for analyzing society' – was not to be wished away. In contrast to King's project of seeking to revive American liberalism by making it live up to its promises, Garvey believed America and its liberal creed to be 'fundamentally racist', a fact that meant that black success relied on black solidarity and self-determination.[18] Though this racial destiny was necessarily separate from that of whites, this did not preclude identifications with Jewish Zionism, which Garvey often invoked as a model for his own Pan-Africanism.

The Nation of Islam – which made a profound impact on Malcolm during his years in prison – is a clear heir to the Garveyite legacy. Seeking to draw Garvey outside of his Judeo-Christian coordinates, the NOI formulated a novel and hybrid variant of Islam in which Garvey's invocation of a black Christ was transplanted to a black Allah. Yet as Melani McAlister explains, the NOI did not discard the stories of the Hebrew bible – most varieties of Islam do of course endow what they usually view as the Old Testament with considerable authority. But these stories were no longer a source of identification with other religious or ethnic groupings. Re-branded by Elijah Muhammad as 'prophecies rather than histories ... they spoke of the contemporary experiences of African Americans rather than the historical experiences of the ancient Hebrews':

> Within this paradigm, Jews were not those whose ancient history was the prototype for contemporary liberation, as was the case for King and other civil rights leaders, but those whose putative status as 'the chosen people' usurped the position of the black people in relation to God.[19]

Thus the ambivalence expressed in Garveyism – about Jews and about the role of slavery in black identity – was collapsed by the NOI's cannibalization of Garveyite ideas, which espoused overt hostility towards Jews and which eschewed the idea that the African American experience originated in a story of oppression. What the NOI offered instead was an alternative site of identification, not with Hebrew slaves but rather with what was seen as a more empowering vision of civilization residing in the Nile valley – one that we might more readily associate with Pharaoh, the master of slaves. In this sense Garvey's attempt to appropriate the resources of Judeo-Christian culture in the interests of African redemption is simplified by an organization seeking to jettison, as McAlister puts it, 'the dominant discourse of Judeo-Christian Americanness'.[20]

The NOI's talent for transforming the lives of former prison inmates thus found particularly fertile ground in Malcolm Little. The organization's unqualified rejection of a racist American culture reconnected him with his Garveyite roots while severing those roots from a Christianity that Malcolm claimed to have always found problematic. As the Haley-inflected Malcolm of the *Autobiography* explains, while his brother Philbert 'loved church ... it confused and amazed me':

> I would sit goggle-eyed at my father jumping and shouting as he preached, with the congregation jumping and shouting behind him, their souls and bodies devoted to singing and praying.

Malcolm contrasts these scenes at church to the Garvey UNIA (Universal Negro Improvement Association) meetings: in the latter the members of the congregation and Malcolm's father 'were more intense, more intelligent and down to earth'. As Malcolm admits, his father's role as Baptist preacher 'fit his association with the back-to-Africa movement, with Marcus Garvey's "Black Train Homeward"'. But this association – between black nationalism and black Christianity – is one that the NOI enabled the newly named Malcolm X to suppress.[21]

Malcolm's later contempt for King and the Civil Rights movement (which would turn to reluctant admiration shortly before his death) seemingly confirmed his earlier sense that a black freedom narrative couched within Christian terms was doomed simply to mimic white culture. In this sense Malcolm was free to articulate the suggestion that necessarily remained latent in many antebellum slave narratives: that Christianity might just be irretrievably contaminated by white racism.[22] As Malcolm writes in the *Autobiography*:

> Where the religion of every other people on earth taught its believers of a God with whom they could identify, a God who at least looked like one of their own kind, the slavemaster injected

his Christian religion into this 'Negro'. This 'Negro' was taught to worship an alien God having the same blond hair, pale skin and blue eyes as the slavemaster.

He goes on to write that 'this religion taught the "Negro" that black was a curse. It taught him to hate everything black, including himself'. Like Du Bois, King and black liberation theologians, Malcolm here critiques the Europeanization of Christianity and the white supremacist claim that Jesus was ethnically white. For Malcolm the rejection of Christianity equates to the rejection of a self-hating and alien ideology foisted onto 'the black man'. The highly gendered language for which Malcolm X and the Nation of Islam are well known is no accident. The suggestion that runs through the NOI's critique of Christianity is that US blacks require a religion that is altogether more muscular. Christianity was used not only to justify the violence of the slavemaster's whip, but it also 'further deceived and brainwashed this "Negro" to always turn the other cheek, and grin, and scrape, and bow, and be humble, and to sing, and to pray and to take whatever was dished out by the devilish white man'. [23] While we need to be careful not to associate Islam with violence and Christianity with pacifism – the violence of the slaveholding Christian illustrates the misleading nature of that idea – it is nonetheless true that, as Sherman Jackson claims, Islam 'had a well-established reputation for resistance and armed struggle'. Moreover, 'it was independent of white people (or at least Europeans), the latter having no authority to define its ethos or its substance'.[24]

In this vein, in 1962, Malcolm X declared to an all-white student assembly:

> We don't have any confidence in the white man ... I am not a white man. I am not a western man. I was brought here by your forefathers. We are the lost found Nation of Islam. We were kidnapped from our Islamic culture by slave traders 400 years ago.[25]

As spokesperson for the NOI, Malcolm's presentation of Islam as 'a special religion for the black man',[26] an indigenous African religion (as opposed to an imposed Christianity designed to teach submission, passivity and black self-hatred) does have some historical grounding. As Amiri YaSin Al-Hadid points out, often overlooked is the fact that large numbers of Muslims did make the Middle Passage: 'Islam first came to the United States on slave ships. Between 1492 and 1865, millions of Muslims from the coast and interior of North West Africa were captured, sold, and transported.' While the exact number of Muslims enslaved and brought to North America remains unknown, 'estimates range between 10 and 40 per cent'.[27]

Yet as with Malcolm's own experience, for most black Americans the passage into Islam would be via conversion. Here again though, the sense that Islam is more hospitable than Christianity to oppressed peoples – and thus more 'authentic' a religion for black people – carries historical weight. Even Edward Wilmot Blyden, the nineteenth-century proto-black nationalist *Christian*, found on his travels to Africa that Islam offered black Africans more freedom by which to interpret and authenticate their own realities than did Christianity. In his 1887 publication *Christianity, Islam and the Negro Race*, Blyden notes that 'the Christian Negro has ... rarely been trained to trust his own judgement or to think that he has anything to say which foreigners will care to hear':

> The Mohammedan Negro is a much better Mohammedan than the Christian Negro is a Christian, because the Muslim Negro, as a learner, is a disciple, not an imitator. A disciple, when freed from leading-strings, may become a producer; an imitator never rises above a mere copyist.[28]

Commenting on these passages, Sherman Jackson concludes that the 'Christianization of the African amounted to a destructive process of Europeanization', whereas 'Islamization in Africa did not entail Arabization'.[29] And it seems that Malcolm X, through his encounter with Elijah Muhammad's organization, similarly understood Islam as a religion that could be shaped by and for the black experience, beyond the experience of Christian colonization.

The geographical displacement of America as a site of possible black American redemption was crucial to the NOI's alternative geographical orientation, which attempted to link the Muslim and African worlds via the bridging trope of 'Egypt'. As argued in Chapter 2, double consciousness, the 'peculiar sensation' that Du Bois suggested afflicts African Americans, is a painful yet at times productive cleavage which yields a heightened awareness via African American 'second sight'. In contrast, for Malcolm it is a thoroughly negative condition engendered by the internalization of racism. Black salvation lies in repudiating this false consciousness and recognizing America as a foreign land. While the NOI agenda did involve claims to independent territory within the US which would in effect end what the organization perceived as the internal colonization of African Americans – according to Malcolm the claim to land was central to the 'black revolution' he envisaged[30] – a psychological revolution was the necessary prerequisite and in fact the focus of much NOI rhetoric.

Through emphasis on a black past defined outside the purview of oppression, Malcolm's rhetoric as NOI spokesperson laid stress on a subjective wholeness afforded to those who could see beyond a history of vulnerability and back to the splendours of Egypt. As McAlister explains, the NOI 'believed emphatically that Egypt was a black nation and that the greatness of ancient Egyptian civilization was proof of the historical greatness of black culture'.[31] This powerful and empowering story of origins restored to the 'black man' a sense of dignity denied by a society that would sooner incarcerate its black citizens than accept them on equal terms. Thus Malcolm's life story is offered up as an example, initially dedicated to 'The Honorable Elijah Muhammad, who found me here in America in the muck and mire of the filthiest civilization and society on this earth, and pulled me out, cleaned me up, and stood me on my feet, and made me the man that I am today'.[32]

And yet Malcolm's story of conversion is considerably complicated by his ejection from the NOI in the March of 1964, when Malcolm instructed Alex Haley to cancel the book's original dedication to the organization's leader. Malcolm's sense of his autobiography's trajectory thus underwent drastic changes during the process of its textual construction, changes that complicate Malcolm's assumption of NOI theology and ideology, including the seemingly neat transition from, as it were, Exodus to Egypt, the shackles of a white racist Christianity to a self-determining black Islam. The immediate circumstances of Malcolm's break with the NOI involved a statement he made to the press on the occasion of John F. Kennedy's assassination – a statement which suggested that the murder of this much-loved US president was a case of 'chickens coming home to roost'. Muhammad silenced Malcolm for 90 days. Yet it was clear that Malcolm had been sidelined within the organization for some time – the NOI newspaper that Malcolm had himself founded, *Muhammad Speaks*, had long ceased to cover the activities of the NOI's most famous member. Malcolm's increasing isolation was mirrored by his own disillusionment: when rumours were confirmed that Elijah Muhammad had fathered at least three illegitimate children, Malcolm loyally turned to the Qu'ran to justify his leader's behaviour. Yet Malcolm's encounters with the Qu'ran apparently only fuelled his increasing discomfort within the NOI.

As Edward Curtis notes, from around 1959, Malcolm was often assailed after speaking engagements by Muslim immigrants citing the Qu'ran to prove that many of the NOI's theological premises were 'un-Islamic'. At the centre of these accusations was the NOI's controversial claim that white people are the work of the devil. Malcolm himself was an enthusiastic advocate of the NOI's notorious 'white devil' thesis, but evidence suggests that he was increasingly troubled by suggestions that this idea did not reflect 'true' Islam.[33] In addition, though the NOI claimed to preach an authentic religion for oppressed African Americans, shunning what it cast as the 'accom-modationist' activities of black Christians increasingly involved in the Civil Rights movement, the NOI emphasized its identity as a religious organization and in general shied away from practical politics. For the narrow brand of black nationalism espoused by Muhammad's NOI in fact betrayed a number of crossovers with black conservative ideologies.[34] In contrast to conservative ideologies, for the NOI white racism, rather than black pathology, was the cause of racial inequalities; yet the organization's nationalist emphasis on self-help, particularly in the moral and economic arena, combined with its aversion to practical politics, made its ethos closer to a conservative individualism than the progressive collective visions that inspired other black nationalist organizations, including the organization later founded by Malcolm X.

So in spite of the NOI's reverence for the 'Egypt' trope – and its radiating Islamic and African contexts – most critics agree that Malcolm was unable to take a truly Pan-African approach until his break with the NOI in 1964. As Manning Marable explains, 'throughout 1960–63, Malcolm frequently spoke at hundreds of public forums' on a number of issues including foreign policy, a subject 'alien to Elijah Muhammad'.[35] So while, as McAlister suggests, the NOI offered its members an 'alternative sacred geography with Mecca as its center',[36] this 'sacred geography' functioned almost entirely on the level of the imaginary. Both 'Africa' and 'Mecca' symbolized a connection with the non-white and decolonizing world, but Elijah Muhammad's vision was an essentially parochial one much more centred on America than he liked to admit.

The section that follows suggests that Malcolm's journey to Mecca, and his post-NOI encounters with Middle East and

African politics, afforded him concrete experiences with religious and political contexts long mythologized by the NOI. Malcolm's travels opened up a worldview that enabled him to nuance the simplified tenets of the NOI, and yet this process also entailed a complication of the neat equation whereby the terms of the NOI's 'Egypt' redeem those of an 'Exodus' contaminated by a racist Judeo-Christian West. This in turn complicates Malcolm's sense that Islam is the natural religion for oppressed African Americans, and leads to an altered understanding of the relationship between religion and black political agency.

SUNNI ISLAM AND THE POLITICS OF PAN-AFRICANISM

Following his break with the NOI, Malcolm formed a new organization, the Muslim Mosque Inc., before departing to Saudi Arabia to make the hajj in April 1964 – this was in many ways the culmination of his second religious conversion. His trip to the Middle East was followed by visits to several African countries, including Egypt, and he then embarked on a much longer trip taking in a number of African states from July to November of 1964. These were not Malcolm's first experiences of the Middle East or Africa. In 1959 Malcolm had travelled to Egypt, Ghana, Sudan, Nigeria, Iran, Syria and the United Arab Republic; as ambassador for the NOI, Malcolm laid the groundwork for the pilgrimage to Mecca Muhammad was to make later that same year, which was then frequently billed as proof that the NOI had been accepted by the wider Muslim community. It is clear though that Malcolm saw something very different once he was able to look beyond the narrow lens of the NOI.

Malcolm's two religious conversions are portrayed in Spike Lee's film as dramatic moments of transformation. In so doing Lee follows and intensifies the account offered in the *Autobiography*, visually capturing both the scenes at Mecca as well as Malcolm's earlier conversion in prison, which comes about after the apparition of a dark-suited man who Malcolm later comes to believe is 'Master W.D. Fard, the Messiah, the one whom Elijah Muhammad said had appointed him – Elijah Muhammad – as His Last Messenger to the black people of North America'.[37] Critics are right to insist that Lee's film exaggerates the suddenness of Malcolm's religious trans-formations, which clearly evolved over time, but Malcolm himself encouraged this view, on several occasions comparing his role in the NOI to Paul's relationship to Christianity – a comparison that draws parallels not only between Malcolm's and Paul's evangelizing roles in establishing a new church but also between Malcolm's prison conversion and Paul's 'thunderbolt' on the road to Damascus.

In many ways the figure of Fard – of 'Asiatic' appearance in Malcolm's account – stands in for the NOI's version of an incarnate God, the archetypal opposite of the white devil who, according to NOI mythology, similarly bears a human face. Yet it becomes increasingly clear in the *Autobiography* that the object of Malcolm's worship during his NOI days was Elijah Muhammad himself. Rather than exhibiting religious devotion to an inaccessible monotheistic God, it seems that Malcolm's faith was displaced through human channels, transferred from the Messiah-figure of Fard to the father-figure of the organization's leader. When Malcolm hears his name coupled with 'death-talk' in NOI circles he realizes that it must 'have been approved of – if not actually initiated – by only one man' and he feels 'as though something in *nature* had failed, like the sun, or the stars. It was that incredible phenomenon to me – something too stupendous to conceive.'[38] That Malcolm experiences the failure of this 'God' as a personal betrayal signals the opening up of the supposedly sealed process of conversion. Malcolm's prison experience was not, it seems, the thunderbolt of the Damascene conversion.

In his discussion of Malcolm's life-writing, Paul John Eakin claims that the revelations about Muhammad and the NOI destroy 'the very premises of the autobiography' Malcolm 'had set out to write'.[39] The multiple levels of narrative voices that emerge in the *Autobiography* from differing periods of the subject's life testify to the fact that the figures of Fard and Muhammad did not set the trajectory for the rest of Malcolm's life as Jesus clearly did for Paul. For increasingly Malcolm came to realize: 'my whole life had been a chronology of *changes*.'[40] In contrast to the absolute certainty of the Pauline conversion, Malcolm affirms his own identity as one of constant flux. And where Paul's sense of Christianity arguably hinges on its oppositional identity in relation to Judaism, I suggest that Malcolm's initiation into Islam as practised in the East in some ways liberated him from the oppositional logic that arguably defined the NOI. Not only did the NOI offer what Marable describes as the 'reverse, yet mirror-like, opposition' to the liberal demand for black inclusion by advocating a 'racial-separatist vision of race relations';[41] it also exemplifies what Dawson describes as the tendency of 'the most extreme forms of black nationalism to tactically ally themselves with the most extreme elements of white racism'.[42] In similar vein

to Marcus Garvey, Malcolm himself was sent by the NOI to talk
with the Ku Klux Klan about how best to ensure the separation of
the races. It is important to note that both Garvey and Malcolm
held the belief at certain points in their careers that there was not
a great deal of difference between the Klan and white liberals, the
former simply being more honest about their investment in white
supremacy. Garvey's and Malcolm's advocacy of racial separation
was a reaction to endemic white racism as opposed to a desire to
secure a superior position within a racist hierarchy. Nonetheless, the
investment in the idea that race is destiny is complicit in the logic
of white supremacy, a complicity that Malcolm's discomfort about
his meeting with the Klan seemed to acknowledge.[43]

In Mecca Malcolm apparently embraced the opposite impulse
when he discovered an ostensible Islamic 'universalism' that
transformed his understanding of racial particularity. Experiencing
what he felt to be a subjective wholeness before the 'Oneness of
God', Malcolm for the first time 'feels like a complete human
being' and glimpses the corollary: the 'Oneness of Man'. Malcolm
insists that 'the American Negro never can be blamed for his racial
animosities – he is only reacting to four hundred years of the
conscious racism of the American whites'. Nonetheless, Malcolm's
contact with what he perceives to be 'the true religion of Islam' in
Mecca engenders in him a reassessment of the NOI's views on race
and religion, crucial to which seemed to be the eschewal of the idea
of a human deity, as well as its flipside.[44] As Louis DeCaro writes,
'one of the least noticed aspects of the legacy of the Nation of Islam
is that in calling white people "the devil," belief in the metaphysical
Satan is nullified.'[45] DeCaro suggests that Malcolm's experience
on the hajj of throwing stones at a metaphysical 'Satan' was a key
moment in his rejection of NOI race doctrines. This moment not
only affirms the otherness of the devil but also the otherness of God,
an otherness that undergirds Malcolm's evolving sense of human
equality, and which subverts the anthropomorphic projection of the
white supremacist idea of a white God as well as the black inversion.

Malcolm's now legendary 'letter from Mecca' reads:

Never have I witnessed such sincere hospitality and the
overwhelming spirit of true brotherhood as is practiced by people
of all colors and races here in this ancient Holy Land, the home
of Abraham, Muhammad and all the other prophets of the Holy
Scriptures. For the past week, I have been utterly speechless and

spellbound by the graciousness I see displayed all around me by people *of all colors*.[46]

We see here an invocation of the Abrahamic lineage that Islam shares with Christianity – Malcolm thus claims a religious identity formed by more than the space of a negation. Quite in contrast to the Oriental fantasy – that by necessity remained a fantasy – of the NOI, Malcolm is here exposed to a concrete experience of religious life in the Islamic world. Malcolm's pilgrimage to Mecca can be seen as the spiritual dimension of his increasing enthusiasm for Pan-African politics and alliances with the wider world of non-white peoples. His assumption of what he felt to be a more 'authentic' form of Islam deepened his sense that Islam was the 'answer' for oppressed African Americans. That Malcolm spent a considerable amount of his time in Africa in Cairo shows that for him, the link with Egypt as a meeting point of African and Muslim worlds was still highly significant, but it was now more than just symbolic. Where Malcolm's Muslim Mosque Inc. reflected his religious trans-formation, the Organization for Afro-American Unity (OAAU), the formation of which Malcolm announced on his return from Saudi Arabia, arguably represented the political face of the same moral vision.

Yet in spite of Malcolm's attempt to portray his new religious and political positions as largely continuous, it seems that Malcolm's embrace of Sunni Islam increasingly came into conflict with his growing interest in black diasporic politics. This potential strain is registered in a letter from Cairo dated 29 August 1964. Malcolm writes that 'being away from America is a blessing in more ways than one' because it has allowed him to view 'the whole picture'. He tells his 'brothers and sisters' back in America that 'our problem has been *internationalized*', hence the need to understand the global 'system of racist exploitation' which is 'bigger and more complicated than many of us realize'. This letter addresses Malcolm's two new organizations, speaking of a unity of purpose between and within them – they are, he claims, bound together by a *'common enemy'* – yet it is clear from the letter that Malcolm is actually attempting to deal with growing rifts in his fledgling organizations. Not only does the letter at moments address the OAAU and the MMI separately – acknowledging that his Muslim following does not necessarily share the same goals as those striving for racial justice – but he also raises the possibility that the 'small differences' emerging within and between each organization could actually destroy them.[47]

Malcolm's correspondence from both the Middle East and Africa speaks constantly of the interconnected nature of structures of oppression fostered by the Christian West, and the sense that 'only Islam could keep white Christianity at bay'.[48] But many indicators suggest that Malcolm was feeling the pressure of competing commitments issuing from a number of not necessarily compatible worldviews. The equation between Islam, Africa and black Americans was not as watertight as Malcolm's rhetoric implied. Malcolm's actual experience of Cairo then in some senses unravelled the component parts of the 'Egypt' metaphor – thus underscoring the rationale behind the isolationist practices of the NOI. It is not that the NOI shunned concrete transnational connections – as Muhammad's pilgrimage to Mecca shows, they relied on these for their public legitimacy – but its highly selective and simplistic rendering of these connections allowed the organization to overlook the contradictions that Malcolm was to confront head on in his later years.

The NOI's reverence for the powerful symbol of anti-colonial nationalism, Egypt's Gamal Abdel Nasser, is a case in point. As C. Eric Lincoln explains in his 1961 study of the NOI, *The Black Muslims in America*, Nasser's portrait 'graces the walls of many Muslim homes and temples'.[49] McAlister describes Nasser as one of the most prominent of a group of anti-colonial figures who 'represented an emotionally explosive convergence of anticolonial defiance and a global racial consciousness'.[50] Nasser's idea of the three overlapping 'circles' of Arabia, Africa and Islam – as outlined in his 1955 publication, *Egypt's Liberation: The Philosophy of the Revolution* – appears to be central to the NOI's spiritual reclamation of the Egypt trope. Yet it is hard not to conclude that this seductive mythology was better able to survive via the avoidance of substantive contact with the complex relationship between politics and religion in the Middle East and Africa.

As Lincoln recounts, Muhammad made a show of the NOI's identification with Nasser and the emerging non-aligned movement – that Nasser cultivated as an alternative to the Cold War binary of allegiance either to the Soviet Union or to the United States – when he sent a telegram to Egypt's president in January 1958, who was at that time hosting the African-Asian conference. Muhammad wrote, '*your long lost Muslim Brothers here in America pray that Allah's divine presence will be felt at this historic African-Asian Conference, and give unity to our efforts for peace and brotherhood.*'[51] Ever the astute leader seeking to bridge Pan-Arab and Pan-African sentiments, Nasser responded in kind: he thanked the '*leader, teacher and spiritual head of the Nation of Islam in the West*' for the message and sent his best wishes '*to our brothers of Africa and Asia living in the West*'.[52] Yet while Nasser's position as the only nominally 'Muslim' leader within the non-aligned movement afforded him great power, his socialist politics of Arab nationalism was largely a secular affair. Muhammad's telegram and Nasser's response maintain the fiction of this theological-political alliance in part because unlike the immigrant Muslim groups denouncing the NOI as un-Islamic in America, Nasser was likely to be less concerned with the organization's theological oddities; in turn, Muhammad was likely to be less concerned with – and may have been wholly ignorant of – the fact of Nasser's political repression of Muslim groups in Egypt itself.

In contrast, Malcolm X's second conversion was overseen by Saudi Muslim missionaries actively engaged in resisting Nasser's brand of Arab populism – in the name of Islam. Curtis claims that Malcolm, in seeking the guidance of Mahmoud Youssef Shawarbi, an Egyptian apparently out of favour with Nasser's regime, 'unknowingly thrust himself into the center' of 'new Saudi-financed missionary activity'.[53] Malcolm thus came under the influence of a group of Pan-Islamists whose politics did not neatly dovetail with Pan-Arab nationalism, Pan-Africanism, or even anti-colonial politics. These tensions register in Malcolm's thinking as his religious and political outlooks undergo something of a bifurcation. As Curtis recounts, in September 1964, Said Ramadan – himself an Egyptian member of the Muslim Brotherhood, a group forcefully repressed in Nasser's Egypt – challenged Malcolm's continued focus on black politics by asking 'how could a man of your spirit, intellect, and worldwide outlook fail to see in Islam' a message that strikes 'at the very root' of 'racial discrimination?'[54] Malcolm rejected the advice from Sunni advisers like Ramadan to devote himself wholly to Islam and trust the work of racial justice to a future Islamic state; despite his sense that 'Islam removes the race problem', his increasing commitment to a largely secular Pan-African politics tells a different story. Arguably then, the bridging symbol of 'Egypt' unravels as Malcolm channels the affairs of blacks and Muslims through two distinct bodies, the religious MMI and secular OAAU.

Curtis suggests that Malcolm's trip to Nigeria in May 1964 – shortly after his Mecca experience – 'might be fruitfully seen as yet a third conversion'.[55] Malcolm's descriptions of Africa are bathed in a similar glow to that which characterizes his account of Mecca; just as Mecca bequeaths him the new name El-Hajj Malik-

El-Shabazz, he is named by students in Nigeria 'Omowale' – 'the child has come home'.[56] According to Curtis, the fact that these two new identities remain distinct – and sometimes conflicting – engenders for Malcolm a new kind of double consciousness. Thus where the NOI enabled Malcolm to resolve the tension between his black identity and American Christianity – by substituting the former, the 'true religion of the black man', for the latter – arguably his post-NOI evolution re-introduces this cleavage by failing to completely reconcile Islam to the imperatives of black politics.

Curtis' suggestion that Malcolm in effect ceded theological authority to Sunni missionaries dovetails with Sherman Jackson's account of the larger tensions between what he sees as black and postcolonial religion. Jackson's *Islam and the Blackamerican* (2005) concerns itself with the transference of authority from the NOI to the Sunni tradition that occurred within black American Islam in the mid to late 1960s and 1970s. In his eventual acceptance of what Jackson characterizes as the 'super-tradition of historical Islam' – one that issues from the Muslim world and is centred on the Middle East – Malcolm X anticipates this trend.

According to Jackson, these new 'foreign' identifications placed black Americans at a distance from their own experiences, for their own realities 'could not be treated directly but only analogously on the basis of conclusions reached in contemplation of the situation in the Muslim world'. In contrast to the NOI, Muslim immigrants were focused on the oppression of Muslims in the Muslim world – over and above the oppression of blacks, Muslims or otherwise, in America. This derived from the sense that 'the *history* of the modern Muslim world' was seen by Sunni communities to 'have a greater claim to be the proper object of Muslim religious thought and effort'.[57] Thus while black Americans, according to Jackson, identified with what he calls 'Immigrant Islam' in part because they saw in its critical posture towards the West a mirror of their own critique of America, this actually conceals a clash between two religious worldviews grounded in distinct histories. Jackson writes:

> Like Black Religion, Post-Colonial Religion is not revealed but a product of history. At its core lies not so much a body of texts or interpretive tradition as does a particular historical *experience* from which its followers desperately seek redemption.[58]

For Jackson 'Black Religion' encapsulates not all but rather the distinctly politicized variants of African American religious expression and practice: 'Black Religion' encapsulates the idea that black Americans 'are quintessentially a "protest people"'.[59] While since slavery, 'Black Religion' has most often manifested itself in a Christian register, what the NOI did so successfully was insist that only through Islam could blacks express themselves authentically. Yet as I have argued, in the eyes of many Sunni Muslims, including – towards the end of his life – Malcolm X, the NOI did not embody an 'authentic' expression of Islam itself. This was in part precisely because it was so transfixed on a particularistic account of 'Black Religion', rather than a supposedly 'universalist' understanding of Islam – an account that would lead early commentators on the NOI like Lincoln to question whether the organization represented 'legitimate religion' at all.[60] Jackson turns this idea on its head; while he critiques what he sees as the particularistic leanings of 'Black Religion', he also argues that by investing in the notion that what was 'truly Islamic' derived from the Middle East and not America, black American Sunni Muslims gave up the right to interpret their own religious and political realities. In this way they submitted to a false universal and an essentialist vision of 'historical Islam' – and thus to another kind of domination. Here we come full circle, from the idea that Islam is 'the true religion of the black man', to the sense that the experience of Islam, like that of white Christianity, is one which potentially devalues the experience of African Americans.

I suggest though that in Malcolm's case the attempt to negotiate these two potentially competing theological-political traditions opens up some productive tensions, tensions that point in a rather different direction to Jackson's negative appraisal. It seems that Curtis is right in his assessment that Malcolm X's second conversion engendered a conflict between two notions of authenticity – one centred on his racial identity, the other on his religious identity. As Malcolm announced to a crowd in Cairo:

> My fight is two-fold, my burden is double, my responsibili-
> ties multiple ... material as well as spiritual, political as well as
> religious, racial as well as non-racial ... I will never hesitate to let
> the entire world know the hell my people suffer from America's
> deceit and her hypocrisy, as well as her oppression.[61]

While Curtis' comparison of this split to double consciousness is convincing, his conclusion seems to be that Malcolm's religious and political identities cease to have a meaningful relationship with one another. In contrast, Du Bois' theory of African American doubleness posits constant interaction between the two competing identifications, and I suggest that this is also the case with Malcolm's conflicting affiliations. Malcolm's later rhetoric links politics and religion while refusing to collapse the one into the other; for he consistently refused the call of either his Sunni or Pan-African advisers that he should focus solely on Islam or black politics. In so doing he partially deconstructs both Sunni Islam and Pan-Africanism as exclusive sites of authority, in turn confirming that his 'people' are Muslims in the Middle East and Africans in Africa, but primarily they are black Americans in the United States.

Malcolm's post-NOI experiences do not in any way reconcile him to America, Christianity, or indeed the political platform of the Civil Rights movement. And he maintained that progressive, anti-racist whites should organize among themselves to enable independent black organizing for black interests, though he did at this stage decide that whites could play a supporting role from the outside. And Malcolm's trips abroad, paradoxically, seem to confirm for him that his principal work lay in the United States and that while he himself remained a Muslim, he would now be willing to work with black Christians. His travels thus seemed to heighten his sense, articulated in April 1964, that the best way to avoid arguments was to 'put your religion at home, in the closet, keep it between you and your God. Because if it hasn't done anything more for you than it has, you need to forget it anyway.'[62] Religion was clearly pivotal in Malcolm's life and politics and so the secular thrust of this statement should be treated with caution. It does though seem that by the end of his life Malcolm, unlike King, was no longer searching for a religious ground for political action. This movement was then much more profound than the switching of religious allegiance from the NOI to Sunni Islam. The absolute certainty which grounded Malcolm's earlier vision was supplanted by an understanding of God that could no longer provide sanction to his political beliefs and actions. Possibly to an even greater extent than King, whose rewriting of Exodus politics incorporated the Judaic ban on images of God in order to undermine the religious certainties of white racists, Malcolm's latter politics was cast as provisional and constantly open to what is other.

BLACK EGYPT AND THE EXORCISM OF COLONIALISM

This chapter has argued that Malcolm X's trajectory challenged what Jackson describes as the 'presumed affinity between Islam, blackness, and oppression',[63] indicating that invocations of a black Egypt do not straightforwardly 'redeem' the problematic possibilities of the Judeo-Christian Exodus narrative, and can in some guises replicate them. While King sought to purge his appropriation of the Exodus narrative of its contamination by the logic of white supremacy – particularly in its anticipation of a discourse of the 'damned' and the 'saved' – Malcolm similarly nuanced the NOI's appropriation of 'Egypt', which had not fully broken away from the racist logic it was reacting to. This section broadens the discussion to the wider contexts of the 1960s that Malcolm's legacy played such a large role in shaping, as well as casting an eye back to the roots of black nationalism. It assesses the extent to which the identification of a black Egypt provided an alternative narrative of decolonization to that modelled on the Exodus narrative.

The NOI itself adopted a highly disciplined and hierarchical structure that in some ways supports the view of later critics of Afrocentrism that the valorization of ancient Egypt can be related to the privileging of elitist and authoritarian modes of organization. As seen in Chapter 1, Wilson Jeremiah Moses critiques 'Egyptocentrism' (though not Afrocentrism as a whole) on the grounds that it romanticizes 'pharaonic dominion',[64] while Paul Gilroy, writing in 1993, states that 'blacks today appear to identify far more readily with the glamorous pharaohs than with the abject plight of those they held in bondage'.[65] Both thus conflate identifications with ancient Egypt with a will to power. In contrast, Melani McAlister uses the Egypt identification as shorthand for the emergence in the 1960s of what she sees as 'a powerful historical alliance' between 'black Islam, Arab nationalism, and African American radicalism'.[66] While McAlister notes tendencies to the contrary, her account is focused on the progressive potentialities of the Egypt identification, in particular its role in enabling a critique of colonialism. McAlister claims that Gilroy 'refuses to see black identifications with the Arab world as anything other than a failure to identify sufficiently with Jewish history';[67] a history that, McAlister argues, is erroneously conflated by Gilroy with the experience of 'suffering and slavery'. McAlister overlooks the fact that Gilroy's account is dealing with a different historical moment and is not considering the difference between Exodus and Egypt as the difference between black identifications with Jews or with Arabs. The difference Gilroy identifies is black identification with Jews or more exclusive identifications with disaporic blacks only. Yet McAlister's account is a useful corrective to Gilroy's in that it guards against anachronistic readings that view identifications with Egypt solely through the prism of 1980s and 1990s Afrocentrism. I suggest that these very different interpretations of the Exodus and Egypt identifications – turning on their respective relationships to mastery and slavery – interestingly mirror the ways in which the mobilization of these allegorical entities often simplifies much more complex realities. Taken together, they illustrate that the two tropes are inescapably linked to one another and so cannot be appropriated as polar opposites.

McAlister's *Epic Encounters* (2005) is an excellent study of US cultural encounters with the Middle East, and her chapter on African American cultural politics (covering the period 1955–72), though it does not focus on Malcolm X explicitly, has formed a crucial point of dialogue for the wider arguments of this chapter. McAlister's account opens by highlighting the 1956 Suez crisis – when Nasser nationalized the Suez canal in an act of defiance against both Israel and the old colonial powers, which then invaded – as a key moment in the transition, touched on in the previous chapter, which saw large numbers of African American activists switch their Middle East identification from the Israelis to the Palestinians. As McAlister recounts, in 1956, against the backdrop of Suez, Martin Luther King found himself in something of a metaphorical contradiction in speaking of 'the Egypt of colonialism and imperialism' and was careful to distinguish contemporary from pharaonic Egypt.[68] And as Chapter 2 outlined, at this same moment Du Bois tempered his enthusiasm for Zionism by casting Israel as the pawn of western nations 'who steal the Negros' land'. In the instance of Suez the US sided with Egypt against the old imperial powers in a show of what Charles Hilliard termed 'benevolent supremacy', so it was not until 1967 that black anti-colonial sentiments could unite with a critique of US foreign policy that seemed to increasingly champion Israel.[69] This switch from, as it were, 'Exodus' to 'Egypt' – in both literal and metaphorical terms – had implications not only for black American relations with American Jews but also for the ways in which US blacks defined their own oppression in America, which, by the late 1960s, was being articulated by Black Power advocates via the theory of internal colonization.

This was another instance in which Malcolm X – this time as a NOI minister – anticipated trends among black American activists. In his 1961 book, Lincoln quotes an interview in which Malcolm told him: 'Jews, with the help of Christians in America and Europe, drove our Muslim brothers (i.e., the Arabs) out of their homeland, where they had been settled for centuries, and took over the land for themselves. This every Muslim resents.' We can assume that this interview took place after Suez but well before the 1967 war. In addition, Malcolm adds that 'in America, the Jews sap the very life-blood of the so-called Negroes to maintain the state of Israel, its armies and its continued aggression against our brothers in the East. This every Black Man resents.'[70] As lead spokesperson for the NOI, Malcolm articulates a link between Palestinians and African Americans both oppressed by America and by Jews. The anti-Semitism that marked much NOI ideology and consequently Malcolm's earlier rhetoric is not explicit in later echoes of this link by Black Power activists in the late 1960s – most of whom were much more careful to distinguish anti-Zionism from anti-Semitism. But Malcolm here raises the idea that African Americans are themselves internally colonized within the US, a move that captures the black nationalist position of seeking to interrupt the repressive powers of the 'state' via a mobilization of 'nation'. Such a move facilitated the comparison between African Americans and Palestinians – one that was perhaps most forcefully articulated by Stokely Carmichael (also known as Kwame Ture) in his essay, 'The Black American and Palestinian Revolutions', which was originally presented as an address to the Organization of Arab Students (OAS) in 1968.[71]

Carmichael was the first to articulate the 'Black Power' slogan as the leader of the Student Non-Violent Coordinating Committee (SNCC) in 1966, during a moment at which the limits of white liberal commitments to the black struggle were increasingly apparent. By 1968, while some Black Power organizations continued to work with white Americans, including American Jews, many were suspicious of the motives behind white involvement and focused instead on building all-black alliances. That many American Jews were openly supportive of Israel's victory in the 1967 war contributed to the demise of leftist alliances between blacks and Jews that had existed in the US since the turn of the century. Carmichael was to claim in this 1968 essay that 'a few years ago I was for the Jewish people of Israel',[72] and he charts the path whereby black Americans came to instead identify with the displaced Palestinian Arabs as fellow non-white victims of colonial oppression. McAlister's academic account follows a similar logic, claiming that while 'suffering and slavery' had historically served as a potent link between blacks and Jews, it gave way to a situation in which 'Jews have come to be identified less by their suffering than by their power, both in Israel and in the United States'.[73] Yet this analysis overlooks the fact that the black nationalist critique of the Civil Rights movement – as exemplified by a range of often diverse nationalist individuals and organizations, from the NOI to the Black Panther Party – was a rejection of what was perceived as a weak and passive movement. 'Black Power' was in many ways a call to reject an identity defined by the memory of 'suffering and slavery'. This is precisely what the Jews in Israel had done. This is not to invalidate the colonial critique of Israel – which since 1967 has carried considerable moral force – but rather to show that the black nationalist rejection of Zionism at this particular historical juncture did entail certain ironies.

Carmichael goes on to dismiss the Zionist claim that Palestine is 'the motherland, the homeland of the Jews' as imperialist propaganda. Yet he then directly compares the Jewish attachment to Israel with black American attachments to Egypt. The Jews, he writes,

> established a state in 1948 and yet they feel such a strong tie with it. There is no difference in black people [from the US] going to fight for and defend Egypt. Egypt is in Africa and Africa is our homeland. The oldest civilization in the world comes from Egypt. We must feel we are part of it. There are many of us who are slowly beginning to prepare for that propaganda and prepare for the actual fight. We intend to fight imperialism wherever it is, in the United States or in our homeland.[74]

The fight then for Carmichael is undeniably against what was perceived as racist imperialism. The problem of Europe's others – the Jews – had paradoxically been 'resolved', in Carmichael's eyes, by the assumption of the guise of a European settler state. But the Zionist aspiration is here without doubt brought into comparison – and competition – with Pan-Africanist sentiments among US blacks. Here again, Carmichael echoes Malcolm, who in a letter from Ghana in May 1964 compared his burgeoning Pan-Africanism to the diasporic consciousness that unites 'world Jewry'.[75] As McAlister points out, Malcolm's 'grudging respect' for Jewish nationalism 'did not translate into emotional identification';[76] and I suggest that this points to a much more profound disarticulation of the black historical and religious identification with Jews than an uncomplicated rejection of Israel on account of its colonial project in Palestine.

Carmichael underlines the centrality of race in the conflict when he claims 'colonization comes into play when there are people of a different race oppressing another race'.[77] He then proceeds to project onto the Middle East conflict the black/white binary that is the most basic element of US race relations. Israeli Jews are allied with the forces of white supremacy in a reflection of the 'whitening' of Jews in post-war America, while the Arab identity of Palestinians is translated onto the opposite side of America's racial divide. In turn Carmichael implies that Palestinian political aspirations are identical to those of Egypt on the grounds of a shared – Arab – ethnicity. In so doing Carmichael overlooks the fact that prior to 1967, Egypt controlled Gaza as an occupying power, and Nasser did not allow the Palestinians living there any real degree of self-government. In fact, Carmichael's analysis was more relevant for the Jews originating from Arab countries who made up just over 50 per cent of the Israeli population until the Russian immigration of the 1990s. Directly inspired by the Black Power movement in the US, groups of 'Eastern' Jews, or 'Misrahim', formed the Israeli Black Panthers in 1971, to fight discrimination within an Ashkenazi-dominated Israel.[78] Carmichael's essay is in many ways prophetic in its emphasis on Palestinian self-determination, support for which unites many otherwise diverse groups of Arab people, if not Arab states, today. But his mobilization of both a literal and mythological black Egypt against Israel failed to realistically capture the nuances of 1967.

The mobilization of the Egypt trope by revolutionary nationalists like Carmichael – who attempted to pick up where Malcolm left off – involved a somewhat simplified black/white binary that arguably played a role in assessments of power differentials in the Middle East. Nonetheless, Carmichael's mobilization of Egypt represents a largely progressive attempt to identify with the oppressed. The proto-cultural nationalists that anticipated Malcolm's NOI days were much more ambiguous about their opposition to the logic of domination. Garvey is the most famous example. Garvey himself championed Zionism so long as it did not conflict with black interests – when in 1939 the British government announced that it would consider the settlement of Jewish refugees in its South American colony of Guiana, Garvey objected on the grounds that this was 'Negro country'.[79] While a critique of white supremacist power was undoubtedly central to the Garveyite movement, Garvey was himself arguably more attracted by the aesthetics of state power than identifications with the oppressed. As Gilroy argues, Garvey was seduced by 'the martial technologies of racial becoming – drill, uniforms, medals, titles, massed display' and defined his brand of nationalism by claiming 'we were the first Fascists'.[80] In 1974, Garvey's oldest son Marcus Garvey Jr wrote a tribute to his father:

> African National Socialism postulates that the children of the Black God of Africa have a date with destiny. We shall recreate the glories of ancient Egypt, Ethiopia and Nubia. It is natural that the children of mother Africa scattered in the great diaspora will cleave together once more. It seems certain that the world will one day be faced with the black cry for an African 'Anschluss' and the resolute demand for African 'Lebensraum.'[81]

This invocation of 'lebensraum' suggests not just the unification but the colonization of African living space under strong leadership. Such a vision – if we bracket the identification with the Nazis that this statement clearly entails – contains echoes of the nineteenth-century proto-black nationalists Edward Wilmot Blyden and Martin Delany, who began their careers in Liberian and Sierre Leone politics as Christian missionaries, and who hoped to 'raise the race' by 'civilizing' the natives.[82] While all of these figures have complex legacies and their ideas evolved over time, they all to an extent internalized some of the logic of western modes of domination that enabled white supremacy. This logic has been mirrored by some later Afrocentrists whose 'search for a glorious African past' has often accepted 'dominant European notions of what that past should look like'. In particular, as E. Frances White suggests, 'the process of elevating Egypt' has often meant the acceptance of the idea that 'the majority of Africans who lived in stateless societies' were 'uncivilized and even savage primitives'.[83] In this sense the symbol of ancient Egypt is potentially part of a hierarchical logic comparable to the notion of divine election central to the Exodus text, an idea that was taken to its most brutal extreme by the Nazis.

The 'desire for a simpler world premised on racial sameness and racial similarities'[84] is a desire that animates the more polemical variants of Afrocentrism that emerged in the 1980s. Indeed, quite apart from embracing links with Islam and Arab nationalism, Islam emerges in the Afrocentric writing of Molefi Kete Asante as an alien and slave-trading religion on a par with Christianity.[85] This is the context for Asante's embrace of 'Malcolm X as cultural hero' which all but ignores his Muslim identity.[86] In this view 'black Egypt' is not a bridging symbol – as it arguably was for the NOI – but rather one that competes with an Arab and Islamic Egypt, in much the same way that the black Zion has so often competed with the Jewish one in black nationalist thought.

As Gilroy notes, Egypt has been an important touchstone for the black imagination of modernity. Du Bois had long been an enthusiastic advocate of the idea that ancient Egypt should be seen as a point of origin for black identity, and this idea received a boost in the 1950s when African historiography began to circulate Cheikh Anta Diop's thesis that the origins of African and European culture lay in Egypt and that 'ancient Egyptian and Pharaonic civilization was a Negro civilization'.[87] But just as Exodus is a tale of the excesses of group identity politics as much as it is a story of liberation, the imagination of a specifically pharaonic Egypt, while providing a powerful counterpoint to the myth of western modernity, does not always offer a contradiction of state power. This is of course a wider risk posed by the crucial call for power that 1960s black nationalists articulated, and the fact that, as Lubiano argues, the black nationalist concern with filling the void left by the state in some cases reinscribes some of the tendencies it ostensibly seeks to resist. The Israeli political situation is a poignant example of the fate of nationalist movements that achieve state power. The progressive potential of US black nationalism seems to lie precisely in its ability to offer an alternative vision to the state, as Malcolm did in his last year.

Rather than succumbing to amnesia about the experience of suffering and slavery that nonetheless acts as a subterranean ground for political legitimacy – a trend that can be found in the most crude forms of Afrocentrism – Malcolm sought to mobilize what Michael Hanchard describes as 'black memory' against 'state memory'.[88] For Malcolm, the experience of suffering in the US is not the sum of black American memory. This is precisely why he pursued religious and political activities beyond America, as well as seeking to take crimes of the United States before the United Nations. For Malcolm the African American experience in part transcends the American state. As this chapter has argued, Malcolm's latter agenda involved a complicated combination of Islamic religious identification, Pan-African politics and African American identity politics, a combination that did not match the seamless interlinking of national, religious – and arguably racial – identity that informs the American civil religion. In this sense Malcolm's reclamation of 'Egypt' as an alternative to the Judeo-Christian 'Exodus' too closely associated with a racist West was not a straightforward redemption of Christianity by Islam, America by Africa, white by black. By the end of his life it represented a hybrid and provisional trope that resisted essentializing cultures or peoples. 'Egypt' was thus appropriated as part of the logic of decolonization but it was not the full story.

No proto-black nationalist illustrates the interlinked legacies of Egypt and Exodus better than Edward Wilmot Blyden. While Blyden early on in his career subscribed to condescending views of African natives, his vision is not one that sought to collapse the variety of his experience into a single entity. Blyden grew up in St Thomas, a Danish colony in the Caribbean, in a predominantly Jewish community. There he witnessed – with 'awe and reverence' – the activities of the local synagogue, and he subsequently came to view the 'Jewish Question' as 'the question of questions', one that might be solved via 'that marvellous movement called Zionism'. As noted earlier in this chapter, while himself a Christian, Blyden regarded Islam as possibly the best religious vehicle for black self-determination. On his first sight of the Pyramids, Blyden felt that 'the blood seemed to flow faster through my veins. I seemed to hear the echo of those illustrious Africans. I seemed to feel the impulse of those stirring characters who sent civilisation to Greece ...' He thus identified intimately with the three Abrahamic religions as well as laying an important foundation for the Pan-African idea. His experience of the Pyramids – which, he imagines, were 'built before the tribes of man had been so generally scattered ... but built by that branch of the descendants of Noah, the enterprising sons of Ham, from which I descended' – captures the images of both mastery and slavery, glimpsing an as yet to be realized universal vision of humanity as well as one defined by racial particularity. While Malcolm X was not the cosmopolitan that Blyden was, his experiences at Mecca and in the Middle East more generally, alongside his travels in Africa, read as distant echoes of Blyden's irreducible vision.[89]

CONCLUSION: MALCOLM AFTER 9/11

The attacks on New York and Washington DC on 11 September 2001 ushered in a period in global politics that decisively crowded out complex visions of the world that fail to show up in the clear lines of black and white. The image of the crumbling twin towers strengthened the already decisive link between Islam and violence in the popular western imagination.[90] The East/West binary seemed to have found new expression in the post-Cold War era, and displays of American patriotism – expressed within the terms of exceptionalist discourse – ostensibly underscored a nation united in mourning and against a common enemy. The events of 9/11 not only mobilized the American civil religion. In many ways the very reference to 9/11 has become a ritual of the civil religion itself.[91] Within this context the March 2008 revelation that Reverend Jeremiah Wright, at that time Obama's pastor, had claimed that 9/11 was a case of 'chickens coming home to roost' – a self-conscious echo of Malcolm's reaction to the assassination of President Kennedy – was branded treasonous by most sections of the US media. While the critique of US foreign policy that Wright's comment entailed can be viewed within the tradition of the black jeremiad and thus read as the highest form of patriotism, the reductive process of media spin encouraged the view that Obama was associated with an anti-American church – one that recalls the threatening popular image of Malcolm X, whose mobilization of Islam represented an explicit challenge to the American political establishment.

The racist idea that there might be some incongruity between 'blackness' and 'Americanness' that circulated during the Wright controversy – and indeed throughout Obama's campaign and into his presidency – was exacerbated by an unwillingness to understand the fact that the experience of American racism makes black Americans more likely to adopt critical positions towards the American state. Data that has attempted to measure the extent to which African Americans identified with post-9/11 US patriotism has varied. While initially anecdotal evidence seemed to suggest that black Americans were just as – if not more – vocal in their condemnations of the attacks,[92] other evidence has suggested that African Americans are more likely than their white American counterparts to point to the provocations of US foreign policy as partial explanation for anti-American sentiment in the Muslim world. As a report on this notes, 'many of the black students who participated in our focus groups felt that American expressions of freedom, equality, and democracy were hypocritical given the country's history of slavery, genocide, colonialism, exploitation and discrimination'.[93] This suggests a possible identification with those on the rough end of US foreign policy and, in turn, a challenge to the rigid binary between the West and the rest. Hamid Dabashi's *Islamic Liberation Theology: Resisting the Empire* (2008) claims Malcolm X's legacy as a symbol of just this transgression – representative of the 'wretched of the earth' both in the US and elsewhere, Dabashi claims that Malcolm's memory bridges the fictional division that 9/11 consolidated.[94]

Well before Wright's comment on 9/11 made the headlines and threatened to thwart Obama's bid for the presidential nomination, another African American figure also profoundly influenced by Malcolm X publicly made a very similar point. Amiri Baraka's poem 'Somebody Blew Up America', penned in October 2001, similarly presents the attacks as the uncanny effect of the 'blowback' of US imperial power. The poem's point of departure is the relationship between what Baraka poses as international and domestic terrorism. The legacies of black slavery and the genocide of Native Americans form the backdrop to a racialized master narrative exposed and condemned by Baraka's incantatory and accusatory repetition of the pronoun 'Who?'

> Who made Bush president
> Who believe the confederate flag need to be flying
> Who talk about democracy and be lying
> WHO/ WHO/ WHOWHO/

Baraka's poem sparked controversy largely on account of the following lines:

> Who knew the World Trade Center was gonna get bombed
> Who told 4000 Israeli workers at the Twin Towers
>   To stay home that day
> Why did Sharon stay away   ?[95]

His poem condemned by the Anti-Defamation League (ADL) as evidence of an anti-Semitic conspiracy theory, Baraka refused to apologize – or heed the call to resign his position as New Jersey state poet laureate, a stance which led to the dissolution of the post of poet laureate itself. Baraka defended himself by claiming that his poem is asking 'who is responsible for this horrible crime and WHY? It is a poem that aims to probe and disturb, but there is not the slightest evidence of Anti-Semitism, as anyone who reads it without some insidious bias would have to agree.'[96] William Harris and Aldon Nielson's interpretation of the poem supports Baraka's claim by stating that the rhetorical complexity of the poem has been overlooked; they claim that 'the interrogating litany of *Who's*' raises 'the question of the status of the utterance, by throwing into question the political and rhetorical ground on which the saying takes place'.[97] As one early line in the poem reads, 'They say (who say? Who do the saying'. A number of literary critics have suggested that while provocative, Baraka's poem is not the one-dimensional anti-Semitic caricature that ADL's critique implies.

Baraka in turn accused ADL of equating anti-Zionism with anti-Semitism, and asserts that this conflation is in fact at the root of ADL's identification of 'Black Anti-Semitism' which, Baraka claims, only became a problem for ADL when Stokely Carmichael and SNCC began to speak out against Israel. It is possible that ADL was partly motivated by Baraka's much earlier and explicitly anti-Semitic statements that he himself admitted and retracted in his 1980 'Confessions of a former Anti-Semite'.

The literary qualities of 'Somebody Blew Up America' do seem to have been overlooked by ADL, which takes the poem at face value. And some of the supposedly offensive statements made by Baraka that ADL lists on its website simply accuse Israel of imperialism on a par with the United States – there is no sense that Jews in particular are being singled out for attack. More problematically, a number of Baraka's statements on his poem call into question the legitimacy of Jewish nationalism. This is an ironic move for a figure so long associated with black nationalism, and one seemingly made by overlooking Jewish claims to be an ethnic and national grouping, and instead treating the designation 'Jewish' as a religious category only. This neither reflects the self-understanding of many Jews nor the motivation behind anti-Semitism – which clearly entails not just religious hatred but race hatred too.

In writing 'Somebody Blew Up America', Baraka provocatively reawakens, deconstructs, and to a certain extent re-invests a string of oppositions between people of colour and the American state, the West and Islam, blacks and Jews. This not only reawakened the spectre of 1960s black radicalism, and particularly Malcolm X as a one-dimensional embodiment of anti-American anger. It also raised more recent memories of the vexed relations between black and Jews, which arguably reached a low point in the 1990s. As outlined in Chapter 1, alongside the perception of anti-black racism among some American Jews, some of the more polemical advocates of Afrocentrism contributed to the perception of anti-Semitism among some black Americans, a perception that is also associated with the ascendancy of Louis Farrakhan. Farrakhan's Nation of Islam – which was formed in 1978 following the death of Elijah Muhammad in 1975 and the migration of many of the organization's members to Sunni Islam – has never commanded huge numbers, but his status as a populist leader among African Americans, despite the ambivalence that he has provoked in black and white Americans, was unparalleled throughout the 1990s and was most vividly on display during his Million Man March in 1995.[98] While Farrakhan's support – much of which came from outside the NOI – was largely based on the fact that he was filling a void in black leadership and striking a chord particularly among young black men with his discourse on the restoration of black male authority,[99] in the press it was Farrakhan's anti-Semitism which drew the most sensationalist headlines. While some of the more well-known anti-Jewish comments made by Farrakhan have been subject to considerable distortions, his rhetoric testifies to an investment in Jewish conspiracy theories. In 1991 the NOI published *The Secret Relationship Between Blacks and Jews*, a report that, on the basis of a series of scholarly distortions, claims that Jews played a disproportionate role in the African slave trade; in addition, according to Farrakhan, 75 per cent of the Jews in the antebellum South owned slaves.[100] During this time the media circulated the idea that Farrakhan is a 'black Hitler' – a designation that was resurrected during Obama's campaign – and this seemed to be a largely hysterical reaction to an atmosphere that Farrakhan's anti-Semitism nonetheless played a part in creating.

What was not re-circulated during Obama's campaign was the fact that within black nationalist circles, Farrakhan's authority has been widely questioned. In the 1990s, Farrakhan came under fire from a number of prominent Afrocentrists for apparently allowing his Muslim loyalties to eclipse his concern for Africa and Africans. Not only did Farrakhan refuse to allow a representative from the International Coalition Against Chattel Slavery to speak for Africans enslaved in the Sudan at the Million Man March; he also held a friendly meeting with Sudan's Omar al-Bashir, the man arguably responsible for the slave trade in Sudan.[101] Events in the Sudan have bolstered the assertion of some Afrocentrists that Islam, in both its historical and contemporary manifestations, is a slave-trading religion incompatible with black nationalism. In 2009 the International Criminal Court (ICC) issued an arrest warrant for Omar al-Bashir on charges of war crimes and crimes against humanity in Darfur. Though the Court did not initially charge him with genocide, an appeals panel resurrected the case against him and in July 2010 the ICC issued a warrant charging Bashir with three counts of genocide against non-Arab populations in Darfur. The perception that his government has sponsored attacks specifically targeted at black Africans – now supported by the ICC – is an issue that has for a number of years galvanized African American activists.

This debate within black nationalist circles is forwarded merely to illustrate that the relationships between black Americans, Africa and Islam are no more continuous today than they were for Malcolm X during the 1960s. The mobilization of post-9/11 Islamophobia and anti-black racism during Obama's campaign created a one-dimensional caricature of a homogeneous black nationalism that held no real coherence. By the time of Obama's inauguration he had been forced to largely renounce the complicated black nationalist ideology that undoubtedly did partly inform his former church and his outlook as a community organizer in the predominantly black areas of Chicago's South Side. As Dianne Feinstein opened the inaugural ceremony she made a point of distinguishing the legacy of the Civil Rights movement from that of the black nationalist ideologies that followed in its wake. She said:

> Those who doubt the supremacy of the ballot over the bullet can never diminish the power engendered by non-violent struggles for justice and equality, like the one that made this day possible. No triumph tainted by brutality could ever match the sweet victory of this hour and what it means to those who marched and died to make it a reality.

In his famous 1964 'The Ballot or the Bullet' speech Malcolm did not advocate violence, contrary to his popular caricature, but rather pointed up the limits of an electoral system for African Americans in which the party that claimed to be the 'friend' of Civil Rights, the Democrats, was simultaneously in the position of appeasing its racist southern wing. Malcolm in this speech called for a 'broader interpretation' of the 'civil-rights struggle' which included acknowledging the fact that 'the political philosophy of black nationalism' had in fact penetrated the black Christian church, along with Civil Rights institutions like SNCC, CORE (Congress of Racial Equality) and even the NAACP (National Association for the Advancement of Colored People). In contrast to the sentiments of Obama's critics who sought to associate him with a monolithic black nationalism, or Feinstein's speech which seeks to place his election squarely within the narrative of the Civil Rights movement purged of any elements that advocated violence in self-defence, Malcolm's last year sought to build bridges between different black nationalist orientations and to bridge the supposed divide between black nationalist and Civil Rights approaches. As Dabashi's account of Malcolm shows, Malcolm's literal and philosophical desire to traverse the distance between East and West enables an account of opposition to American state power that transcends the mutually reinforcing positions of what Dabashi characterizes as the illegitimate violence perpetuated by both the Bush administration and Al Qaeda.

Dabashi's post-9/11 appropriation of Malcolm as a 'Muslim revolutionary' overplays the role of Islam in Malcolm's latter politics, but he does point to the illuminating coincidence that in the same year that Malcolm was introduced to Islam in prison, the Egyptian Sayyid Qutb – whose view of America would have a lasting impact on the development of Islamist ideology in the decades preceding 9/11 – arrived in the US.[102] During his stay in the US Qutb formed his now well-known views on American decadence; on his return to Egypt Qutb joined the Muslim Brotherhood and formulated a critique of the West that would violently return to the US in September 2001. For Dabashi these developments represent the exhaustion within Islamist ideology of what was a genuine campaign of resistance against European colonialism and US imperialism that emerged in the nineteenth century. In contrast to those who have attempted to rescue Islam in the aftermath of 9/11 by confining its role to the private sphere, Dabashi claims Islam as a religion of protest to which the triumphalist imagery of 9/11 could not do justice.[103] Malcolm's resistance to 'America', on the other hand, offered something far more complex than its mirror image, and so did not subvert itself in this way. While initially drawn to the NOI which, like some variants of Islamist ideology, drew much of its energy from an inverse relationship to American ideology, Malcolm's later phase accumulated the myriad influences he was exposed to in the Middle East and Africa and came to view the US as, in Dabashi's words, 'a microcosm of the world at large'. Ultimately Malcolm's outlook relied on no singular, unquestioned site of authority. As is evident from the way he shed 'one revolutionary skin after another', Malcolm's worldview cannot be characterized by the moral complacency and ideological certainty that comes with occupying the flipside of the adversary's coin.[104]

President Obama's June 2009 Cairo speech arguably celebrated a vision of America's relationship to the rest of the world, and particularly to Islam, that is not so out of keeping with Malcolm's legacy. And yet, as argued in Chapter 1, as head of state, Obama is unable to adopt a critical stance towards America comparable to that of Malcolm – who, in 'The Ballot or the Bullet', reiterated his long-held view that 'I'm not an American. I'm one of the 22 million black people who are the victims of Americanism.'[105] The relationship between black America and American ideology, the possibility that liberation movements do not always sufficiently break away from the logic they are reacting to – and indeed the ways in which any pledge to represent 'change' can be coopted by the system – is the subject of Toni Morrison's *Paradise* (1998), explored in the next chapter as a form of commentary on the ideas forwarded in this book so far. Like Malcolm's complicated reclamation of 'Egypt', it points to the ultimately self-defeating nature of forms of resistance that adopt totalizing ideologies grounded in singular understandings of group identity, while affirming the moral and psychological need to reclaim an understanding of 'home', if not 'paradise', from the wreckage of white supremacy.

5
Transcending the Nation: Toni Morrison's *Paradise*

INTRODUCTION: LOOKING BACK TO THE FUTURE

At the centre of Toni Morrison's *Paradise* (1998) lies a powerful story of origins cast in the contours of the biblical Exodus. Like unqualified constructions of the 'Egypt' trope discussed in the previous chapter, Exodus functions as a founding myth in *Paradise* that authorizes a particular vision of racial and national community, and which delimits the imagination of the future. In so doing the novel returns to the theme of Morrison's 1987 novel, *Beloved*, by engaging with the question of black memory and the simultaneous need to remember the slave past without allowing it to imprison the future. Where the slave narrative traced in *Beloved* looks back to antebellum America, Emancipation is the starting point for the story of exodus in *Paradise*. The narrative present is 1976, the Bicentennial of the Declaration of Independence, and the black community that forms the novel's focus is clearly heir not only to the legacies of Civil Rights and Black Power but also to the contradictions of the nation's founding. While this community initially believes that their all-black town is a promised land that has delivered them from the evils of white racism, Morrison's text strongly suggests that theirs is the time of the wilderness.

In this way *Paradise* can be read as a working through of the ideological implications of the dramatic shifts in black America's relationship to the state ushered in by the 1960s. Morrison's focus is on the beneficiaries of the movement. *Paradise* portrays a community plagued by the possibility that its own roots in resistance to oppression have been forgotten, that its newfound middle-class status has led to a privileging of the material over the spiritual world, that its separatist stance in some ways offers a mirror image to the exclusionary logic of white supremacy – one that has fostered an African American exceptionalism that unwittingly accepts the corrupt premises of the exceptionalist myth of America's founding. The novel's highly allegorical nature is thus suggestive of a liberation movement that has failed to fully account for the oppressive logic it seeks to challenge. Most notable perhaps is the novel's suggestion that the legacies of Civil Rights and Black Power are inadequate for addressing patriarchy, and have in some ways reinforced the problematic gender norms of Euro-America. In this sense Morrison's novel can be read not only as commentary on preceding chapters, which have explored black Exodus rhetoric as a religious and political conversation about the dilemmas of US citizenship and the grounds for variously imagined forms of black political agency. *Paradise* also acts as an important corrective to these conversations by suggesting that an over-investment in masculine authority is part of the process whereby a slave narrative comes to resemble that of the master.

While Morrison's novel provocatively opens with the line 'they shoot the white girl first',[1] *Paradise* is not a novel about so-called 'reverse racism'. The power of the all-black community in *Paradise* is strictly limited to its territorial boundaries in Oklahoma, and menacingly figured beyond this geography is a racist nation in which particularly young black men are incarcerated and die. Rather, this is an exploration of a reaction to the pain of white supremacy. Just as Morrison's debut novel, *The Bluest Eye* (1970), featured a young girl who prays to a Christian God for blue eyes, the community in *Paradise* respond to a racist white religion by creating what some see as a 'gospel of blackness'.[2] Their sense that they have been chosen by God is an attempt to counteract the internalized sense of inferiority that has been of particular concern to black nationalist groupings – concerns that Morrison's work shares.

Morrison has very consciously worked in the shadows of racialized oppression that she regards as intrinsic to modernity, and *Paradise* is no exception, but her work has also been drawn to a symbol of Africa – not as a 'pure' origin for black identity but as a crucial point of orientation for African Americans. Notably, Morrison has embraced the thesis of Martin Bernal's *Black Athena* (1987), which, as mentioned in Chapter 1, argues that racist nineteenth-century historiography wrote the role of ancient Egypt out of the story of ancient Greece in order to affirm a purely European origin for western civilization. Bernal proposes the substitution of this latter 'Aryan Model' for a revised version of the 'Ancient Model' that he argues predominated in scholarship prior to this chauvinistic rendering of ancient history.[3] Bernal's 'revised Ancient Model', that re-affirms Egypt as the cradle of civilization, has been greeted enthusiastically by Afrocentric scholars, but Morrison embraces the thesis on rather different terms: she takes up Bernal's suggestion that there was no 'pure childhood' to European culture and that in fact, western civilization is the result of a mixture of native European, African and Semitic heritage.[4] Just as Bernal's work seeks to counteract the 'purifying' force of racist nineteenth-century historiography, *Paradise* challenges its protagonists and readers to re-think the purifying drives that have shaped the United States. The primary vehicle for the purifying mission that takes place in *Paradise* appears to be Christianity, but the following reading also suggests that Morrison's fictive all-black town's embrace of some of the central symbols of ancient Athens points to a communal suppression of all things African. In this sense, along with attention to sexist and heterosexist patriarchal norms, the novel calls for a more thorough re-negotiation of the component parts of double consciousness, and a fuller embrace of the African dimension of the African American experience.

Paradise tells the story of a fictive all-black town named Ruby. Ruby is the second incarnation of Haven, a town that was settled by a group of African Americans migrating out of Mississippi after the failure of the post-Emancipation Reconstruction period in the South, that had allowed blacks brief inroads into the political, social and economic fabric of southern society. On their journey this group was rejected by other white and Indian settlements and, most damaging, they were also rejected by another all-black town – on account of their abject poverty and, some members of the town believe, their exceptionally dark, '8-rock' black skin. They name this experience 'the Disallowing', an experience that is then in part redeemed by the creation of their own separatist town. The inhabitants of Ruby come to mythologize the journey that takes them to their patch of land in Oklahoma as one overseen by the will of God, in much the same way that the Hebrews' journey from bondage to freedom in Exodus is the result of divine providence. The town's origins are therefore rooted in a sacralized narrative of suffering and redemption, one that breeds a peculiarly insular mentality that threatens to paralyse those in the story who choose to live by it. That is until a group of women take up residence in a convent on the town's periphery and threaten to undermine the town's integrity. Not only does the convent appear to foster a community beyond patriarchal control, it also introduces elements of racial and religious difference – and ambiguity – into a town founded on notions of purity and stability. The novel thus opens with a powerful and shocking scene in which the men of Ruby arrive at the convent on a decidedly religious mission to exorcize these disruptive forces by killing the women that live there. The novel ends with the curious – spectral – return of the convent women.

This chapter focuses on Morrison's construction of the Exodus narrative as a story of national founding. I suggest that the novel traverses a range of possible interpretations in a way that enables it to act as commentary on the engagements with national, racial and religious identity that I have explored through Du Bois, King, Malcolm X and, in a different register, Obama. The chapter offers a series of interconnected readings of *Paradise* that imagines various points of 'origin' as vehicles through which to understand the novel's vision of the future. The first explores the evolution of Ruby's slave narrative, and the way in which the town's story of origin – imagined in the shape of the biblical Exodus – comes to be haunted by the logic of oppression that it seeks to negate. This provides the opportunity to re-visit what Morrison seems to be suggesting are the fundamentally incomplete legacies of Civil Rights and Black Power. In this vein, I propose, *Paradise* offers a critical appraisal of the new black middle class, suggesting that some have embraced a religious orientation closer to the prosperity gospel than black liberation theology. The reading that follows suggests that in assuming a religious outlook that favours the status quo, Morrison's fictive community is closer to American Christian evangelical conservatives focused on so-called morality issues, than to the social justice mission that has historically animated many black churches. In particular, the invocation of Revelation in the novel authorizes acts of purgatory and misogynistic violence that seem to parody the violence of the frontier myth that shaped the United States. The next section suggests that Morrison's novel tempers this violence by offering a revisionist account of the creation myth of Genesis, one that can be compared to both Du Bois' anti-theodic musings as well as to King's emphasis on the ultimately provisional nature of political solutions in a finite world. This is part of the project outlined in this book, whereby black American thinkers have sought to rein in Christianity's potential to support a violent white supremacy, and instead put it to work for anti-racism.

As the fourth reading suggests, these various interpretations of the novel speak to the parallels between the black and Jewish narratives of oppression and resistance, one of the themes that has animated this book. In particular the novel can be read as commentary on the religious aspects of the Jewish settlement of modern Israel – a commentary that provides the opportunity to compare the US and Israeli contexts vis-à-vis African American politics, a comparison that has implicitly informed much of the discussion about Israel's changing image in previous chapters. *Paradise*'s critique of the cycles of violence that have unfolded from the Exodus myth has implications both for the United States and the State of Israel – as well as for the violent suppression of Native Americans, black Americans and the Palestinians. While presenting a powerful critique of group identity politics, *Paradise* does not propose a moral equivalence between state violence and reactive violence, and neither does the novel deconstruct the logic of narrative altogether. This idea is explored in a fifth reading which provides a reflection on this book's exploration of 'Africa' in the African American imagination. This reading suggests that the text rescues a notion of redemption that derives not from the certainty of Pauline Christianity – a certainty that, as we have seen, has been mobilized in the name of white supremacy – but rather from a Christianity supplemented by magical elements derived from West African spirituality. Significantly, this is a spirituality preserved and passed on by the novel's female characters.

The concluding section reads the novel in the context of 'America' today, in ways that cannot have been imagined for it by its author. For I suggest that though published in 1998, *Paradise* can be read as a poignant comment on the post-9/11 resurgence of covenantal theology in the US, which gained a certain rhetorical centrality within the Bush administration of 2001 to 2009. The novel's rigorous critique of worldviews based on religious certainties is, above all, aimed at the tyranny of state violence that forwards agendas that have literally and metaphorically pitted 'white' against 'black'. The neglect of narrative possibility that is a clear theme in the novel thus finds its real-world echo in the macho 'frontier' mentality fostered by the Bush administration. Barack Obama's use of rhetoric as a political tool, as well as his insistence on the often conflicting possibilities of historical narrative, throws this dangerously simplified worldview into sharp relief. For his own life story contradicts the myth of American origins which casts the United States as an inherently postcolonial nation innocent of the imperialist tendencies from which it fled. While Obama's narrative presents a challenge to this particular national vision, *Paradise* memorably transcends it.

EXODUS

Paradise traces the painful ironies embodied in the 'Exoduster' movement, which saw large numbers of African Americans migrate out of the South in 1879 after witnessing the region's failure to deliver on the promises of equality, political rights and physical safety to its black population. This was the beginning of the post-Reconstruction – or, as some southern whites saw it, 'Redemption' – period in the South that would later form the centre of Du Bois' elegiac protest in *The Souls of Black Folk* (1903). The portrayal of Ruby in *Paradise* seems to be heavily influenced by Norman Crockett's *The Black Towns* (1979), which charts the development of the all-black towns that were created as a consequence of this first wave of migrations out of the South. This was not the Great Migration of the interwar years, but rather the migration which spanned from the end of the Civil War until the start of the First World War. 'The problem', Crockett writes, echoing Du Bois, 'was how to be both black and American.'[5]

Crockett explains that many of the black Americans who chose not to make the 'exodus to Canada, Africa, or some other country' instead opted for 'self-segregation inside the United States within the protective confines of an all-black community'. The majority of these towns were located in Oklahoma, also the scene of Morrison's novel. Crockett's case studies of five black towns demonstrate that these settlers resolve the painful conflict engendered by double consciousness by investing in a sacralized understanding of race pride in an attempt to hold the prejudices of white Americans at both a physical and psychological distance. These towns thus adopted what would become Booker T. Washington's formula of 'self-help, moral uplift, and racial solidarity', while rejecting the accommodationism that would be central to his vision by opting for a much more complete version of segregation than the one proposed in Washington's famous 'Atlanta Compromise' speech of 1895. As a song sung by early settlers of one all-black town expressed it: 'Be courageous, brother, and forget the past – the great and mighty problem of race has been solved at last.' This sense of absolute certainty about the future is translated into Morrison's fictive community, who echo the inhabitants of Boley – one of Crockett's case studies – in their sense that their town 'is the salvation of the Negro race'.[6]

Crockett's is a sympathetic account of the way in which the black towns internalized racist discourses from the white world that surrounded them, and in so doing marked the failure of their separatist project. As Crockett explains, 'promoters committed a serious blunder by using the white belief in black inferiority as a means to attract settlers and to hold them'; those who did try to leave were branded traitors to their race. 'Few groups', writes Crockett, 'have succeeded by attempting to duplicate the ideas and methods of their oppressor.'[7] In an intensification of Crockett's theme, Morrison's protagonists are left asking themselves 'how could so clean and blessed a mission devour itself and become the world they had escaped?'[8] *Paradise* imagines the survival of its fictive all-black community well beyond the Great Depression that put an end to most of the historical black towns. The novel's mythic continuation of this historical phenomenon exacerbates the problematic features of the original towns, and the narrative of Exodus that Morrison's fictive community appropriates steers a path back to a metaphorical 'Egypt'.

Sitting on the town's edge, the convent is a place of refuge for a group of 'lost' women who come to function as pariah figures against which the town defines itself. Their murder by Ruby's leaders is justified in the name of protecting a hard-won and seemingly fulfilled dream:

> Freedmen who stood tall in 1889 dropped to their knees in 1934 and were stomach-crawling by 1948. That is why they are here in this Convent. To make sure it never happens again. That nothing inside or out rots the one all-black town worth the pain.[9]

Ruby's inhabitants' desire to wall in their home against seemingly invasive forces issues from the fact that the community's story originates in a primary tale of rejection, a tale that comes to be mythologized in the town and known as 'the Disallowing'. 'The humiliation did more than rankle; it threatened to crack open their bones.' The novel does not offer the subsequent story to the reader whole, but rather offers fragments that can be pieced together: 'Thrown out and cast away' by those they perceive to be their own people, the future founders of the first settlement, Haven, come to form a 'tight band of wayfarers bound by the enormity of what had happened to them'. In exile they find themselves 'going into Indian country with no destination and winter on the way'. And yet from this seemingly hopeless wilderness period emerges a leader, Zechariah, who, like his biblical namesake, similarly wishes to rebuild the temple of a shattered promise. Thus Zechariah 'would not name himself after Joshua, the king, but after the witness to whom God and angels spoke on a regular basis about things' he 'knew something about'.[10]

The parallels with the Hebrew exodus out of Egypt are unmistakeable. Having declared that 'this is God's time', the protagonists of *Paradise* take possession of their chosen space: 'this is our place'. For they perceive that 'here freedom was a test administered by the natural world that a man had to take for himself every day. And if he passed enough tests long enough, he was king.' Yet like Crockett's account of the historical black towns, this original settlement, symbolically named 'Haven', does not survive the Great Depression. Ruby is thus the result of Haven's second incarnation, founded by Haven's descendants when that first town fails. What these descendants have inherited is a story of 'shame' that continues to haunt the narrative present – as one character muses almost a century later, 'the thought of that level of helplessness made him want to shoot somebody'. The town's painful beginnings in suffering and slavery are what drive Ruby's narrative to become increasingly 'a story that explained why neither the founders of Haven nor their descendants could tolerate anybody but themselves'.[11]

The aptly named characters Steward and Deacon, who form Ruby's 'twinned leadership', are heirs to the prophetic lineage assumed by their grandfather Zechariah, and consequently behave 'as if God were their silent business partner'. A partner, moreover, who has not come good on the terms of their 'deal'; after Deacon's sons Easter and Scout are shipped home from Vietnam in caskets, 'they understood the terms and conditions of the deal much better'. In the absence of a providential history that bears witness to their election, the people of Ruby in effect elect themselves to act as representatives of God's will on earth. Steward and Deacon thus become 'stiffer, prouder with each misfortune, the details of which were engraved into the twins' powerful memories'. Thus recoiling from the evidence of a broken covenant that appears to be its fate, Ruby memorializes its founding story in a parallel of the Israelites' injunction to remember and recount the story of their going out from Egypt. But the mythic register of *Paradise* takes this narrative much further than the initial biblical correlate. The town firmly believes that 'Ruby's different' from the outside world, and the absence of deaths in the young town has led its inhabitants to conclude that the reaper is 'barred entry'.[12] Ruby's subsequent exceptionalist account of itself equally lays claim to all that is immortal. As Sarah Aguiar argues, 'the citizens of Ruby have re-created Eden to their own specifications; and like the original death-less Eden, nobody dies in Ruby. Yet nobody "lives" in Ruby either, as the town exists within the isolated parameters of its citizens' powerfully executed will.'[13] The promised land is thus made over into a 'paradise' resistant to change and to knowledge of its own finitude.

Thus where Eddie Glaude's study of the Exodus motif in nineteenth-century black America argues that it 'enabled black individuals to make themselves over in the image of God and thereby escape the debilitating relation of master and slave',[14] Morrison's is a cautionary tale that suggests that the result can in fact be the opposite. Ruby's former slaves do not escape this relation; rather their attempt to assume mastery over their own destiny – precisely by making 'themselves over in the image of God' – is the road to self-destruction. The town's leaders in *Paradise* thus occupy a complex relationship to the fault line that has driven understandings of the African American religious experience. As Glaude summarizes: 'in Du Bois's view, black religious life oscillated between a form of deep religious fatalism and a pragmatically driven social ethic, that is, an other-worldly escapism and a this-worldly sense of racial advocacy.'[15] Morrison's approach arguably pierces this dichotomy by suggesting that the 'active' elements of the black religious tradition, those elements valorized by Glaude as potentially supportive of an empowering 'nation language', can become as reactionary as they were once radical.

Nowhere is this better exemplified in *Paradise* than in the town's debate about its sacred script, the 'words attached to the lip of the Oven'.[16] The Oven is an ambivalent and curious icon which sits at the centre of the town. As Tessa Roynon has argued, the location of the Oven in Ruby is analogous to the site of 'Greek religious and civic pride' in ancient Athens, for the Oven itself is the equivalent of the '*koine hestia* or communal hearth that was housed in the *prytaneion* ('symbolic centre') of the Greek polis'.[17] The powerful men in the town gather at the Oven to make decisions about Ruby's future, but rather than being the centre of a flourishing democracy, the Oven becomes the focus of a 'blocked' dialogue about the town's relationship to God and to politics. Though passed on via memory, the words on the Oven have been effaced by time to the point that the first, crucial word can no longer be deciphered. This leads to a debate between the older generation, who claim that the Oven's 'command' reads 'Beware the Furrow of His Brow', and the younger generation who claim the saying as a 'motto' that instead should read 'Be the Furrow of His Brow'. Deacon, apparently unaware of the irony, tells the youth of the town 'that Oven already has a history – it doesn't need you to fix it'. Attempts to counter this are then branded 'backtalk'. The Reverend Richard Misner argues on the side of the town's youth and claims that 'it's because they do know the Oven's value that they want to give it new life'; opening up the question of dialogue it is asked of Ruby's rigid older generation 'what is talk if it's not "back"?'[18]

At the heart of this debate is not only the role of language and interpretation but also the question of human versus divine agency. The irony is that both sides in fact stage the relationship between human and divine in the same way: the older generation's objections to the ostensibly more militant rendering of the words on the part of the town's youth is disingenuous. While their version of the script apparently points to their submission to an all-powerful God, like the town's youth they in fact seek to appropriate 'the mystery of God's justice' as their own.[19] This intergenerational debate has interesting parallels with the split that occurred in the Civil Rights movement in the mid to late 1960s. Younger activists, made up largely of increasingly radicalized students, became disillusioned with what they saw as a moderate vision that seemed to issue from the movement's Christian tenor. Though in Morrison's novel the young reject not Christianity but rather the idea that they should rely on divine providence, their criticism nonetheless highlights the idea that religion can lead to political quietism. The desecration of the Oven by a fist, 'jet black with red fingernails', is blamed not only on the convent's malevolent influence on the town's youth, but also on the political contexts that radiate beyond Ruby's borders, suggesting that Black Power ideology is infiltrating the town and offering ideological alternatives to the singular narrative promoted by the town's leadership.[20]

Yet *Paradise*'s many layers also enable us to read this debate as an internal one within the Black Power movement itself, as well as black nationalist circles more generally. The separatist vision on which the town is founded, alongside its politically conservative emphases on issues of individual behaviour and morality, yields similarities with many cultural nationalist groupings, including the Nation of Islam (NOI). According to some characters, the town is fixated on its supposedly superior '8-rock' blood, a characteristic in some ways analogous to the NOI's race doctrines that hold up a mirror to American racial hierarchies. In addition, the misogyny of the town's male leaders recalls that of the NOI and the masculine bias of nationalisms – black and white, American and non-American – in general. These emphases contrast with revolutionary nationalists like the Black Panther Party, which was politically active, made conscious efforts to embrace gender equality, and which, while promoting black solidarity, emphasized class relations alongside race relations. In capturing these alternatives *Paradise* underscores the possibility of a sharp cleavage in Black Power ideology.

Glaude claims that 'the rhetorical excesses of Black Power sought to offer many African Americans a glimpse of paradise, a way of seeing beyond the immediacy of evil (white folk)', and this is precisely the vision that the all-black town of Ruby appears to offer its inhabitants.[21] Yet Glaude also cites Cornel West's contention that, 'beneath the rhetoric of Black Power, black control, and black self-determination was a budding, "new," black, middle class hungry for power and starving for status'.[22] This new black middle class, one that has in part exhausted its adversarial stance to the racist mainstream, seems to form one of the novel's critical horizons. For *Paradise* points to the idea that 'black power' in some circumstances might just mean black capitalism. The town's leaders, Steward and Deacon, run a bank. Ruby's reverence for material goods can be seen not only in the opulent homes but also in the cars that particularly the men of the town parade as status symbols. While these symbols ostensibly redeem the abject poverty of the town's initial settlers, they are also reminiscent of the way in which conservative federal governments – notably, the Nixon administration – have openly championed 'black self-determination' as 'black capitalism', and have thus coopted black nationalism's critique of the state for the state.[23]

In Glaude's account of the contradictions of aspects of Black Power ideology, he claims that the black nationalist 'search for a pristine cultural history' ironically involved stepping outside of history, moves which grounded ahistorical understandings of an all-pervasive 'blackness'. This 'politics of blackness' in turn 'took on a commodity form. African Americans could literally buy their salvation.'[24] This leap both dissolves the powerful class critique central to some Black Power groups and tells a contrary message to what is usually seen as the major religious outlook to have evolved from the Black Power movement: black liberation theology. Instead, the commodification of 'blackness' becomes the corollary for a version of the prosperity gospel which teaches that wealth is evidence of God's blessing. This certainly resonates with Ruby, which not only invests in a racial identity rooted in a frozen past, but which also pairs the supposedly 'prophetic wisdom' of Deacon with the 'magical way he (and his twin) accumulated money'.[25] The apparently redemptive racial ideology of Morrison's protagonists is similarly bound up with capitalistic commodity values.

Melissa Harris-Lacewell's comparison of the messages of black liberation theology and the prosperity gospel suggests that while they logically seem to move in opposing directions, in fact both fall on the 'this-worldly' side of the this-worldly/other-worldly line that has shaped understandings of African American faith. This bears interesting parallels to the theological debate in *Paradise* that, as suggested above, highlights a split between a commitment to political activism and a default political quietism, but which in fact sees both sides seeking to appropriate God for their particular worldview. Harris-Lacewell takes up the case of T.D. Jakes who 'reinterprets the Exodus narrative that has been central to African American religion since slavery as salvation from scarcity into a land of prosperity'. As Harris-Lacewell elaborates, because T.D. Jakes' prosperity gospel emphasizes material independence, his rendition of Exodus is one in which 'God frees his people from dependency, not oppression'. This interpretation fits with that of Ruby's leadership. While believing that they have been delivered into a land of milk and honey, they view the town's constitutive experience of the 'Disallowing' more as a source of shame than evidence of injustice.[26]

While the difference between the prosperity gospel and black liberation theology cannot be straightforwardly mapped onto the two rival churches in *Paradise*, the contrast does bear parallels. Where Reverend Pulliam tells his congregation 'God is not interested in you', Reverend Richard Misner believes that 'not only is God interested in you; He *is* you.' Pulliam's distant God accords with the God of the prosperity gospel who is known mostly through the Old Testament stories and Paul's epistles, where Richard's is the Christ of the Gospels who is with his people in their oppression. Pulliam's notion that 'you have to earn God' and that the love God enables 'is a diploma'[27] echoes what Harris-Lacewell characterizes as Jakes' understanding of Christ as 'an investment strategy';[28] this individualistic orientation contrasts sharply with Richard's clear identification with the collective strategies of the movement and particularly with the figure of Martin Luther King – who, as we have seen, made as much of an impact on black liberation theology as did the Black Power movement.

This is not to suggest that these contrasting theological orientations were Morrison's primary sources, though as Harris-Lacewell's account demonstrates, mass African American attendance at megachurches preaching the prosperity gospel did emerge in the mid to late 1990s just prior to *Paradise*'s publication. As Harris-Lacewell explains, commentators on this phenomenon argued that these churches had 'lost sight of the black religious tradition' by de-emphasizing religion's role in social justice work. Harris-Lacewell elaborates:

> Without the identity of Christ as liberator, there is no moral imperative for social action. This is especially true when we consider that the prosperity gospel's audience is largely middle-class and suburban blacks with a lot at stake in the status quo.[29]

Harris-Lacewell agrees with critics that the prosperity gospel 'is not a uniquely black religious tradition' and that 'the major figures in the American prosperity gospel are charismatic white evangelicals'. Nonetheless she emphasizes that not only is the prosperity gospel an 'international phenomenon that is also prevalent in Africa and Latin America', it also appeals to a specifically black, largely middle-class tradition of racial uplift ideology.[30] This undoubtedly seems to be the case for the characters in *Paradise* too, although, and similar to Crockett's black towns, their invocations of race pride seem to mask their internalization of discourses of inferiority bequeathed to them by the racist, capitalist mainstream.

Where in Glaude's account Black Power's commodified 'blackness' captures an understanding of racial identity grounded in a timeless 'Africa' – or, indeed, 'Egypt' – the inhabitants of Ruby largely reject Africa as a source of identity. In this sense the protagonists of *Paradise* are much closer than comparable strains of Black Power ideology to performing a repetition of hegemonic US discourse. That Ruby mimes the process of nation-building is clear when Soane, Deacon's wife, tries to fend off criticism of their rapidly evolving fortress by declaring: 'We are making something.'[31] In Hegelian vein, the town prophesies its own redemption through work and, like Crockett's description of the town-building process, Ruby's all-black community emerges as an isolated 'laboratory' that unwittingly becomes a microcosm of the wider nation. In this sense what began as a counter-discourse of black Exodus politics becomes difficult to distinguish from the rendition of Exodus perpetuated by the American state.

REVELATION

As Channette Romero writes, 'beginning the chronology in 1755 and setting the main action of the text in the Bicentennial, July 1976, urges readers to consider how closely tied these characters are to the values and exclusions used to create this nation.'[32] Morrison's text is haunted both by slavery and by the near erasure of the nation's indigenous peoples. Ruby's founders are themselves the victims of this process, but the way that their tale of communal founding mimes the process of nation-building is indicative of the fact that they have assimilated problematic aspects of the wider national mythology that their separatist project sought to keep at bay. Like the Puritan settlers that *Paradise* seems to allude to, the original settlers of Haven have to engage in long negotiations with 'State Indians' before their land is 'free and clear'.[33] And the way that Ruby's founding fathers compromise their vision of freedom with an apparent investment in racial hierarchies appears to be a distant echo of the founding fathers of the United States, who polluted their ideal of freedom with the reality of racialized slavery. Ruby's leaders' internalization and subsequent inversion of the violent logic of Euro-America is reflected in the town's exclusive foundations, most painfully revealed in the misogynistic suppression and then murder of the convent women. The massacre is the culmination of Ruby's own exodus out of the Egypt of the South and into the promised land of Oklahoma. That theirs becomes the violent myth of the frontier shows the inhabitants of Ruby to uncannily repeat the violent circumstances of the nation's founding.

Revelation is the generative text of Christian apocalyptic thought. While it is open to multiple readings, it is often read as a battle of Armageddon between the forces of 'good' and 'evil', one which separates the 'sinners' from the 'saved' and isolates the latter behind the gates of a 'holy city'. The massacre of the convent women seems to self-consciously incorporate elements of this story. The convent is perceived as a source of disruption in a once 'peaceable kingdom', and Ruby's patriarchs conceive of their mission to kill as one of protection and of cleansing. For 'the mess is seeping back into *our* homes, *our* families'.[34] Their mission to root out the elements of 'sin' that they believe to be infecting their town shows the men of Ruby to have come a long way from the injunction in Exodus that: 'thou shalt not oppress a stranger: for ye know the heart of a stranger, seeing ye were strangers in the land of Egypt' (Exodus, 23:9). Revelation arguably subverts this injunction by conflating the figures of outsider and enemy. For those that may enter 'through the gates into the city' are 'blessed', and 'without are dogs, and sorcerers, and whoremongers, and murderers, and idolaters, and whosoever loveth and maketh a lie' (Revelation, 22:15). In the eyes of Ruby's leaders the convent women are precisely these 'dogs': 'Bitches. More like witches', the men accuse them of acts involving 'revolting sex, deceit and the sly torture of children'. Thus the branding of 'good' and 'evil' that occurs in Revelation also takes place in the New Jerusalem dreamed up by Morrison's protagonists. In thus purging the town of its perceived evil, in taking the laws of God into their own hands, they believe that they are 'men on their way to Paradise'.[35]

In an interview following *Paradise*'s publication, Morrison contended that

> our view of Paradise is so limited: it requires you to think of yourself as the chosen people – chosen by God, that is. Which means your job is to isolate yourself from other people. That's the nature of Paradise: it's really defined by who is not there as well as who is.[36]

This view is reflected by Richard in the novel, who observes, a 'hard-won heaven defined only by the absence of the unsaved, the unworthy and the strange'.[37] This narrative, which I suggest charts a path from the town's rendition of Exodus to a moment which resonates with Revelation, also picks up on earlier moments of the New Testament. The town's annual nativity play writes over the story of Mary and Joseph by making the 'original families' over into 'holy families'. Just as Jesus embodies the exemplary life, Ruby's self-presentation is that of an exceptional community. Where Jesus underwent the ultimate sacrifice for the sake of his example, Ruby has already nullified itself in its first apparition. The failure of the first settlement, Haven, instigated the second journey. Ruby is therefore resistant to change because it believes itself to exist in the form of a second coming. As Megan Sweeney argues, while the founding fathers initially conceive of themselves as 'crucified Christs', *Paradise* emphasizes their 'movement from the position of crucified to the position of crucifier',[38] a movement that perhaps suggests a slippage between the gentle message of the Gospels to the violent possibilities of self-authorization enabled by Revelation.

In his discussion of America's postcolonial experience, Jon Stratton claims that 'where colonialist Europe has constituted itself in terms of self-identity, troped by the idea of home, the settler colonies have always experienced themselves in terms of displacement'. Stratton argues that the American preoccupation with an unsettled identity plays itself out along the frontier and finds its most powerful expression in the imagination of apocalypse. According to Stratton, the Puritan search for a new Zion evolved into a project bent on extending the frontier: 'in this millenarian view the frontier literalizes the moment of transition from an earthly world of imperfect reality to a heavenly world of perfection.' While Ruby's troubled self-identity is in many ways a reaction to the original violence that made up the context of the frontier myth, its inhabitants' desire to domesticate their own territory in contrast to a menacing 'Out There' bears similarities with this utopian vision. Morrison's characters ultimately engage in just the fantasy Stratton describes: 'chaos and decimation performs a cleansing on the people out of which only the chosen survive.'[39] *Paradise* reads:

> Ten generations had known what lay Out There: space, once beckoning and free, became unmonitored and seething; became a void where random and organized evil erupted when and where it chose.[40]

Where for the Puritans this generalized fear of the wilderness attached itself to the figure of the 'Indian', in *Paradise* it takes shape primarily in the form of a female other. So while Ruby is itself imagined as a sanctuary for female purity – a place where lone females can walk about at night – the town's leaders imagine the end of the town via a fantasy of sexually transgressive females congregating in the convent. In this way *Paradise* mirrors the misogynistic impulses of the racist frontier mentality, which also combined agendas to protect women and punish them as agents of miscegenation. In this way Ruby's leaders unwittingly reveal crossovers between white supremacy and patriarchy.

As Katrine Dalsgård argues, by 'bringing itself to the point of apocalypse through its failure to live up to its founding ideals', Morrison's fictive world mirrors the Puritan anxieties about their errand into the wilderness, those anxieties that created the template for the jeremiad. Dalsgård argues that in showing Ruby's patriarchs to appropriate Puritan-derived covenantal theology, 'Morrison invites us critically to acknowledge the presence of one of the most canonical European American narratives – that of American exceptionalism, in African American discourse'. Rather than reinscribing the exceptionalist narrative as does the traditional jeremiad, Dalsgård claims that 'Morrison deconstructs the original ideal, suggesting that it is inevitably entwined with a violent marginalization of its non-exceptionalist other' – a non-exceptionalist other that is, in *Paradise*, primarily female. In this way it is clear that Morrison's rumination in *Paradise* is not a critique of black resistance movements as such, but rather of the hegemonic discourse that inevitably forms the horizon of that resistance – including the misogynistic impulses of patriarchal power.[41]

The perception on the part of Ruby's patriarchs that the convent women are both 'abortionists' and lesbians raise two of the key so-called 'morality' issues that animate many contemporary black Christian conservative churches, churches that can be related not just to the prosperity gospel but to the larger evangelical project of 'soul-saving'. As Chapter 3 demonstrated, the exclusive focus on spiritual matters over and above material need was an approach condemned by both Martin Luther King and James Cone as religious orientations that favour the powerful. The ironic coincidence of an ostensible focus on issues of the spirit with an overt materialism resonates both with the Puritan legacy and the agenda of right-wing evangelical Christians that were major political players in 1998 when *Paradise* was published, as they are today. Though reflective of a set of beliefs held by thousands of Americans living well below the poverty line, the so-called 'religious right' has long been spear-headed and funded by powerful political and media interests that have focused attention away from material inequality and onto issues like abortion and homosexuality.[42] Indeed, as Chapter 3 also argued, the emphasis on 'soul-saving' among white southern Baptist traditions – traditions to which Revelation is central – was historically part of a strategy by which the bible was mobilized in support of slavery and segregation.

In a bid to break out of the cycle whereby the resistance movement self-defeatingly mirrors hegemonic discourse, *Paradise*, I argue below, breaks the bounds of the traditional jeremiad that maintains absolute faith in the American project. In the same vein as Du Bois, Morrison's text bears distinctly anti-theodic tendencies that subvert understandings of redemption that follow the seductive desire to simply turn a negative into a positive. This considerably complicates one of the most prevalent religious readings of *Paradise* – that sees in the novel an allegory of the transition from an Old Testament 'God of justice' to the New Testament 'God of mercy', and the corresponding redemption of the former by the latter. Critic Gail Fox exemplifies this reading by characterizing the clash between the patriarchs of Ruby and the convent women as one which 'mirrors the New Testament conflict between Jewish leaders, who lived by the law and saw God as wrathful and religion as exclusive to their people, and Christ, who brought a message of reconciliation, love and redemption for all'. Thus 'the Convent represents God's redemption' of Ruby just as in the Christian story the New Testament redeems the Old.[43] Philip Page echoes Fox's simplistic conclusions when he states that the convent women 'are Christ figures, who must die so that others may soar'.[44] I will return to the issue of the convent women's apparent resurrection later in this chapter. The section that follows deals with the way in which Morrison's text introduces multiplicity into the town's otherwise singular self-narration. I argue that this does not follow the trajectory of the Christian redemption story, and that in many ways Morrison reverses the supersessionist logic by tracing a backwards flight through the Judeo-Christian bible. In a logic that has interesting crossovers with King's critique of religious violence, *Paradise* turns the implications of the Christian Revelation on its head.

GENESIS

The vision of a battle between the forces of good and evil that will once and for all wipe the world clean of 'sin' is not only far from the gentle message of a merciful God that might be read from the Gospels, it also contradicts the tendency of a writer whose work insists on the redemptive possibilities of mining the historical narrative. This project consists not just in resurrecting the ghosts of slavery but also in noting the importance, as Morrison puts it, of 'the ancestor as foundation', the sense that 'nice things don't always happen to the totally self-reliant if there is no conscious historical connection'.[45] In this way Morrison's treatment of Christianity in *Paradise* can be compared to King's insistence that Christianity address the sins of America's past as well as its own founding disavowal: the violent rejection of Judaism itself. That *Paradise* might follow part of King's theological trajectory by subverting the supersessionist narrative is apparent when, following the convent massacre, Deacon comes to deeply regret 'having become what the Old Fathers cursed: the kind of man who set himself up to judge, rout and even destroy the needy, the defenseless, the different'.[46] This does not support a reading that sees the world of the old fathers as lacking New Testament mercy; rather it suggests that somewhere along the way the vision inherited from the old fathers has gone horribly wrong. What this indicates is that while the initial vision of the town, rooted in its founding narrative of Exodus and religious election, may have sown the seeds of its downfall, this vision may also hold out the promise of redemption. I suggest below that *Paradise* enacts a return to the book of Genesis in a way that bears striking similarities with King's sense that the violent potentialities of Christianity – as evidenced in its critical role in constructing white supremacy – might in part be subverted by a return to its Hebraic roots.

As Richard reflects in the novel, 'Ruby, it seemed to him, was an unnecessary failure. How exquisitely human was the wish for permanent happiness, and how thin human imagination became trying to achieve it.'[47] This desire for permanent happiness, for the stability of place and the security of home, has also led to a dangerous embrace of stasis, an embrace that has quite literally brought Ruby's story to a standstill:

About their own lives they shut up. Had nothing to say, pass on. As though past heroism was enough of a future to live by. As though, rather than children, they wanted duplicates.[48]

This clear reference to the powerful and insistent closing lines of *Beloved* – 'it was not a story to pass on', 'this is not a story to pass on'[49] – speaks to the significance of Richard's rumination here in *Paradise*. This line from *Beloved* highlights a friction between form and meaning: it articulates an intention that its form betrays, the story is passed on in the very articulation of its prohibition. The suggestion seems in part to be that what is needed is not to discard founding narratives but rather to revisit them in order to open them up to new possibilities of reading and interpretation. Ruby may be 'deafened by the roar of its own history',[50] but unblocking the passage to the future nonetheless lies in a re-examination of the past. This re-examination takes place in the novel via an exploration of some of the central tropes of the creation myth in Genesis.

The convent women become in large part external scapegoats for a process of unravelling that infects the heart of the town itself. For Ruby's 'barren silence' – its static self-narration – seems to be intimately linked to the fact that Ruby's families are no longer reproducing themselves. The town's family trees are recorded in the pages of the bible itself – in the form of endless lists of 'who begat whom'. But as Patricia Best – who assigns herself the role of town historian – notes when studying the Morgan family bible, 'these later Morgans were not as prolific as the earlier ones'. Thus 'a population that needed and prided itself on families as large as neighbourhoods', and that sees itself bound by the 'law of continuance and multiplication' articulated in Genesis, is fast going into decline. While the novel seems to suggest that through the act of writing itself into sacred script, Ruby has interrupted the life-cycle inaugurated in the first book of the bible, the town at large blames Lone DuPres, the town's midwife who is increasingly isolated and coupled with bad luck on the grounds that she 'practices', and her co-conspirators in magic at the convent who are similarly condemned as 'abortionists'. Patricia thus concludes her examination of Ruby's depleting family trees with the realization that 'everything that worries them must come from women'.[51]

In this vein Morrison's novel enlists the female characters, particularly the group of racially and sexually ambivalent women who reside at the convent, as agents of disruption who essentially deconstruct Ruby by illustrating the fact that the town has always already been ejected from its Edenic fantasy. Far from being the town's archetypal opposite – and thus its redemptive 'solution' – the convent too is home to dreams of immortality, but dreams that have been thwarted by the reality of actual death. For, following Sarah Aguiar's compelling suggestion, just as *Beloved* includes 'dead characters cohabiting with the living, the possibility that all or some of the convent women – Mavis, Gigi, Seneca, and Pallas – are dead before they reach the Convent is a viable one'. Thus where the men of Ruby refuse to accept death and dialogue, the women of the town possibly do countenance it in their embrace of the convent women. As Aguiar points out, Mavis arrives at the convent in the Cadillac that became a tomb for her two dead children, Gigi arrives in a hearse, Seneca has been abused and Pallas arrives with memories of drowning. All the women flee violent histories and are 'refugees from life'. And yet like the inhabitants of Ruby, they have taught themselves to deny the deaths of others: Mavis insists that her dead twins grow and develop, Gigi runs away from the death she witnesses, and Consolata keeps Mary Magna alive without her knowledge. As Aguiar suggests, 'if they are dead but have not "passed on," perhaps they are not yet prepared for death'.[52]

As with the ejection from Eden, the convent women's ultimate acceptance of finitude is intimately bound up with the possibility of narrative. Connie appears to be the conduit for their preparation for death – via language – as she transforms herself into 'Consolata' and sets the scene for the eventual 'loud dreaming' through which she leads them before they meet their deaths. The 'half-tales and the never-dreamed' that 'escaped from their lips' act as a therapeutic externalization of desires – 'it was never important to know who said the dream or whether it had meaning'.[53] The identities of the convent women open as they articulate and let go of their haunted pasts. Thus Consolata, herself in many ways deprived of the means to express her own sense of loss, becomes a vehicle through which the other women exorcize their demons. Following the logic of Morrison's spectral understanding of history, the men of Ruby fail to kill off what the convent women represent. The linguistic fixity that supports a memorialized past is in fact turned upside down by the violent resolution of the town's 'blocked dialogue':

> Bewildered, angry, sad, frightened people pile into cars, making their way back to children, livestock, fields, household chores and uncertainty. How hard they had worked for this place; how far away they once were from the terribleness they have just witnessed. How could so clean and blessed a mission devour itself and become the world they had escaped?[54]

The shock of the massacre of the convent women results in a variety of rapidly proliferating and incompatible versions of the story: 'every one of the assaulting men had a different tale and their families and friends (who had been nowhere near the Convent) supported them, enhancing, recasting, inventing misinformation.' That the multiplicity of stories leads Reverend Misner to reject all its versions rapidly 'becoming gospel' as not 'sermonizable' is highly significant. The notion of 'altered truth' that Ruby's actions bring upon itself questions the very basis upon which the town's own 'Gospel' is founded.[55]

Paradise, then, stages a linguistic fall that scatters the logic of the town's monolithic founding narrative in a notably Babelian performance. In so doing, Morrison re-signifies the scattering of Babel along the lines described in her Nobel lecture:

> The conventional wisdom of the Tower of Babel story is that the collapse was a misfortune. That it was the distraction or the

weight of many languages that precipitated the tower's failed architecture. That one monolithic language would have expedited the building, and heaven would have been reached. Whose heaven, she wonders? And what kind? Perhaps the achievement of Paradise was premature, a little hasty if no one could take the time to understand other languages, other views, other narratives. Had they, the heaven they imagined might have been found at their feet. Complicated, demanding, yes, but a view of heaven as life; not heaven as post-life.[56]

The scattering of Babel is thus the maintenance of the knowledge of human finitude that began with the ejection from Eden, one that is signified by Morrison not as 'sin' but rather as necessity. For the sexual knowledge of Eden is, after all, the origin of reproduction. Such a vision is close – though not identical – to currents in the Judaic tradition that, as Gabriel Josipovici explains, see idolatry in the concept of the tower and celebrate the separation between heaven and earth, the ruthless differentiation of human tongues, as that which is life.[57] In contrast, the predominant Christian interpretation of the failure of the tower mourns the separations that God imposes between human and the divine as the result of 'original sin'. Morrison's Nobel speech does not reject the idea of paradise altogether – rather she sees its achievement as 'premature' – but she reads the tower's collapse not as a misfortune but rather a necessary stage on the way to the genuine achievement of understanding between different human beings.

A similar trajectory can be traced in Morrison's novel. Like conventional Christian readings of the collapse of Babel, Ruby too has mourned the gap between human and divine through an idolatrous fantasy of union. Yet as with the biblical Exodus, which teeters on the moment of communal founding and casts its culmination and its promise into an ever-receding future, *Paradise* ultimately denies its protagonists their dream of freedom as self-mastery and invokes instead Moses' dying glimpse of the promised land. This moment comes at the end of the novel as its protagonists realize the fragile foundations of their 'hard-won heaven' and are forced back into a position of self-questioning and doubt. This period of critical self-awareness and dialogue can be likened both to the scene of fraught communication invoked by Morrison's Nobel speech and to the exiled Israelites in the book of Exodus, who remain throughout that text condemned to the wilderness.

Ruby's interrupted self-narration is ultimately forced to tell not of paradise's realization but rather of its loss. In this sense Morrison's novel dramatizes the violence that ensues from faith in a God that prohibits multiplicity; but in fact her text also offers a site from which the potential of Genesis might be renewed. This potential lies not in a reading of Genesis which mourns the exile from the Garden of Eden, but rather one that embraces that exile as the necessary condition for narrative and thus survival. In this sense the women of the convent are the 'bodacious black Eves unredeemed by Mary' that the men think they are.[58] Not because they are the sexually licentious figures of the men's imaginations – most of the women living in the convent are themselves the victims of sexual violence – but because like Eve, they break the spell of Eden. As the misogynistic rendering of Genesis demonstrates, the Edenic paradise consists of a purity violated by a transgressive Eve who dares to introduce difference. This is also precisely the fear of miscegenation. In casting the female 'others' as sexually transgressive Eves who threaten the town's purity, the men of Ruby not only buy into a sexist and racist frontier mentality, as outlined above, they also embrace a logic of exclusion that has a specifically Christian origin.

Misogynistic readings of the bible in general and Genesis in particular are of course not unknown within the field of Jewish hermeneutics – though the Judaic emphasis on strict separations between the finite and the infinite has often meant that the expulsion from Eden, like the scattering of Babel, has been appraised differently in the Jewish tradition. By calling into question this orthodox reading of Genesis, *Paradise* recalls a brand of rabbinic hermeneutics interested not in closing down the possibilities of sacred text – as is the case in Revelation, which claims to be the final word – but rather in opening it up to multiplicity and otherness. Thus rather than confirming a Christian reading of the bible which sees the Old Testament redeemed by the New, Morrison supplements the Christian story that runs through *Paradise* with a Jewish 'ancestor', and in so doing re-reads the exclusions of the Christian narrative. This process deconstructs the 'fictions that found' Ruby, insinuating uncertainty into its rendition of the Exodus narrative that becomes in the text, to borrow Jean-Luc Nancy's phrase, a 'myth interrupted'.[59] When Richard and Kate see glimpses of an opening – a door or a window – suggesting 'another realm' they ask themselves and each other the only question they can ask: 'what on earth would it be? What on earth?'[60] The idea of this 'beyond' acts in *Paradise* as an insistent reminder of the provisionality that conditions worldly understanding. This echoes the anti-theodic strains of Du Bois as well as King's insistence that the current world is unredeemed, and subverts the theological certainties that previous chapters have suggested are supported by a specifically Pauline rendering of Christianity.

By interrupting the direction of travel of Christian supersessionist accounts, and returning the authors of an apocalyptic tale to the scene of Genesis, Morrison invokes what Theophus Smith describes as 'the lonely God' of Genesis, 'a God who yearns to coinhabit a world of other beings'. Smith likens this deity to the conjuror figure in African American folk tradition, and claims that the creation myth of Genesis is central for a tradition that has from its inception sought to 'conjure God for freedom'.[61] The lonely conjuror figure offers a way in to understanding the function of the divine in *Paradise*. The issue of this magical supplement to the Judeo-Christian bible will be picked up after a brief discussion of the ways in which a Hebraic rendering of religion in *Paradise* speaks to the ostensibly redemptive foundations of the Jewish state, as well as to the parallels between black and Jewish suffering.

ISRAEL

If *Paradise* was primarily concerned with critiquing Judaism and celebrating the event of Christianity as some critics suggest, Morrison's critique of American racism would be largely redundant. American Christianity has demonstrated time and again that it is no guarantee against white supremacy and racial violence. Yet while Morrison's seems not to be a novel aimed at critiquing the chauvinism that haunts the heart of a specifically Jewish understanding of election, I suggest that the exploration of narratives of communal founding in *Paradise* illuminates the theological-political origins of the State of Israel and the comparison of black and Jewish suffering that has formed a subtext of this book. This brief discussion attempts to illustrate the way in which *Paradise* speaks not only to identity politics in the United States but also – and differently – to those often violently articulated in the Middle East. In this way, the novel can be seen to intervene in – and indeed complicate – the debate that occurred in black activist circles in the 1960s about Israel's relationship to racism and colonialism.

In his article 'The Jews of Ruby, Oklahoma', James Mellard argues that the convent women, who I have suggested symbolically point to victimization at the hands of both sexist and racist violence

– against women, blacks and Native Americans – embody what Slavoj Žižek describes as 'the conceptual Jew', a fantasmatic figure that has haunted the mind of the anti-Semite and occupied the position of the archetypal other in western culture. While Mellard's argument is pitched on a philosophical and psychological level rather than a political and historical one, his account is suggestive of the idea that Morrison may have had Jewish persecution in mind when conceptualizing some aspects of *Paradise*. The epigraphs to Mellard's article juxtapose Morrison's opening passage – 'they shoot the white girl first' – with a description of Jews being herded out of a ghetto and shot. He suggests that as scapegoats for all that goes wrong in Ruby, the convent women function as Jews did in Nazi Germany.[62]

Certainly the way the men of Ruby behave towards the convent women conforms to some of the well-known theories of anti-Semitism. Theodor Adorno and Max Horkheimer's contention that anti-Semitism is primarily the result of a projection of the disavowed aspects of the self onto the other matches the way in which the repressed sexual life of the town is imaginatively played out on the bodies of its pariahs. Moreover, the ritualized behaviour of Ruby's patriarchs is expressed in their fear of the rituals they imagine to go on at the convent – 'graven idols were worshipped here'[63] – in a way that mirrors Adorno's and Horkheimer's understanding of anti-Semitic mimicry. Adorno and Horkheimer suggest that while the Jew becomes the symbol of 'forbidden magic and bloody ritual', this is precisely the behaviour that anti-Semitism enables in the form of ritualized group activities: 'they cannot stand the Jews, yet imitate them.'[64] These are of course features that can also be identified in anti-black racism. White supremacists have long projected onto black people their own fantasies about black sexuality, and the rituals of the Ku Klux Klan, mobilized primarily against blacks but also historically against Jews, suggest these traits can be routinely identified among hate groups.

Mellard's suggestion that some of the imagery of the convent massacre recalls anti-Jewish pogroms is convincing, as is his implication that Patricia's theory about Ruby's unspoken 'blood rule' fulfils a comparable ideological function to eugenics in Nazi Germany – though the fear that the purity of '8 rock' blood might be polluted is in fact much closer to being a straightforward inversion of America's 'one-drop rule' that defines blackness as any deviation from a supposedly pure whiteness. An important gloss to Mellard's article is that Morrison's novel seems to be in no danger of collapsing the enormous difference between the behaviour of Ruby's patriarchs and that of the Nazis. Rather, a more compelling suggestion raised by *Paradise* is that the inhabitants of the town – including its leaders – are themselves comparable to the victims of the Nazis, just as they are the victims of white supremacy. Specifically, their settlement of Ruby recalls the post-Holocaust establishment of Israel – which similarly mobilized the bible as a transhistorical 'controlling story' through which historical trauma might be redeemed.

The narrative of Exodus assumed by Morrison's fictive community echoes Glaude's characterization of the story's rendition in nineteenth-century black American discourse. Glaude writes:

> What Isaiah Berlin clearly saw as the constitutive element of nationalisms generally, collective humiliation, was the principal element of African American uses of nation language in the early nineteenth century: the reality of pain, suffering, and collective humiliation caused by a violently racist nation.[65]

The 'Disallowing' functions in *Paradise* as the constitutive event for the grounding of Ruby's group identity politics, identity politics that project an imagined community not dissimilar to a nation, just as the isolated town is run as a unit that resembles a state. While the Disallowing seems to work as an echo of the traumas already inflicted on the future settlers as a result of slavery, their plight might also be compared to the Jewish experience precisely because they are rejected by what they assumed to be their 'kin', that is, other black people. It has of course historically been the fate of Jewish people to be branded as exterior to the myriad national identities they have felt themselves to be a part of. Thus mirroring the trajectory set by the Jewish experience of persecution in Europe, those that come to be Ruby's founding fathers are described by Morrison as a 'band of wayfarers' rejected as 'other' by every settlement they attempt to enter. As Mellard suggests, this 'negative event becomes a positive one' in Ruby's account of its own origins. That this traumatic experience might somehow be redeemed via the town's founding resonates with the role the Holocaust has played in the founding and development of the Israeli state. As outlined in Chapter 3, and as will be elaborated below, while from both a moral and religious perspective there are profound problems with the idea that the establishment of the state might somehow redeem the history of Jewish persecution, including the horrors of the Holocaust, this idea nonetheless has functioned as an authorizing discourse in Israel.

Jacqueline Rose contends that the logic of Jewish messianism shapes dominant Zionist accounts of the state's founding: 'redemption arises on the ruins of history. Disaster must be meaningful if it is to be borne.'[66]

In mirroring some of the contradictions of the State of Israel's founding in her narrative of communal founding in *Paradise*, Morrison provides illustration for Wilson Jeremiah Moses' contention that traditions of black messianism, while echoing 'the utopianism and isolationism that have characterized so much of American life', derive from the Judaic idea that Jewish suffering might redeem the rest of the world and, in turn, show Israel to be a 'light unto the nations'.[67] King's explicit identification with Judaism provides apt illustration of this. But as Rose suggests of modern Israel, the irony of the messianic investment is that 'the future that is meant to redeem you borrows the most dreaded trait of the past' (and again, there are traces of this irony in the fact that King's non-violent philosophy relies on the initial generation of violence). Describing precisely Morrison's fictive scenario in *Paradise*, Rose suggests that in modern Israel, 'suffering, not just the response to real and present danger, becomes something like a national disgrace'. The translation of the diaspora Jew into the 'New Jew' of the Israeli frontier myth thus involves the sublimation of suffering in a way that countenances, according to Rose, the suffering of others: 'we live in a time when the means of combating "evil" seem to take on the colors of what they are trying to defeat.' By this reading the women of the convent can be compared not just to Jews themselves but also to the 'victims of the victims', the Palestinians who have been brutally suppressed by the Israeli Jewish narrative.[68]

As Mellard recounts, Morrison originally wanted to name her 1998 novel 'War', in part because, as she told an interviewer, 'I was interested in the kind of violent conflict that could happen as a result of efforts to establish a Paradise'.[69] In so doing she has created a striking parallel with Rose's account of Zionism: 'no enemy will survive in combat against Israel, but inside the circle of the chosen, or at least in the person of the Messiah, the barriers scandalously crumble between man and the divine.'[70] As my account of *Paradise* has stressed, it is the 'scandalous' assumption of the 'mystery of God's justice' that is the object of Morrison's critique of the violent potential of human agency. In thus locating the violent potential of the Israeli state, and in particular its creation and oppression of its own form of pariah, Rose follows Edward Said in his sense that the authorizing logic of modern Israel is primarily religious.

This is where my reading of *Paradise* – as a sideways glance at the founding of the Israeli state – differs from Rose's account of Jewish nationalism.

In a 1985 debate with Michael Walzer that turned on allegorical readings of the Exodus narrative, Edward Said claimed that 'the text of Exodus *does* categorically enjoin victorious Jews to deal unforgivingly with their enemies, the prior native inhabitants of the Promised Land'. Against what Said sees as Walzer's anaemic account of the role of the Exodus narrative – which claims it as a this-worldly paradigm for revolutionary politics – Said names the 'Indian-killing Puritans in New England' and the 'South African Boers claiming large swatches of territory held by Blacks' as characteristic of those inspired by what he sees as a violently sectarian text.[71] In response to Walzer's view that Zionism was 'primarily nonreligious and often, among its leftist cadres, fiercely antireligious',[72] Said claims that 'while it contained important secular elements', Zionism 'was primarily religious and imperialist'. As the Puritan 'mission' brutally colonized parts of America and the 'Exodus' of the South African Boers usurped much black African territory, Zionism – from Said's perspective – conquered Palestinian lands with similar zeal. Just over ten years after Stokely Carmichael characterized Israel as an outpost of western imperialism (as explored in the previous chapter), Said, in his 1979 essay, 'Zionism from the Standpoint of its Victims', claims that 'Zionism',

> ... (like the view of America as an empty land held by Puritans) was a colonial vision unlike that of most other nineteenth-century European powers, for whom the natives of outlying territories were *included* in the redemptive *mission civilisatrice*.[73]

Locating his own voice within this so-called 'empty' space, Said designates his response to Walzer a 'Caananite reading', one that pinpoints the exclusions that continue to unfold from the legacy of this religious text. I suggest though that while we might also identify *Paradise* as a 'Canaanite reading' in sympathy with Said's rejection of the chauvinism of the idea of the 'chosen people', Morrison's treatment of Exodus is much more ambivalent than Said's; and in fact it points up, as I demonstrate below, a contrast between the Puritan mission and the Zionist project.

Where Said reads Exodus as primarily an apologia for the present-day State of Israel, Morrison is dealing with the tradition of black Exodus rhetoric in America, a discourse that has always been posed as adversarial to the state. This puts the inhabitants of Ruby in a very different position to Israeli Jews. Indeed, Morrison's work is well-known for its attention to the contrasting treatment accorded to the historical traumas of blacks compared to Jews: her 1987 novel, *Beloved*, sparked controversy by the fact that it was dedicated to the 'Sixty Million and more' who died in the African slave trade, a figure that Morrison failed to account for in interviews and which some claimed was designed to bring slavery into comparison with the Holocaust which saw the death of six million Jews. In so doing she contrasted an experience that has been properly assimilated into the historical memory of the West with one that remains 'disremembered and unaccounted for'.[74] Nonetheless, Morrison's is ultimately a sympathetic account of a variant of black separatist politics – that provides a rationale for the community's reactionary violence without condoning it – and in creating a parallel with the settlement of Israel, brings the defensive strategies of black nationalism and Jewish nationalism into comparison. The fictive pain suffered by the convent women and the very real violence inflicted on the Palestinians notwith-standing, rather than inviting us into a world of moral relativism in which reactive violence is conflated with originary violence, state violence with non-state violence, *Paradise* seems to be asking us to think the differences between them. Despite the myriad allegorical frames in which the novel can be read, it provides readers with the resources to make distinctions between white supremacy and the sometimes problematic racial politics of the black nationalist response, the suffering of black people and the suffering of Jews, the state terrorism perpetuated by the Israelis and the much more deadly variants spear-headed by the Nazis, the relative power and status of the Israeli national narrative today as compared to the lack of recognition accorded Palestinian self-determination.

The very different reading of Exodus that emerges in *Paradise* as compared to that offered by Said derives in part from very different readings of religion. For Said, who follows the Marxian dictum that all criticism begins with the criticism of religion, religion and nationalism both enable the violent expression of sectarian identity politics. In this vein, Zionism is a primarily religious movement, a view also posited by Rose who claims 'without messianism, no nation'.[75] Rose recognizes that for many religious Jews who believe that this world remains unredeemed, worldly return to the biblical lands posed problems – a dilemma discussed in Chapter 3 in relation to Martin Luther King – but she argues that 'traces of messianic redemption, even in its acute form, can be found in the language of those who in many ways struggled hardest to defeat it'. Emmanuel Levinas' philosophical meditations on Zionism illustrate Rose's point. Despite the fact that his work consistently refers to the need to distinguish 'the work of justice' – which is for him intimately linked to the religious domain – from 'the work of the state', he frames his discussion of the 'passion' of Israel at Auschwitz in sacrificial terms, as the basis for a 'new beginning' in a resurrected state.[76] In so doing he oversteps the safeguards of his own thinking (as King did in his reaction to the 1967 war). And yet the fact that Levinas here mobilizes Christological motifs to describe the state's materialization – its 'resurrection' and 'incarnation' – is indicative of the dissonance between Judaism and the language of worldly fulfilment, Jewish religion and Jewish nationalism. A similar dissonance is insinuated into the narrative of *Paradise*.

The story initially presents us with a scenario in which Ruby's leaders have translated the wandering – diasporic – existence of its founding fathers into a condition of stasis and fulfilment. Morrison depicts Steward and Deacon fondly recalling formative moments from their childhood, 'sitting on the floor in a firelit room, listening to war stories',

> to stories of great migrations – those who made it and those who did not; to the failures and triumphs of intelligent men – their fear, their bravery, their confusion; to tales of love deep and permanent. All there in the one book they owned then. Black leather covers with gold lettering; the pages thinner than young leaves, than petals. The spine frayed into webbing at the top, the corners fingered down to the skin. The strong words, strange at first, becoming familiar, gaining weight and hypnotic beauty the more they heard them, made them their own.[77]

The very physicality of the book here is deeply implicated in this act of claiming the biblical migratory tradition as 'their own'; the book is shaped by their hands, 'fingered down' to what is the book's own yet connective 'skin'. The 'hypnotic' powers of biblical language conform to the 'monologic reading of Scripture' that Susan Handelman characterizes as 'the province of the Church Fathers'.[78] Pointing towards an ultimate fusion of body with text, the twins find in these words the final destination for this wandering trajectory – and thus an end to the interpretive process. Yet as I have argued, Morrison disrupts the town's founding certainties not by rejecting religion as such but rather by tracing a backwards flight through the Judeo-Christian bible. What she arrives at is comparable to the Judaic struggle against idolatry – a struggle to formulate, in Josh Cohen's words, 'a thought of God' that 'puts in question rather than resolves the meaning of experience'.[79]

Interestingly, Cohen's is a description of the idea of God that emerges in Emmanuel Levinas' work. While as I have outlined, Levinas has himself transgressed this thought by collapsing the difference between the real and the ideal – a fact that seemingly enabled him to refuse to condemn Israel's tacit approval in 1982 of the Sabra and Shatila massacre of Palestinians in a Lebanese refugee camp – his Judaic philosophy has proved fertile grounds for those wanting to deconstruct Israel's absolute claim to the entirety of the so-called 'bible lands', particularly Jerusalem. The religious relation that thus structures Levinas' sense of the ethical relation is one, I suggest, that speaks to the understanding of God in *Paradise*:

> To be drawn towards the Good is to be turned away from it: this is the constitutive paradox that structures the religious relation. The approach to the Absolute – God or the Good – takes the form of an infinite detour towards the other human being.[80]

Cohen suggests that Levinas sets up the terms in which Jewish religion might interrupt the culmination of Jewish nationalism – not by questioning the state's existence but by questioning the redemptive terms on which many justify its actions. Thus in contrast to the Hegelian impulse to collapse the difference between religious authority and the state – an impulse that we saw Du Bois resisting in Chapter 1 – Cohen here posits a separation between 'Israel' and 'State'. The settler myth portrayed in *Paradise*, which presents an overt critique of the conflation of the will of God with that of human beings, speaks in a not dissimilar vein. Its complex politics of reading, which interrupts the possibility of epistemological certainty, recalls, I have argued above, the tendency of some strains of Judaism to embrace hermeneutic uncertainty, an uncertainty that undermines Judaism's ability to play an authorizing role in worldly action.

That some traditions of Jewish religion might harbour a passivity at odds with the active impulses of Jewish nationalism points up the profoundly complex role Jewish tradition has played in African American discourse. On the one hand, Jewish religious emphases on an unredeemed world bolstered King's critique of the US as a nation that has always claimed a redemptive horizon; on the other, its conflicting nationalist tendencies have held out a model for black nationalists in search of land. The apparent fusion between the two discourses in the establishment of the State of Israel put King in the position of granting redemptive sanction to state violence, and black nationalists in the position of condemning a national project – as a manifestation of western imperialism – that mirrored many of their own aspirations. What is productive about these contradictions at the heart of the Israeli state itself, as I have argued, is that they suggest a potential dissonance between religion and state, and it is precisely this dissonance that a host of black American thinkers have attempted to insinuate into the US context – where hegemonic discourses have much more flagrantly and seamlessly appropriated religion for the state. Comparison of the US and Israeli contexts – wherein religion has played contrasting roles in their respective projects of national founding – thus illuminates the dual function of religion both as authorizing discourse *and* critique. This duality has been of crucial importance for all of the thinkers considered in this book.

This duality follows Derrida's insight that 'religion' plays a double function in both binding and unbinding the 'social nexus', an understanding that Derrida derives in large part from Levinas' reformulation of the Jewish religious tradition.[81] This bringing together within religion of a 'scruple' as well as an affirmative impulse complicates Said's sense that critique is always a 'secular' affair. For Said, the 'secular' consciousness is acutely aware of its own self-positioning and will always 'trouble the quasi-religious authority of being comfortably at home among one's people, supported by known powers and acceptable values, protected against the outside world'.[82] This notion of 'the secular' is in fact remarkably similar to Morrison's notion of 'the religious' in *Paradise*. For Said posits an approach to national culture that is simultaneously a withdrawal from it. This notion of a connection earned via painful separation mirrors Said's own exile from Palestine, the circumstance that leads him to imagine a relation to national culture that is also 'a condition of terminal loss', of mourning.[83] In this sense a 'secular' relationship with one's heritage lies in its simultaneous transcendence – a relationship that paradoxically echoes Levinas' notion of the 'adieu' as the simultaneous approach to and withdrawal from God, and that constitutes *Paradise*'s 'religious' critique.

This double structure allows Morrison to critique the dogmatism that Said identifies at the heart of *all* religious thinking, while affirming, in Said's words, the 'noncoercive knowledge' that might enable the articulation of some kind of identity politics. For while Said lays stress on the condition of alienation as the only standpoint for the secular critic, his own work has powerfully demanded the 'permission to narrate' a Palestinian national identity.[84] In the same vein *Paradise* is not a text that denies the logic of identity politics altogether. For while *Paradise* deconstructs the power of Christianity via the 'rebellion' of its Judaic 'ancestor', the novel also reconstructs a notion of agency through its evocation of magic. In this way Morrison stages a fascinating encounter between surviving remnants of West African religion and the founding text of western culture.

AFRICA

The most direct references to Africa in the novel come from the Baptist preacher Richard Misner. 'Africa is our home', he insists to Patricia, 'whether you like it or not.' In response to Patricia's suggestion that he is simply seeking 'some kind of past with no slavery in it', Richard responds with a short sermon linking a pre-slavery Africa with a mythic 'Genesis time':

> Can't you even imagine what it must feel like to have a true home? I don't mean heaven. I mean a real earthly home. Not some fortress you bought and built up and have to keep everybody locked in or out. A real home. Not some place you went to and invaded and slaughtered people to get. Not some place you claimed, snatched because you got the guns. Not some place you stole from the people living there, but your own home, where if you go back past your great-great-grandparents, past theirs, and theirs, past the whole of Western history, past the beginning of organized knowledge, past pyramids and poison bows, on back to when rain was new, before plants forgot they could sing and birds thought they were fish, back when God said Good! Good! – there, right there where you know your own people were born and lived and died. Imagine that, Pat. That place. Who was God talking to if not to my people living in my home?[85]

Richard's vision of a pre-lapsarian Africa recalls the image of Africa in the writing of some Afrocentrists who have posited the continent as a holistic symbol that might cure the alienation of blacks in America. Kwame Anthony Appiah forwards the standard critique of this image of Africa, arguing that 'it is surely preposterous to suppose that there is a single African culture, shared by everyone from the civilizations of the Upper Nile thousands of years ago to the thousand or so language-zones of contemporary Africa'.[86] Richard's vision in *Paradise* makes no claim to contemporary Africa, but for reasons comparable to Appiah's, Morrison's novel pointedly resists the seductions of appropriating Africa – or indeed Egypt – as an Edenic origin for African American identity. Yet Morrison's is not Appiah's straightforward dismissal of the Afrocentric idea. *Paradise* similarly rejects Patricia's view that 'slavery *is* our past' as one-dimensional, and instead the novel navigates a different course 'back to Africa'.[87] This course is a process of retrieval whereby Morrison rescues fragments of West African traditions that have survived the slave experience. In this way *Paradise* might be read as a response to the sometimes problematic elevation of ancient Egypt in the black nationalist imagination; one that deconstructs the patriarchal and indeed statist values that tend to circulate around the 'Egypt' construct, while centralizing the importance of the African dimension of African American double consciousness. This emphasis on an African heritage makes its mark on the novel, I suggest, primarily through the invocation of magic, which potentially fulfils the role of mediating the more damaging aspects of America's racial and moral binaries.

When Consolata Sosa discovers her 'gifts', Lone DuPres, the town's midwife who also 'practices', tells Consolata that Christianity is not necessarily enough: 'sometimes folks need more … You stuck on dividing Him from His works. Don't unbalance His world.' For Consolata's 'in-sight' becomes a medium through which she transcends the mind/body dualism that trammels Christian thinking and which has wrought havoc in her own life. While the town gains its 'magic' through the Christian narrative in which its inhabitants write themselves as living gods, Consolata gains her magic via an authority decidedly forbidden by the Christian church; it is a magic that supposedly pollutes the town's purity and brings about a tide of guilt in Consolata for 'everything holy forbade its claims to knowingness and its practice'. And in this way Consolata similarly subjugates nature to her will by 'stepping in' between people and their mortality.[88]

As La Vinia Delois Jennings suggests, Morrison's portrayal of Consolata – whose race remains unknown but who was found in a Brazilian slum by the Catholic nuns who adopted her – recalls the racially ambiguous figure of Tituba, a practitioner of voodoo who purportedly ignited the hysteria of the Salem witch trials of 1692. In stark contrast to the Puritanism of Ruby's patriarchs, who clearly view the convent as a coven, Consolata is a composite figure whose gifts seem to carry into the narrative present memories of Candomblé derived from African-Brazilian culture. As Jennings suggests, the text 'establishes the site of Consolata's body as the historical juxtaposing of the European and African religions and Catholicism's attempt to displace the African-derived religion', but she speaks powerfully to Protestantism's exclusions as well. For these exclusions often issue directly from the sharp binary that Judeo-Christian thinking so often posits between good and evil, a binary that Morrison rejects.[89]

As Morrison explained in a 1975 interview in relation to her novel *Sula* (1973), 'Black people never annihilate evil. They don't run it out of their neighbourhoods, chop it up, or burn it. They don't have witch hangings. They accept it.'[90] This contention supports Jennings' sense that part of Ruby's problem in *Paradise* lies in its rejection of its African heritage – and an embrace of the dualistic theodicy that structures American Christianity. Thus where in Africa Consolata would have been accepted and possibly even revered, in Ruby she is misogynistically deemed 'unholy, anti-male, anti-maternal' and 'anti-reproductive';[91] the leader of a group of 'bodacious black Eves unredeemed by Mary' who 'don't need men and ... don't need God'.[92] In its suggestion that it is the male characters who betray their African heritage, *Paradise* is an interesting intervention into the debates about gender equality that often pit black feminists and black nationalists against one another. Morrison's novel can be read as a feminist revision of the ideology of 'complementarity' between the sexes formulated by some Afrocentrists who claim to base their ideas on interpretations of African family life. While Afrocentrists like Ron Karenga have suggested that the collective needs of black families rely on women adopting 'complementary' and unequal roles in relation to men, Morrison's novel, while refusing to surrender the ideal of equality, suggests that part of Ruby's downfall is that the men of the town have failed to complement the practices of the women, and in so doing have 'unbalanced' their world.[93] This lack of balance arguably has its real-world correlate in the gender inequalities – and imbalances – that remained unchallenged during the 1960s black freedom movements, and which in *Paradise* seem to have given rise to a self-certain male embrace of a sharp binary between good and evil.

In his study of the influences of conjure practices on black Christianity, Theophus Smith supports Morrison's sense that, in contrast to the stark division between good and evil that defines

Puritan-derived covenantal theology, a very different understanding of morality has been carried into black spirituality by way of African religion. Smith explains that the practice of magic asserts both 'tonic and toxic' elements in a way that both refuses its own redemption and, by extension, conjoins elements of good and evil that appear radically separate in their Christian manifestation.[94] Such a view is underscored by the nature of the convent women's 'magical' return which, I suggest, considerably strains readings that cast the conclusion of *Paradise* in the light of the Christian resurrection story.

As argued above, the suggestion throughout the text is that the convent women are suspended between the lands of the living and the dead, fulfilling the angelic role of communicating between human beings and an ultimately uncertain beyond. At the novel's end the women return to key scenes of suffering in their former lives. The spirit of their return is only ambivalently cast as one of forgiveness, and the warrior-like clothing they don suggests that Billie Delia's hope that they return to avenge their deaths might be closer to the truth. In this sense they ambiguously recall both the merciful Christ of the Gospels and the avenging Christ who arguably animates Revelation, leaving the impression that they adequately represent neither. Rather than redeeming the men's actions through forgiveness or revenge, the returned convent women, as Mellard suggests, mark the site of a crime, while they themselves have been placed by Morrison 'in a space beyond the abuse, the violence, and the brutalization'.[95] I suggest that this space should be understood in the context of a specifically black Christianity derived from slave religion. Harold Bloom claims that:

> West African religion exalted a distant God, while providing for a crowded intermediate realm where lesser gods mingled with the ongoing spirits of dead ancestors. This vibrant atmosphere of diffused power survives in African-American congregations until this day.[96]

I suggest that the resurrection of the convent women owes as much to this intermediate realm as it does to Christianity's foundational myths. In this way Morrison suspends the novel's conclusion between the poles of exile and redemption – the reappearance of the convent women seems neither to reject nor redeem the logic of Ruby's continuance. *Paradise* thus harnesses the conjunctive aspect of magic – that embraces a model of power both tonic and toxic – to show that the dialectic between the God of mercy and the God of justice need not be a Hegelian one that will always privilege a higher term. Thus contrary to the views of some critics that the convent represents the transfigured 'paradise' of a merciful and comforting God, I suggest that the convent inhabits a supplementary in-between space capable of transforming Ruby precisely because it is not the absolute 'other' that the town's men believe it to be. Just as the town is full of examples of the confusion between human and divine, the convent too is replete with idols that reflect the women's yearning to conjure tangible representations of divinity. The difference between Ruby and the convent is that where the former claims redemption via a story of self-empowerment, the latter ultimately achieves a form of self-empowerment via a partial embrace of exile. This latter structure might also be mapped onto Morrison's understanding of the role of Africa in African American culture. There is no sense that the convent might ultimately represent 'Africa' while Ruby stands in for 'America', but the relation is similar – 'Africa' mediates 'America' and guards against the uncritical embrace of mainstream American values. This is precisely the model of identity that Du Bois, Malcolm, and arguably King came to envisage as prerequisite for African American freedom.

An essay by Gillian Rose speaks forcefully to this difference – between the convent and Ruby, Africa and America – which is emphatically not an opposition. In 'Athens and Jerusalem: A Tale of Three Cities', Gillian Rose describes a painting by Poussin, *Gathering the Ashes of Phocion*. It features two women gathering the ashes of a dead husband and master who, having offered himself as a model of civic virtue in Athenian public life and then having been unjustly accused of treason, is condemned to death, his ashes banished to the outside of the city walls. The classical architecture of Athens looms behind and frames the image of the mourning women, of whom Rose asks:

> Do they bring to representation an immediate ethical experience, 'women's experience', silenced and suppressed by the law of the city, and hence expelled outside its walls? No. In these delegitimate acts of tending the dead, these acts of justice, against the current will of the city, women reinvent the political life of the community.[97]

Rose categorically rejects the notion that through their act of defiance the women have somehow abandoned old Athens for a

New Jerusalem; and it seems that an equivalent rejection should be made for *Paradise*, which vividly depicts the violence inherent to just this kind of claim. To argue that the convent women's opposition to Ruby is a declaration of a 'New Jerusalem' would be to valorize a reinscription of precisely the move made by the town's patriarchs; as Rose contends in relation to Poussin's painting – to do so would be 'completely to efface the politics' of their resistance.[98]

Rose argues that 'the unsparing revulsion against the fallen idols and the rush to espouse their formerly degraded "others" perpetuate dualisms in which all the undesirable features of the original term are reinforced and reappear in its ostensibly newly revealed and valorised "other"'.[99] I suggest that a similar sentiment motivates *Paradise*, which does not seek to unequivocally condemn the men of Ruby and elevate the women as ethical 'others'. As Morrison writes, her notion of 'home' seeks to move 'the job of unmattering race away from pathetic yearning and futile desire; away from an impossible future or an irretrievable and probably non-existent Eden to a manageable, doable, modern human activity.'[100] Thus *Paradise* does not capture an idealized presentation of 'Judaism as the sublime other of modernity' – a characteristic Rose attributes to the 'ethical turn' of postmodern thought. And neither does it seek to replace the 'Greek' lineage claimed by the men of Ruby – notably via their elevation of the Oven – with 'Egypt', or to elevate 'Africa' over 'America'. Like Rose, Morrison's terrain is this '*third city*' – 'the city in which we all live and with which we are too familiar';[101] yet as Morrison writes, 'if I had to live in a racial house, it was important, at the least, to rebuild it'.[102] To this end Morrison enlists a notably transfigured Christianity in *Paradise*. *Paradise* does not rule out the idea at the heart of its name, rather it insists on its constant re-imagining. In this sense *Paradise* conjures the kind of 'redemptive critique' identified by Paul Gilroy as the hallmark of the black Atlantic aesthetic, consisting of 'both a hermeneutics of suspicion and a hermeneutics of memory'.[103] In this way the novel distils an angle of vision that Du Bois, King, Malcolm and Obama have in common: a refusal of the kind of religious dogmatism that has so often lent itself to racial violence, but a refusal that simultaneously embraces the redemptive possibilities of the black experience, including its religious traditions. The challenge of this vision is the precarious balancing act required to prevent the affirmation of the latter from coming to mirror the certainties of the former.

What we get in *Paradise* then is a glimpse of redemption. This glimpse is brought to us through the portrait of a woman, Piedade, the text's comforter, singing to another woman in her lap. The novel's final lines read: 'Around them on the beach, sea trash gleams. Discarded bottle caps sparkle near a broken sandal':

> There is nothing to beat this solace which is what Piedade's song is about, although the words evoke memories neither one has ever had: of reaching age in the company of the other; of speech shared and divided bread smoking from the fire; the unambivalent bliss of going home to be at home – the ease of coming back to love begun.
>
> When the ocean heaves sending rhythms of water ashore, Piedade looks to see what has come. Another ship, perhaps, but different, heading to port, crew and passengers, lost and saved, atremble, for they have been disconsolate for some time. Now they will rest before shouldering the endless work they were created to do down here in paradise.[104]

We are left with an image comparable to Lurianic Kabbalah's breaking of the vessels. The luminous shards of creation are scattered, fragmented, and yet they invite, tempt, even charge human hands with the task of healing the rupture. Morrison's vision insists on human work, which involves diving back into the historical record to rescue the shards that have been discarded. Her invocations of black America's African past are thus mediated by both time and space. To name these origins Morrison designates 'hybrid' would be to posit a prior state of purity that overlooks the sense written all over Morrison's oeuvre that the particular is bound to a universal that has always already resisted this opposition.

CONCLUSION: AMERICA

Barack Obama's invocation of the need for human work in the task of American renewal led Toni Morrison to publicly endorse his candidacy while he was fighting for the Democratic nomination. Arguably President Obama's December 2009 Nobel acceptance address showcased the qualities of candidate Obama that may well have appealed to Morrison. Though of course couched in a very different register to *Paradise*, Obama's announcement to the Nobel committee nonetheless recalls its message: 'Let us reach for the world that ought to be – that spark of the divine that stirs within each of our souls.' As Chapter 1 discussed, Obama's entire Nobel speech was punctuated with the Niebuhrian distinction between man and God, but his understanding of the 'spark of the divine' that might equip us to face the 'challenge' of 'our work here on Earth' might be characterized, on reading *Paradise*, Morrisonian as well.[105] Obama's well-known advocacy of a flexible approach to the interpretation of the nation's founding documents[106] – which did of course enshrine the right to own black slaves at the centre of the new republic – seems to follow from his understanding of human fallibility, and contrasts sharply with the desire of Morrison's fictive community to sacralize their founding script and to thus evade the risks of dialogue.

In spite of her long-time support of the Clintons, in 2008 Morrison decided that Obama possessed something that she did not see in other candidates: 'That something is a creative imagination which coupled with brilliance equals wisdom. It is too bad if we associate it only with gray hair and old age. Or if we call searing vision naivete.' It is perhaps not surprising that Morrison would be drawn to a candidate whose evident respect for word-craft and narrative makes him a much more literary president than most. Morrison rejects age, experience, race and gender as categories that might have determined her decision – she claims to have not much cared for Hillary Clinton's gender, who she very much admires, and in the same way she tells Obama 'nor do I care very much for your race[s]. I would not support you if that was all you had to offer or because it might make me "proud."'[107] Indeed, in 1998 Morrison famously described Bill Clinton as 'our first black president', suggesting here an understanding of blackness premised on political identification rather than skin colour.[108]

This latter statement was made in the midst of the Lewinsky affair when Morrison named the situation a coup d'etat: 'the Presidency is being stolen from us.' Similarly her outspoken endorsement of Obama was made amidst what Morrison perceived to be 'multiple crises'. The nation, she claimed in this 2008 letter, needs 'someone who understands what it will take to help America realize the virtues it fancies about itself, what it desperately needs to become in the world?' For the interlude between the nation's first black president and Barack Obama, Morrison's letter seems to suggest, has called for an urgent focus on the nation's future: 'unleashing the glory of that future will require a difficult labor, and some may be so frightened of its birth they will refuse to abandon their nostalgia for the womb.' While only implicit, there is the suggestion here that the presidency of George W. Bush is this nostalgia. In so doing Morrison creates a metaphor for contemporary American nationalism that contrasts sharply with Edward Said's notion of an irremediably exiled relation to national culture, and instead powerfully recalls the communal vision of her 1998 novel, *Paradise*, which also looked back to the birth of a nation.

Morrison's 1998 novel is the third in a trilogy which explores excessive love – *Beloved* (1987) explores excessive maternal love, *Jazz* (1992) looks at excessive romantic love and *Paradise*, though ostensibly about excessive religious love, in fact seems to chart the way in which excessive love of God can become excessive love of the self. In his article on *Paradise* Mellard conveys the political consequences of this narcissism by citing Slavoj Žižek's contention that:

> Insofar as all organic visions of a harmonious Whole of society rely on a fantasy, democracy thus appears to offer a political stance which 'traverses the fantasy,' that is, which renounces the impossible ideal of a non-antagonistic society.[109]

Just as in *Beloved*, Sethe's murderous desire to reincorporate her daughter into her womb is subverted by a necessary separation enacted by Morrison's narrative, in *Paradise* Morrison ejects her protagonists from their Edenic fantasy and subjects their self-defeating vision of wholeness to the reality of antagonistic forces. In exploring what Morrison has elsewhere described as the 'house/home antagonism'[110] – how to imagine a home without simultaneously constructing a prison – *Paradise* not only meditates on the origins of America but unwittingly anticipates her 2008 reflection on the leadership of the Bush years, which similarly appears to reflect on the failure of democracy. As Richard in *Paradise* wonders, 'who will protect them from their leaders?'[111] When was the last time, Morrison wonders in 2008, that the country was led by 'someone whose moral center was un-embargoed? Someone with courage instead of mere ambition? Someone who truly thinks of his country's citizens as "we," not "they"?'

The Bush administration was not explicitly nostalgic for the white supremacist vision of the nation's birth conjured by D.W. Griffith's 1915 film. Rather, this virulently racist nostalgia has surfaced more recently in the form of a right-wing revolt against Obama's presidency – made up of those who, as Morrison's letter in part predicted, refuse 'to abandon their nostalgia for the womb'. Nonetheless, following 9/11 the Bush administration played out its own version of the 'purifying' frontier myth. Appropriating the

nation's Puritan-derived covenantal theology in order to justify
military actions against religious and racial groups branded 'other'
by a Manichean and ultimately false clash of civilizations theory,
the Bush government projected onto the world stage what Michael
Northcott has characterized as an apocalyptic understanding of
American empire.[112] Responding to what was a clear desire to
humiliate America by penetrating its symbols of economic and
military power, combined with devastating loss of life, the US
launched badly targeted acts of revenge. It is worth re-stating
that *Paradise* should primarily be understood within the specific
historical coordinates that the novel provides: the leaders of Ruby
are not the founding fathers of the United States and neither are they
Israeli settlers, Nazis, nor the mirror image of the Bush administration. Nonetheless, the novel's richly allegorical nature enables us
to read the traits of its mythic community across a diverse range
of historical experience. And I suggest that the Bush administration's mobilization of 9/11 for the subsequent 'war on terror', its
activation of the nation's founding exceptionalist discourse – in
particular the idea that America is a 'chosen nation' – and its
flagrant transgression of the rule of law resonates with *Paradise*'s
exploration of group identity politics and power; which features a
community that similarly mythologizes a traumatic event that leads
to the sacralization of myths of origin, justifies acts of violence and
oversees the stagnation of democratic modes of self-government.

   As Roynon argues, *Paradise* not only parodies American exceptionalism but also reflects the founding fathers' 'well-documented
belief in their project's analogical relationship to both the Athenian
Democracy and the Roman Republic'.[113] This analogy harbours
numerous ironies for Morrison's protagonists. The romanticized
vision of a virtuous ancient classical world – that exists prior to
its decline into corruption – overlooks the fact that both Greece
and Rome were slave-holding societies; a fact that was consistently
mobilized in the antebellum South in support of slavery. Thus while
Morrison's novel invokes this well-known narrative of declension to
signify Ruby's increasing political stagnation, her implication is that
there are no pure origins to return to. This caveat was not at work
in the resurrection of this narrative by politicians and scholars after
9/11. Responding to the erosion of civil liberties and unprecedented
extension of executive powers under the Bush presidency, critics
not only articulated a dissenting jeremiad that compared the US
to ancient Israel but also invoked this parallel with ancient Rome.
As Margaret Malamud explains, following the example of the late

West Virginia Senator Robert C. Byrd, a number of contemporary US politicians have filtered their understanding of Roman political power through the lens of modern America, claiming that it was when the Roman Senate relinquished control to Caesar that Rome ceased to be a republic and became an imperium.[114]

Critics of the Bush administration were responding not only to post-9/11 foreign and domestic policy, but also to the climate that paved the way for policy: the resurgence of the national civil religion. Fritz Breithaupt claims that while the US media posed as a vessel of national healing in 9/11's aftermath, by continually replaying the footage of the planes crashing into the World Trade Center it kept the event alive and created a unified 'ideology of trauma' in which all US citizens could share, thus establishing an enduring narrative of American innocence.[115] The widespread ritual of national flag-waving was thus bolstered by the circulation of key images. One of the best-known images of 9/11 is that in which men from the emergency services resurrect the US flag on the site of Ground Zero. This image captures conventional redemptive motifs of courage, sacrifice and rebirth that undergird the modern nation-state. Very different treatment was accorded to another striking image taken on 11 September 2001. The image of the falling man captured by photographer Richard Drew was deemed so shocking that it soon vanished from public view and did not take its place among the iconic images that now define 9/11. The picture offers a glimpse into the lonely journey of one of the many individuals who jumped to their deaths from the windows of the World Trade Center to escape the flames. As the journalist Tom Junod discovered, the unbearably sad quality of this picture – which makes what seems to be an intensely private moment very public – was not the only reason for its suppression. There was also a sense that it somehow did not fit with the scenes of heroism and rebirth that 9/11 inspired.[116] The falling man does not contradict the images of bravery deemed more suitable for public consumption, but the image does trouble the narrative of national redemption. In complexly capturing a display of human vulnerability and strength that seems to transcend the imaginary of any nation, the picture is affecting precisely because, rather than promoting the narrative of American innocence coalescing around a sense of outraged virtue, it implicates us all. In so doing it subverts the holistic fantasy of union promoted by the national civil religion in 9/11's aftermath, a fantasy that, in Morrison's terms, displayed a marked nostalgia for the womb.

This disavowed image of 9/11 seems to capture the spirit of Morrison's oeuvre, which has sought to challenge the national amnesia of a racist state. It also recalls a tragedy that occurred just four years later that similarly could not be made to service the national narrative in any comfortable way. Where a censored 9/11 narrative was in many ways the making of an illegitimate Bush presidency – one in part forged on the denial of African American voting rights in Florida – Hurricane Katrina, the subject of the concluding chapter, played a large role in his administration's undoing. Testimony to the neglect of successive neoliberal governments, the post-Katrina experience of the majority-black city of New Orleans is a poignant commentary on the fundamentally incomplete nature of the 1960s freedom movements. The widespread displacement of African Americans following the storm highlights the material coordinates within which the imagery of Exodus becomes comprehensible in the black tradition. Post-Katrina New Orleans also provides, I suggest below, a symbolic and consequential opportunity for the genuine reckoning with the nation's past that many hoped would be the result of an Obama presidency. Certainly Morrison's letter of endorsement seems to suggest that rather than mobilizing a narrative that captures an idealized image of America's origins, Obama's vision might be capable of imagining a future that genuinely transcends the painful circumstances of the nation's birth.

Conclusion: Exodus and Return in Post-Katrina New Orleans

INTRODUCTION: KATRINA AS BLACK MEMORY

The scenes of post-Hurricane Katrina New Orleans in the late summer of 2005 revealed like no other event in recent history the 'unhomely' quality of the American experience for large sections of the nation's black population. New Orleans narrowly escaped the catastrophe of a direct hit from the eye of the storm – which smashed into the Mississippi coast obliterating entire towns – but breaches of the New Orleans levees on 29 August led to the flooding of over 80 per cent of the city. One only had to cast an eye over the images beamed all around the world to realize that African Americans had borne the brunt of the devastating storm damage. Consequently most of the one million people evacuated from the city in the aftermath of the storm, many separated from family and friends and scattered across the United States, were black. The exodus out of the drowning city resurrected imagery that has long played a role in the black religious imagination. While Katrina affected people of all racial groups, its disproportionate impact on African Americans means that its memory has in part been assimilated to the wider narrative of the black experience on US soil.

New Orleans is a home to which many of the large number of black Americans who live there have strong attachments, but it is no promised land. Making up over 67 per cent of the city's pre-Katrina population, African Americans are statistically more likely than their white counterparts to suffer from some of the worst public schools in the nation, high rates of unemployment and low incomes. It is important to recognize that poverty affects all racial groups in New Orleans as it does elsewhere, but it is equally important to note that poverty is undeniably racialized in the city.[1] The majority of those who lived in cheaper flood-prone areas, and who lacked the transportation to evacuate the city, were African Americans. The rollback of the Civil Rights achievements in the 1970s, 1980s and 1990s are well-documented;[2] but it is hard to think of more powerful testimony to their limitations than the sea of predominantly black faces that populated the Superdome and Convention Center – the 'places of last resort' for those unable to adhere to the mandatory evacuation order – during the five days in which the city was in effect abandoned by the federal government. Most of those who suffered the indignity caused by government neglect are not members of the black middle class that was in large part created by the successes of the 1960s freedom movement. They are rather those who remain the victims of inner city decay and ghettoization – the very constituencies that shaped the political visions of Malcolm X and the Black Power movement, and which convinced Martin Luther King that civil and political rights are no guarantee of social and economic outcomes.

The plight of New Orleans' black poor in the aftermath of Katrina was a poignant illustration of the fact that the forty years between King's assassination and Obama's election were indeed wilderness years. The 'shameful condition' that inspired King's dream in August 1963 was all too apparent in the late summer of 2005. King's speech identified a 'lonely island of poverty in the midst of a vast ocean of material prosperity' in which black Americans 'still languished in the corners of American society', in 'exile' in their 'own land'.[3] The portrait of New Orleans that Katrina uncovered provided evidence for King's later sense that the dream might itself be bankrupt. This possibility was compounded by the reaction to the storm on the part not just of a criminally negligent state but also on the part of religious figures and large sections of the US media – many of which pathologized the victims of the storm rather than probing the underlying causes for their suffering. In this way Katrina not only exposed the 'unhomely' reality of much of the black American experience, but it also occasioned an 'unhomely' moment for the larger narrative of national self-understanding. The storm powerfully revealed that the reality of the post-Civil Rights experience for the majority of African Americans has not been assimilated as part of America's official story – which has chosen to embrace King but not his final message. In this sense Katrina pointed not only to the Du Boisian double consciousness of black America – involving the experience of a cognitive dissonance between 'black' and dominant 'American' understandings of the storm while belonging to both categories. It also pointed to the possibility of a disavowed double consciousness at work in white Americans, a possibility that in many ways fuelled the development of King's Civil Rights campaign.

The word 'unhomely' comes from Freud's definition of the 'uncanny' – the literal translation from the German being 'unhomely' – which, Freud argues, is a state of discomfort that comes about via the transformation of '*das Heimliche*', or that which is 'homely', 'familiar', 'into its opposite, *das Unheimliche*; for this uncanny is in reality nothing new or alien, but something which is familiar and old-established in the mind and which has become alienated from it only through the process of repression.'[4] Post-Katrina New Orleans similarly offered a glimpse of the United States through the refracted lens of the uncanny, vividly revealing that American freedom and prosperity have long been parasitic on the experiences of slavery and poverty. The myriad ways in which commentators claimed that the scenes of post-Katrina New Orleans were somehow 'unfamiliar' to the American experience were problematic for a number of reasons, not least because they represented distancing moves that colluded in a desire to repress the event's American provenance. For the America Katrina revealed was one that had betrayed its exceptionalist founding claim to have transcended the hierarchies that shape European societies.

In pointing up the troubling underside of the circumstances of America's birth, Katrina momentarily returned the nation to a point of origin that cannot be invoked as a redemptive template for the future. For, as Nicholas Royle suggests, the uncanny occasions 'another thinking of beginning: the beginning is already haunted.'[5] This concluding chapter argues that the storm carried with it the knowledge that the nation's founding promises were betrayed at the very moment of their articulation. The Katrina narrative thus challenges America's self-perception as a new promised land and has instead, as I suggest below, inspired a counter-discourse that might be partially understood within the tradition of black Exodus rhetoric. Indeed, Chokwe Lumumba, founder of the Malcolm X Grassroots Movement, has described Katrina as the 'Emmett Till of our generation'.[6] In so doing Lumumba mobilizes Civil Rights memory in order to 'make claims in contemporary life about the relationship between present inequalities and past injustices'. As Michael Hanchard elaborates:

> Black memory has mostly served the purpose of keeping visible the actual or imagined experiences of black peoples that would have been otherwise forgotten or neglected.[7]

Hanchard makes an important distinction between 'black memory' and the 'representation of black memory', though it is hard to see how the former could ever be accessible if not via some form of the latter. Nonetheless, his sense that memory, as opposed to memorialization, 'eludes total capture' and cannot be packaged in 'heritage' site museums and ceremonies – which, he claims, 'often veer (at least in my view) into kitsch' – is helpful for understanding the mobilization of black memory in Katrina's aftermath.[8] This not only encompassed the reawakening of Civil Rights memory, it also resurrected what was simultaneously the catalyst for the movement and the underside of what that movement has come to represent: slave memory. Describing the post-Katrina 'scattering' of her family in Spike Lee's epic documentary, *When the Levees Broke* (2006), Gina Montana says: 'I felt like it was an ancient memory as if we had been up on an auction block.'[9] Montana was not the only commentator to feel that the scenes in which families and friends were shipped away in different directions were 'akin to slavery'. Contemplating the dispersal of black people following the inept federal response, Michael Eric Dyson writes that 'the deadly waters of slavery's middle passage flooded the black collective memory'.[10]

Hanchard explains that 'in cases of kitsch or near-kitsch, a reference is confused with a lived-in occurrence'. In contrast, the widespread invocations of slavery in Katrina's aftermath were prompted by the intimacy between the pain of two lived experiences, as opposed to a gratuitous desire to reproduce or sell representations of the past. According to Hanchard, 'racism, slavery, reparations, nationalism and anticolonial struggle, and migration could be identified as some of the constitutive themes of black memory'.[11] All of these elements of black memory have been mobilized in Katrina's wake, which compelled even George W. Bush to talk about the legacy of slavery – if not the need for direct reparations. Katrina has also re-animated theories among black activists about internal colonization and the need for independent black organization to resist the damage caused by a racist state. And Dyson locates Katrina's aftermath within a series of black migrations or 'exodus events', with slavery and then the Great Migration being the most significant. He distinguishes between forced exoduses that uproot black communities from their homes and voluntary exoduses in which black people move in search of a better life. Dyson here thus supplements Martin Luther King's sense that the biblical Exodus is an event which spirals throughout history in a movement towards freedom with the thought that this trajectory towards freedom is always a back and forth; in the bible too, though the trajectory of the Exodus narrative is towards the promised land, this symbol of fulfilment is framed by the wilderness period and the later experience of dispersal. In thus opposing the official national narrative, in which the Civil Rights movement is appropriated as indicative of America's inevitably progressive direction of travel, these instances of post-Katrina black memory are at odds with state memory.[12]

The distinction between black memory and state memory, borrowed from Michael Hanchard, is one that I have deployed throughout this book as a way to understand not just the difference between the dominant national rendition of Exodus and the black counter-narrative, but also as a way of thinking through the extent to which the latter can sometimes inadvertently identify with the values of the former, and in so doing reinscribe tendencies it ostensibly seeks to resist. I have described these as moments of inversion which mirror – turn upside down – the original discourse. These examples of mirroring are better understood not as attempts to enact the reversal of the terms of the dominant discourse – of racial, national, religious or gendered hierarchies – but rather as instances of forgetting.

As Benedict Anderson claims, and as Toni Morrison's *Paradise* vividly demonstrates, forgetting is central to the processes by which national communities imagine themselves into being.[13] Inevitably the Obama administration is now thoroughly invested in just these processes. The extent to which it is able to act on the evidence of the counter-narrative that played such a large part in delivering Obama into the White House – and begin the journey out of the wilderness – remains to be seen. Before considering the significance of the current administration's attitudes towards post-Katrina New Orleans and beyond – in an attempt to make some tentative suggestions about its ability to genuinely address the nation's compromised origins – this concluding chapter will survey the ways in which Katrina registered within what we might understand as the nation's 'master narrative', and will then consider the possibility that the grassroots response has genuinely surpassed the economy of the jeremiad and thus the boundaries of state-sanctioned dissent.

EXILE

On 17 January 2006, New Orleans' African American mayor Ray Nagin – who lost office in May 2010 – gave a speech on Martin Luther King Day in which he ventriloquized King and suggested that Hurricane Katrina had shown that 'God is mad' not only at 'America' but also, and in particular, at 'black America'. Nagin's intervention into prophetic politics was intended to galvanize the city's displaced residents to return to make New Orleans a 'chocolate' city, a 'majority-African American city' – 'it's the way God wants it to be', he told the crowd. Yet instead his rhetoric played into the line spun by conservative religious voices, who also saw the hurricane as a divine judgement on New Orleans – and often, though usually implicitly, black New Orleanians – and who were contributing to arguments against the city's restoration.[14]

As Dyson recounts, 'not long after Katrina made landfall, voices from every corner of the religious map weighed in on how God had used the hurricane to punish the nation'. An Orthodox Israeli rabbi claimed that God was punishing President Bush for supporting the August 2005 withdrawal of Jewish settlers from Gaza; Al Qaeda in Iraq claimed that 'God attacked America and the prayers of the oppressed were answered'; Louis Farrakhan agreed that God was punishing the nation for its warmongering and racism. These commentators overlooked the fact that those hardest hit by Katrina had long been oppressed by the American state. Like Nagin, their rhetoric colluded with conservative Christians who strongly identified with the Bush administration and who, as Dyson suggests, 'battered the victims of Katrina all over again' by claiming that the disaster was God's design. A host of conservative ministers named the storm divine retribution for a city of 'sin' – 'the epitome of a place where they mock God'. The characterization of New Orleans as a haven for decadence and 'sin' dates back to the nineteenth century, and in 2005 conservative Christians mobilized its key consensus issues – homosexuality and abortion – along with the racialized spectre of 'welfare dependency', to suggest that the storm was sent to cleanse the city. Indeed, recalling the apocalyptic violence invoked in *Paradise*, which in turn refers to the myth of Manifest Destiny, several pointed out that Katrina means 'to purify'.[15]

The fact that close to 70 per cent of the city's pre-Katrina population was black, combined with the fact that African Americans are more likely to be unemployed than white Americans, means that these right-wing evangelical ministers were projecting God's apocalyptic anger not only onto gay people and women who seek abortions but onto poor black people as well. This narrative, which casts Katrina in the role of God's violent messenger, vividly illustrates the fact that the story of decline from virtuous origins in the form of the jeremiad has been mobilized not only in the name of social justice but has also been appropriated by conservative forces that, as George Shulman argues, have used prophetic language to authorize 'imperial power, racial domination, and patriarchal codes'. Shulman argues that prophetic language is '*inherently* a problematic genre for democratic politics' because it is articulated by people who 'speak in the name of a God whose higher authority is beyond question'.[16] As this book has argued, while the central figures treated here have deployed a structure of protest that sometimes invokes the jeremiad – in the name of social justice – they have on the whole eschewed the position whereby human beings speak in the name of God, while at the same time throwing into question the virtue of the nation's first principles. Yet though these 'safeguards' may be central strands of black intellectual and religious thought, they are not the only ones. And while, contra Shulman's reading, many understandings of the notion of prophecy stress the fact that it conveys the mediated – and decidedly not the direct – voice of God,[17] the temptation to collapse the word of the prophet into the word of God is always a real one. As Dyson points out, black conservative ministers were not immune to the line of argument that overlooked the structural 'sins' of racism and economic oppression in order to categorically condemn New Orleans and its inhabitants in theological terms. Dyson suggests that many of these black ministers were very much part of a 'right-wing evangelical faith' that 'sanctifies the state, worships the market, and genuflects before conservative government'.[18]

Black Baptist minister Dwight McKissic contributed to a very specific discourse of 'othering' the city when he claimed that 'they openly practice voodoo and devil worship in New Orleans'.[19] Here McKissic refers to West African spiritual traditions that still make their mark on the city's religious culture. This xenophobic attitude towards New Orleans' status as America's 'most African city' has a long history,[20] and must be understood, alongside the larger discourse of US anti-black racism, as context for the highly racialized discourse circulated by the media in the storm's immediate aftermath. The sensationalist coverage, which complemented the authorities' prioritization of 'law and order' over the imperatives of 'search and rescue', focused not on the plight of those trapped in unsanitary conditions without food or water, but rather on the rumours of widespread looting, rioting and violence. The vast majority of these rumours turned out to lack any foundation, and as many subsequent commentators have suggested, this imagery played into racist stereotypes that have long criminalized the black poor.[21] Yet the particularly virulent quality of the racist reaction to Katrina is arguably related to New Orleans' key location in black Atlantic culture. Once a slave port, New Orleans is also America's cultural and economic gateway to the black Caribbean.[22] As sociologist James Petras observed, given the nature of the commentary on the post-Katrina scenes in the city, 'it is surprising that "cannibalism" wasn't included in the media's list of "outrages" committed by the "Africanized" destitute'.[23]

In a 2007 article for *American Quarterly*, Anna Brickhouse draws a compelling comparison between the media treatments of post-Katrina New Orleans in 2005 and the responses of US journalists to the catastrophic fire that destroyed 50 per cent of the buildings in the Haiti capital of Port-au-Prince in 1866. The descriptions of the two events are strikingly similar: both emphasize the 'wild' potential of a resident black 'mob' that requires containment by outside forces. In contrast to these reactions, Brickhouse cites a poem written in response to the Haiti fire by Adolphe Duhart, a francophone Creole living in New Orleans. As Brickhouse points out, the fact that many New Orleans Creoles are descendants of free peoples of colour who left what was formerly Saint-Domingue following the Haitian revolution has often led commentators to cast Creoles as elites who identified with the French aristocracy. Yet Duhart's 'L'Ouragan de Flammes' or 'Hurricane of Flames' stages a very clear identification with the suffering Haitians. Brickhouse argues that this reflects the internationalist outlook of *La Tribune de la Nouvelle Orleans* for which Duhart was writing, which offered 'a record of francophone radicalism centered on an alternative discourse of racial politics – one that was not premised primarily on U.S. national identity, but was instead crystallized through a dense set of transatlantic and transamerican historical and literary ties'.[24]

The suggestion that Duhart's 'transamerican' identification with the victims of the Haiti fire might open up a new framework within which to understand the narrative generated by Hurricane Katrina is even more compelling in the light of the devastating earthquake that struck Haiti in January 2010. As one commentator put it in Spike Lee's 2010 sequel to *When the Levees Broke*, *If God is Willing and Da Creek Don't Rise*, in comparison to the devastation of the Haiti earthquake, Katrina was a 'garden party'.[25] Yet the sister cities of New Orleans and Port-au-Prince, as Sean Penn points out in the film, both hosted natural disasters severely exacerbated by extreme levels of poverty that might easily have been checked by the world's only superpower – Penn asserts that in both cases, race explains this neglect. Certainly the comparison between Haiti and New Orleans throws light on the way in which New Orleans' distinct colonial history played a role in shaping reactions to Katrina.

As Brickhouse recounts, former Haitian president, Jean-Bertrand Aristide – who had recently accused the US of sponsoring the coup d'état that ousted him from power in 2004 – invoked in his post-Katrina statement of condolence historical ties between Haiti and Louisiana that issue from the fact that the Haitian revolution, as he put it, 'occasioned' the Louisiana Purchase of 1803. In this way he alluded to the paradox that the first successful slave revolt in history had delivered to the United States a vast proportion of its continental empire, including the crucial port of New Orleans. While Aristide thus interpreted New Orleans within the wider context of the foreign relations that brought it into being as an object of US empire, Fidel Castro and Hugo Chávez emphasized the city's regional status which again highlighted the international, as opposed to national, coordinates of the post-Katrina city. Despite – or perhaps because of – poor diplomatic relations with the US, both Cuba and Venezuela offered the US government much-needed medical and humanitarian aid. Castro in particular pitched this aid as a transamerican effort, invoking, as Brickhouse summarizes, 'a shared Caribbean ecological history linking New Orleans and Cuba'. Castro's public recognition that, as he put it, people were 'in urgent need of medical care' provided him with the opportunity to stress that 'regardless of how rich a country may be', no nation, not even the United States of America, is beyond the need of aid from the international community. Not surprisingly, these offers of aid were turned down, though eventually the US did accept Mexico's offers of help. As Brickhouse explains, the arrival of Mexican troops on US soil prompted the mainstream press to observe 'a kind of *reconquista* in the spectacle, noting that armed Mexican troops had not been on U.S. soil since 1846, during the U.S.–Mexican War'.[26]

In efforts to combat the impression that the US was not in control of the Gulf Coast region and particularly New Orleans, the Bush administration repeatedly insisted, against the media tendency to mislabel storm evacuees 'refugees', that Katrina was a 'national tragedy'. Yet Bush's own efforts to assimilate the disaster into an overarching national narrative were unconvincing. When Bush finally travelled to New Orleans to complete an aerial tour of the city – which, as many noted, did not involve him setting foot on Louisiana soil or confronting a single human being affected by the storm – he cast the region in a peculiarly ambiguous register. He remarked 'I've just completed a tour of some devastated country';

he also claimed to 'know the people of this part of the world are suffering …' People 'from this part of the world', Bush insisted, would not be forgotten.[27] The president's apparent alienation from the region found expression in the idea, repeatedly raised by the media, that post-Katrina New Orleans presented the unsettling image of a third world disaster zone; as Brickhouse puts it, the press spoke of the hurricane as though it had enacted a 'quasi-sublime revelation of a national paradox—a mystifying Third-World/First-World convergence at the nation's very doorway'.[28] This apparent alienation from the Gulf Coast region in general and the Crescent City in particular was subsequently reflected back in the other direction: many New Orleanians experienced the arrival of federal troops in the city as a foreign invasion. One interviewee in *When the Levees Broke* hesitantly draws parallels between the military 'occupation' of Louisiana and the invasion of Iraq; another describes Louisiana as a 'colony of the federal government', a 'place to extract resources'.

The rhetorical moves by which the media distanced the storm zone and its victims from the larger national imaginary were thus consistent with both the strategies deployed by the federal responders to the storm and a narrative that has long marginalized the region and particularly its principal city. Stephanie Houston Grey explains that 'the federal response to Katrina demonstrated that the catastrophe was not to be addressed via outreach and rescue but through strategies of containment'. This strategy involved federal responders establishing 'a periphery around the city that blocked access to its main staging areas for at least five days'; rather than seeing such a policy – which effectively abandoned people amidst unbearable heat and without food and medical supplies – as an aberration, Grey describes it as 'a logical extension of existing urban rationality' that specifically targets ethnic minorities. This rationality was perhaps most vividly on display on 31 August 2005, when armed police prevented a group of predominantly African American evacuees from crossing a bridge from New Orleans into the city of Gretna. This incident, which saw the suspension of freedom of movement on US soil in the midst of a supposed 'national tragedy', supports Grey's analysis that New Orleans plays a special role in this narrative of racialized urban control: 'residing as it does at the mouth of the Mississippi River, the city of New Orleans has been historically characterized as a site of expulsion, waste, and excess.' Whether or not Grey's 'geographical allegory of waste, pollution, and ethnic permeation' really did play a decisive role in the way the storm survivors were treated, it is hard not to agree with her conclusion that on some level, this strategy of regional containment, working both on a literal and metaphorical level, smoothed the process whereby human beings were viewed as somehow 'disposable'.[29]

The contrast between the treatment of Katrina victims and those who suffered in 9/11 is striking, and can perhaps in part be explained by the fact that where an external enemy struck New York and Washington DC in 2001, in 2005, while Katrina itself was the official and 'natural' cause of the disaster, the real enemy on display in New Orleans seemed to come from within US society. The social conditions exposed by the storm played a central role in most accounts of Katrina's aftermath, but the burden of responsibility in these accounts often substituted cause for effect, blaming the victims of racialized poverty as opposed to its conditions of possibility. Studies have conclusively shown that attitudes towards Katrina victims diverge sharply according to race, suggesting that the storm has become a flashpoint issue revealing what Michael Dawson and Melissa Harris-Lacewell identify as a 'black counterpublic'. A post-Katrina study conducted by Dawson, Harris-Lacewell and Cathy Cohen found that 84 per cent of black people in their sample felt that the federal government would have responded faster if the victims had been white, where only 20 per cent of white people felt the same way. This same study also suggested that 'the dominant frame of early reports, which showed African American victims and referred to them as refugees may have reduced the political will among white Americans to hold the federal government responsible for rebuilding'.[30]

The aggressive process of gentrification that took place in the years immediately after Katrina subsequently denied many evacuees the right to return home. As Naomi Klein noted on a visit to the city shortly after the storm, 'New Orleans' public sphere was not being rebuilt, it was being erased'.[31] Nagin's call for the return of a 'chocolate city' was ostensibly designed to resist not simply those voices that were suggesting New Orleans ought not to be built back at all, but also the possibility that the reconstruction process might become, as some feared, a de facto process of ethnically cleansing the city. Yet as mayor from 2002 to 2010, Nagin was complicit in the business-driven approach to the city's reconstruction which has made it so difficult for the city's poorer and mostly black residents to reclaim New Orleans and the culture that the city's historically black neighbourhoods have played such a central role in creating.

Nagin's statements on Martin Luther King Day thus speak to the fact that while so many have paid lip-service to the idea that New Orleans is a 'cultural gem' that must be restored, its relationship to the nation's colonial and slave history accord the city an unsettling place in the national imaginary.

RETURN

Contemplating what might be the fate of Katrina memory in 2006, David Dante Troutt suggests that 'soon this history will become black, not American'.[32] This section explores the ways in which some of the social protest narratives that have evolved in Katrina's wake have addressed, if not resolved, this perceived tension between 'blackness' and 'Americanness'. This is a tension that I have argued was exacerbated by the rhetoric of government, media and religious representatives, many of whom seemed to react to the specificities of the city's racial, colonial and regional history by in effect disowning New Orleans and its victims in national and theological terms.

Just days after Katrina hit, on 3 September 2005, Reverend Al Sharpton called on the media to stop referring to evacuees as 'refugees'. He claimed that refugees are 'some others from somewhere lost, needing charity'. Seeking instead to locate Katrina evacuees squarely within American national life, Sharpton insisted on their citizenship and their subsequent rights to protection; sarcastically he exclaimed: 'activate the national guard, activate the military. Oh I forgot, they were in Iraq making democracy free for those abroad, while those at home had nothing.'[33] Sharpton here was referring to the fact that federal forces took five days to reach storm-struck Louisiana, while large numbers of troops were stationed in Iraq. By refuting the de-nationalizing implications of the 'refugee' status, and by emphasizing national over international imperatives, Sharpton's comments attempt to reinsert Katrina evacuees into the identifiable and privileged terrains of American citizenship and identity. Yet by emphasizing American benevolence abroad as compared with the neglect of a vulnerable home front, Sharpton reveals the conservative thrust of his own critique – which condemns the war but upholds the government line on it. He thus side-steps a more thorough critique of US power in favour of assuming an exceptionalist rhetoric – and in so doing restricts the economy of his own protest to one that still serves the national ideology. This restricted economy was also evident when Sharpton insisted that most of those affected by the storm were 'viable' tax-payers, thus emphasizing the storm victims' adherence to the national Protestant work ethic at the expense of acknowledging that the storm uncovered the fact that high levels of unemployment among African Americans has led to extreme levels of racialized poverty in the city. Sharpton's jeremiad typifies a trend of African American resistance to the racist discourses unleashed by the storm, one that reverberates with sections of the Civil Rights movement that shaped Sharpton's political context.

Tonya Williams of the US Human Rights Network suggests that this negative attitude towards the 'refugee' label – which not only rejects the label as a false denial of citizenship status but which also forecloses on identifications with 'foreigners' who are denied the right to claim protection from the state in which they reside – results from the desire on the part of some African Americans to hold at a distance the 'visual pictures of Africans who have been displaced because of conflict'. The rejection of this implied analogy, Williams asserts, derives from a larger discourse whereby 'African descendant peoples' in the US have 'conceptualized themselves against continental Africans'.[34] In an approach that challenges this discourse, Williams began the work of coordinating a campaign to have Katrina survivors recognized by the US government as Internally Displaced Persons, a move that turns the appeal to national identity on its head by underscoring the inadequacy of current US law. This campaign has been fuelled by the post-Katrina neglect of the economic, social and cultural rights of survivors across the Gulf Coast, and particularly in New Orleans.

Behind much human rights organizing in and around New Orleans is a desire to resist what some have described as 'disaster exceptionalism'. This orientation instead 'understands "disaster" to be different in degree, not in kind, from the ongoing experience of social inequality in the United States'.[35] For what Katrina exposed was a city still rigidly divided along the lines of race decades after the Civil Rights movement, and the storm's aftermath has accelerated the vulnerability of those already suffering as a result of racialized poverty. Signs that federal, state and city authorities in New Orleans were not only doing little to aid the return of the city's most vulnerable populations, but were in fact actively preventing their return, became clear in late 2006 when the Department of Housing and Urban Development announced the demolition of a number of New Orleans' public housing projects. As the prominent civil rights lawyer and social justice activist William Quigley suggested at the time, these proposals would lead to 'a government-sanctioned diaspora of New Orleans's poorest African American citizens'.[36]

In February 2008 the UN confirmed the prescience of Quigley's statement by calling for a halt to the demolition of public housing in the city, highlighting the human rights of African Americans as a particular cause for concern. In so doing the UN invoked an international frame of reference that had been called on almost as soon as it became clear that those charged with the task of reconstructing New Orleans were imagining a radically transformed city. In particular, developers had their eyes on the prime real estate adjacent to the city's tourist hub that is also home to large numbers of lower-income residents. In this context, as Quigley states, 'no principle has proven more helpful to Gulf Coast advocates than the international "right of return." The right to return has no parallel in U.S. law, which makes it even more important in advocacy and analysis.'[37] A central plank in the UN's Guiding Principles on Internal Displacement, the right of return outlines an obligation on the part of national governments to enable those displaced in post-conflict and post-disaster situations to return home.[38] This deployment of international law does not involve embracing the 'refugee' label which, applied to most Katrina survivors, was incorrect. But many human rights activists do see the international coordinates in which they work as an explicit refutation of American exceptionalism. The US Human Rights Network explains on its website that

> underlying all human rights work in the United States is a commitment to challenge the belief that the United States is inherently superior to other countries of the world, and that neither the US government nor the US rights movements have anything to gain from the domestic application of human rights.[39]

As suggested below, this understanding of human rights discourse reveals the ways in which aspects of the post-Katrina human rights narrative can be seen as heir to the internationalist perspective that has historically animated significant sections of the black freedom narrative.

In her analysis of the roots of the contemporary US human rights movement, Dorothy Thomas suggests that the African American struggle against racism has played a crucial role in highlighting the challenge human rights discourse potentially poses to American exceptionalism. At the core of the contemporary movement, she suggests, 'is the question of racism or, more broadly, supremacy':

Its nearest roots lie in the sharp conflict of the mid-1940s and 1950s between the principles of human rights and the practice of discrimination based on race. At the time, the U.S. government chose explicitly and aggressively to protect domestic racial segregation at the cost of its own adherence to human rights, despite the origin of those rights in much of its own leadership and tradition.[40]

Here Thomas refers to the fact that shortly after Franklin Delano Roosevelt's famous articulation of the 'four freedoms' in 1941 – freedom of speech and worship, and freedom from want and fear – southern Democrats in concert with allies in the Republican Party began to charge that the US Constitution and America were under attack from human rights. The UN was cast, in the words of Carol Anderson, as 'that foreigner-dominated organization set out to subvert American values with socialistic, even communistic, ideas about freedom and democracy'. Their primary concern was the protection of Jim Crow in southern states, and in particular they feared that 'the Genocide Convention, if ratified', could 'transform lynching into an international crime, and obligate the federal government to prosecute those who had, heretofore, killed black Americans with impunity'.[41] It was within this context that W.E.B. Du Bois and the NAACP recognized the UN as a potential ally in the fight against racial injustice. Although the NAACP under Walter White gave in to pressure to desist bringing evidence of state-sanctioned racism before the UN, and instead moved to an exclusive focus on fighting for civil rights within the parameters of US law, Du Bois continued to espouse the view that individuals have rights that transcend the nation-state.

Du Bois' sentiments were in many ways echoed in the later rhetoric of Malcolm X. In his 1964 speech 'The Ballot or the Bullet', Malcolm envisaged an expansion of 'the civil-rights struggle to the level of human rights' and advocated taking 'the case of the black man in this country before the nations in the U.N.'. Malcolm saw the exposure of American crimes before this 'world court' as a way of enlisting help from African, Asian and Latin American 'brothers' for the African American struggle against racism, which would then come into view alongside anti-colonial movements.[42] Talal Asad characterizes Malcolm's mobilization of human rights rhetoric as an apparently secular alternative to the prophetic language deployed by Martin Luther King. As Asad points out, the political tradition of invoking the (Exodus) story of captivity, deliverance and decline from virtuous origins

> allows, even encourages, the identification of social crises and the condemnation of social injustice, both by those who occupy the ideological center of American liberalism and by those who stand outside it as its critics.[43]

It is precisely because the jeremiad is a discourse sanctioned by American political traditions, Asad suggests, that King was able to use it with such effect, whereas Malcolm's emphasis on human rights failed to recognize the power of the state over and above the international community. The irony of this, Asad seems to suggest, is that the apparently universalist language of human rights discourse is the 'secular' manifestation of the culturally specific language of American prophecy. For Asad claims that human rights language draws on 'the idea that "freedom" and "America" are virtually interchangeable – that American political culture is (as the bible says of the Chosen People) "a light unto the nations"'. By this reading, quite apart from challenging exceptionalist discourse, Malcolm's mobilization of human rights rhetoric inadvertently and paradoxically invests in the assumptions of what Asad reads as 'the global moral project of America'.[44]

While Asad's account helpfully highlights the false universals at work in human rights discourse, his analysis of Malcolm and King overlooks the wider contexts of their linguistic investments. While Asad notes that King's discourse of redemption can be distinguished from that of the state he was opposing, his characterization of King reinforces historical accounts that situate the Civil Rights movement as a domestic affair invested in Cold War exceptionalism. In so doing Asad misses the fact that King's prophetic rhetoric was itself increasingly mobilized in the name of human rights over and above Civil Rights – as King became focused on issues related to class and poverty. This illustrates Asad's point that there is indeed an overlap between prophetic rhetoric and human rights discourse, which arguably points to a common American provenance (though this overlap might be more properly identified as Judeo-Christian). But King's interventions in prophetic rhetoric are also a prime example of a black American tradition that has long resisted the dominant culture by exposing that culture to uncanny re-articulations of some of its most valued narratives. In similar vein to King's 'unhomely' account of the Exodus story, Malcolm X's desire to 'bring human rights home' represented a similarly estranging process which proposed that the nation view itself through the refracted lens of double consciousness.

Asad does note the paradox that while 'the U.S. government has been a major force behind the attempt to globalize human rights ... inside the United States the human rights language has had comparatively little purchase'.[45] The human rights movement in post-Katrina New Orleans thus might be seen as an attempt to bring the United States to a fuller recognition of its own, often ugly, reflection. Comparable to the jeremiad, this involves emphasizing a culturally specific western narrative that, like prophetic rhetoric, emphasizes the difference between the real and the ideal. But the very fact that the human rights work going on in and around New Orleans highlights Katrina as a disaster that might be compared to the 2004 Asian tsunami or the earthquake in Haiti throws doubt on the idea that America itself is the redemptive vehicle for the purportedly universalist category of the 'human'. Rather, the suggestion that America might just be a nation among nations brings home the 'unhomely' idea that the human rights of US citizens require protection from the state.

Rachel Luft argues that the post-Katrina human rights work going on in New Orleans represents the convergence of three disparate traditions – 'the Black Liberation Movement (BLM), the United Nations (UN) and nongovernmental organizations (NGOs)'.[46] As she suggests, what is striking about the mobilization of activism and community organizing in New Orleans and across the Gulf Coast is that it is not a mainly middle-class phenomenon as was the 1960s Civil Rights movement, but has instead involved many of the working poor whose lives have been most directly affected. In this sense the post-Katrina human rights work might be seen as heir to King's vision of an interracial coalition to fight poverty. And arguably, New Orleans itself, partly because of its unique cultural status within the wider nation, is an environment that is uniquely receptive to cultures of resistance.

As Clyde Woods explains, the community organizing in post-Katrina New Orleans can be understood in the context of a city that has long hosted a thriving network of community institutions that have resisted the repressive and racist policies of its ruling elite. Woods characterizes this as a 'dialectic of Bourbonism and the Blues'. Bourbonism points back to a French and Spanish monarchical dynasty 'whose famed indifference to human suffering led them to create one disaster after another'; transported to the New World, Bourbonism traces the lineage of Louisiana's oligarchy that enabled some of the most brutal forms of slavery and then racism in the post-Louisiana Purchase Union. 'Many of the fundamental principles of Bourbonism', Woods claims, 'have emerged on the national stage as neoliberalism.' The Blues tradition, on the other hand, stands in for the myriad forms of resistance to this system. In the nineteenth century New Orleans became a hub of insurrectionary activity on the part of both black and Native Americans, as well as becoming a major centre of diverse African diasporic cultural traditions and a revolutionary black Christian social gospel. These are the contexts, Woods suggests, of 'Katrina's world'. The questions thus raised by Katrina are profound: 'did we know we were witnessing the destruction of a global cultural center? Did we know that those impoverished Black communities were the center of this center?'[47]

CONCLUSION: REBUILDING AMERICA

Numerous commentators have suggested that the process of rebuilding New Orleans offers a poignant vision for Obama's America. Obama took office on the understanding that the nation was 'sick' and in need of recovery. He has repeatedly insisted that this recovery must be enacted through partnerships between government and civil society, particularly faith-based groups – an idea that extends back to his Chicago days as a community organizer and into his post-election campaigning body, 'Organizing for America'. Nowhere is this vision more fully realized than in post-Katrina New Orleans. On the four-year anniversary of Hurricane Katrina the president cast New Orleans and the Gulf Coast more generally as a site of renewal:

> On this day, we commemorate a tragedy that befell our people. But we also remember that with every tragedy comes the chance of renewal. It is a quintessentially American notion – that adversity can give birth to hope, and that the lessons of the past hold the key to a better future.[48]

The extent to which those lessons of the past extend to the racial truths revealed by the storm will inevitably be an important test of Obama's presidency. Immediately after Katrina, Obama resisted the idea that the federal response to the storm was slow and incompetent because the victims were predominantly black, pointing out that the situation was in fact much more complex. He did though suggest that the administration's planning 'showed a degree of remove from, and indifference toward, the problems of inner-city poverty'.[49] Whether his administration will address those problems – integral to which is systemic racism – has become a focus of concern amidst the growing chorus of voices that claim Obama's presidency is not living up to the promises of his campaign. This criticism is inevitable for any president, but the stakes are particularly high for one whose campaign not only borrowed from the language and the spirit of the Civil Rights movement, but which also strongly implied that an Obama presidency would continue, if not complete, the journey that Civil Rights began.

Obama's campaign speeches repeatedly referenced the New Orleans levee breaches. The reasons for this are obvious. The mismanagement of the storm's aftermath caused Bush's approval ratings to plummet. Writing in *The Nation* in March 2009, Melissa Harris-Lacewell and James Perry argued that 'the televised suffering in New Orleans set the stage for the Democratic win in 2006 and Obama's victory in 2008'; 'Democratic victory was possible because the people of New Orleans suffered. This is a debt Democrats must repay.'[50] Studies suggest that Katrina played a major role in turning the tide of public opinion against the war in Iraq, but the ways in which the storm revealed the most reviled aspects of the Bush administration should not just be seen in terms of the gross neglect of the domestic front. Shortly after the storm – reflecting the authorities' sense of post-Katrina New Orleans as a threatening location in need of containment rather than a site of vulnerability in need of rescue – the city was flooded with armed security details, including guards from private firms like Blackwater. In this way Katrina enacted the uncanny return to the home front of some of the most sinister symbolism of the Bush administration's foreign policy. This is vividly captured in Dave Eggers' imaginative account of the real-life experience of Abdulrahman Zeitoun, who was held without charges in 'Camp Greyhound' – a makeshift prison made up of cage-like structures built in New Orleans' bus station in Katrina's wake. The traumatic nature of this experience for the Syrian-born immigrant, who had apparently done nothing to provoke suspicion apart from staying behind in the flooded city to help abandoned residents, is encapsulated by Zeitoun's sense that this 'vast outdoor prison ... looked precisely like the pictures he'd seen of Guantanamo Bay'. The suggestion that Zeitoun's transgression might be his ethnic identity haunts the patriotic American immigrant, and this suggestion is heightened by the symbolism that shadows his transferral to a high security prison, Angola, where he was held for weeks and denied access to a lawyer. As Eggers' text recounts,

> Angola, the country's largest prison, was built on an eighteen-thousand-acre former plantation once used for the breeding of slaves ... Historically the inmates were required to do backbreaking labor, including picking cotton, for about four cents an hour. In a mass protest decades ago, thirty-one prisoners cut their Achilles tendons, lest they be sent again to work. [51]

Zeitoun's experience is an illustration of the underside of state power revealed by Katrina, the 'war on terror' and the mass incarceration of black men in US prisons. Zeitoun's story points to the racist discourses that link these narratives, and is suggestive not only of the gulf between a rights-bearing 'citizen' and the apparently empty vessel of 'non-citizen' in the eyes of the state, but also the fact that these positions are separated by a precariously thin line. As Kevin Gaines suggests, the mass incarceration of prisoners within the US and the detention and torture of terror suspects abroad similarly gesture back to the traumatic circumstances of America's birth: 'the supercarceral state and society we have become remind us we have yet to transcend the origins of a country founded on the theft of land and the sale of human beings for profit.' Gaines here echoes Morrison's message in *Paradise* by claiming that a critical examination of the nation's origins is crucial for democracy. He cautions that 'even as we celebrate the election of Barack Obama, we are condemning many of our children to become the latter-day slaves of the twenty-first century'.[52]

The fact that, as Gaines points out, the racist attacks on Obama issue from a convergence of older discourses of white supremacy with post-9/11 xenophobia, makes a confrontation with the origins of the 'war on terror' and Katrina all the more significant for his presidency. Indeed, New Orleans itself raises questions about American identity that have been central to the personal story that Obama has made so crucial to his political persona. As Shirley Thompson argues, New Orleans' complex Creole heritage, which self-consciously insinuates Africa, Europe and the wider colonial and slave histories into the American experience, means that the city 'demonstrates in microcosm the challenges and contradictions of becoming American'. For this reason Thompson suggests that 'in the face of American forgetfulness and notions of relentless progress,

New Orleanians have embraced their ruins, becoming the nation's premier "city of collective memory"'.[53]

Commentators from both right and left have been quick to identify in Obama's administration a 'forgetfulness' relating not just to the 'ruins' of America's past that the president seems so uniquely placed to address, but also to the more recent spectre of the Bush presidency. The war in Afghanistan has thus been made over by the media into 'Obama's war', while the devastating BP (British Petroleum) oil spill in the Gulf of Mexico that resulted from an explosion on the Deepwater Horizon oil rig in April 2010 – which killed eleven people and which will almost certainly lead to the long-term material and psychological suffering of many more – has frequently been dubbed 'Obama's Katrina'. This label seems to be gratifying to Obama's opponents because it projects onto the current administration what was possibly the worst nemesis of the Bush years. But the irony of the suggestion that Obama is just as capable of creating the very disaster that played a large role in ousting the Republicans from office is compounded by the unspoken fact that Katrina is a highly racialized spectre which has been partially assimilated into the archive of black memory. I suggest that this accusation – 'Obama's Katrina' – plays into a subterranean discourse of racial betrayal that commentary from both right and left has played a role in shaping.

While Obama's election brought to the fore unambiguous examples of public racism, the Obama presidency works in the shadows of a largely unarticulated discourse about race that does not speak its name. Obama has in the past supported various affirmative action measures, but the role race has played in the presidency so far suggests the political expediency of his stated position that 'an emphasis on universal, as opposed to race-specific, programs isn't just good policy; it's also good politics.'[54] This position was re-articulated in relation to the health care bill, which Obama stressed was a universal measure that would nonetheless disproportionately help ethnic minorities, including large numbers of African Americans. In turn, health care was billed by Obama's right-wing critics as slavery reparations by stealth, while those on the left condemned the president's supposed timidity. Both health care reform and the stimulus package allocated specific funds to the Gulf Coast, and some claim that the new administration gave momentum to the rebuilding process in New Orleans. But Obama has also been criticized for failing to take decisive steps in post-Katrina New Orleans that would reverse the consequences of gentrification that some have claimed amounts to ethnic cleansing. It is too soon to judge what can only be a long-term strategy in New Orleans and the Gulf Coast region as a whole. But certainly in his four-year anniversary address the president did not offer even a veiled allusion to the fact that the persistent reality of racialized poverty was one of the most important 'lessons of Katrina'. Indeed, in his five-year anniversary address, while Obama condemned the 'shameful breakdown in government' that Katrina exposed, he concluded by invoking the theme of renewal in the book of Job, and declared that 'New Orleans is blossoming again'.[55] Undeniably there is much to celebrate in post-Katrina New Orleans, and the strengthened communal bonds that Obama's speech mentions are part of that picture. But that community solidarity has been forged in the face of government neglect and arguably is being put to work to carry out tasks that are ultimately the responsibility of the state. In this sense Obama's upbeat message threatens to pave over this reality, just as the claim that his election represents a victory for anti-racism threatens to pave over the reality of persistent racism. This dilemma is that brought into focus by the 'split screen' that Obama wrote of in 2006, in what seems to be a formulation of the jeremiad shot through with the knowledge of Du Boisian double consciousness:

> To think clearly about race, then, requires us to see the world on a split screen – to maintain in our sights the kind of America that we want while looking squarely at America as it is, to acknowledge the sins of our past and the challenges of the present without becoming trapped in cynicism or despair.[56]

While the Obama campaign was able to draw on the redemptive message of the Civil Rights movement, it seems highly unlikely that his government is going to fully address the painful history of the nation's past. Indeed, Obama's success in mobilizing Civil Rights rhetoric seemed to be in part because he was able to universalize its triumphant message across racial lines. Michael Hanchard suggests that:

> While the people in a particular national society can have many, often competing, versions of the national narrative, a national-state can only have one narrative about the nation's origins, founding, and maintenance, without appearing contradictory, feeble, and indecisive.[57]

As Chapter 1 argued, Obama's inaugural address unambiguously re-activated America's revolutionary origins as a site of renewal, if not redemption. By this account the conditions of possibility for slavery's eventual overcoming were always already part of the national narrative. Obama's political progression from his days as a community organizer on Chicago's South Side show a painstaking attempt to calculate where he might most effectively bring about change. As conversations with his former mentor Jerry Kellman suggest, he was fully aware of the dangers of becoming an 'insider' in the corridors of power and being coopted by the system; Obama asked Kellman, 'Can you join the system and not lose your sense of what is just?'[58] When on the campaign trail Obama presented himself to a black congregation in Selma as part of the promise of King's Exodus vision, he claimed to 'worry sometimes that the Joshua generation in its success forgets where it came from'; as he pointed out, among a string of problems facing black communities, 'you've got Katrina still undone'.[59] In so explicitly placing himself in the lineage of a black political tradition – and identifying so closely with black political interests – Obama leaves himself open to the accusation that he himself is guilty of this very forgetfulness. Eugene Goodheart is right when he claims that 'the disillusionment with Obama on the Left proceeds from what can only be characterized as a disappointed messianic expectation'.[60] These are though expectations that Obama himself raised.

As Goodheart suggests, Obama infuriates his liberal base because his agenda for 'change' seems not to be their agenda but rather encompasses the desire to transcend party lines in order to overcome the 'gridlock that paralyzes government' and prevents the implementation of major reform.[61] This suggestion might be extended to the particular disaffection with Obama from his black constituency. Obama has consistently rejected what he disconcertingly describes as the (racial) 'politics of grievance'. While figures like Martin Luther King, Jesse Jackson and Jeremiah Wright enabled his political rise, Obama's engagement with black politics has consistently involved translating its insights into worlds beyond the black experience and indeed beyond the American experience more generally. And while the Civil Rights movement, from which Obama drew so much inspiration, set its sights on an expanded understanding of freedom, Obama's pursuit of elected office signalled a desire to invest in the inevitably compromised process of 'nation-building'. Obama's election campaign did have some legitimate claim to the movement – the mass voter registration drive focused in particular on mobilizing

the black vote in a way that not only repudiated the disenfranchise-
ment of black voters in Florida in 2000 but which also gestured
back to a movement that made it possible for southern blacks to
vote at all. But Obama's administration must translate the poetry
of the campaign into the prose of governing, a difference that can
immediately be detected in the contrast between Obama's energetic
and inspirational election night speech and the sombre tones of his
inaugural address. 'Organizing for America', Obama's post-election
campaigning body, is an attempt to sustain the momentum of
the astonishing campaign that brought Obama into office and
provide his government with much needed support against the
right-wing backlash. Yet Obama now represents not a grassroots
movement but the most powerful country in the world. His not
insignificant legislative achievements are part of the mundane world
of secular politics, and the language of redemptive hope seems more
appropriately placed outside the centre of government.[62]

Obama does of course continue to articulate and transform a
narrative of American exceptionalism. Arguably, while he famously
announced to appreciative crowds in Berlin in July 2008 that
he was 'a citizen of the world', Obama's vision of a 'world that
stands as one' is collapsed back into the 'endless frontier' of his
American-centred political imagination.[63] And yet the fact that
Obama's vision of America is so open to worlds beyond America
paradoxically undermines the story of American uniqueness, just as
the articulation of human rights discourse in relation to US practices
in post-Katrina New Orleans might be seen as the uncanny – and
thus discomforting – return of American exceptionalism as much
as it is part of the 'global moral project of America'. Nonetheless,
the black Exodus rhetoric that I have argued has shaped Obama's
political vision is much less apparent in the language of a man
seeking to follow in the footsteps not of Martin Luther King but
of transformative – though perhaps inevitably flawed – presidents
like Abraham Lincoln and Franklin Delano Roosevelt.

Critics who compare Obama unfavourably to Roosevelt often
view the latter through a rose-tinted lens that overlooks the fact
that it took the Second World War to lift the US out of the Great
Depression. Nonetheless, Roosevelt's vision of a New Deal for the
American people envisaged the kind of radical transformation called
for by the enormous inequalities revealed by Katrina. Beyond the
politics of identity, the storm exposed cleavages along the lines of race
and class that illustrated the global coordinates of environmental

and social vulnerability. It demonstrated the prophetic nature of the luminaries of the 1960s black freedom movement who saw that the direction of the struggle must be towards global and class-based alliances. This vision is alive among the myriad forms of post-Katrina organizing.

In the meantime, and in the absence of a New Deal for the Gulf Coast, it has been the historically black church that has stepped into the gaping breach left by government in the five years since the storm. Reverend Donald Boutte claims that after a few decades in which the black church stepped away from its prophetic calling, it is once again focused on social justice. Boutte and other church leaders in New Orleans thus provide health care and social workers to communities otherwise abandoned to their fate – in much the same way, Boutte points out, that the Trinity United Church of Christ created by Reverend Jeremiah Wright serves the communities of Chicago's South Side. Their interventions constitute much more than influencing policy; as Boutte puts it, through their social and spiritual work, particularly black preachers are tasked with the job of 'restoring hope' where there is none.[64]

This message of 'hope' was also that which became Barack Obama's political mantra – derived not from the supposed 'paradise' of Hawaii but from an African-centred church located in an urban wasteland stalked by poverty and crime; the very antithesis of the American dream and the 'promised land' that Chicago represented for so many African Americans who made the Great Migration north, including Michelle Obama's family.[65] The twentieth-century exodus of African Americans out of the South exposed many to one of the most racist cities in the North, a city that saw the rise of the Nation of Islam and the death of many of Martin Luther King's dreams. Marking the southernmost point of the Mississippi, the endpoint of the mythological route into ever worse forms of slavery, New Orleans occupies a comparably pivotal place in the southern black imagination. In telling a much less forgiving account of America's origins, the post-Katrina portrait of New Orleans is a reminder not only of the fact that black American leaders have historically borne witness to a dream deferred, an exodus yet to come. It also highlights the crucial role an ideologically and religiously diverse black American counterpublic has historically played in the task of renewing democracy and speaking truth to power. Obama himself stands for an idea of America where there is no conflict between blackness and Americanness. It is the role of social movements on the outside of government to contradict the reactionary chorus of voices that identify Obama's administration with 'reverse racism', and to instead keep reminding the president that realities both within and beyond America have yet to catch up with the ideal of an 'America-in-the-world' that his rhetoric has so compellingly captured.

Notes

INTRODUCTION: REWRITING EXODUS

1. Reverend Donald Boutte, interview with Anna Hartnell, 27 May 2009.
2. George W. Bush quoted by Naomi Wolf, 'Fake Patriotism', *The Huffington Post*, 2 October 2008, http://www.huffingtonpost.com/naomi-wolf/fake-patriotism_b_131401.html (accessed 29 October 2010).
3. Ronald Reagan, 'Farewell Address to the Nation', *RonaldReagan.com*, 11 January 1989, http://www.ronaldreagan.com/sp_21.html (accessed 29 October 2010).
4. Robert Bellah, 'Civil Religion in America' in *American Civil Religion*, ed. Donald G. Jones and Russell E. Richey (San Francisco: Mellen Research University Press, 1990), 21–44.
5. Roderick D. Bush, *The End of White World Supremacy: Black Internationalism and the Problem of the Color Line* (Philadelphia, PA: Temple University Press, 2009), 6.
6. G.W.F. Hegel, *The Philosophy of History*, trans. J. Sibree (Amherst, MA: Prometheus Books, 1991), 86.
7. Michael Hanchard, 'Black Memory versus State Memory: Notes Toward a Method', *small axe*, 26 (2008): 45–62 (46).
8. Robin D.G. Kelley, *Freedom Dreams: The Black Radical Imagination* (Boston, MA: Beacon Press, 2002), 14.
9. W.E.B. Du Bois, *The Souls of Black Folk* (New York: The Modern Library, 2003), 5.
10. Malcolm X quoted by C. Eric Lincoln, *The Black Muslims in America* (Boston, MA: Beacon Press, 1961), 225.
11. Hanchard, 48.
12. Paul Gilroy, *Between Camps: Nations, Cultures and the Allure of Race* (London: Penguin, 2000), 231–237.
13. Du Bois, *Souls*, 5.
14. Hazel V. Carby, *Race Men* (Cambridge, MA: Harvard University Press: 1998), 4–6.
15. See, for example, Toni Morrison, 'Rootedness: The Ancestor as Foundation' in *Black Women Writers (1950-1980)*, ed. Mari Evans (Garden City, NY: Anchor Press/Doubleday, 1984), 339–345 (344).
16. Melissa Harris-Lacewell, *Barbershops, Bibles, and BET* (Princeton, NJ: Princeton University Press, 2004), 19.
17. See Michael C. Dawson, *Black Visions: The Roots of Contemporary African-American Political Ideologies* (Chicago: University of Chicago Press, 2001), xii; 1–43.
18. Du Bois, *Souls*, 13.
19. Henry Louis Gates Jr and Cornel West, *The African-American Century: How Black Americans Have Shaped Our Country* (New York: Touchstone, 2000), xii–xvi.

241

20. George Shulman, *American Prophecy: Race and Redemption in American Political Culture* (Minneapolis: University of Minnesota Press, 2008), 8.
21. Sacvan Bercovitch, *The American Jeremiad* (Wisconsin: University of Wisconsin Press, 1978), xiv.
22. See Shulman, 13.
23. Eddie S. Glaude Jr, *Exodus! Religion, Race, and Nation in Early Nineteenth-Century Black America* (Chicago: University of Chicago Press, 2000), 53.
24. Du Bois, *Souls*, 144.
25. Shulman, 11.
26. Wilson Jeremiah Moses, *Black Messiahs and Uncle Toms: Social and Literary Manipulations of a Religious Myth* (University Park: Pennsylvania State University Press, 1993), 30–31.
27. Kelley, xi.
28. Toni Morrison, 'On the Backs of Blacks' in *Arguing Immigration: The Debate Over the Changing Face of America*, ed. Nicolaus Mills (New York: Touchstone, 1994), 97–100 (98).
29. Thomas J. Sugrue, *Not Even Past: Barack Obama and the Burden of Race* (Princeton, NJ: Princeton University Press, 2010), 100–101.
30. See Roxanna Harlow and Lauren Dundes, '"United" We Stand: Responses to the September 11 Attacks in Black and White', *Sociological Perspectives* 47.4 (2004): 439–464 and Michael Dawson, Melissa Harris-Lacewell and Cathy Cohen, '2005 Racial Attitudes and the Katrina Disaster Study' (Chicago: Center for the Study of Race, Politics and Culture, 2006), http://www.melissaharrislacewell.com/docs/Katrina_Initial_Report.pdf (accessed 29 October 2010).
31. Manning Marable, *Beyond Black and White: Transforming African-American Politics* (London: Verso, 2009), xiv.
32. Dawson, 3.
33. Martin Luther King quoted by Richard Lischer, *The Preacher King: Martin Luther King, Jr. and the Word that Moved America* (New York: Oxford University Press, 1995), 121.
34. Moses, *Black Messiahs and Uncle Toms*, xiii.
35. *Malcolm X*, dir. Spike Lee, DVD (Pathe Distribution, 2001).

1   RE-READING AMERICA: BARACK OBAMA

1. See Francis X. Clines, 'The Closing of a Circle', *New York Times*, 19 January 2009, http://www.nytimes.com/2009/01/20/opinion/20tue4.html (accessed 29 October 2010).
2. Jonathan Freedland, 'All the Conservative Trappings Freed Obama to Frame a Radical Message', *Guardian*, 20 January 2009, http://www.guardian.co.uk/commentisfree/cifamerica/2009/jan/20/obama-inauguration-barackobama1 (accessed 29 October 2010).
3. Barack Obama, 'Remarks of President-Elect Barack Obama: Election Night', *Organizing for America*, 4 November 2008, http://www.barackobama.com/2008/11/04/remarks_of_presidentelect_bara.php (accessed 29 October 2010).
4. Martin Luther King Jr, *A Testament of Hope: The Essential Writings and Speeches of Martin Luther King, Jr.*, ed. James Melvin Washington (New York: Harper Collins, 1991), 286.

5. It should be noted that Obama employs a team of speech writers led by Jon Favreau. Favreau, who was just 27 years old at the time of Obama's inauguration and who happens to be white, has been employed by Obama since 2004 and has had a hand in all of his major public addresses. While this fact somewhat complicates the question of the authorship of Obama's speeches, much more than many presidents Obama works closely with his ghost writer, dictating the themes of his speeches and editing and re-writing the drafts. Favreau himself is said to have closely studied Obama's memoir, *Dreams From My Father*, and certainly the voice of Obama's public addresses bears marked similarities to that which animates the memoir that Obama penned prior to his political career.

6. Andrew Young quoted by Gwen Ifill, *The Breakthrough: Politics and Race in the Age of Obama* (New York: Doubleday, 2009), 35.

7. See, for example, the essays in *Barack Obama and African American Empowerment: The Rise of Black America's New Leadership*, ed. Manning Marable and Kristen Clarke (New York: Palgrave Macmillan, 2009).

8. Young quoted by Ifill, 50.

9. See Michael Hanchard, 'Black Memory versus State Memory: Notes Toward a Method', *small axe*, 26 (2008): 45–62.

10. See Ifill.

11. Barack Obama, *Dreams From My Father: A Story of Race and Inheritance* (Edinburgh: Canongate, 2007), xvi.

12. George W. Bush, 'Inaugural Address of George W. Bush', *The Avalon Project* at Yale Law School, 20 January 2001, http://avalon.law.yale.edu/21st_century/gbush1.asp (accessed 29 October 2010).

13. George W. Bush, 'Second Inaugural Address of George W. Bush', *The Avalon Project* at Yale Law School, 20 January 2005, http://avalon.law.yale.edu/21st_century/gbush2.asp (accessed 29 October 2010).

14. Jonathan Raban, 'The Golden Trumpet', *Guardian*, 24 January 2009, http://www.guardian.co.uk/world/2009/jan/24/barack-obama-inauguration-speech-presidency-president-review-jonathan-raban (accessed 29 October 2010).

15. Barack Obama, 'President Barack Obama's Inaugural Address', *The White House*, 20 January 2009, http://www.whitehouse.gov/blog/inaugural-address/ (accessed 29 October 2010).

16. Barack Obama, 'Renewing American Leadership', *Foreign Affairs*, July/August 2007, http://www.foreignaffairs.com/articles/62636/barack-obama/renewing-american-leadership (accessed 29 October 2010).

17. David Howard-Pitney, *The African American Jeremiad: Appeals for Justice in America* (Philadelphia, PA: Temple University Press, 2005), 5.

18. Obama, 'Election Night'.

19. For the Obama–Niebuhr connection see David Brooks, 'Obama, Gospel and Verse', *New York Times*, 26 April 2007, http://select.nytimes.com/2007/04/26/opinion/26brooks.html?_r=1 (accessed 29 October 2010).

20. Reinhold Niebuhr quoted by Carl Pederson, *Obama's America* (Edinburgh: Edinburgh University Press, 2009), 135.

21. Obama quoted by Pederson, 154.

22. Barack Obama, 'Remarks by the President at the Acceptance of the Nobel Peace Prize', *The White House*, 10 December 2009, http://www.whitehouse.gov/the-press-office/remarks-president-acceptance-nobel-peace-prize (accessed 29 October 2009).

23. Barack Obama, 'Keynote Address at the 2004 Democratic National Convention', *Organizing for America*, 27 July 2004, http://www.barackobama.com/2004/07/27/keynote_address_at_the_2004_de_1.php (accessed 29 October 2010).
24. Barack Obama, 'Remarks of Senator Barack Obama: 99th Annual Convention of the NAACP', *Organizing for America*, 14 July 2008, http://www.barackobama.com/2008/07/14/remarks_of_senator_barack_obam_93.php (accessed 29 October 2010).
25. Obama, 'Keynote Address at the 2004 Democratic National Convention'.
26. Obama, 'Acceptance of the Nobel Peace Prize'.
27. Obama, 'Inaugural Address'.
28. Obama, 'Inaugural Address'.
29. Cedric J. Robinson, *Black Movements in America* (New York: Routledge, 1997), 20.
30. Obama, 'Inaugural Address'.
31. Martin Luther King quoted by Eddie S. Glaude Jr, 'Black Power Revisited' in *Is it Nation Time? Contemporary Essays on Black Power and Black Nationalism*, ed. Eddie S. Glaude Jr (Chicago: University of Chicago Press, 2002), 1–21 (6).
32. Obama, *Dreams*, x.
33. Bush, 'The Second Inaugural Address of George W. Bush'.
34. Obama, *Dreams*, x.
35. Obama, *Dreams*, x.
36. Obama, *Dreams*, x.
37. David Remnick, *The Bridge: The Life and Rise of Barack Obama* (London: Picador, 2010), 119; 117.
38. Rickey Hill, 'The Race Problematic, the Narrative of Martin Luther King, Jr., and the Election of Barack Obama' in *Barack Obama and African American Empowerment*, 133–147 (136).
39. Remnick, 240.
40. Elizabeth Chang, 'Why Obama Should Not Have Checked "Black" on His Census Form', *Washington Post*, 29 April 2010, http://www.washingtonpost.com/wp-dyn/content/article/2010/04/28/AR2010042804156.html?referrer=emailarticle (accessed 29 October 2010).
41. Remnick, 235.
42. Obama, *Dreams*, 394.
43. Remnick, 248.
44. Obama, *Dreams*, 414.
45. Obama, *Dreams*, 86.
46. Remnick, 254–255.
47. See Henry Louis Gates Jr, *The Signifying Monkey: A Theory of African-American Literary Criticism* (New York: Oxford University Press, 1988).
48. Obama, *Dreams*, 437–438.
49. James T. Kloppenberg, *Reading Obama: Dreams, Hope, and the American Political Tradition* (Princeton, NJ: Princeton University Press, 2011), 252–253.
50. Malcolm X quoted by Michael C. Dawson, *Black Visions: The Roots of Contemporary African-American Political Ideologies* (Chicago: University of Chicago Press, 2001), 240.
51. Obama, *Dreams*, 439.

52. Jodi Kantor, 'The Obama's Marriage', *New York Times*, 26 October 2009, http://www.nytimes.com/2009/11/01/magazine/01Obama-t.html (accessed 29 October 2010).

53. Remnick, 4–25.

54. Barack Obama, 'Remarks by the President in Address to the Nation on the Way Forward in Afghanistan and Pakistan', *The White House*, 1 December 2009, http://www.whitehouse.gov/the-press-office/remarks-president-address-nation-way-forward-afghanistan-and-pakistan (accessed 29 October 2010).

55. Barack Obama, *The Audacity of Hope: Thoughts on Reclaiming the American Dream* (Canongate: Edinburgh, 2007), 198.

56. Obama, *Dreams*, 294.

57. Obama, *Dreams*, 394.

58. Melissa Harris-Lacewell, *Barbershops, Bibles, and BET* (Princeton, NJ: Princeton University Press, 2004), 35.

59. Eddie Glaude Jr, 'The Black Church is Dead', *The Huffington Post*, 24 February 2010, http://www.huffingtonpost.com/eddie-glaude-jr-phd/the-black-church-is-dead_b_473815.html (accessed 12 August 2010).

60. 'Our History', *Trinity United Church of Christ*, http://www.trinitychicago.org/index.php?option=com_content&task=view&id=12&Itemid=27 (accessed 29 October 2010).

61. It is important to note that the work of early black liberation theologians like Cone, Albert Cleage and J. Deotis Roberts has been followed by important revisionist works by womanist theologians.

62. James H. Cone, *Black Theology and Black Power* (New York: Seabury Press, 1969), 127.

63. Albert B. Cleage Jr, *The Black Messiah* (New York: Search Book Edition, 1969), 3–9.

64. Jeremiah A. Wright Jr, 'An Underground Theology' in *Black Faith and Public Talk: Critical Essays on James H. Cone's Black Theology and Black Power*, ed. Dwight N. Hopkins (Waco, TX: Baylor University Press, 2007), 96–102 (96).

65. Melissa Harris-Lacewell, 'From Liberation to Mutual Fund: Political Consequences of Differing Conceptions of Christ in the African American Church' in *From Pews to Polling Places: Faith and Politics in the American Religious Mosaic*, ed. J. Matthew Wilson (Washington, DC: Georgetown University Press, 2007), 131–160 (156).

66. See E. Franklin Frazier and C. Eric Lincoln, *The Negro Church in America/ The Black Church since Frazier* (New York: Schocken Books, 1974); for an analysis of this tendency, see Harris-Lacewell, *Barbershops, Bibles, and BET*, 35–39.

67. Jeremiah A. Wright Jr, *What Makes You So Strong? Sermons of Joy and Strength from Jeremiah A. Wright Jr.* , ed. Jini M. Kilgore (Valley Forge, PA: Judson Press, 1993), 107.

68. Darryl Pinckney, 'Obama and the Black Church', *New York Review of Books*, 17 July 2008, http://www.nybooks.com/articles/21611 (accessed 30 July 2009).

69. See Max Blumenthal, 'Obama Nation Author Jerome Corsi's Racist History Exposed', *The Nation*, 20 August 2008, http://www.thenation.com/doc/20080901/blumenthal (accessed 2 October 2009).

70. *Unfit for Publication*, 14 August 2008, http://www.politico.com/static/
    PPM104_080814_unfit_cover.html (accessed 2 October 2009).
71. Jerome R. Corsi, *The Obama Nation: Leftist Politics and the Cult of
    Personality* (New York: Threshold Editions, 2008), ix–xvi.
72. Colin Powell quoted by Grant Farred, 'The Ethics of Colin Powell' in *Barack
    Obama and African American Empowerment*, 105–120 (107).
73. Corsi, 50.
74. Obama, *Audacity*, 208.
75. Obama, *Dreams*, 287.
76. Barack Obama, 'A More Perfect Union', *Organizing for America*, 18 March
    2008, http://my.barackobama.com/page/content/hisownwords (accessed 30
    July 2009).
77. Sheryl Gay Stolberg, 'Obama Gives Fiery Address at N.A.A.C.P.', *New
    York Times*, 16 July 2009, http://www.nytimes.com/2009/07/17/us/
    politics/17obama.html (accessed 29 October 2010).
78. See Barack Obama, 'Father's Day 2008' in *Change We Can Believe In: Barack
    Obama's Plan to Renew America's Promise* (Edinburgh: Canongate, 2009),
    243–251.
79. Barack Obama, 'Remarks by the President to the NAACP Centennial
    Convention', *The White House*, 17 July 2009, http://www.whitehouse.
    gov/the_press_office/Remarks-by-the-President-to-the-NAACP-Centennial-
    Convention-07/16/2009/ (accessed 29 October 2010).
80. Samuel G. Freedman, 'Call and Response on the State of the Black Church',
    New York Times, 16 April 2010, http://www.nytimes.com/2010/04/17/
    us/17religion.html (accessed 13 August 2010).
81. Harris-Lacewell, *Barbershops, Bibles, and BET*, 137.
82. See Kevin Gaines, *Uplifting the Race: Black Leadership, Politics, and Culture
    in the Twentieth Century* (Chapel Hill: University of North Carolina Press,
    1996).
83. Hill, 144.
84. Robinson, 96; 98.
85. Malcolm X, *Malcolm X Speaks*, ed. George Breitman (New York: Grove
    Press, 1990), 26.
86. Dawson, 117.
87. Wilson Jeremiah Moses, *Afrotopia: The Roots of African American Popular
    History* (Cambridge: Cambridge University Press, 1998).
88. Penny M. Von Eschen, *Race Against Empire: Black Americans and
    Anticolonialism, 1937–1957* (Ithaca, NY: Cornell University Press, 1997).
89. Moses, *Afrotopia*, 5–11.
90. Stephen Howe, *Afrocentrism: Mythical Pasts and Imagined Homes* (London:
    Verso, 1998), 202.
91. Paul Gilroy, *The Black Atlantic: Modernity and Double Consciousness*
    (London: Verso, 1993), 205; 207.
92. Barack Obama, 'Remarks by the President at Cape Coast Castle', *The White
    House*, 11 July 2009, http://www.whitehouse.gov/the_press_office/Remarks-
    By-The-President-At-Cape-Coast-Castle/ (accessed 29 October 2010).
93. Obama, *Audacity*, 98.
94. Obama, *Audacity*, 97.
95. Obama, 'Acceptance of the Nobel Peace Prize'.

96. Barack Obama, 'Remarks by the President in Commencement Address at the University of Notre Dame', *The White House*, 17 May 2009, http://www. whitehouse.gov/the_press_office/Remarks-by-the-President-at-Notre-Dame-Commencement/ (accessed 29 October 2009).

97. Barack Obama, 'Remarks of Senator Barack Obama: AIPAC Policy Conference', *Organizing for America*, 4 June 2008, http://www.barackobama. com/2008/06/04/remarks_of_senator_barack_obam_74.php (accessed 30 July 2008).

98. It should be noted that Obama did ultimately gain 78 per cent of the Jewish vote.

99. John Pilger, 'The Danse Macabre of US-style Democracy', *New Statesman*, 24 January 2008, http://www.newstatesman.com/north-america/2008/01/ pilger-presidential-webb (accessed 23 October 2009).

100. Farred, 116.

101. John Pilger, 'The Smile on the Face of the Tiger', *New Statesman*, 11 June 2009, http://www.newstatesman.com/middle-east/2009/06/pilger-obama-israel (accessed 23 October 2009).

102. Barack Obama, 'Remarks by the President on a New Beginning', *The White House*, 4 June 2009, http://www.whitehouse.gov/the_press_office/Remarks-by-the-President-at-Cairo-University-6-04-09/ (accessed 29 October 2010).

103. Barack Obama, 'Remarks by the President to the Ghanaian Parliament', *The White House*, 11 July 2009, http://www.whitehouse.gov/the_press_office/ Remarks-by-the-President-to-the-Ghanaian-Parliament/ (accessed 29 October 2009).

104. Marieme Helie Lucas, 'Obama Speech Omits Women and Secularists', *Pambazuka News*, 437, 11 June 2009, http://www.pambazuka.org/en/ category/features/56867/print (accessed 29 October 2010).

105. Obama, 'NAACP Centennial Convention'.

106. Pederson, 163–170; 125.

107. Robert Fisk, 'Words that Could Heal Wounds of Centuries', *The Independent*, 5 June 2009, http://www.independent.co.uk/opinion/commentators/fisk/ robert-fisk-words-that-could-heal-wounds-of-centuries-1697417.html (accessed 29 October 2010).

108. Harris-Lacewell, *Barbershops, Bibles, and BET*, 3.

109. Naomi Klein, 'Minority Death Match: Jews, Blacks and the "Post-Racial" Presidency', *Harper's Magazine* (September 2009): 53–67 (54).

110. See Remnick, 265.

111. Dawson, 119.

112. Manning Marable, *Beyond Black and White: Transforming African-American Politics* (London: Verso, 2009), 258.

113. Marable, *Beyond Black and White*, 256–257.

114. Robin D.G. Kelley, *Freedom Dreams: The Black Radical Imagination* (Boston, MA: Beacon Press, 2002), 129.

115. Barack Obama, '99th Annual Convention of the NAACP'.

116. Wilson Jeremiah Moses, *Black Messiahs and Uncle Toms: Social and Literary Manipulations of a Religious Myth* (University Park: Pennsylvania State University Press, 1993), xiii.

117. Kevin Gaines, 'Of Teachable Moments and Specters of Race', *American Quarterly*, 62.2 (2010), 195–213 (195; 204). Unfortunately, this anti-government chorus is not confined to the fringe of 'Tea Party' activists who

are currently pushing the Republican Party further and further to the right; conservative thinker Dinesh D'Souza argues in his recent book that Obama has 'embraced his father's ideals and decided to live out the script of his father's unfulfilled life'; this entails taking up 'the black man's burden' and imposing a socialist, anti-colonial agenda 'with vengeance on America and the world'. D'Souza's arguments are particularly ironic given that the claim that the US is itself an anti-imperialist endeavour is a standard ingredient of American exceptionalism. Indeed, the Tea Party movement takes its name from an event that was not only about repudiating government taxation but also the British Empire. See Dinesh D'Souza, *The Roots of Obama's Rage* (Washington, DC: Regnery Publishing, 2010), 17–35.

118. Obama, *Audacity*, 97–98.

2 DOUBLE CONSCIOUSNESS AND THE MASTER/SLAVE DIALECTIC: W.E.B. DU BOIS

1. Orlando Patterson, *An Absence of Ruins* (1967), quoted by James Ngugi, 'The African Writer and his Past' in *Perspectives on African Literature*, ed. Christopher Heywood (London: Heinemann, 1971), 3–8 (5).
2. For analysis see Charles M. Blow, 'Obama's "Race" War', *New York Times*, 30 July 2010, http://www.nytimes.com/2010/07/31/opinion/31blow.html?_r=2&th&emc=th (accessed 13 August 2010) and 'For Obama, Race Means Repeated Distractions', *Black Politics on the Web*, 24 July 2010, http://blackpoliticsontheweb.com/2010/07/24/for-obama-race-means-repeated-distractions/ (accessed 13 August 2010).
3. Kevin Gaines, 'Of Teachable Moments and Specters of Race', *American Quarterly*, 62.2 (2010): 195–213 (204).
4. David Theo Goldberg, *The Threat of Race: Reflections on Racial Neoliberalism* (Malden, MA: Wiley-Blackwell, 2009), 25.
5. Lisa Palmer, '"Obamanation!" Navigating Race and Blackness in "Post-racial America"', unpublished conference paper delivered at 'Obama: 300 Days', University of Birmingham, 29 October 2009.
6. W.E.B. Du Bois, *The Souls of Black Folk* (New York: The Modern Library, 2003), 5.
7. For an account, see Edward J. Blum, *W.E.B. Du Bois: American Prophet* (Philadelphia: University of Pennsylvania Press, 2007), 61–97.
8. Du Bois, *Souls*, 111–112; 116–122; 127.
9. Du Bois, *Souls*, 117–118.
10. Du Bois, *Souls*, 144.
11. See Michael Hanchard, 'Black Memory versus State Memory: Notes Toward a Method', *small axe*, 26 (2008): 45–62.
12. Richard H. King, *Race, Culture, and the Intellectuals 1940–1970* (Washington, DC and Baltimore, MD: Woodrow Wilson Center Press and Johns Hopkins University Press, 2004), 46.
13. W.E.B. Du Bois, *Du Bois on Religion*, ed. Phil Zuckerman (Walnut Creek, CA: AltaMira Press, 2000).
14. W.E.B. Du Bois, *Dusk of Dawn: An Essay Toward an Autobiography of a Race Concept* (New Brunswick, NJ: Transaction Books, 1984), xxix–xxx.
15. Du Bois, *Souls*, xli.

16. Richard King, 37–45.
17. W.E.B. Du Bois, 'Jacob and Esau' in *Du Bois on Religion*, 187–196 (188–189).
18. Du Bois, 'Jacob and Esau', 189–194.
19. Du Bois, 'Jacob and Esau', 195.
20. W.E.B. Du Bois, *Darkwater: Voices from Within the Veil* (London: Dodo Press, 2006), 17–31 (17; 29).
21. Du Bois, *Darkwater*, 21.
22. Du Bois quoted by Richard King, 47.
23. For a summary see Richard King, 14; 45–48.
24. Du Bois, *Darkwater*, 23.
25. Richard King, 41.
26. Du Bois, *Dusk of Dawn*, 137.
27. Du Bois, *Dusk of Dawn*, 116.
28. Paul Gilroy, *The Black Atlantic: Modernity and Double Consciousness* (London: Verso, 1993), 111–145 (113).
29. Segun Gbadesgesin, 'Kinship of the Dispossessed: Du Bois, Nkrumah, and the Foundations of Pan-Africanism' in *W.E.B. Du Bois on Race and Culture*, ed. Bernard W. Bell, Emily Grosholz and James B. Stewart (New York: Routledge, 1996), 219–242 (224).
30. Richard King, 41.
31. Du Bois, *Dusk of Dawn*, 141.
32. Du Bois quoted by Manning Marable, 'The Pan-Africanism of W.E.B. Du Bois' in *W.E.B. Du Bois on Race and Culture*, 193–218 (199).
33. Arnold Rampersad, *The Art and Imagination of W.E.B. Du Bois* (Cambridge, MA: Harvard University Press, 1976), 19.
34. Blum, 65–76.
35. Robert Young, *White Mythologies: Writing, History and the West* (London: Routledge, 1990).
36. Du Bois, *Darkwater*, 20.
37. Jemima Pierre and Jesse Weaver Shipley, 'African/Diaspora History: W.E.B. Du Bois and Pan-Africanism in Ghana' in *Ghana in Africa and the World: Essays in Honor of Adu Boahen*, ed. Toyin Falola (Trenton, NJ: Africa World Press, 2003), 731–753 (733).
38. Du Bois, *Darkwater*, 21.
39. G.W.F. Hegel quoted by David Gunkel, 'Escape Velocity: *Exodus* and Postmodernism', *Soundings: An Interdisciplinary Journal*, 81.3–4 (1998): 437–459 (437).
40. Du Bois, *Souls*, 8–13.
41. Du Bois, *Souls*, 10.
42. Blum, 3–4.
43. G.W.F. Hegel, *Phenomenology of Spirit*, trans. A.V. Miller (Oxford: Oxford University Press, 1977), 113–116.
44. Du Bois, *Souls*, 5.
45. Orlando Patterson, *Slavery and Social Death* (Cambridge, MA: Harvard University Press, 1982), 335.
46. Hegel, *Phenomenology of Spirit*, 130–133.
47. Du Bois, *Souls*, 5.
48. Frantz Fanon, *Black Skin, White Masks* (London: Pluto, 1986), 109–140.
49. Du Bois, *Souls*, 4–6.
50. Hegel, *Phenomenology of Spirit*, 131.

51. Du Bois, *Souls*, 7; 200.
52. Alexandre Kojève, *Introduction to the Reading of Hegel: Lectures on the Phenomenology of Spirit*, assembled by Raymond Queneau, ed. Alan Bloom, trans. James H. Nichols Jr (Ithaca, NY: Cornell University Press, 1980), 53.
53. Shamoon Zamir, *Dark Voices: W.E.B. Du Bois and American Thought, 1888–1903* (Chicago: University of Chicago Press, 1995), 141.
54. Joel Williamson, *The Crucible of Race: Black–White Relations in the American South Since Emancipation* (New York: Oxford University Press, 1984), 409.
55. Du Bois, *Souls*, 4–5; 13; 6.
56. Kojève, 46.
57. Williamson, 403.
58. Du Bois, *Souls*, 5.
59. Du Bois, *Darkwater*, i–ii.
60. Blum, 64.
61. Zamir, 136.
62. Du Bois, *Souls*, 6.
63. Werner Sollors, *Beyond Ethnicity: Consent and Descent in American Culture* (New York: Oxford University Press, 1986), 49.
64. Rowan Williams, 'Logic and Spirit in Hegel' in *Post-Secular Philosophy: Between Philosophy and Theology*, ed. Phillip Blond (London: Routledge, 1998), 116–130 (126).
65. Phillip Blond, 'Introduction: Theology before Philosophy' in *Post-Secular Philosophy*, 1–66 (18).
66. J.N. Findlay, 'Analysis of the Text' in *Phenomenology of Spirit*, 495–591 (585).
67. Findlay, 590.
68. Kojève, 67.
69. Du Bois, *Souls*, 190–208.
70. Du Bois, *Souls*, 197.
71. Du Bois, *Souls*, 207–208.
72. Kojève, 67.
73. Blond, 18.
74. Blond, 18.
75. Du Bois, *Souls*, 211.
76. Du Bois, *Souls*, 211–216.
77. Gunkel, 445.
78. David Levering Lewis, 'Introduction' in *The Souls of Black Folk*, xi–xxxiii (xxii–xxiii).
79. Du Bois, *Souls*, 211.
80. Lewis, xxii.
81. See Blum, 89.
82. Du Bois, *Souls*, 215.
83. Gilroy, *The Black Atlantic*, 63.
84. Du Bois, *Souls*, 227.
85. Williamson, 405.
86. Du Bois, *Souls*, 150.
87. Patterson, 342.
88. Du Bois, *Souls*, 8.
89. Du Bois, *Darkwater*, 45.

90. Du Bois quoted by Benjamin Sevitch, 'W.E.B. Du Bois and Jews: A Lifetime of Opposing Anti-Semitism', *Journal of African American History*, 87 (2002): 323–337 (326).
91. Sevitch, 328.
92. Du Bois quoted by Sevitch, 334.
93. Du Bois quoted by Robert G. Weisbord and Richard Kazarian Jr, *Israel in the Black American Perspective* (Westport, CT: Greenwood Press, 1985), 30.
94. W.E.B. Du Bois, 'The Negro and the Warsaw Ghetto' in *Du Bois on Religion*, 197–201 (199).
95. See Weisbord and Kazarian, 93–119.
96. Du Bois, *Darkwater*, 64.

3 EXCAVATING THE PROMISED LAND: MARTIN LUTHER KING

1. Martin Luther King Jr, 'I Have a Dream', 28 August 1963, in *A Testament of Hope: The Essential Writings and Speeches of Martin Luther King, Jr.*, ed. James Melvin Washington (New York: Harper Collins, 1991), 217–220 (219).
2. Jeremy Olshan and Geoff Earle, 'Temple of Dem on Mt. O-lympus', *New York Post*, 28 August 2008, http://www.nypost.com/p/news/national/item_6opMriwkG5qfmPLfggQisN (accessed 13 November 2010).
3. Richard Lischer, *The Preacher King: Martin Luther King, Jr. and the Word that Moved America* (New York: Oxford University Press, 1995), 7.
4. King quoted by Michael Eric Dyson, *I May Not Get There with You: The True Martin Luther King, Jr.* (New York: The Free Press, 2000), 30.
5. King, *A Testament of Hope*, 317.
6. King points to 'racist blindness' in 'A Testament of Hope' in *A Testament of Hope*, 313–328 (326).
7. King, *A Testament of Hope*, 318.
8. Barack Obama, 'Remarks of Senator Barack Obama: The American Promise', *Organizing for America*, 28 August 2009, http://www.barackobama.com/2008/08/28/remarks_of_senator_barack_obam_108.php (accessed 13 November 2010).
9. Keith Miller, *Voice of Deliverance: The Language of Martin Luther King, Jr., and its Sources* (Athens: University of Georgia Press, 1998), 14.
10. See Peter J. Paris, 'Comparing the Public Theologies of James H. Cone and Martin Luther King, Jr.' in *Black Faith and Public Talk: Critical Essays on James H. Cone's Black Theology and Black Power*, ed. Dwight N. Hopkins (Waco TX: Baylor University Press, 2007), 218–231 (222).
11. James H. Cone, *A Black Theology of Liberation* (Maryknoll, NY: Orbis Books, 1986), 128.
12. Timothy P. Caron, *Struggles over the Word: Race and Religion in O'Connor, Faulkner, Hurston, and Wright* (Macon, GA: Mercer University Press, 2000), 12.
13. King quoted by Taylor Branch, *Pillar of Fire: America in the King Years 1963–65* (New York: Simon and Schuster, 1998), 24.
14. James H. Cone, *Black Theology and Black Power* (New York: Seabury Press, 1969), 124.
15. Jerry Falwell quoted by Lewis V. Baldwin, 'On the Relation of the Christian to the State: The Development of a Kingian Ethic' in *The Legacy of Martin*

Luther King, Jr.: The Boundaries of Law, Politics, and Religion, ed. Lewis V. Baldwin, Rufus Burrow Jr, Barbara A. Holmes and Susan Holmes Winfield (Notre Dame, IN: University of Notre Dame Press, 2002), 77–123 (92).

16. Martin Luther King Jr, *Why We Can't Wait* (New York: Signet Books, 1964), 91.
17. King, *A Testament of Hope*, 26.
18. King quoted by Paris, 221.
19. That is, the Christian claim to have superseded – replaced – Judaism.
20. Eugene Genovese, *Roll, Jordan, Roll: The World the Slaves Made* (New York: Vintage, 1976), 252.
21. Martin Luther King Jr, *The Papers of Martin Luther King, Jr.: Volume 1: Called to Serve, January 1929–June 1951*, ed. Clayborne Carson (Berkeley: University of California Press, 1992), 269.
22. King, *The Papers of Martin Luther King*, 246.
23. King quoted by Baldwin, 'On the Relation of the Christian to the State', 85.
24. Howard Thurman, *Jesus and the Disinherited* (Boston, MA: Beacon Press, 1996), 31.
25. See in particular the character of Gail Hightower in Faulkner's *Light in August* (1932).
26. See Michael Northcott, *An Angel Directs the Storm: Apocalyptic Religion and American Empire* (London: I.B. Tauris, 2004), 61–68.
27. King, *The Papers of Martin Luther King*, 260–262.
28. King, *The Papers of Martin Luther King*, 262.
29. Editorial note, *The Papers of Martin Luther King*, 257.
30. Cone, *A Black Theology of Liberation*, 118.
31. King, *The Papers of Martin Luther King*, 229; 271.
32. Alain Badiou, *Saint Paul: The Foundation of Universalism*, trans. Ray Brassier (Stanford, CA: Stanford University Press, 2003).
33. Thurman, 12–13; 33.
34. Albert B. Cleage Jr, *The Black Messiah* (New York: Search Book Editions, 1969), 4.
35. Slavoj Žižek, *The Puppet and the Dwarf: The Perverse Core of Christianity* (Cambridge, MA: MIT Press, 2003), 31–33.
36. King, *The Papers of Martin Luther King*, 245.
37. King, *The Papers of Martin Luther King*, 197.
38. King, *The Papers of Martin Luther King*, 245.
39. Vincent Harding, 'Foreword' in *Jesus and the Disinherited*, 1.
40. Thurman, 24.
41. Melissa Harris-Lacewell, 'From Liberation to Mutual Fund: Political Consequences of Differing Conceptions of Christ in the African American Church' in *From Pews to Polling Places: Faith and Politics in the American Religious Mosaic*, ed. J. Matthew Wilson (Washington, DC: Georgetown University Press, 2007), 131–160 (138).
42. Thurman, 11.
43. Badiou, 27.
44. Badiou, 103.
45. King, *The Papers of Martin Luther King*, 265.
46. King, *Why We Can't Wait*, 86.
47. King, *Why We Can't Wait*, 120.
48. Badiou, 103.

49. For a full account of the debate about the 'Jewish Jesus', see Susannah Heschel, *Abraham Geiger and the Jewish Jesus* (Chicago: University of Chicago Press, 1998).

50. Sigmund Freud, *Moses and Monotheism, an Outline of Psycho-Analysis and Other Works*, Standard Edition 23, ed. and trans. James Strachey (London: Vintage, 2001), 86; 135.

51. Martin Luther King Jr, *Stride Toward Freedom: The Montgomery Story* (New York: Harper and Row, 1958), 99–100.

52. Susannah Heschel, 'Theological Affinities in the Writings of Abraham Joshua Heschel and Martin Luther King, Jr.' in *Black Zion: African American Religious Encounters with Judaism*, ed. Yvonne Chireau and Nathaniel Deutsch (New York: Oxford University Press, 2000), 168–186 (168–169).

53. See, for example, King, *Why We Can't Wait*, 82–83.

54. James Baldwin quoted by Jonathan Kaufman, *Broken Alliance: The Turbulent Times Between Blacks and Jews in America* (New York: Charles Scribner's Sons, 1988), 2.

55. Kaufman, 32.

56. King quoted by Marc Schneier, *Shared Dreams: Martin Luther King, Jr. and the Jewish Community* (Woodstock: Jewish Lights Publishing, 1999), 35.

57. Account of Albert Vorspan quoted by Schneier, 41.

58. Schneier, 45.

59. See Edward S. Shapiro, 'World War II and American Jewish Identity', *Modern Judaism*, 10.1 (1990): 65–84.

60. For an account of the 1967 war – which argues that the war was the culmination of a series of diplomatic miscalculations on both sides, meaning that 'of all the Arab–Israeli wars, the June 1967 war was the only one that neither side wanted' – see Avi Shlaim, *The Iron Wall: Israel and the Arab World* (London: Penguin, 2000), 218–264 (236).

61. King quoted by Schneier, 165–169.

62. See Chapter 5 for an elaboration of this argument.

63. See Shlomo Avineri, *The Making of Modern Zionism: The Intellectual Origins of the Jewish State* (London: Weidenfeld and Nicolson, 1981), 3–4.

64. Zachary Braiterman, *(God) After Auschwitz: Tradition and Change in Post-Holocaust Jewish Thought* (Princeton, NJ: Princeton University Press, 1998), 71.

65. Leela Gandhi, 'Concerning Violence: The Limits and Circulations of Gandhian *Ahimsa* or Passive Resistance', *Cultural Critique*, 35 (1996–97): 105–147 (106).

66. King, *Stride Toward Freedom*, 97.

67. Leela Gandhi, 107.

68. King, *Stride Toward Freedom*, 99.

69. *Muhammad Speaks*, quoted by Gary E. Rubin, 'African Americans and Israel' in *Struggles in the Promised Land: Toward a History of Black–Jewish Relations in the United States*, ed. Jack Salzman and Cornel West (New York: Oxford University Press, 1997), 357–370 (358).

70. Edward W. Said, *Out of Place* (London: Granta, 1999), 141.

71. Penny M. Von Eschen, *Race Against Empire: Black Americans and Anticolonialism, 1937–1957* (Ithaca, NY: Cornell University Press, 1997), 3.

72. Thurman, 13–15.

73. See Martin Luther King Jr, *Where Do We Go from Here: Chaos or Community?* (London: Hodder and Stoughton, 1968), 176.
74. King, *Where Do We Go From Here?*, 170–175.
75. Lewis Baldwin, 'Martin Luther King, Jr., a "Coalition of Conscience," and Freedom in South Africa' in *Freedom's Distant Shores: American Protestants and Post-Colonial Alliances with Africa*, ed. R. Drew Smith (Waco, TX: Baylor University Press, 2006), 53–82 (54).
76. See Robert G. Weisbord and Richard Kazarian Jr, *Israel in the Black American Perspective* (Westport, CT: Greenwood Press, 1985), 100.
77. George Orwell quoted by Geoffrey Wheatcroft, 'On Trying to be Portugal', *London Review of Books*, 6 August 2009, 35.15, http://www.lrb.co.uk/v31/n15/whea03_.html (accessed 13 November 2010).
78. Orwell quoted by Wheatcroft.
79. King, *A Testament of Hope*, 257.
80. Ed Pilkington, 'Chicago's Murdered Children', *Guardian*, 11 August 2009, http://www.guardian.co.uk/world/2009/aug/11/chicago-children-murders (accessed 13 November 2010).
81. King, 'I See the Promised Land', 3 April 1968, in *A Testament of Hope*, 279–286 (280).
82. Lischer, 158–159.
83. Lischer, 158–159.
84. Dyson, *I May Not Get There with You*, 32–34.
85. King, *A Testament of Hope*, 317.
86. King, *A Testament of Hope*, 318.
87. King, *A Testament of Hope*, 328.
88. Barack Obama, 'The American Promise'.
89. Algernon Austin, *Achieving Blackness: Race, Black Nationalism and Afrocentrism in the Twentieth Century* (New York: New York University Press, 2006), xi.
90. See Michael Hanchard, 'Black Memory versus State Memory: Notes Toward a Method', *small axe*, 26 (2008): 45–62.
91. See Margaret Malamud, *Ancient Rome and Modern America* (Chichester: Wiley-Blackwell, 2009).
92. King, *A Testament of Hope*, 219.

4   RECLAIMING 'EGYPT': MALCOLM X

1. Malcolm X, *By Any Means Necessary*, ed. George Breitman (New York: Pathfinder, 1992), 46.
2. Richard Lischer, *The Preacher King: Martin Luther King, Jr. and the Word that Moved America* (New York: Oxford University Press, 1995), 161–162.
3. Michael Eric Dyson, *I May Not Get There with You: The True Martin Luther King, Jr.* (New York: The Free Press, 2000), 31.
4. Carolyn Gerald quoted by Richard H. King, *Race, Culture, and the Intellectuals 1940–1970* (Washington, DC and Baltimore, MD: Woodrow Wilson Center Press and Johns Hopkins University Press, 2004), 282.
5. Michael C. Dawson, *Black Visions: The Roots of Contemporary African-American Political Ideologies* (Chicago: University of Chicago Press, 2001), 60.

6. See Claybourne Carson, ed., *The Autobiography of Martin Luther King, Jr.* (London: Abacus, 2000).
7. Barack Obama, *Dreams From My Father: A Story of Race and Inheritance* (Edinburgh: Canongate, 2007), 86.
8. Obama, *Dreams*, 86.
9. *Malcolm X*, dir. Spike Lee, DVD (Pathe Distribution, 2001; first released 1992).
10. See Nia-Malika Henderson, 'Blacks, Whites Hear Obama Differently', *Politico*, 3 March 2009, http://www.politico.com/news/stories/0309/19538.html (accessed 13 November 2010).
11. Wahneema Lubiano, 'Standing in for the State: Black Nationalism and "Writing" the Black Subject' in *Is it Nation Time? Contemporary Essays on Black Power and Black Nationalism*, ed. Eddie S. Glaude Jr (Chicago: University of Chicago Press, 2002), 156–164 (158).
12. Lubiano, 157.
13. See Dawson, 111.
14. Eddie S. Glaude Jr, *Exodus! Religion, Race, and Nation in Early Nineteenth-Century Black America* (Chicago: University of Chicago Press, 2000).
15. Dawson, 87.
16. Wilson Jeremiah Moses, *The Golden Age of Black Nationalism 1850–1925* (Hamden, CT: Archon Books, 1978), 9–12.
17. David Howard-Pitney quoted by Dawson, 103.
18. Dawson, 87.
19. Melani McAlister, *Epic Encounters: Culture, Media, and U.S. Interests in the Middle East since 1945* (Berkeley: University of California Press, 2005), 98.
20. McAlister, 94.
21. Malcolm X, *The Autobiography of Malcolm X*, with the assistance of Alex Haley (London: Penguin, 1968), 83–85.
22. See Frederick Douglass, 'Narrative of the Life of Frederick Douglass, an American Slave' in *The Classic Slave Narratives*, ed. Henry Louis Gates Jr (New York: Mentor, 1987), 243–331; this text was first published in 1845.
23. Malcolm X, *Autobiography*, 257.
24. Sherman A. Jackson, *Islam and the Blackamerican: Looking Toward the Third Resurrection* (New York: Oxford University Press, 2005), 44.
25. Malcolm X quoted by Louis A. DeCaro Jr, *On the Side of My People: A Religious Life of Malcolm X* (New York: New York University Press, 1996), 173.
26. Malcolm X, *Autobiography*, 320.
27. Lewis V. Baldwin and Amiri YaSin Al-Hadid, *Between Cross and Crescent: Christian and Muslim Perspectives on Malcolm and Martin* (Gainesville: University Press of Florida, 2002), 66.
28. Edward Wilmot Blyden quoted by Jackson, 63–65.
29. Jackson, 64–66.
30. See Dawson, 97.
31. McAlister, 99.
32. Alex Haley, 'Foreword' in *The Autobiography of Malcolm X*, 11–78 (14).
33. Edward E. Curtis, *Islam in Black America: Identity, Liberation, and Difference in African-American Islamic Thought* (Albany: State University of New York Press, 2002), 89–90.

34. For an analysis of the ideological crossovers between black nationalism and black conservatism, see Melissa Harris-Lacewell, *Barbershops, Bibles, and BET* (Princeton, NJ: Princeton University Press, 2004), 137.

35. Manning Marable, 'Malcolm as Messiah: Cultural Myth vs. Historical Reality in *Malcolm X*', *Cineaste* 19.4 (1993): 7–9 (9).

36. McAlister, 98.

37. Malcolm X, *Autobiography*, 282–285.

38. Malcolm X, *Autobiography*, 411–414.

39. Paul John Eakin, 'Malcolm X and the Limits of Autobiography' in *African American Autobiography*, ed. William L. Andrews (Englewood Cliffs, NJ: Prentice Hall, 1993), 151–161 (156).

40. Malcolm X, *Autobiography*, 454.

41. Manning Marable, *Beyond Black and White: Transforming African-American Politics* (London: Verso, 2009), 210.

42. Dawson, 104.

43. For an account of Malcolm's meeting with the Klan, see DeCaro, *On the Side of My People*, 180–181.

44. Malcolm X, *Autobiography*, 452–456.

45. Louis A. DeCaro Jr, *Malcolm and the Cross: The Nation of Islam, Malcolm X, and Christianity* (New York: New York University Press, 1998), 1.

46. Malcolm X, *Malcolm X Speaks*, ed. George Breitman (New York: Grove Press, 1990), 59.

47. Malcolm X, *By Any Means Necessary*, 125–129.

48. Malcolm X, *Autobiography*, 486.

49. C. Eric Lincoln, *The Black Muslims in America* (Boston, MA: Beacon Press, 1961), 224.

50. McAlister, 90.

51. Elijah Muhammad quoted by Lincoln, 224.

52. Gamal Abdel Nasser quoted by Lincoln, 225.

53. Curtis, *Islam in Black America*, 93.

54. Said Ramadam quoted by Curtis, *Islam in Black America*, 104–105.

55. Curtis, *Islam in Black America*, 97.

56. See *Malcolm X Speaks*, 62.

57. Jackson, 78.

58. Jackson, 77.

59. Jackson, 29–32.

60. Lincoln, 210–226.

61. Malcolm quoted by Edward E. Curtis, 'Islamism and its African American Muslim Critics: Black Muslims in the Era of the Arab Cold War', *American Quarterly*, 59.3 (2007): 683–709 (696).

62. Malcolm X, *By Any Means Necessary*, 196.

63. Jackson, 27.

64. Wilson Jeremiah Moses, *Afrotopia: The Roots of African American Popular History* (Cambridge: Cambridge University Press, 1998), 5.

65. Paul Gilroy, *The Black Atlantic: Modernity and Double Consciousness* (London: Verso, 1993), 207.

66. McAlister, 91.

67. McAlister, 122.

68. McAlister, 84.

69. See McAlister, 47.

70. Malcolm quoted by Lincoln, 166.
71. See Stokely Carmichael, *Stokely Speaks: Black Power Back to Pan-Africanism* (New York: Random House, 1971), 131–143.
72. Carmichael, 136.
73. McAlister, 123.
74. Carmichael, 141.
75. *Malcolm X Speaks*, 62–63.
76. McAlister, 99.
77. Carmichael, 132–133.
78. See Arie Bober, ed., *The Other Israel: The Radical Case Against Zionism* (Garden City, NY: Anchor Books, 1972), 24–30.
79. Robert G. Weisbord and Richard Kazarian Jr, *Israel in the Black American Perspective* (Westport, CT: Greenwood Press, 1985), 19.
80. Paul Gilroy, *Between Camps: Nations, Cultures and the Allure of Race* (London: Penguin, 2000), 231–237.
81. Marcus Garvey Jr, quoted by Gilroy, *Between Camps*, 236.
82. See Gilroy, *The Black Atlantic*, 24.
83. E. Frances White, 'Africa on My Mind: Gender, Counter Discourse, and African American Nationalism' in *Is it Nation Time?*, 130–155 (132).
84. Gilroy, *Between Camps*, 237.
85. See, for example, Molefi Kete Asante, *Afrocentricity: The Theory of Social Change* (Buffalo, NY: Amulefi Publishing, 1980), 5.
86. See Molefi Kete Asante, *Malcolm X as Cultural Hero and other Afrocentric Essays* (Trenton, NJ: Africa World Press, 1993).
87. Cheikh Anta Diop quoted by Richard King, 240.
88. Michael Hanchard, 'Black Memory versus State Memory: Notes Toward a Method', *small axe*, 26 (2008): 45–62.
89. See Gilroy, *The Black Atlantic*, 208–209; for a more extensive account of Blyden see Curtis, *Islam in Black America*, 21–43; for Jewish connections see Weisbord and Kazarian, *Israel in the Black American Perspective*, 7–10.
90. See Edward W. Said, *Covering Islam* (London: Vintage, 1997).
91. See Ronald L. Grimes, *Rite out of Place: Ritual, Media, and the Arts* (Oxford: Oxford University Press, 2006), 74–86.
92. See, for example, Roopali Mukherjee, 'Between Enemies and Traitors: Black Press Coverage of September 11 and the Predicaments of National "Others"' in *Media Representations of September 11*, ed. Steven Chermak, Frankie Y. Bailey and Michelle Brown (Westport, CT: Praeger, 2003), 29–46.
93. Roxanna Harlow and Lauren Dundes, '"United" We Stand: Responses to the September 11 Attacks in Black and White', *Sociological Perspectives*, 47.4 (2004): 439–464 (456). Though this sentiment is likely to be similar among other minority groups within the US, as Harlow and Dundes point out, a 1997 study found that African Americans are less patriotic than Latinos and Asian Americans, not just whites.
94. Hamid Dabashi, *Islamic Liberation Theology: Resisting the Empire* (New York: Routledge, 2008), 234–253.
95. Amiri Baraka, 'Somebody Blew Up America', *Amiri Baraka* (2001), http://www.amiribaraka.com/blew.html (accessed 13 November 2010).
96. Amiri Baraka, 'I Will not "Apologize," I Will not "Resign!"', *Amiri Baraka*, http://www.thetalkingdrum.com/amiri.html (accessed 13 November 2010).

97. William J. Harris and Aldon Lynn Nielson, 'Somebody Blew Off Baraka', *African American Review*, 37.2/3 (2003): 183–187 (184).

98. See Amy Alexander, 'Introduction: Our Brother, the Other: Farrakhan and a Vigil for New Black Leadership' in *The Farrakhan Factor: African-American Writers on Leadership, Nationhood, and Minister Louis Farrakhan*, ed. Amy Alexander (New York: Grove Press, 1998), 1–17.

99. See Harris-Lacewell, *Barbershops, Bibles, and BET*, 210–218.

100. See Henry Louis Gates Jr, 'The Charmer' in *The Farrakhan Factor*, 18–51 (38–39).

101. See Gates, 'The Charmer', 46.

102. Dabashi, 241–244.

103. Dabashi, 214.

104. Dabashi, 243–244.

105. *Malcolm X Speaks*, 26.

5   TRANSCENDING THE NATION: TONI MORRISON'S *PARADISE*

1. Toni Morrison, *Paradise* (London: Vintage, 1999), 3.

2. I borrow this term from Phillip Brian Harper's essay 'Nationalism and Social Division in Black Arts Poetry of the 1960s' in *Is it Nation Time? Contemporary Essays on Black Power and Black Nationalism*, ed. Eddie Glaude Jr (Chicago: University of Chicago Press, 2002), 165–188.

3. Martin Bernal, *Black Athena: The Afroasiatic Roots of Classical Civilization, Volume 1: The Fabrication of Ancient Greece 1785–1985* (New Brunswick, NJ: Rutgers University Press, 1987).

4. Toni Morrison, 'Unspeakable Things Unspoken: The Afro-American Presence in American Literature' in *Criticism and the Color Line: Desegregating American Literary Studies*, ed. Henry B. Wonham (New Brunswick, NJ: Rutgers University Press, 1996), 16–29 (20–21).

5. Norman L. Crockett, *The Black Towns* (Lawrence: The Regents Press of Kansas, 1979), xi.

6. Crockett, xii; 51; 40; 181.

7. Crockett, 187.

8. Morrison, *Paradise*, 292.

9. Morrison, *Paradise*, 5.

10. Morrison, *Paradise*, 95; 188; 189; 98; 192.

11. Morrison, *Paradise*, 98; 99; 96; 13.

12. Morrison, *Paradise*, 143; 113; 14; 117; 296.

13. Sarah Appleton Aguiar, '"Passing On" Death: Stealing Life in Toni Morrison's *Paradise*', *African American Review*, 38.3 (2004): 513–519 (513).

14. Eddie S. Glaude Jr, *Exodus! Religion, Race, and Nation in Early Nineteenth-Century Black America* (Chicago: Chicago University Press, 2000), 44.

15. Glaude, *Exodus*, 30.

16. Morrison, *Paradise*, 83.

17. Tessa Roynon, 'Toni Morrison and Classical Tradition', *Literature Compass*, 4/6 (2007): 1514–1537 (1522).

18. Morrison, *Paradise*, 83–86.

19. Morrison, *Paradise*, 109.

20. Morrison, *Paradise*, 101.

21. Eddie Glaude, 'Black Power Revisited' in *Is it Nation Time?*, 1–21 (10).

22. Cornel West quoted by Glaude, 'Black Power Revisited', 10.
23. See Cornel West, 'The Paradox of the African American Rebellion' in *Is It Nation Time?*, 22–38.
24. Glaude, 'Black Power Revisited', 11.
25. Morrison, *Paradise*, 107.
26. Melissa Harris-Lacewell, 'From Liberation to Mutual Fund: Political Consequences of Differing Conceptions of Christ in the African American Church' in *From Pews to Polling Places: Faith and Politics in the American Religious Mosaic*, ed. J. Matthew Wilson (Washington, DC: Georgetown University Press, 2007), 131–160 (143–144).
27. Morrison, *Paradise*, 141–147.
28. Harris-Lacewell, 'From Liberation to Mutual Fund', 143.
29. Harris-Lacewell, 'From Liberation to Mutual Fund', 149.
30. Harris-Lacewell, 'From Liberation to Mutual Fund', 141.
31. Morrison, *Paradise*, 240.
32. Channette Romero, 'Creating the Beloved Community: Religion, Race, and Nation in Toni Morrison's *Paradise*', *African American Review*, 39.3 (2005): 415–430 (420).
33. Morrison, *Paradise*, 98–99.
34. Morrison, *Paradise*, 276.
35. Morrison, *Paradise*, 276; 8; 201–202.
36. Toni Morrison quoted by James Marcus, 'This Side of Paradise', Interview with Toni Morrison, http://www.amazon.com/gp/feature.html?ie=UTF8&docId=7651 (accessed 29 October 2010).
37. Morrison, *Paradise*, 306.
38. Megan Sweeney, 'Racial House, Big House, Home: Contemporary Abolitionism in Toni Morrison's *Paradise*', *Meridians*, 4.2 (2004): 40–67 (43).
39. Jon Stratton, 'The Beast of the Apocalypse: The Postcolonial Experience of the United States', *New Formations*, 21 (1993): 35–63 (39; 51; 36).
40. Morrison, *Paradise*, 16.
41. Katrine Dalsgård, 'The One All-Black Town Worth the Pain: (African) American Exceptionalism, Historical Narration, and the Critique of Nationhood in Toni Morrison's *Paradise*', *African American Review*, 35.2 (2001): 233–248 (237; 233–234; 237).
42. It should though be noted that many commentators have identified a leftwards drift in American evangelical Christianity that has entailed increasing emphases on issues like poverty and climate change. See R. Marie Griffith and Melani McAlister, 'Introduction: Is the Public Square Still Naked?', *American Quarterly*, 59.3 (2007): 527–563.
43. Gail Fox, 'Biblical Connections in Toni Morrison's *Paradise*', *Notes on Contemporary Literature*, 34.3 (2004), 7–8 (8).
44. Philip Page, 'Furrowing All the Brows: Interpretation and the Transcendent in Toni Morrison's *Paradise*', *African American Review*, 35.4 (2001): 637–649 (646).
45. Toni Morrison, 'Rootedness: The Ancestor as Foundation' in *Black Women Writers (1950–1980)*, ed. Mari Evans (Garden City, NY: Anchor Press/Doubleday, 1984), 339–345 (344).
46. Morrison, *Paradise*, 302.
47. Morrison, *Paradise*, 306.
48. Morrison, *Paradise*, 161.

49. Toni Morrison, *Beloved* (London: Picador, 1988), 274–275.
50. Morrison, *Paradise*, 306.
51. Morrison, *Paradise*, 187; 191; 279; 217.
52. Aguiar, 514.
53. Morrison, *Paradise*, 264.
54. Morrison, *Paradise*, 292.
55. Morrison, *Paradise*, 297.
56. Toni Morrison, *The Nobel Lecture in Literature, 1993* (New York: Alfred A. Knopf, 1996), 19.
57. Gabriel Josipovici, *The Book of God: A Response to the Bible* (New Haven, CT: Yale University Press, 1988), 175.
58. Morrison, *Paradise*, 18.
59. See Jean-Luc Nancy, 'Myth Interrupted' in *The Inoperative Community*, trans. Peter Connor (Minneapolis: University of Minnesota Press, 1991), 43–70.
60. Morrison, *Paradise*, 305.
61. Theophus H. Smith, *Conjuring Culture: Biblical Formations of Black America* (New York: Oxford University Press, 1994), 28.
62. James M. Mellard, 'The Jews of Ruby, Oklahoma: Politics, Parallax, and Ideological Fantasy in Toni Morrison's *Paradise*', *Modern Fiction Studies*, 56.2 (2010): 349–377.
63. Morrison, *Paradise*, 9.
64. Theodor W. Adorno and Max Horkheimer, *Dialectic of Enlightenment*, trans. John Cummings (London: Verso, 1979), 180–186.
65. Glaude, *Exodus*, 9.
66. Jacqueline Rose, *The Question of Zion* (Princeton, NJ: Princeton University Press, 2005), 19.
67. Wilson Jeremiah Moses, *Black Messiahs and Uncle Toms: Social and Literary Manipulations of a Religious Myth* (University Park: Pennsylvania State University Press, 1993), 2.
68. Jacqueline Rose, 20; 130; 27.
69. Morrison quoted by Marcus.
70. Jacqueline Rose, 17.
71. Edward W. Said, 'Michael Walzer's *Exodus and Revolution*: A Caananite Reading' in *Blaming the Victims: Spurious Scholarship and the Palestinian Question*, ed. Edward W. Said and Christopher Hitchens (London: Verso, 1988), 161–178 (166–167).
72. Edward Said, 'An Exchange of Letters between Michael Walzer and Edward Said' in William Hart, *Edward Said and the Religious Effects of Culture* (Cambridge: Cambridge University Press, 2000), 187–199 (191).
73. Edward W. Said, *The Edward Said Reader*, ed. Moustafa Bayoumi and Andrew Rubin (London: Granta, 2001), 126.
74. Morrison, *Beloved*, 275.
75. Jacqueline Rose, 45.
76. See Emmanuel Levinas, 'From the Rise of Nihilism to the Carnal Jew' in *Difficult Freedom: Essays on Judaism*, trans. Seán Hand (Baltimore, MD: Johns Hopkins University Press, 1997), 221–225.
77. Morrison, *Paradise*, 110–111.
78. Susan A. Handelman, *The Slayers of Moses: The Emergence of Rabbinic Interpretation in Modern Literary Theory* (Albany: State University of New York Press, 1982), 81.

79. Josh Cohen, *Interrupting Auschwitz: Art, Religion, Philosophy* (New York: Continuum, 2003), 91.

80. Cohen, 93.

81. See Jacques Derrida, *Acts of Religion*, ed. Gil Anidjar (New York: Routledge, 2002); in particular see the essay 'Faith and Knowledge: The Two Sources of "Religion" and the Limits of Reason Alone', 42–101.

82. Edward W. Said, *The World, the Text, and the Critic* (Cambridge, MA: Harvard University Press, 1983), 16.

83. Edward W. Said, *Reflections on Exile* (London: Granta, 2001), 173.

84. See, for example, Said, 'Permission to Narrate' (1984) in *The Edward Said Reader*, 243–266.

85. Morrison, *Paradise*, 213.

86. Kwame Anthony Appiah, 'Europe Upside Down: Fallacies of the New Afrocentrism' in *Perspectives on Africa: A Reader in Culture, History and Representation*, ed. Roy Richard Grinker, Stephen C. Lubkemann and Christopher B. Steiner (Sussex: Wiley-Blackwell, 2010), 48–54 (50) (a version of this article was first published in 1993).

87. Morrison, *Paradise*, 210.

88. Morrison, *Paradise*, 244.

89. La Vinia Delois Jennings, *Toni Morrison and the Idea of Africa* (New York: Cambridge University Press, 2008), 71–80.

90. Morrison quoted by Jennings, 24.

91. Jennings, 78.

92. Morrison, *Paradise*, 18; 276.

93. For a discussion of Karenga's idea of 'complementarity', see E. Frances White, 'Africa on My Mind: Gender, Counter Discourse, and African American Nationalism' in *Is it Nation Time?*, 130–155.

94. Smith, 76.

95. Mellard, 371.

96. Harold Bloom, *The American Religion: The Emergence of the Post-Christian Nation* (New York: Simon and Schuster, 1992), 245.

97. Gillian Rose, *Mourning Becomes the Law: Philosophy and Representation* (Cambridge: Cambridge University Press, 1996), 35.

98. Gillian Rose, 25.

99. Gillian Rose, 3.

100. Toni Morrison, 'Home' in *The House that Race Built*, ed. Wahneema Lubiano (New York: Pantheon Books, 1997), 3–12 (3–4).

101. Gillian Rose, 37; 34.

102. Morrison, 'Home', 4.

103. Paul Gilroy, *The Black Atlantic: Modernity and Double Consciousness* (London: Verso, 1993), 71.

104. Morrison, *Paradise*, 318; Although the final word 'paradise' appears in the upper case in this edition, it has been amended to the lower case here because, as Morrison stated in an interview, 'I wanted the book to be an interrogation of the idea of paradise and I wanted to move it from its pedestal of exclusion and to make it more accessible to everybody. Thus, I meant, but forgot, to make the last word begin with a small letter. I have asked the publisher to correct that in subsequent printings'; see 'Toni Morrison', *Time*, 21 January 1998, http://www.time.com/time/community/transcripts/chattr012198.html (accessed 29 October 2010).

105. Barack Obama, 'Remarks by the President at the Acceptance of the Nobel Peace Prize', *The White House*, 10 December 2009, http://www.whitehouse. gov/the-press-office/remarks-president-acceptance-nobel-peace-prize (accessed 29 October 2010).

106. See Barack Obama, *The Audacity of Hope: Thoughts on Reclaiming the American Dream* (Canongate: Edinburgh, 2007), 71–100.

107. Toni Morrison, 'Toni Morrison's letter to Barack Obama', *New York Observer*, 28 January 2008, http://www.observer.com/2008/toni-morrisons-letter-barack-obama (accessed 13 November 2010).

108. Toni Morrison, 'The Talk of the Town: Comment', *The New Yorker*, 5 October 1998, http://www.newyorker.com/archive/1998/10/05/1998_10_0 5_031_TNY_LIBRY_000016504 (accessed 13 November 2010).

109. Slavoj Žižek quoted by Mellard, 349.

110. Morrison, 'Home', 5.

111. Morrison, *Paradise*, 306.

112. Michael Northcott, *An Angel Directs the Storm: Apocalyptic Religion and American Empire* (London: I.B. Tauris, 2004).

113. Roynon, 1522.

114. Margaret Malamud, *Ancient Rome and Modern America* (Chichester: Wiley-Blackwell, 2009), 3.

115. Fritz Breithaupt, 'Rituals of Trauma: How the Media Fabricated September 11' in *Media Representations of September 11*, ed. Steven Chermak, Frankie Y. Bailey and Michelle Brown (Westport, CT: Praeger, 2003), 67–81.

116. See Tom Junod, 'The Falling Man', *Esquire*, 8 September 2009, http://www. esquire.com/features/ESQ0903-SEP_FALLINGMAN (accessed 13 November 2010).

CONCLUSION: EXODUS AND RETURN IN POST-KATRINA NEW ORLEANS

1. See, for examples, the essays in *Seeking Higher Ground: The Hurricane Katrina Crisis, Race, and Public Policy Reader*, ed. Manning Marable and Kristen Clarke (New York: Palgrave Macmillan, 2008).

2. See Manning Marable, *Race, Reform, and Rebellion: The Second Reconstruction and Beyond in Black America, 1945–2006* (New York: Palgrave Macmillan, 2007).

3. Martin Luther King Jr, 'I Have a Dream', 28 August 1963, *A Testament of Hope: The Essential Writings and Speeches of Martin Luther King, Jr.*, ed. James Melvin Washington (New York: Harper Collins, 1991), 217–220 (217).

4. Sigmund Freud, 'The Uncanny' in *An Infantile Neurosis and Other Works*, Standard Edition 17, ed. and trans. James Strachey (London: Vintage, 2001), 219–256 (241).

5. Nicholas Royle, *The Uncanny* (Manchester: Manchester University Press, 2003), 1.

6. Chokwe Lumumba quoted by Rachel E. Luft, 'Beyond Disaster Exceptionalism: Social Movement Developments in New Orleans after Hurricane Katrina', *American Quarterly*, 61.3 (2009): 499–527 (502).

7. Michael Hanchard, 'Black Memory versus State Memory: Notes Toward a Method', *small axe*, 26 (2008): 45–62 (48).

8. Hanchard, 55.
9. *When the Levees Broke: A Requiem in Four Acts*, dir. Spike Lee, DVD (HBO, 2006).
10. Michael Eric Dyson, 'Great Migrations?' in *After the Storm: Black Intellectuals Explore the Meaning of Hurricane Katrina*, ed. David Dante Troutt (New York: The New Press, 2006), 75–84 (75).
11. Hanchard, 55, 47.
12. Dyson, 'Great Migrations?', 75–84.
13. Benedict Anderson, *Imagined Communities: Reflections on the Origin and Spread of Nationalism* (London: Verso, 1991).
14. Ray Nagin, 'Transcript of Nagin's speech', *The Times-Picayune*, 17 January 2006, http://www.nola.com/news/t-p/frontpage/index.ssf?/news/t-p/stories/011706_nagin_transcript.html (accessed 13 November 2010).
15. Michael Eric Dyson, *Come Hell or High Water: Hurricane Katrina and the Color of Disaster* (New York: Basic Civitas, 2006), 179–181.
16. George Shulman, *American Prophecy: Race and Redemption in American Political Culture* (Minneapolis: University of Minnesota Press, 2008), x–xi.
17. See, for example, Abraham Joshua Heschel, *The Prophets* (New York: Harper Collins, 2001); first published in 1962, this book became popular among Christian Civil Rights activists.
18. Dyson, *Come Hell or High Water*, 197.
19. Dwight McKissic quoted by Dyson, *Come Hell or High Water*, 180.
20. For discussion of that status, see Spike Lee's *When the Levees Broke*, Act 3.
21. See Cheryl L. Harris and Devon W. Carbado, 'Loot or Find: Fact or Frame?' in *After the Storm*, 87–110.
22. See Anna Brickhouse, '"L'Ouragan de Flammes" ("Hurricane of Flames"): New Orleans and Transamerican Catastrophe, 1866/2005', *American Quarterly*, 59.4 (2007): 1097–1127 (1100).
23. James Petras quoted by Brickhouse, 1100.
24. Brickhouse, 1106.
25. *If God is Willing and Da Creek Don't Rise*, Part 1, dir. Spike Lee (HBO, 2010).
26. Brickhouse, 1100–1102.
27. George W. Bush, 'Bush's Remarks in New Orleans', *New York Times*, 2 September 2005, http://www.nytimes.com/2005/09/02/national/nationalspecial/02BUSH-NOTEXT.html (accessed 13 November 2010).
28. Brickhouse, 1100.
29. Stephanie Houston Grey, '(Re)Imagining Ethnicity in the City of New Orleans: Katrina's Geographical Allegory' in *Seeking Higher Ground*, 129–140.
30. Michael Dawson, Melissa Harris-Lacewell and Cathy Cohen, '2005 Racial Attitudes and the Katrina Disaster Study' (Chicago: Center for the Study of Race, Politics and Culture, 2006), http://www.melissaharrislacewell.com/docs/Katrina_Initial_Report.pdf (accessed 29 October 2010).
31. Naomi Klein, *The Shock Doctrine: The Rise of Disaster Capitalism* (London: Penguin, 2008), 415.
32. David Dante Troutt, 'Many Thousands Gone, Again' in *After the Storm*, 3–27 (19).
33. See *When the Levees Broke*.
34. Tonya Williams, interview with Anna Hartnell, 1 April 2009.
35. Luft, 500.

36. Julia Cass and Peter Whoriskey, 'New Orleans to Raze Public Housing', *The Washington Post*, 8 December 2006, http://www.washingtonpost.com/wp-dyn/content/article/2006/12/07/AR2006120701482.html (accessed 13 November 2010).

37. William P. Quigley, 'Thirteen Ways of Looking at Katrina: Human and Civil Rights Left Behind Again', *Tulane Law Review*, 81.4 (2007): 955–1017 (1007).

38. See United Nations, 'Guiding Principles on Internal Displacement', http://www.unhcr.org/43ce1cff2.html (accessed 29 October 2010).

39. US Human Rights Network, http://www.ushrnetwork.org/about_us (29 October 2010).

40. Dorothy Q. Thomas, 'Against American Supremacy: Rebuilding Human Rights Culture in the United States' in *Bringing Human Rights Home: From Civil Rights to Human Rights*, ed. Cynthia Soohoo, Catherine Albisa and Martha F. Davis (Westport, CT: Praeger, 2008), 1–23 (1–2).

41. Carol Anderson, 'A "Hollow Mockery": African Americans, White Supremacy, and the Development of Human Rights in the United States' in *Bringing Human Rights Home: A History of Human Rights in the United States*, ed Cynthia Soohoo, Catherine Albisa and Martha F. Davis (Westport, CT: Praeger, 2008), 75–101 (90–91).

42. Malcolm X, *Malcolm X Speaks*, ed. George Breitman (New York: Grove Press, 1990), 34–35.

43. Talal Asad, *Formations of the Secular: Christianity, Islam, Modernity* (Stanford, CA: Stanford University Press, 2003), 145.

44. Asad, 140–148.

45. Asad, 140–141.

46. Luft, 500.

47. Clyde Woods, 'Katrina's World: Blues, Bourbon, and the Return to the Source', *American Quarterly*, 61.3 (2009): 427–453.

48. Barack Obama, 'President Obama Marks Fourth Anniversary of Hurricane Katrina', *The White House*, 29 August 2009, http://www.whitehouse.gov/the_press_office/Weekly-Address-President-Obama-Marks-Fourth-Anniversary-of-Hurricane-Katrina-Will-Visit-New-Orleans-Later-This-Year/ (accessed 13 November 2010).

49. Barack Obama, *The Audacity of Hope: Thoughts on Reclaiming the American Dream* (Canongate: Edinburgh, 2007), 229–230.

50. Melissa Harris-Lacewell and James Perry, 'Obama's Debt to New Orleans', *The Nation*, 30 March 2009, http://www.thenation.com/article/obamas-debt-new-orleans (accessed 13 November 2010).

51. Dave Eggers, *Zeitoun* (San Francisco: McSweeney's Books, 2009), 228–229; 320.

52. Kevin Gaines, 'Of Teachable Moments and Specters of Race', *American Quarterly*, 62.2 (2010): 195–213 (208).

53. Shirley Elizabeth Thompson, *Exiles at Home: The Struggle to Become American in Creole New Orleans* (Cambridge, MA: Harvard University Press, 2009), 7–8.

54. Obama, *Audacity*, 247.

55. Barack Obama, 'Remarks by the President on the Fifth Anniversary of Hurricane Katrina in New Orleans, Louisiana', *The White House*, 29 August 2010, http://www.whitehouse.gov/the-press-office/2010/08/29/remarks-

president-fifth-anniversary-hurricane-katrina-new-orleans-louisi (accessed 13 November 2010).

56. Obama, *Audacity*, 233.

57. Hanchard, 47.

58. See David Remnick, *The Bridge: The Life and Rise of Barack Obama* (London: Picador, 2010), 139.

59. Obama quoted by Remnick, 21–22.

60. Eugene Goodheart, 'Obama On and Off Base', *Dissent*, Summer 2010, http://www.dissentmagazine.org/article/?article=3268 (accessed 13 November 2010).

61. In this way, and as James Kloppenberg argues, Obama's well-known commitments to democratic deliberation and compromise should be read in the light of philosophical pragmatism, rather than a 'vulgar pragmatism' that simply seeks the path of least resistance. See James T. Kloppenberg, *Reading Obama: Dreams, Hope, and the American Political Tradition* (Princeton, NJ: Princeton University Press, 2011), 83.

62. For an account of the legislation passed during Obama's first year, see Jonathan Alter, *The Promise: President Obama, Year One* (London: Simon and Schuster, 2010).

63. See Barack Obama, 'A World that Stands as One' in *Change We Can Believe In: Barack Obama's Plan to Renew America's Promise* (Edinburgh: Canongate, 2009), 271–281; also see page 7 of this text where Obama writes of America's 'endless frontier'.

64. Reverend Donald Boutte, interview with Anna Hartnell, 27 May 2009.

65. See Milton C. Sernett, *Bound for the Promised Land: African American Religion and the Great Migration* (Durham, NC: Duke University Press, 1997).

Select Bibliography

Adorno, Theodor W. and Max Horkheimer, *Dialectic of Enlightenment*, trans. John Cummings (1947; London: Verso, 1979).

Aguiar, Sarah Appleton, '"Passing On" Death: Stealing Life in Toni Morrison's *Paradise*', *African American Review*, 38.3 (2004): 513–519.

Alexander, Amy, ed., *The Farrakhan Factor: African-American Writers on Leadership, Nationhood, and Minister Louis Farrakhan* (New York: Grove Press, 1998).

Alter, Jonathan, *The Promise: President Obama, Year One* (London: Simon and Schuster, 2010).

Anderson, Benedict, *Imagined Communities: Reflections on the Origin and Spread of Nationalism* (1983; London: Verso, 1991).

Andrews, William L., *African American Autobiography* (Englewood Cliffs, NJ: Prentice Hall, 1993).

Appiah, Kwame Anthony, 'Europe Upside Down: Fallacies of the New Afrocentrism' in *Perspectives on Africa: A Reader in Culture, History and Representation*, ed. Roy Richard Grinker, Stephen C. Lubkemann and Christopher B. Steiner (Sussex: Wiley-Blackwell, 2010), 48–54.

Asad, Talal, *Formations of the Secular: Christianity, Islam, Modernity* (Stanford, CA: Stanford University Press, 2003).

Asante, Molefi Kete, *Malcolm X as Cultural Hero and other Afrocentric Essays* (Trenton, NJ: Africa World Press, 1993).

—— *Afrocentricity: The Theory of Social Change* (Buffalo, NY: Amulefi Publishing, 1980).

Austin, Algernon, *Achieving Blackness: Race, Black Nationalism and Afrocentrism in the Twentieth Century* (New York: New York University Press, 2006).

Avineri, Shlomo, *The Making of Modern Zionism: The Intellectual Origins of the Jewish State* (London: Weidenfeld and Nicolson, 1981).

Badiou, Alain, *Saint Paul: The Foundation of Universalism*, trans. Ray Brassier (Stanford, CA: Stanford University Press, 2003).

Baldwin, James, *The Fire Next Time* (London: Michael Joseph, 1963).

Baldwin, Lewis, 'Martin Luther King, Jr., a "Coalition of Conscience," and Freedom in South Africa' in *Freedom's Distant Shores: American Protestants and Post-Colonial Alliances with Africa*, ed. R. Drew Smith (Waco, TX: Baylor University Press, 2006), 53–82.

Baldwin, Lewis V. and Amiri YaSin Al-Hadid, *Between Cross and Crescent: Christian and Muslim Perspectives on Malcolm and Martin* (Gainesville: University Press of Florida, 2002).

Baldwin, Lewis V., Rufus Burrow Jr, Barbara A. Holmes and Susan Holmes Winfield, eds, *The Legacy of Martin Luther King, Jr.: The Boundaries of Law, Politics, and Religion* (Notre Dame, IN: University of Notre Dame Press, 2002).

Baraka Amiri, 'Somebody Blew Up America', *Amiri Baraka* (2001), http://www.amiribaraka.com/blew.html (accessed 13 November 2010).

Bell, Bernard W., Emily Grosholz and James B. Stewart, eds, *W.E.B. Du Bois on Race and Culture* (New York: Routledge, 1996).

Bellah, Robert, 'Civil Religion in America' in *American Civil Religion*, ed. Donald G. Jones and Russell E. Richey (San Francisco: Mellen Research University Press, 1990), 21–44.

Bercovitch, Sacvan, *The American Jeremiad* (Wisconsin: University of Wisconsin Press, 1978).

Bernal, Martin, *Black Athena: The Afroasiatic Roots of Classical Civilization, Volume 1: The Fabrication of Ancient Greece 1785–1985* (New Brunswick, NJ: Rutgers University Press, 1987).

Bhabha, Homi, 'The World and the Home', *Social Text*, 31/32 (1992): 141–153.

Blond, Phillip, ed., *Post-Secular Philosophy: Between Philosophy and Theology* (London: Routledge, 1998).

Bloom, Harold, *The American Religion: The Emergence of the Post-Christian Nation* (New York: Simon and Schuster, 1992).

Blum, Edward J., *W.E.B. Du Bois: American Prophet* (Philadelphia: University of Pennsylvania Press, 2007).

Bober, Arie, ed., *The Other Israel: The Radical Case Against Zionism* (Garden City, NY: Anchor Books, 1972).

Braiterman, Zachary, *(God) After Auschwitz: Tradition and Change in Post-Holocaust Jewish Thought* (Princeton, NJ: Princeton University Press, 1998).

Branch, Taylor, *Pillar of Fire: America in the King Years 1963–65* (New York: Simon and Schuster, 1998).

Brickhouse, Anna, '"L'Ouragan de Flammes" ("Hurricane of Flames"): New Orleans and Transamerican Catastrophe, 1866/2005', *American Quarterly*, 59.4 (2007): 1097–1127.

Bush, Roderick D., *The End of White World Supremacy: Black Internationalism and the Problem of the Color Line* (Philadelphia, PA: Temple University Press, 2009).

Carby, Hazel V., *Race Men* (Cambridge, MA: Harvard University Press, 1998).

Carmichael, Stokely, *Stokely Speaks: Black Power Back to Pan-Africanism* (New York: Random House, 1971).

Caron, Timothy P., *Struggles over the Word: Race and Religion in O'Connor, Faulkner, Hurston, and Wright* (Macon, GA: Mercer University Press, 2000).

Carson, Claybourne, ed., *The Autobiography of Martin Luther King, Jr.* (London: Abacus, 2000).

Chermak, Steven, Frankie Y. Bailey and Michelle Brown, eds, *Media Representations of September 11* (Westport, CT: Praeger, 2003).

Chireau, Yvonne and Nathaniel Deutsch, eds, *Black Zion: African American Religious Encounters with Judaism* (New York: Oxford University Press, 2000).

Cleage, Albert B. Jr, *The Black Messiah* (1968; New York: Search Book Edition, 1969).

Cohen, Josh, *Interrupting Auschwitz: Art, Religion, Philosophy* (New York: Continuum, 2003).

Cone, James H., *Martin and Malcolm and America: A Dream or a Nightmare* (Maryknoll, NY: Orbis Books, 1991).

—— *A Black Theology of Liberation* (Maryknoll, NY: Orbis Books, 1986).

—— *Black Theology and Black Power* (New York: Seabury Press, 1969).

Corsi, Jerome R., *The Obama Nation: Leftist Politics and the Cult of Personality* (New York, Threshold Editions, 2008).

Crockett, Norman L., *The Black Towns* (Lawrence: The Regents Press of Kansas, 1979).

Curtis, Edward E., *Islam in Black America: Identity, Liberation, and Difference in African-American Islamic Thought* (Albany: State University of New York Press, 2002).

Dabashi, Hamid, *Islamic Liberation Theology: Resisting the Empire* (New York: Routledge, 2008).

Dalsgård, Katrine, 'The One All-Black Town Worth the Pain: (African) American Exceptionalism, Historical Narration, and the Critique of Nationhood in Toni Morrison's *Paradise*', *African American Review*, 35.2 (2001): 233–248.

Dawson, Michael C., *Black Visions: The Roots of Contemporary African-American Political Ideologies* (Chicago: University of Chicago Press, 2001).

Dawson, Michael, Melissa Harris-Lacewell and Cathy Cohen, '2005 Racial Attitudes and the Katrina Disaster Study' (Chicago: Center for the Study of Race, Politics and Culture, 2006), http://www.melissaharrislacewell.com/docs/Katrina_Initial_Report.pdf (accessed 29 October 2010).

DeCaro, Louis A., Jr, *Malcolm and the Cross: The Nation of Islam, Malcolm X, and Christianity* (New York: New York University Press, 1998).

—— *On the Side of My People: A Religious Life of Malcolm X* (New York: New York University Press, 1996).

Derrida, Jacques, *Acts of Religion*, ed. Gil Anidjar (New York: Routledge, 2002).

D'Souza, Dinesh, *The Roots of Obama's Rage* (Washington, DC: Regnery Publishing, 2010).

Du Bois, W.E.B., *Darkwater: Voices from Within the Veil* (1920; London: Dodo Press, 2006).

—— *The Souls of Black Folk* (1903; New York: The Modern Library, 2003).

—— *Du Bois on Religion*, ed. Phil Zuckerman (Walnut Creek, CA: AltaMira Press, 2000).

—— *Dusk of Dawn: An Essay Toward an Autobiography of a Race Concept* (1940; New Brunswick, NJ: Transaction Books, 1984).

Dyson, Michael Eric, *Come Hell or High Water: Hurricane Katrina and the Color of Disaster* (New York: Basic Civitas, 2006).

—— *I May Not Get There With You: The True Martin Luther King, Jr.* (New York: The Free Press, 2000).

Eggers, Dave, *Zeitoun* (San Francisco: McSweeney's Books, 2009).

Fanon, Frantz, *Black Skin, White Masks* (1952; London: Pluto, 1986).

Fox, Gail, 'Biblical Connections in Toni Morrison's *Paradise*', *Notes on Contemporary Literature*, 34.3 (2004), 7–8.

Frazier, E. Franklin and C. Eric Lincoln, *The Negro Church in America/The Black Church since Frazier* (New York: Schocken Books, 1974).

Freud, Sigmund, 'The Uncanny' in *An Infantile Neurosis and Other Works*, Standard Edition 17, ed. and trans. James Strachey (London: Vintage, 2001), 219–256.

—— *Moses and Monotheism, An Outline of Psycho-Analysis and Other Works*, Standard Edition 23, ed. and trans. James Strachey (London: Vintage, 2001).

Gaines, Kevin, 'Of Teachable Moments and Specters of Race', *American Quarterly*, 62.2 (2010): 195–213.

—— *Uplifting the Race: Black Leadership, Politics, and Culture in the Twentieth Century* (Chapel Hill: University of North Carolina Press, 1996).

Gandhi, Leela, 'Concerning Violence: The Limits and Circulations of Gandhian *Ahimsa* or Passive Resistance', *Cultural Critique*, 35 (1996–97): 105–147.

Gates, Henry Louis, Jr, *The Signifying Monkey: A Theory of African-American Literary Criticism* (New York: Oxford University Press, 1988).

—— ed., *The Classic Slave Narratives* (New York: Mentor, 1987).

Gates, Henry Louis, Jr and Cornel West, *The African-American Century: How Black Americans Have Shaped Our Country* (New York: Touchstone, 2000).

Genovese, Eugene, *Roll, Jordan, Roll: The World the Slaves Made* (New York: Vintage, 1976).

Gilroy, Paul, *Between Camps: Nations, Cultures and the Allure of Race* (London: Penguin, 2000).

—— *The Black Atlantic: Modernity and Double Consciousness* (London: Verso, 1993).

Glaude, Eddie S., Jr, 'The Black Church is Dead', *The Huffington Post*, 24 February 2010, http://www.huffingtonpost.com/eddie-glaude-jr-phd/the-black-church-is-dead_b_473815.html (accessed 12 August 2010).

—— ed., *Is it Nation Time? Contemporary Essays on Black Power and Black Nationalism* (Chicago: University of Chicago Press, 2002).

—— *Exodus! Religion, Race, and Nation in Early Nineteenth-Century Black America* (Chicago: University of Chicago Press, 2000).

Goldberg, David Theo, *The Threat of Race: Reflections on Racial Neoliberalism* (Malden, MA: Wiley-Blackwell, 2009).

Gooding-Williams, Robert, *Look, a Negro! Philosophical essays on Race, Culture and Politics* (New York: Routledge, 2006).

Griffith, R. Marie and Melani McAlister, eds, *American Quarterly* Special Issue: 'Religion and Politics in the Contemporary United States', 59.3 (2007).

Grimes, Ronald L., *Rite out of Place: Ritual, Media, and the Arts* (Oxford: Oxford University Press, 2006).

Gunkel, David, 'Escape Velocity: *Exodus* and Postmodernism', *Soundings: An Interdisciplinary Journal*, 81.3–4 (1998): 437–459.

Hanchard, Michael, 'Black Memory versus State Memory: Notes Toward a Method', *small axe*, 26 (2008): 45–62.

Handelman, Susan A., *The Slayers of Moses: The Emergence of Rabbinic Interpretation in Modern Literary Theory* (Albany: State University of New York Press, 1982).

Harlow, Roxanna and Lauren Dundes, '"United" We Stand: Responses to the September 11 Attacks in Black and White', *Sociological Perspectives*, 47.4 (2004): 439–464.

Harris, William J. and Aldon Lynn Nielson, 'Somebody Blew Off Baraka', *African American Review*, 37.2/3 (2003): 183–187.

Harris-Lacewell, Melissa, 'From Liberation to Mutual Fund: Political Consequences of Differing Conceptions of Christ in the African American Church' in *From Pews to Polling Places: Faith and Politics in the American Religious Mosaic*, ed. J. Matthew Wilson (Washington, DC: Georgetown University Press, 2007), 131–160.

—— *Barbershops, Bibles, and BET* (Princeton, NJ: Princeton University Press, 2004).

Hart, William, *Edward Said and the Religious Effects of Culture* (Cambridge: Cambridge University Press, 2000).

Hegel, G.W.F., *The Philosophy of History*, trans. J. Sibree (1837; Amherst, MA: Prometheus Books, 1991).

—— *Phenomenology of Spirit*, trans. A.V. Miller (1807; Oxford: Oxford University Press, 1977).

Heschel, Abraham Joshua, *The Prophets* (1962; New York: Harper Collins, 2001).

Heschel, Susannah, *Abraham Geiger and the Jewish Jesus* (Chicago: University of Chicago Press, 1998).

Hesse, Barnor, ed., *Un/settled Multiculturalisms: Diasporas, Entanglements, Transruptions* (London: Zed Books, 2000).

Hopkins, Dwight N., ed., *Black Faith and Public Talk: Critical Essays on James H. Cone's Black Theology and Black Power* (Waco, TX: Baylor University Press, 2007).

Howard-Pitney, David, *The African American Jeremiad: Appeals for Justice in America* (Philadelphia, PA: Temple University Press, 2005).

Howe, Stephen, *Afrocentrism: Mythical Pasts and Imagined Homes* (London: Verso, 1998).

Ifill, Gwen, *The Breakthrough: Politics and Race in the Age of Obama* (New York: Doubleday, 2009).

Jackson, Sherman A., *Islam and the Blackamerican: Looking Toward the Third Resurrection* (New York: Oxford University Press, 2005).

Jennings, La Vinia Delois, *Toni Morrison and the Idea of Africa* (New York: Cambridge University Press, 2008).

Josipovici, Gabriel, *The Book of God: A Response to the Bible* (New Haven, CT: Yale University Press, 1988).

Kaufman, Jonathan, *Broken Alliance: The Turbulent Times Between Blacks and Jews in America* (New York: Charles Scribner's Sons, 1988).

Kelley, Robin D.G., *Freedom Dreams: The Black Radical Imagination* (Boston, MA: Beacon Press, 2002).

King, Martin Luther, Jr, *The Papers of Martin Luther King, Jr.: Volume 1: Called to Serve, January 1929–June 1951*, ed. Clayborne Carson (Berkeley: University of California Press, 1992).

—— *A Testament of Hope: The Essential Writings and Speeches of Martin Luther King, Jr.*, ed. James Melvin Washington (New York: Harper Collins, 1991).

—— *Where Do We Go From Here: Chaos or Community?* (1967; London: Hodder and Stoughton, 1968).

—— *Why We Can't Wait* (New York: Signet Books, 1964).

—— *Stride Toward Freedom: The Montgomery Story* (New York: Harper and Row, 1958).

King, Richard H., *Race, Culture, and the Intellectuals 1940–1970* (Washington, DC: Woodrow Wilson Center Press and Baltimore, MD: Johns Hopkins University Press, 2004).

Klein, Naomi, *The Shock Doctrine: The Rise of Disaster Capitalism* (London: Penguin, 2008).

—— 'Minority Death Match: Jews, Blacks and the "Post-Racial" Presidency', *Harper's Magazine* (September 2009): 53–67.

Kloppenberg, James T., *Reading Obama: Dreams, Hope, and the American Political Tradition* (Princeton, NJ: Princeton University Press, 2011).

Kojève, Alexandre, *Introduction to the Reading of Hegel: Lectures on the Phenomenology of Spirit*, assembled by Raymond Queneau, ed. Alan Bloom, trans. James H. Nichols Jr (1947; Ithaca, NY: Cornell University Press, 1980).

Levinas, Emmanuel, *Difficult Freedom: Essays on Judaism*, trans. Seán Hand (Baltimore, MD: Johns Hopkins University Press, 1997).

—— *Totality and Infinity: An Essay on Exteriority*, trans. Alphonso Lingis (1961; Pittsburgh: Duquesne University Press, 1969).

Lincoln, C. Eric, *The Black Muslims in America* (Boston, MA: Beacon Press, 1961).

Lischer, Richard, *The Preacher King: Martin Luther King, Jr. and the Word that Moved America* (New York: Oxford University Press, 1995).

Malamud, Margaret, *Ancient Rome and Modern America* (Chichester: Wiley-Blackwell, 2009).

Marable, Manning, *Beyond Black and White: Transforming African-American Politics* (London: Verso, 2009).

—— *Race, Reform, and Rebellion: The Second Reconstruction and Beyond in Black America, 1945–2006* (New York: Palgrave Macmillan, 2007).

Marable, Manning and Kristen Clarke, eds, *Barack Obama and African American Empowerment: The Rise of Black America's New Leadership* (New York: Palgrave Macmillan, 2009).

—— eds, *Seeking Higher Ground: The Hurricane Katrina Crisis, Race, and Public Policy Reader* (New York: Palgrave Macmillan, 2008).

McAlister, Melani, *Epic Encounters: Culture, Media, and US Interests in the Middle East since 1945* (Berkeley: University of California Press, 2005).

Mellard, James M., 'The Jews of Ruby, Oklahoma: Politics, Parallax, and Ideological Fantasy in Toni Morrison's *Paradise*', *Modern Fiction Studies*, 56.2 (2010): 349–377.

Miller, Keith D., *Voice of Deliverance: The Language of Martin Luther King, Jr., and its Sources* (Athens: University of Georgia Press, 1998).

Morrison, Toni, *Paradise* (1998; London: Vintage, 1999).

—— 'Home' in *The House that Race Built*, ed. Wahneema Lubiano (New York: Pantheon Books, 1997), 3–12.

—— 'Unspeakable Things Unspoken: The Afro-American Presence in American Literature' in *Criticism and the Color Line: Desegregating American Literary Studies*, ed. Henry B. Wonham (New Brunswick, NJ: Rutgers University Press, 1996), 16–29.

—— *The Nobel Lecture in Literature, 1993* (New York: Alfred A. Knopf, 1996).

—— 'On the Backs of Blacks' in *Arguing Immigration: The Debate Over the Changing Face of America*, ed. Nicolaus Mills (New York: Touchstone, 1994), 97–100.

—— *Playing in the Dark: Whiteness and the Literary Imagination* (London: Picador, 1993).

—— *Beloved* (1987; London: Picador, 1988).

—— 'Rootedness: The Ancestor as Foundation' in *Black Women Writers (1950–1980)*, ed. Mari Evans (Garden City, NY: Anchor Press/Doubleday, 1984), 339–345.

Moses, Wilson Jeremiah, *Afrotopia: The Roots of African American Popular History* (Cambridge: Cambridge University Press, 1998).

—— *Black Messiahs and Uncle Toms: Social and Literary Manipulations of a Religious Myth* (1982; University Park: Pennsylvania State University Press, 1993).

—— *The Golden Age of Black Nationalism 1850–1925* (Hamden, CT: Archon Books, 1978).

Ngugi, James, 'The African Writer and his Past' in *Perspectives on African Literature*, ed. Christopher Heywood (London: Heinemann, 1971), 3–8.

Niebuhr, Reinhold, *The Irony of American History* (1952; Chicago: University of Chicago Press, 2008).

Northcott, Michael, *An Angel Directs the Storm: Apocalyptic Religion and American Empire* (London: I.B. Tauris, 2004).

Obama, Barack, *Change We Can Believe In: Barack Obama's Plan to Renew America's Promise* (2008; Edinburgh: Canongate, 2009).
—— 'Renewing American Leadership', *Foreign Affairs*, July/August 2007, http://www.foreignaffairs.com/articles/62636/barack-obama/renewing-american-leadership (accessed 29 October 2010).
—— *The Audacity of Hope: Thoughts on Reclaiming the American Dream* (2006; Canongate: Edinburgh, 2007).
—— *Dreams From My Father: A Story of Race and Inheritance* (1995; Edinburgh: Canongate, 2007).
Page, Philip, 'Furrowing All the Brows: Interpretation and the Transcendent in Toni Morrison's *Paradise*', *African American Review*, 35.4 (2001): 637–649.
Patterson, Orlando, *Slavery and Social Death* (Cambridge, MA: Harvard University Press, 1982).
Pederson, Carl, *Obama's America* (Edinburgh: Edinburgh University Press, 2009).
Pierre, Jemima and Jesse Weaver Shipley, 'African/Diaspora History: W.E.B. Du Bois and Pan-Africanism in Ghana' in *Ghana in Africa and the World: Essays in Honor of Adu Boahen*, ed. Toyin Falola (Trenton, NJ: Africa World Press, 2003), 731–753.
Quigley, William P., 'Thirteen Ways of Looking at Katrina: Human and Civil Rights Left Behind Again', *Tulane Law Review*, 81.4 (2007): 955–1017.
Rampersad, Arnold, *The Art and Imagination of W.E.B. Du Bois* (Cambridge, MA: Harvard University Press, 1976).
Remnick, David, *The Bridge: The Life and Rise of Barack Obama* (London: Picador, 2010).
Robinson, Cedric J., *Black Movements in America* (New York: Routledge, 1997).
Romero, Channette, 'Creating the Beloved Community: Religion, Race, and Nation in Toni Morrison's *Paradise*', *African American Review*, 39.3 (2005): 415–430.
Rose, Gillian, *Mourning Becomes the Law: Philosophy and Representation* (Cambridge: Cambridge University Press, 1996).
Rose, Jacqueline, *The Question of Zion* (Princeton, NJ: Princeton University Press, 2005).
Royle, Nicholas, *The Uncanny* (Manchester: Manchester University Press, 2003).
Roynon, Tessa, 'Toni Morrison and Classical Tradition', *Literature Compass* 4/6 (2007): 1514–1537.
Said, Edward W., *Reflections on Exile* (London: Granta, 2001).
—— *The Edward Said Reader*, ed. Moustafa Bayoumi and Andrew Rubin (London: Granta, 2001).
—— *Out of Place* (London: Granta, 1999).
—— *Covering Islam* (1981; London: Vintage, 1997).
—— *Culture and Imperialism* (1993; London: Vintage, 1994).
—— *Orientalism: Western Conceptions of the Orient* (1978; London: Penguin, 1995).
—— 'Michael Walzer's *Exodus and Revolution*: A Caananite Reading' in *Blaming the Victims: Spurious Scholarship and the Palestinian Question*, ed. Edward W. Said and Christopher Hitchens (London: Verso, 1988), 161–178.
—— *The World, the Text, and the Critic* (Cambridge, MA: Harvard University Press, 1983).
Salzman, Jack and Cornel West, *Struggles in the Promised Land: Toward a History of Black–Jewish Relations in the United States* (New York: Oxford University Press, 1997).

Schneier, Marc, *Shared Dreams: Martin Luther King, Jr. and the Jewish Community* (Woodstock: Jewish Lights Publishing, 1999).

Sernett, Milton C., *Bound for the Promised Land: African American Religion and the Great Migration* (Durham, NC: Duke University Press, 1997).

Sevitch, Benjamin, 'W.E.B. Du Bois and Jews: A Lifetime of Opposing Anti-Semitism', *Journal of African American History*, 87 (2002): 323–337.

Shapiro, Edward S., 'World War II and American Jewish Identity', *Modern Judaism*, 10.1 (1990): 65–84.

Shlaim, Avi, *The Iron Wall: Israel and the Arab World* (London: Penguin, 2000).

Shulman, George, *American Prophecy: Race and Redemption in American Political Culture* (Minneapolis: University of Minnesota Press, 2008).

Smith, Theophus H., *Conjuring Culture: Biblical Formations of Black America* (New York: Oxford University Press, 1994).

Sollors, Werner, *Beyond Ethnicity: Consent and Descent in American Culture* (New York: Oxford University Press, 1986).

Soohoo, Cynthia, Catherine Albisa, and Martha F. Davis, eds, *Bringing Human Rights Home: From Civil Rights to Human Rights* (Westport, CT: Praeger, 2008).

—— eds, *Bringing Human Rights Home: A History of Human Rights in the United States* (Westport, CT: Praeger, 2008).

Stratton, Jon, 'The Beast of the Apocalypse: The Postcolonial Experience of the United States', *New Formations*, 21 (1993): 35–63.

Strawson, John, *Partitioning Palestine: Legal Fundamentalism in the Palestinian–Israeli Conflict* (London: Pluto, 2010).

Sugrue, Thomas J., *Not Even Past: Barack Obama and the Burden of Race* (Princeton, NJ: Princeton University Press, 2010).

Sweeney, Megan, 'Racial House, Big House, Home: Contemporary Abolitionism in Toni Morrison's *Paradise*', *Meridians*, 4.2 (2004): 40–67.

Thompson, Shirley Elizabeth, *Exiles at Home: The Struggle to Become American in Creole New Orleans* (Cambridge, MA: Harvard University Press, 2009).

Thurman, Howard, *Jesus and the Disinherited* (1949; Boston, MA: Beacon Press, 1996).

Troutt, David Dante, ed., *After the Storm: Black Intellectuals Explore the Meaning of Hurricane Katrina* (New York: The New Press, 2006).

Von Eschen, Penny M., *Race Against Empire: Black Americans and Anticolonialism, 1937–1957* (Ithaca, NY: Cornell University Press, 1997).

Walzer, Michael, *Exodus and Revolution* (New York: Basic Books, 1985).

Weisbord, Robert G. and Richard Kazarian Jr, *Israel in the Black American Perspective* (Westport, CT: Greenwood Press, 1985).

Williamson, Joel, *The Crucible of Race: Black–White Relations in the American South Since Emancipation* (New York: Oxford University Press, 1984).

Woods, Clyde, ed., *American Quarterly* Special Issue 'In the Wake of Hurricane Katrina: New Paradigms and Social Visions', 61.3 (2009).

Wright, Jeremiah A., Jr, *What Makes You So Strong? Sermons of Joy and Strength from Jeremiah A. Wright Jr.*, ed. Jini M. Kilgore (Valley Forge, PA: Judson Press, 1993).

X, Malcolm, *By Any Means Necessary*, ed. George Breitman (New York: Pathfinder, 1992).

—— *Malcolm X Speaks*, ed. George Breitman (New York: Grove Press, 1990).

—— *The Autobiography of Malcolm X*, with the assistance of Alex Haley (1965; London: Penguin, 1968).

Young, Robert, *White Mythologies: Writing, History and the West* (London: Routledge, 1990).
Zamir, Shamoon, *Dark Voices: W.E.B. Du Bois and American Thought, 1888–1903* (Chicago: University of Chicago Press, 1995).
Žižek, Slavoj, *The Puppet and the Dwarf: The Perverse Core of Christianity* (Cambridge, MA: MIT Press, 2003).

WEBSITES

Trinity United Church of Christ, http://www.tucc.org/ (accessed 13 November 2010).
The White House, http://www.whitehouse.gov/ (accessed 13 November 2010).
Organizing For America, http://www.barackobama.com/ (accessed 13 November 2010).

FILMS

If God is Willing and Da Creek Don't Rise, dir. Spike Lee (HBO, 2010).
When the Levees Broke: A Requiem in Four Acts, dir. Spike Lee, DVD (HBO, 2006).
Malcolm X, dir. Spike Lee, DVD (Pathe Distribution, 2001) (First released 1992).

Index

Compiled by Sue Carlton

Page numbers followed by n refer to the notes

Lumumba, Chokwe 217
lynching 90, 229

McAlister, Melani 138, 141, 142, 145,
    146, 151, 156–7, 158, 159
McCain, John 137
Malamud, Margaret 212–13
Malcolm X 8–9, 43, 133–70, 216
    and Africa as 'land of the future' 4,
        13
    after 9/11 163–70
    attitude towards King 132, 142
    Autobiography 32, 136, 138,
        139–40, 142–3, 147, 148
    biopic by Lee 15–16, 137, 147
    and black nationalism 38, 133–4,
        138, 156
    and Christianity 133, 140, 142–3,
        155
    contrasted with King 133–6, 138,
        139, 155, 156
    and Egypt trope 138, 139, 151,
        155–63
    and Garveyism 140–2
    and House Negro and Field Negro
        48, 50
    human rights rhetoric 229–31
    influence on Obama 32, 49, 136–7
    internationalism 138, 150
    and Islam 139, 141–2, 143–4, 169
    and Jews/Judaism 157–8, 159
    and Nation of Islam 134, 135, 138,
        141–2, 143, 144–9
    and Pan-Africanism 133, 139, 146,
        150, 152, 155, 159, 162
    and the Qu'ran 146
    and religious conversions 147–8
    and slave narratives 140
    and Sunni Islam 135, 139, 147–55
    and US race relations 50
Malcolm X Grassroots Movement 217
Malcolm X (Lee) 15–16, 137, 147
Manifest Destiny 30, 220
Marable, Manning 15, 62, 146, 148
master/slave dialectic 7, 20, 66–97, 98,
    103, 131, 133, 139
Mau Mau rebellion, Kenya 37
Miller, Perry 12
Million Man March 167

Mohamed, Amina 61
Montgomery 104, 120, 126, 135
Morrison, Toni 4, 10–11, 14,
    171–214
    see also Paradise (Morrison)
Moses, Wilson Jeremiah 14, 15, 50–1,
    63–4, 140, 156, 197
Moss, Reverend Otis 40
Muhammad, Elijah 141, 144, 145–6,
    147–8, 151–2, 166
Muslim Brotherhood 152, 169
Muslim Mosque Inc. (MMI) 147, 150

NAACP (National Association for the
    Advancement of Colored People)
    25, 46–7, 63, 168, 229
Nagin, Ray 219–20, 225–6
Nancy, Jean-Luc 193
Nasser, Gamal Abdel 95, 151–2, 157,
    160
Nation of Islam (Farrakhan's) 166–7
Nation of Islam (NOI) 42, 44, 47, 51,
    141–2, 156, 180–1, 239
    and anti-Zionism 123
    identification with Nasser 151–2
    and Malcolm X 134, 135, 138,
        141–2, 143, 144–9
National Black Politics Study (1994)
    42
Nazis/Nazism 73–4, 121, 130–1, 161,
    195–6, 199
New Orleans (post-Hurricane Katrina)
    9–10, 214, 215–40
    and black Exodus rhetoric 217–19
    evacuees labelled refugees 223, 225,
        226–7
    and exile 220–6
    and foreign aid 223
    and human rights narrative 228–31
    and national narrative 223–4,
        226–7
    and racist narratives 1, 9, 232–4
    and rebuilding America 232–40
    and reconstruction 10, 225, 227–8
    and return 226–32
    treatment of survivors 224–5
    see also Hurricane Katrina
Niebuhr, Reinhold 24, 25, 54, 117,
    122

3305663R00157

Printed in Great Britain
by Amazon.co.uk, Ltd.,
Marston Gate.